D0844619

ALL THE COUNTRIES OF THE WORLD

ALL THE COUNTRIES OF THE WORLD

Annelise Hobbs

CHARTWELL
BOOKS, INC.

Published in 2006 by
Chartwell Books, Inc.
A division of Book Sales, Inc.
114 Northfield Avenue
Edison, New Jersey 08837
U.S.A

**Copyright 2006 Regency
House Publishing Ltd**

For all editorial enquiries please contact:
Regency House Publishing at
www.regencyhousepublishing.com

All rights reserved. No part of this book may be
reproduced in any form or by any electronic or
mechanical means, including information, storage
and retrieval systems, without permission in
writing from the publisher.

ISBN 13: 978-0-7858-2072-7

ISBN 10: 0-7858-2072-8

Printed in China

*The publisher would like to thank Helene Rogers
of the Art Directors and Trip Photo Library for
supplying the photographs in this book.
(See back of book for full photographic
acknowledgements.)*

*All flags, maps and statistics are reproduced by
kind permission of Lovell Johns Limited*

INDEPENDENT COUNTRIES

AFGHANISTAN
ALBANIA
ALGERIA
ANDORRA
ANGOLA
ANTIGUA &
BARBUDA
ARGENTINA
ARMENIA
AUSTRALIA
AUSTRIA
AZERBAIJAN
BAHAMAS
BAHRAIN
BANGLADESH
BARBADOS
BELARUS
BELGIUM
BELIZE
BENIN
BHUTAN
BOLIVIA
BOSNIA &
HERZEGOVINA
BOTSWANA
BRAZIL
BRUNEI
BULGARIA
BURKINA FASO
BURMA (SEE
MYANMAR)
BURUNDI
CAMBODIA
CAMEROON
CANADA
CAPE VERDE
CENTRAL AFRICAN
REPUBLIC
CHAD
CHILE & EASTER
ISLAND
CHINA
COLOMBIA
COMOROS &
MAYOTTE
CONGO (Democratic
Republic of)

CONGO (Republic of)
COSTA RICA
CÔTE D'IVOIRE
CROATIA
CUBA
CYPRUS
CZECH REPUBLIC
DENMARK
DJIBOUTI
DOMINICA
DOMINICAN
REPUBLIC
ECUADOR & THE
GALAPAGOS
ISLANDS
EGYPT
EL SALVADOR
ENGLAND
EQUATORIAL
GUINEA
ERITREA
ESTONIA
ETHIOPIA
FIJI
FINLAND
FRANCE
GABON
GAMBIA
GEORGIA
GERMANY
GHANA
GREECE
GRENADA
GUATEMALA
GUINEA
GUINEA-BISSAU
GUYANA
HAITI
HONDURAS
HUNGARY
ICELAND
INDIA
INDONESIA
IRAN
IRAQ
IRELAND (Republic
of, and NORTHERN

IRELAND)
ISRAEL
ITALY
JAMAICA
JAPAN
JORDAN
KAZAKHSTAN
KENYA
KIRIBATI
KOREA (NORTH)
KOREA (SOUTH)
KUWAIT
KYRGYZSTAN
LAOS
LATVIA
LEBANON
LESOTHO
LIBERIA
LIBYA
LIECHTENSTEIN
LITHUANIA
LUXEMBOURG
MACEDONIA
MADAGASCAR
MALAWI
MALAYSIA
MALDIVES
MALI
MALTA
MARSHALL
ISLANDS
MAURITANIA
MAURITIUS
MEXICO
MICRONESIA
MOLDOVA
MONACO
MONGOLIA
MOROCCO
MOZAMBIQUE
MYANMAR
NAMIBIA
NAURU
NEPAL
NETHERLANDS
NEW ZEALAND
NICARAGUA

NIGER
NIGERIA
NORWAY
OMAN
PAKISTAN
PALAU
PALESTINE
PANAMA
PAPUA NEW
GUINEA
PARAGUAY
PERU
PHILIPPINES
POLAND
PORTUGAL
QATAR
ROMANIA
RUSSIA
RWANDA
ST KITTS & NEVIS
ST LUCIA
ST VINCENT & THE
GRENADINES
SAMOA &
AMERICAN SOMOA
SAN MARINO
SÃO TOMÉ &
PRÍNCIPE
SAUDI ARABIA
SCOTLAND
SENEGAL
SERBIA &
MONTENEGRO
SEYCHELLES
SIERRA LEONE
SINGAPORE
SLOVAKIA
SLOVENIA
SOLOMAN ISLANDS
SOMALIA
SOUTH AFRICA
SPAIN
SRI LANKA
SUDAN
SURINAME
SWAZILAND
SWEDEN

SWITZERLAND
SYRIA
TAJIKISTAN
TANZANIA
THAILAND
TIMOR-LESTE
TOGO
TONGA
TRINIDAD &
TOBAGO
TUNISIA
TURKEY
TURKMENISTAN
TUVALU
UGANDA
UKRAINE
UNITED ARAB
EMIRATES
UNITED STATES OF
AMERICA
URUGUAY
UZBEKISTAN
VANUATU
VATICAN CITY
VENEZULA
VIETNAM
WALES
YEMEN
ZAMBIA
ZIMBABWE

DEPENDENCIES

ANGUILLA
ANTARCTICA
ARUBA &
NETHERLANDS ANTILLES
BERMUDA
CAYMAN ISLANDS
COOK ISLANDS
FALKLAND ISLANDS
FRENCH GUIANA
GIBRALTAR
GREENLAND
GUADELOUPE
GUAM &
NORTH MARIANA ISLANDS
HONK KONG
MACAU
MARTINIQUE
NEW CALEDONIA
PITCAIRN ISLANDS
PUERTO RICO
RÉUNION
TAHITI &
FRENCH POLYNESIA
TURKS &
CAICOS ISLANDS
VIRGIN ISLANDS (British and US)
WESTERN SAHARA

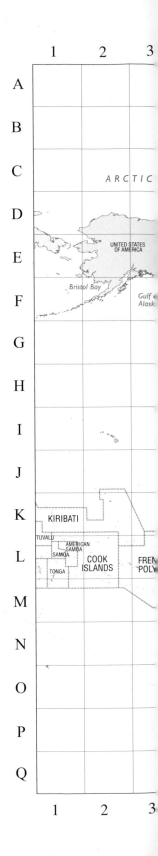

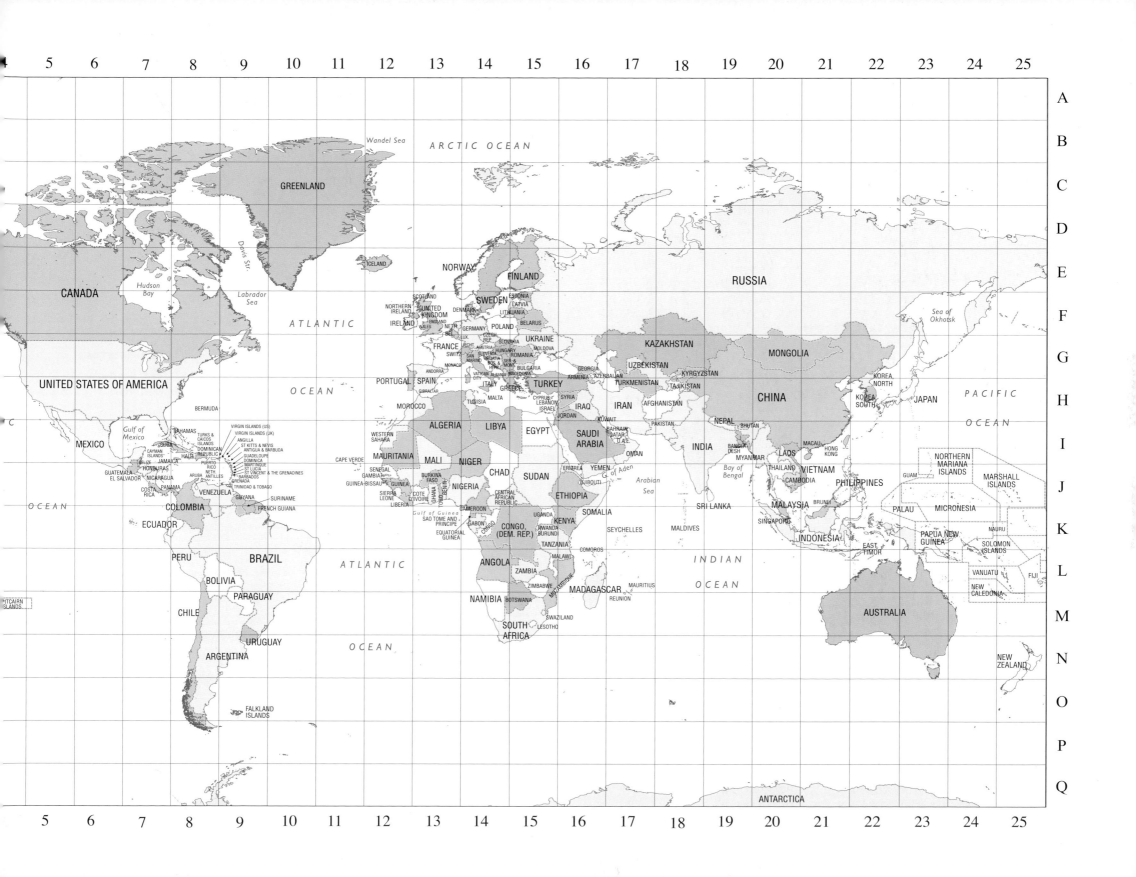

AFGHANISTAN

Location:	18 H
Capital:	Kabul
Area:	249,346sq m (645806km²)
Population:	29,928,987 July 2005
Main Languages:	Dari-Persian, Pashtu
Main Religions:	Sunni Muslim 80%, Sh'ia Muslim 19%
Currency:	1 afghani = 100 puls
Climate:	Hot summer, warm winter, cold in mountains, rains Mar–May

LEFT: The Friday mosque, Herat, a prime example of Islamic architecture.

OPPOSITE: The austere beauty of mountains and lakes near Jalalabad.

Once a part of the ancient Persian Mogul Empire, landlocked Afghanistan lies to the north-west of Pakistan. It is also bordered by Turkmenistan, Uzbekistan and Tajikistan to the north, Iran to the west and China to the east. The terrain is almost entirely mountainous, with grasslands in the north, the remainder being desert or semi-desert. Irrigation allows some crops to be grown, such as wheat and the controversial opium poppy. The majestic Hindu Kush rises to 24,000ft (7300m) in the north-east. The Khyber Pass was long regarded as the back door to Russia and the route by which invading armies were able to penetrate India.

Situated at the crossroads of Central Asia, Afghanistan was strategically located along the legendary Silk Road, an ancient caravan route linking China with the Mediterranean. With its colourful and eventful history and rich diversity of culture, Afghanistan has seen more than its fair share of empire-builders, wars, prophets and poets, and the modern era is no exception.

Afghanistan, as it is known today, came into existence in 1746, but control was ceded to Britain until King Amanullah came to the throne in 1919. During this time, ethnic Pashtun territories were divided by the Durand Line, causing tensions between Afghanistan and British India. Since 1900 there have been 11 rulers of Afghanistan and all were removed by undemocratic or illegal means. The last period of stability was between 1933 and 1973 under the rule of King Zahir Shah. He was replaced in a coup by his brother-in-law, who was murdered, along with his entire family in 1978, when a Marxist regime seized power.

The Soviet invasion and occupation of 1979, and the resulting civil war, left Afghanistan devastated and its once glorious cities in a state of dereliction. The Soviet withdrawal in 1988–89 left the country in a state of turmoil, with various Islamic factions struggling for power. Much of Afghanistan succumbed to the fundamentalist Taliban, which was criticized for its repression of women and violation of other human rights, and which captured Kabul in 1996. In 1998, the US launched missile strikes against the mountain bases of Osama bin-Laden, head of al-Quaeda, an outlaw organization bent on destroying Western values, though he remains elusive to this day. In 2001, the US and Britain attacked Afghanistan, when it refused to hand over bin-Laden, who by now had been implicated in the 11 September terrorist attacks on the US. The following month, opposition forces captured Kandahar, the last bastion of the Taliban, and Hamid Karzai formed a democratic government.

One of the poorest countries in the world, Afghanistan's economy has begun to improve since the fall of the Taliban, when infusions of foreign aid began. Herding and subsistence agriculture are the main activities, though Afghanistan's mineral wealth remains to be exploited.

ALBANIA

Location:	14 G
Capital :	Tirana
Area:	11,101sq m (28752km²)
Population:	3,563,112 July 2005
Main Languages:	Albanian, Greek
Main Religions:	Sh'ia Muslim 45%,
	Sunni Muslim 20%,
	Albanian Orthodox 25%
Currency:	1 lek = 100 qindars
Climate:	Mediterranean, Jan 54°F
	(12ºC), Jul 86°F (30ºC)

Albania, or Shqiperia, the Land of the Eagle, is part of the Balkan peninsula that extends into the Mediterranean Sea. It is bordered by Serbia & Montenegro to the north, Macedonia to the east and Greece to the south. The Dinaric Alps cover the greater part of the country, whose forested slopes are inhabited by wolves and wild boar, and swift streams water the fertile lowlands that border the Adriatic Sea to the west. The Ionian Sea lies off the coast to the south-east.

The original inhabitants of the area that is now Albania were probably people of pre-

Indo-European origin that once occupied the coastal areas of most parts of the Mediterranean. These were overrun by proto-Hellenic tribes that were also active in Greece and southern Macedonia. As part of Illyria, an ancient kingdom that once occupied Dalmatia and other parts of the Adriatic coast, and of which little is known, forays were made into the Greek kingdom of the Molossians, but the Illyrians were eventually repulsed by Philip II of Macedonia, the father of Alexander the Great. Illyria was conquered by the Romans in 167 BC, when it was known as the province of Illyricum; it was later divided as Pannonia and Dalmatia. It eventually became part of the Eastern Roman Empire, established by Augustus in 27 BC; this was divided by Theodosius in AD 395 into the Western or Latin, or Eastern or Greek or Byzantine Empires.

By the Middle Ages, the area was roughly equivalent to modern Albania and had assumed a national identity. After years of resistance under the leadership of Gyorgi Skanderbeg, the Albanian national hero, Albania fell to the Turks in 1468. Albania remained part of the Ottoman Empire until 1912, when, following the First Balkan War, it became an independent principality. It became a republic in 1925, its president, Abu Beg Zogu, becoming king in 1928. Albania was ruled by King Zog until 1938, when it became a puppet state of Italy.

Communists came to power under the leadership of Enver Hoxha after the Second World War, when Albania was governed by one of the most repressive regimes in Europe; Albania claimed to be the first atheist state following the closure of churches and mosques. Relations with the USSR were severed in 1969, and Albania's involvement with China cooled after the Sino-American detente in the 1970s, when Enver Hoxha adopted a stictly isolationist policy: Albania was run as a Communist state but with little contact with the outside world.

Hoxha died in 1985 and was replaced by Ramiz Ali, who at first saw Hoxha as an leader to be emulated; by now, however, changes were afoot in Europe. Gorbachev's *perestroika* and the end of the hateful regime of Ceausescu in Romania gave the signal for Alia to change, and human rights were improved and other reforms were made. The 1992 general elections were won by the Democratic Party, who polled two-thirds of the votes. Since then, Albania has become a member of the Council of Europe, and has requested membership of NATO. President since 2002 is Alfred Moisiu, with Sali Berisha the prime minister since 2005.

Though still Europe's poorest country, with much of the population engaged in agriculture or still working abroad (from whom much of Albania's income is derived), Albania has become more open to the rest of the world. However, oil and gas reserves remain to be explored and the infrastructure is gradually being improved.

OPPOSITE: Berat Castle, central Albania.

LEFT: The Skanderbeg monument to Albania's national hero, with mosque and clock tower.

ALGERIA

Location:	13 H
Capital:	Algiers
Area:	919,595sq m (2381751km²)
Population:	3,2531,853 July 2005
Main Languages:	Arabic, Berber
Main Religions:	Sunni Muslim 98%
Currency:	1 Algerian dinar = 100 centimes
Climate:	Hot summer, humid in the north, cooler on the coast, winter mild. Jan 61°F (16ºC), Jul 82°F (28ºC)

Algeria is a country of the Maghreb, a region of North and North-West Africa that stretches from the Atlantic Ocean to Egypt. This comprises the Mediterranean coastal plain and the Atlas Mountains of Morocco, together with Algeria and Tunisia, and sometimes includes Tripolitania. Most of Algeria's coastline is hilly or mountainous, the area to the south being fertile land that rises to the Atlas Mountains. Much of the rest of Algeria is covered by the Sahara Desert.

Berbers, including Tuaregs, were the

indigenous population of Algeria since at least 10000 BC. In 1000 BC Carthaginians began to settle the coastal area, and the Berber kingdom of Numidia was absorbed into Carthage. Numidia tried to extricate itself, only to be seized by Rome in 200 BC. On the collapse of the Roman Empire,

Vandals assumed control but were expelled by the Byzantine Emperor Justinian I, who retained control until Islam arrived in the 7th century. The Fatimids rapidly established an empire in the north-east, but following the *Reconquista*, Spain began to attack Algerian coastal cities in the 15th and 16th centuries,

prompting help from the Ottoman Empire.

France invaded Algeria in 1830 and the process of colonization began. In 1954 the National Liberation Front (FLN), that was to dominate Algerian politics for the next 40 years, launched a war claiming 350,000 lives. In 1962 Algeria gained independence,

and Ahmed Ben Bella came to power. He was overthrown in a coup by Col. Houari Boumédienne in 1965, who established a military council and began reforms, among them a national health service. In 1991 the Fundamentalist Islamic Salvation Front (FIS) won a surprise victory from the FLN, and violent civil strife ensued. This escalated into an insurgency resulting in 100,000 deaths between 1992 and 1998. Abdelazi Bouteflika became president in 1999 in doubtful elections, but was backed by a landslide victory in 2004. The FIS's Islamic Salvation Army was disbanded in 2000, though small numbers of militants persisted in attacking villages.

In spite of its history of instability, and continued political unrest, there are signs that the country is beginning to rally. The economy is based on hydrocarbons, petroleum, and natural gas.

OPPOSITE: The sand dunes of the Sahara Desert.

ABOVE LEFT: An Algerian nomad.

ABOVE: Children collecting dates in Le M'zab.

ANDORRA

Location:	13 G
Capital:	Andorra la Vella
Area:	177sq m (468km²)
Population:	70,549 July 2005
Main Languages:	Catalan
Main Religions:	Roman Catholic 79%
Currency:	1 euro =100 cents
Climate:	Warm summer, cold winter, abundant snow

ABOVE: A restaurant at Borda Xixerella.

LEFT: Skiing at Pals Ski Station.

BELOW: Pont de Estarell in the Ordino Valley.

A small, landlocked country, the Principality of Andorra lies in the eastern Pyrenees between France and Spain. The terrain is characterized by craggy gorges and narrow valleys surrounded by high mountains, and is probably why Andorra has stayed independent for so long.

According to tradition, Andorra was ganted a charter by Charlemagne in the 8th century for its help in defeating the Moors. In 1278 it came under the joint suzerainty of the French Comtes de Foix and the Spanish bishops of La Seu d'Urgell. Since 1607, power has been invested in the presidents of France, though the bishops still retain their prerogatives. Head of state since 1995 is the French Coprince Jacques Chirac, represented by Philippe Massoni since 2002; the joint head of state since 2003 is the Spanish Coprince Bishop Joan Enric Vives y Sicilía, represented by Nemesi Marques y Oste. Head of government since May 2005 is Executive Council President Albert Pintat.

Even though it remained isolated and impoverished for centuries, Andorra has achieved considerable prosperity through its tourist industry since the Second World War. Visitors are also attracted by its duty-free status, though the advantages have lessened since lower tariffs have been made available to its neighbours. Andorra also has an international banking sector and has become something of a tax haven in recent years.

ANGOLA

Location: 14 L
Capital: Luanda
Area: 481354sq m (1246700km²)
Population: 11,190,786 July 2005
Main Languages: Portuguese
Main Religions: Christian 64%,
Animist 34%
Currency: 1 kwanza = 100 lwei
Climate: Hot wet summer, cooler dry
winter, hot all year in the
south

A republic located on the western coast of southern Africa, Angola has land borders with Congo and DR Congo to the north, Zambia to the east and Namibia to the south. The Atlantic coastal area is flat, unhealthy and unproductive, though there is a vast fertile plateau beyond.

Angola became a possession of Portugal in the 16th centre, when it supplied slaves to Brazil. In the 1950s nationalists began to demand independence; the Popular Movement for the Liberation of Angola (MPLA) was formed, drawing its support from *mestizos* and the Mbundu tribe. In

RIGHT: Coastal view of Luanda.

BELOW RIGHT: School children in the shanty-town area of Luanda.

1961 the MPLA led a revolt in Luanda that was quashed by Portuguese troops, and other nationalist movements developed between different ethnic groups. Independence was granted in 1975 but a power struggle developed among rival nationalist forces. The Marxist MPLA formed a government but troops of the National Union for the Total Independence of Angola (UNITA) launched a civil war that lasted for 16 years. A treaty was signed in 1991 and multi-party elections were held the following year.

Civil strife continued, however, when the MPLA, now no longer Marxist, was victorious and UNITA would not accept the result. In accord with the Lusaka Protocol, a government of national unity was formed in 1994, with leaders from both parties. Dos Santos remained president but UNITA's Jonas Savimbi rejected the vice-presidency, which led to continued fighting. This resulted in UN sanctions being imposed on UNITA in 1997, but the fighting did not stop. In 2002 government forces killed Savimbi and a ceasefire was agreed.

To most people, Angola is synonymous with bloodshed, its association with Portugal and the acquisition of diamonds and crude oil being responsible for this in equal measure. Civil war has hampered development and impoverished the country, even though its mineral resources are a potential for prosperity.

ANGUILLA

Location:	9 I
Capital:	The Valley
Area:	39sq m (102km²)
Population:	13,254 July 2005
Main Languages:	English
Main Religions:	Anglican 29%, Methodist 24%, other Protestant 30%
Currency:	East Caribbean dollar
Climate:	Tropical, moderated by north-east trade winds

The most northerly of the Leeward Islands, Anguilla consists of five Caribbean islands lying east of Puerto Rico, the largest being the island of Anguilla itself. These coral or limestone islands are devoid of interest, being flat, scrubby and unproductive, but they are surrounded by blue waters and have beautiful beaches.

In Spanish, the word *anguilla* means 'eel', possibly the name given to it by Columbus to describe the long, thin shape of the atoll, which he discovered in 1493. Anguilla was colonized by English settlers in 1650, and was incorporated into a single British dependency, along with the islands of St Kitts and Nevis, in the 19th century. This arrangement was not popular, and Anguilla's secession was formerly recognized in 1980. It remains a self-governing dependency of the UK. Head of state since 1952 is Queen Elizabeth II, represented by Governor Alan Eden Huckle since 2004. Head of government since 2000 is Osbourne Fleming.

The economy relies heavily on tourism, offshore banking and lobster fishing.

Anguilla: a typical beach scene.

ANTARCTIA

Location:	20 Q
Area:	5,404,000sq m (14,000,000km²)
Population:	no permanent
Main Languages:	N/A
Main Religions:	N/A
Currency:	N/A
Climate:	Severe, low temperatures

ANTARCTICA

Antarctica lies almost entirely within the Antarctic Circle and is the fifth-largest continent after Asia, Africa, and North and South America; it is larger than both Australia and the sub-continent of Europe. It is bordered by the Southern Ocean and the southern parts of the Atlantic, Pacific and Indian Oceans. Antarctica consists of a high plateau of ancient rocks (similar to some found in New Zealand and South America) that reaches its highest point of 16,000ft (4880m) in the Vinson Massif. Around 95 per cent of the continent is covered with ice throughout the year.

Captain Cook was the first to cross the Antarctic Circle in 1772–75, but the presence of land was not confirmed until

Nathaniel Palmer reached the Antarctic Peninsula in 1820. By 1840 the American, Charles Wilkes, had seen enough of the coast to prove a continent, rather than a group of islands, existed, and the British explorer James Clark Ross mapped the area. In 1911 Roald Amundsen beat Captain Scott by a month in the race to the South Pole, and Richard E. Byrd was the first to view Antarctica from the air.

By the early 19th century, there was much commercial interest in the area. Seals and whales were in abundance, attracted to the krill-rich Southern Ocean. By the end of the century Antarctica had become a centre of the whaling industry and the focus of scientific experiment, when permanent research stations began to appear.

The Antarctic Treaty of 1959 pledged international scientific co-operation, and came into force in 1991. It banned commercial exploitation of the continent, but also formulated a legal framework in which the different nations could operate. However,

The harsh, bleak, but strangely beautiful landscape of Deception Island, located in the Drake Passage, off the Antarctic Peninsula.

it neither denies nor recognizes existing territorial claims, but continues to administer Antarctica by meetings of the consultative member nations in accordance with their own national laws. There is no indigenous population and economic activity is limited to large-scale fishing and tourism, both controlled from outside Antarctica.

ANTIGUA & BARBUDA

Location:	9 I
Capital:	St John's
Area:	171sq m (443km²)
Population:	68,722 July 2005
Main Languages:	English
Main Religions:	Protestant
Currency:	1 East Caribbean dollar = 100 cents
Climate:	Warm all year

Two of the Leeward Islands, Antigua & Barbuda, together with the other Leeward Islands of Anguilla and St Kitts & Nevis, lie in the Caribbean Sea, with the North Atlantic Ocean to their east. The territory also includes the island of Redondo to Antigua's south-east. They are low-lying coral or limestone islands, with higher, volcanic areas. There are no rivers or forests on Antigua, though Barbuda is wooded.

The Siboney were the original inhabitants of the islands, but Christopher Columbus found Arawak and Carib Indians

when he arrived in 1493. The islands were subsequently settled by the Spanish and the French, who were followed by the British, who established a colony in 1667, bringing in slave labour to work the sugar plantations on Antigua; slavery was abolished in 1834. The islands became self-governing in 1967 and independent within the Commonwealth in 1981. Head of state since 1952 is Queen Elizabeth II, represented by Governor-

OPPOSITE: A palm beach on Barbuda.

ABOVE: Priest holding a child, St Johns.

ABOVE RIGHT: Saturday market on St John's.

RIGHT: Stone jetty at Nelson's Dockyard.

General Sir James Carlisle since 1993. Head of government since 2004 is Prime Minister Winston Baldwin Spencer.

Tourism is by far the most important sector of the economy, and accounts for more than half the country's GDP. Its continuing success depends largely on what is happening to the US economy, America being the main supplier of visitors to the islands. Because of the limited water supply, and a shortage of labour, lost to the tourist industry, agriculture is limited to the domestic market. However, some diversification has been made away from tourism and towards manufacturing, which includes petroleum products, textiles, handicrafts and electronic components. Other occupations are livestock rearing and lobster fishing.

ARGENTINA

Location:	8 N
Capital :	Buenos Aires
Area:	1,068,297sq m
	(2,766,890km²)
Population:	39,537,943 July 2005
Main Languages:	Spanish
Main Religions:	Roman Catholic 93%
Currency:	1 peso = 100 centavos
Climate:	Hot and wet all year in
	north; hot summer, cool
	winter in centre; cold all
	year in south

Argentina stretches from the Tropic of Capricorn to Tierra del Fuego, and is the second-largest country in South America. The high Andes, that run along Argentina's border with Chile, contain Aconcagua at 22,834ft (6960m), while between the Paraná and Colorado rivers lie the rolling pampas grasslands that support great herds of cattle producing huge quantities of beef. To the south lies the rolling plateau of Patagonia; here the terrain is dry and barren and the climate becomes progressively colder as it approaches Antarctica.

The original inhabitants of Argentina – the Land of Silver – were wandering hunters called the Amerindians, who resisted first the Incas and then the Spanish in the 16th century. Sadly, they had almost disappeared by the time Argentina finally won its independence from Spain in 1816. Later that century, European settlers, mostly from the Latin countries, began to flow into the country. Until the end of the Second World War there were conflicts between liberals and conservatives and civilians and the military.

In 1944, Ramón Castillo was overthrown in a military coup by General Juan Perón. Helped by his wife, Eva, he established a popular dictatorship that progressively became more severe, until he was deposed in 1955. However, a Perónist movement, which in 1973 led to a new Perónist regime, but which became increasingly corrupt, was overthrown by a military junta and thousands of opponents were tortured or disappeared (*los desaparecidos*) between 1976 and 1982.

General Leopoldo Galtieri, president from 1981, gained fleeting popularity after the invasion of the Falkland Islands in 1982, but his failure to hold them against the British led to a more conventional government. Since 2003, the head of state and head of government has been President Néstor Kirchner. He became president by default when the former Perónist Carlos Saúl Menem, who was president from 1989–99, withdrew his candidacy on the eve of the election.

Argentina has generous natural resources, a well-educated population and an export-oriented agricultural section that includes wheat and beef. However, it has had many troubles over the past ten years, not the least of which has been inflation and massive withdrawals from banks as consumer and investor confidence declined.

LEFT: The Perito Moreno glacier in Los Glaciares National Park, Patagonia.

BELOW: The Plaza Mayor, Buenos Aires.

OPPOSITE: The Iguaçu Falls on the River Paraná.

ARMENIA

Location:	16 G
Capital:	Yerevan
Area:	11,490sq m (29800km²)
Population:	2,982,904 July 2005
Main Languages:	Armenian
Main Religions:	Armenian Orthodox
Currency:	1 dram = 100 lumma
Climate:	Warm summer, cold winter

Armenia's fateful location, between the Black and Caspian Seas, the Caucasus, and the plateau of Iran and Asia Minor, has historically subjected it to war and occupation by Assyrians, Persians, Greeks, Romans, Arabs, Mongols and Turks. The land is mostly mountainous, with fast-flowing rivers and few forests. Mount Ararat, regarded by the Armenians as rightfully theirs, fell to Turkey in 1915.

Armenia was under Turkish rule in the 16th century, but when the Ottoman Empire fell, it was divided between Turkey, Iran and Russia. In what is termed the Armenian Genocide of 1915, it is thought that the Turks forcibly deported nearly two million Armenians to the deserts of Syria and Mesopotamia, with more than half a million perishing on forced marches along the way. Russian Armenia was absorbed into the USSR in 1922, gaining independence as a member of the Commonwealth of Independent States in 1991.

This exacerbated the conflict that began in 1988 with Muslim Azerbaijan over

ABOVE: The monastery at Gegard, parts of which are carved out of the rock.

ABOVE RIGHT: Yerevan with Mount Ararat in the background.

RIGHT: The straw house of people protecting the harvest in Artashat.

Nagorno-Karabakh, which, despite a ceasefire in 1994, has still not been resolved.

Head of state since 1998 is President Robert Kocharian; Prime Minister Andranik Margaryan has been head of government since 2000.

Armenia is still recovering from a disastrous earthquake in 1988, when more than 25,000 people lost their lives. The break-up of the USSR also led to severe economic decline in a country based on industry, having received raw materials and energy from the Soviets in return for its products. However, progress began to be made in 1995, which has encouraged international aid and foreign investment, and there has been diversification into new sectors, such as jewellery, IT and tourism.

ARUBA & NETHERLANDS ANTILLES

Location: Aruba 8 J
Capital: Oranjestad
Area: 75sq m (194km²)
Population: 71,566 July 2005
Main Languages: Dutch
Main Religions: Roman Catholic 82%,
Protestant 8%
Currency: Aruban guilder/florin
Climate: Tropical marine

Location: Netherlands Antilles 8 J
Capital : Willemstad
Area: 309sq m (800km²)
Population: 221,000
Main Languages: Dutch
Main Religions: Roman Catholic,
Protestant
Currency: Netherlands Antilles
florin
Climate: Tropical marine

The Netherlands Antilles consists of a group
of islands in the West Indies, off the coast of
Venezuela, which form an autonomous
region of the Netherlands. They consist of

Aruba, Curaçao,
Bonaire, St
Eustatius, Saba and
part of St Maarten.
Discovered and
settled by the
Spanish in 1499,
the islands were captured by the Dutch in
the 17th century. Their colonial status altered
in 1954, when they became part of the
kingdom of the Netherlands. In 1986,
however, Aruba seceded, and was given
status aparte from the others. Progression
towards full independence was halted at
Aruba's request in 1990.

The islands all originated from volcanic
activity, and being hilly have no agriculture.

ABOVE: Oranjestad main square.

*RIGHT: Overview of St Eustatius, with the
The Quill mountain in the background.*

The overall head of state since 1980 is
Queen Beatrix of the Netherlands,
represented in the Netherlands Antilles by
Governor-General Frits Goedgedrag since
2002. The head of government since 2004 is
Prime Minister Etienne Ys. On Aruba, the
queen has been represented since 2004 by
Governor-General Fredis Refunjol. Head of
government since 2001 is Prime Minister
Nelson O Oduber.

The islands are prosperous compared
with other nations in the area, and tourism,
oil refining and the transshipment of
petroleum are the mainstays of the economy.

AUSTRALIA

Location:	22 M
Capital:	Canberra
Area:	2,967,896sq m
	(7686850km²)
Population:	20,090,437 July 2005
Main Languages:	English
Main Religions:	Christian 74%, Muslim,
	Jewish, Buddhist
Currency:	1 Australian dollar = 100
	cents
Climate:	Hot in north with rain,
	hot summer, mild winter
	elsewhere

Australia is a large island located in the Southern Hemisphere. It is the world's smallest continent but the sixth-largest country. It lies between the Pacific, Indian and Southern Oceans, the Timor and Arafura seas separating it from Asia to the north-east. The island of Tasmania, part of the Commonwealth of Australia, is separated from the south-eastern coast of Australia by the Bass Strait.

Australia is the driest inhabited continent; it is also the flattest, and has the

LEFT: Uluru (Ayres Rock).

BELOW: State Parliament House, Melbourne.

OPPOSITE: Sydney Opera House.

PAGE 26, LEFT: The Sydney Harbour Bridge, with ferries.

PAGE 26, RIGHT: A waterhole in the MacDonnell ranges, Northern Territory.

PAGE 27: A forest that has regenerated after a fire, Queensland.

oldest, least-fertile soil. The continent has distinct divisions: the narrow eastern coastal plain, on which several of the most important towns are situated and where much of the population is concentrated; the western plateau – an area composed of semi-desert; the central plains, where cattle and sheep-rearing are predominant, and which relies for water on the Great Artesian Basin, that underlies 20 per cent of the continent and is the world's largest underground reservoir. This division also includes the wheat and cattle lands of the Murray and Darling basins to the south-east; the Great Dividing Range of the eastern highlands; the the coast of Queensland in the north-east, protected by the Great Barrier Reef, a chain of coral 1,250ft (2,000km) long, and visible only at low tide. This has a true tropical climate, and sugar and cotton are grown.

Legends of *terra australis incognita* – an unknown southern land – are thought to date from Roman times. The name Australia came into being in a work by the navigator Matthew Flinders in 1814, and Governor Lachlan Macquarie of New South Wales began to use it in dispatches to England soon after. Australia became the official name of the continent in 1824.

The original inhabitants of Australia are the Aborigines, believed to have been here since time immemorial (hence the name), but who may have come from Asia in prehistoric times. These people have a rich heritage of song, ritual and legend, centred on the Dreamtime, a time when man first appeared on Earth and when the animal spirits of totemic ancestors wandered abroad. Today, the long mistreatment of

Native Australians remains a contentious issue. In 1993 an act was passed, restoring land rights to traditional Native Australian hunting grounds and sacred areas.

Europeans did not arrive until the early 17th century, when Dutch explorers charted the western and northern coastlines of what they called New Holland, but did not settle. In 1770, Captain James Cook mapped the eastern coast, called it New South Wales, and claimed it for Britain. This led to the establishment by the British of a penal colony on the site of present-day Sydney in 1788, to which criminals, previously sent to the American colonies, now lost, were transported instead. In the 19th century free settlers began to arrive and the economy, based on mining and sheep-rearing, began to develop rapidly.

In 1901, the country was divided into colonies, which eventually became the states of New South Wales, Queensland, South Australia, Victoria and Western Australia; these federated to form the Commonwealth of Australia. In 1911, the Northern Territory joined the federation, and the federal capital of Canberra and the Australian Capital Territory joined in 1927, each state and territory with their own legislature. Queen Elizabeth II is represented in each state by a governor, by an administrator in the Northern Territory, and by the Governor-General in the Australian Capital Territory.

LEFT: A kookaburra, a large Australian kingfisher that feeds on terrestrial prey.

OPPOSITE: The Blue Mountains of New South Wales.

Most of the population is from British stock and Australians fought with the Allies in two World Wars; but a later wave of immigration from Europe and Asia in the 20th century has substantially changed the ethnic mix. Now that Britain is more involved with the EU, her links with Australia have weakened, and Australia is looking increasingly to Asia, and especially to Japan, for trade. It is thought by many that Australia will eventually sever its ties with Britain, abandoning the British monarchy and becoming a republic in its own right. However, in a referendum in 1999, Australia voted to remain as it is.

The most powerful office in the Commonweath of Australia is that of prime minister. The prime minister is appointed by the Governor-General, and is nearly always the leader of the political party with majority support in the House of Representatives. Since 1996 the holder of the office has been John Howard of the Liberal Party,

Australia has a prosperous, mixed economy similar to those of the West. It is a major producer and exporter of cattle, wheat, wool, and wine, and minerals such as bauxite, coal, copper, gold, silver, iron, manganese and tungsten are in good supply. Australia also has a highly-developed manufacturing industry, and tourism is becoming increasingly important.

RIGHT: Kangaroo are marsupials found only in Australia and New Guinea.

OPPOSITE: Lake Wood in the Northern Territory.

AUSTRIA

Location:	14 G
Capital :	Vienna
Area:	32,377sq m
	(83,859km²)
Population:	818,4691 July 2005
Main Languages:	German
Main Religions:	Roman Catholic 78%,
	Protestant 5%
Currency:	euro
Climate:	Cold winters,
	warm summers

A landlocked country of Central Europe, Austria (Österreich) is bordered by Germany, the Czech Republic, Slovakia, Hungary, Croatia, Slovenia, Italy, Switzerland and Liechtenstein.

Geographically, Austria can be split into two: the Alpine zone to the south-west, and the Danube lowlands with the Vienna plain to the north-east. Here the land rises towards the Bohemian Forest and Moravian heights of Slovakia. The Austrian Alps are lower and more accessible than those of Switzerland, and are dissected by the long, wide, Brenner, Arlberg, Semmering and Schöber passes.

Prehistorically, Austria was inhabited by Celtic tribes, but it was later conquered by the Romans and incorporated into the Roman Empire in 14 BC. After the empire fell in the 5th century, Austria fell prey to Vandals, Goths, Huns, Lombards and Avars, but when Charlemagne conquered the Avars in 791, the East Mark, the basis of the Austrian empire, was established. From the middle of the 13th century, Austria was dominated by the Habsburg family. Rudolf of Habsburg became King of the Romans and Holy Roman Emperor in 1273 and seized Austria, investing his son archduke from 1282 and ensuring the continuance of the Habsburg line. This ceased to be following the victory of Napoleon at the Battle of Austerlitz in 1806. Maria Theresa came to the throne in 1740, which prompted the War of the Austrian Succession. The revolution of 1848 forced the succession of

OPPOSITE: Salzburg, Mozart's birthplace and the location of the famous music festival.

LEFT: Hallstatt viewed from the lake. The town features on UNESCO's World Heritage list as a place of outstanding beauty.

Franz Joseph, and Austrian power continued to decline after the Austro-Prussian War of 1866. In 1867 Austria and Hungary became autonomous states under one sovereign. Through expansion, the Austro-Hungarian Empire became a massive entity, but its disregard for individual nations precipitated the First World War. It was dissolved under the Treaty of Versailles in 1919.

Engelbert Dollfüss established a totalitarian state, but was unable to prevent the rise of Germany, which annexed Austria in 1938. Austria was occupied by the Allies after the Second World War, but regained its sovereignty in 1955, when union with Germany was forbidden and perpetual neutrality for Austria was established. Head of state since 2004 is President Heinz Fischer; head of government since 2000 is Chancellor Wolfgang Schuessel.

A prosperous, democratic country, Austria joined the EU in 1995. It has a well-developed market economy, having modern agricultural and industrial sectors, and a high standard of living. Dairy and livestock farming are main agricultural activities, its main industry being metal manufacture. It has a thriving tourist scene, based around its historic cities and winter sports facilities.

AZERBAIJAN

Location:	16 G
Capital:	Baku
Area:	33,430sq m (86600km²)
Population:	7,911,974 July 2005
Main Languages:	Azeri
Main Religions:	Muslim 88%, Christian
Currency:	1 manat = 100 gyapiks
Climate:	Warm summer, cold winter, rain in west

A country of south-western Asia on the western shore of the Caspian Sea, between Iran and Russia. The terrain is mainly flat, apart from the Caucasus in the north and the Little Caucasus in the south-west.

Azerbaijan is still very much a part of old Asia and was once a larger region that included part of Persia (Iran). In 1917 there was an attempt to form a Transcaucasion Federation with Armenia and Georgia. When this failed Azerbaijan was absorbed into the Soviet Union in 1922, gaining independence on the break-up of the USSR in 1991. Since 2003, the head of state has been President Ilham Aliyev; head of

RIGHT: Watching the world go by, Baku.

BELOW: Shirvanashakhov Palace with mosque and minaret.

government is Prime Minister Artur Rasizade.

Azerbaijan's most important export is oil, but long-term prosperity will depend on world oil prices, new pipelines and Azerbaijan's ability to manage the revenue it receives from oil. A dispute between Azerbaijan and Armenia arose in 1985 over separatist Nagorno-Karabakh, which remains largely unresolved (see Armenia), and which continues to be a drain on the economy.

BAHAMAS

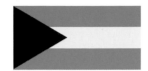

Location:	8 I
Capital:	Nassau
Area:	5,382sq m (13939km²)
Population:	301,790 July 2005
Main Languages:	English
Main Religions:	Christian (various denominations) 95%
Currency:	1 Bahamian dollar = 100 cents
Climate:	Hot summer, warm winter, risk of hurricanes

Situated off the south-east coast of Florida, the Bahamas are a chain of islands in the Caribbean.

There are hundreds of islands and cays, of which about 30 or so are inhabited. They are flat coral formations with some hills. Hurricanes and tropical storms are a hazard.

Columbus made his first landfall here in his search for the New World (October 1492). The islands were held alternately by the British and Spanish in the 17th and 18th centuries, until they finally became British in 1783, gaining independence within the Commonwealth in 1973. Head of state since

1952 is Queen Elizabeth II, represented since 2002 by Governor-General Dame Ivy Dumont; Prime Minister Perry Christie is head of government, also since 2002.

The Bahamas have a stable, developing economy that relies almost entirely on tourism, offshore banking, and financial services. Nowadays it is a firm favourite with Americans, who make up 80 per cent of all visitors. This makes the Bahamas vulnerable to what is happening in the US economy, particularly as Bahamian agriculture and manufacturing show little growth, despite government incentives.

LEFT: Junkanoo, a local festival held in Bay St, Nassau, on 26 December.

ABOVE: Balmoral Island, Bahamas.

35

BAHRAIN

Location:	17 I
Capital:	Manama
Area:	262sq m (678km²)
Population:	688,345 July 2005
Main Languages:	Arabic
Main Religions:	Muslim 85%, Christian 7%
Currency:	1 Bahraini dinar = 100 fils
Climate:	Hot dry summer, cooler winter

An archipelago of islands, strategically located in the Persian Gulf, 25 miles (15m) from the mainland of Saudi Arabia. Bahrain, the largest island, is linked to the Saudi mainland by a causeway. The terrain consists of a low-lying desert plain, that rises slightly towards the central escarpment.

Once one of the ancient world's great trading empires, Bahrain was ruled by the Portuguese and Persians in the 16th and 17th centuries before becoming a British protectorate in 1861. It gained its independence from Britain in 1971. Tensions between the majority Shi'a and the Sunni have existed for some time, the former demanding the return of an elected National Assembly, and they are also pressing for an Islamic state.

Head of state since 1999 is the present emir, whose family has governed Bahrain since the late 18th century. The emir proclaimed himself King Hamad bin Isa al-Khalifa in February 2002, when a new constitution was introduced. Later that year, Bahrainis were able to choose new members of the bicameral lower house of the reconstituted House of Assembly in the first election for 27 years. Head of government is Prime Minister Khalifa bin Salman al-Khalifa.

Oil was discovered in 1932 and petroleum production and refining have been instrumental in making Bahrain prosperous. However, since the 1970s oil reserves have

been running low, but Bahrain has managed to transform itself into a centre for international banking. It is now home to many multinational companies with business in the Gulf, and Bahrain's aluminium-smelting plant is the largest industrial complex in the area. In 2004 Bahrain signed a Free Trade Agreement with the US, which makes it unique among the Gulf states.

ABOVE: A souk in Manama.

LEFT: Manama's financial district.

OPPOSITE: The Grand Mosque in Manama, Bahrain's capital city.

BANGLADESH

Location:	19 I
Capital:	Dhaka
Area:	55,600sq m (144000km²)
Population:	144,319,628 July 2005
Main Languages:	Bengali
Main Religions:	Muslim 87%, Hindu 12%
Currency:	1 taka = 100 poisa
Climate:	Hot all year, monsoon Apr–Oct

A country of the Indian sub-continent, lying on the Bay of Bengal and the Indian Ocean, Bangladesh is located between India and Myanmar (Burma). It occupies part of the alluvial plain of the Ganges-Brahmaputra river, where rainfall is high; the great delta is frequently flooded, destroying lives, homes and crops. Nevertheless, the flooding leaves behind a rich and fertile silt that allows up to three rice crops a year to be grown, as well as high-quality jute. It is hilly in the south-east.

The history of Bangladesh is synonymous with that of Bengal, which embraced Islam in the 13th century, and was part of the vast Mogul empire from the 16th

century. In the late 18th century Bengal came under the control of the British East India Company and was eventually a province of British India. In 1905 Britain divided Bengal into East Bengal and West Bengal. When India became independent in 1947, an Islamic state was formed called Pakistan. This consisted of two geographical units, with East Bengal becoming part of Pakistan as East Pakistan, while West Bengal remained part of the new state of India. This meant that Pakistan (West Pakistan) now had two provinces separated by 1,000 miles (1500km), one to the north-west of India, the other to the north-east.

The desire for autonomy arose because East Pakistan was dissatisfied with its smaller share of Pakistan's development funds, even though its jute industry was significantly contributing to Pakistan's balance of payments; moreover, it had the larger population. Sheikh Mujibar Rahman proclaimed secession in 1971 and civil war followed. During nine months of fighting, more than a million East Pakistanis lost their lives and millions more were forced into exile, mainly to India. Helped by India, East Pakistan was able to defeat Pakistan. East Pakistan (East Bengal) became the independent state of Bangladesh (The Bengal Nation) from 1972, with Sheik Rahman as its president, and ten million refugees returned across the Indian border.

In 1976 Sheik Rahman was assassinated in a military coup and martial law was declared, the military holding power for the next 15 years. In 1991 Bangladesh held its first free elections since independence. In 1996 the Awami League, led by Rahman's daughter Hasina Wazed, was elected and completed the first full term of office in the country's history. She was succeeded as prime minister by Rahman's wife, Begum Khaleda Zia. Head of state since 2002 is President Iajuddin Ahmed.

Besides cyclones and flooding, Bangladesh has other problems, in that it is the most highly-populated country in the world. Many of the people are without land and are forced to live on and cultivate land that is prone to flooding, facing the danger of waterborne diseases. Agriculture employs half the workforce and rice is the main crop. The most important export is jute.

OPPOSITE: The Lalbagh fort-mosque, built in 1680 by the Mogul Governor of Bengal.

BELOW LEFT: Loading building materials on the Padma river at Faridpur.

BELOW: A ricefield tended by young people.

BARBADOS

Location:	9 J
Capital:	Bridgetown
Area:	166sq m (430km²)
Population:	279,254 July 2005
Main Languages:	English
Main Religions:	Protestant 71%, Roman Catholic 5%
Currency:	1 Barbados dollar = 100 cents
Climate:	Warm and dry all year, showers Jul–Nov

Barbados is the most easterly of the Windward Islands of the West Indies, lying to the north-east of Venezuela. The island is limestone with a layer of coral, giving rise to an astonishing network of caves, caverns and underground waterfalls.

Barbados was settled by the British from 1627, when sugar plantations began to spring up, worked by African slave labour; this continued until slavery was abolished 200 years later. Barbados achieved independence within the Commonwealth from 1966. Head of state since 1952 is

OPPOSITE: South Winds Sailing Club at Dover Beach, Christchurch.

ABOVE: Barbadians in traditional dress.

FAR RIGHT: The Bridgetown Holetown Tuk band.

Queen Elizabeth II, represented since 1996 by Governor-General Sir Clifford Husbands. Head of government since 1994 is Prime Minister Owen Seymour Arthur.

Sugar, rum and molasses have long been the traditional products of Barbados. However, tourism and mnufacturing began to overtake the sugar industry in the 1990s, and offshore banking and information services are important revenue earners.

41

BELARUS

Location:	15 F
Capital:	Minsk
Area:	80,154sq m (207600km²)
Population:	10,300,483 July 2005
Main Languages:	Belarusian, Russian
Main Religions:	Eastern Orthodox 80%;
	Roman Catholic, Protestant,
	Jewish and Muslim 20%
Currency:	1 rouble = 100 kopeks
Climate:	Warm, moist summer, cold
	winter

A landlocked country in Eastern Europe, Belarus is bordered by Poland, Lithuania, Latvia, Russia and Ukraine. It is a low-lying and marshy country, with extensive peat bogs and many lakes. The colder north has birch, alder and pine forests, and oak and ash grow in the warmer south. Farmland and pasture have replaced some of the original forests.

Must of Belarus' turbulent history is attributable to its geographical position in Eastern Europe, though it has managed to survive. Settled by Slavic peoples from the 6th to the 8h century, in the following

42

century the area was part of the first East Slavic state of Kieven Rus, that was originally centred on Kiev in Ukraine. In the 13th century it was overrun by the Golden Horde and became part of the Mongol Empire. From the 14th century the area was successively part of Lithuania, Poland and Imperial Russia. It was left devastated by the retreating armies during the Napoleonic Wars in 1812, and much the same thing happened to it in the First World War. It declared itself independent from Russia in 1918, but was declared a socialist republic the following year. By the Treaty of Riga in 1921, the western part was given to Poland and the east became the Belorussian SSR. (The word 'Belorussia' is translated in many languages as 'White Russia', but is more correctly 'White Ruthenia'.) During the Stalinist era, a policy of Russification was adopted and Belorussian culture and the use of its language was severely discouraged. In 1939 the Soviet Union annexed the part of Belorussia held by Poland, as a result of the Molotov-Ribbentrop Pact.

During the Second World War Belorussia became a theatre of war once again, when a quarter of the population perished and most of the Jewish population was killed by the Nazis; it took until 1971

for the population to reach its pre-war level.

As the Republic of Belarus it became a founder member of the Commonwealth of Independent States on the break-up of the Soviet Union in 1991. Despite allegations of autocracy and violation of human rights, the head of state since 1994 has been President Aleksandr Lukashenko, having gained a second term of office in 2001; head of government since 2003 is Prime Minister Sergei Sidorsky. As a result of these allegations Belarus has been excluded from joining the Council of Europe

Belarus' economy has grown substantially in recent years, but it continues to suffer high inflation and trade deficits. Besides being a largely agricultural economy, with dairy and livestock farming, it also has an important petrochemical industry, though it is reliant on Russia for energy. Russia is also its most important trading partner.

OPPOSITE: Victory Square, Minsk.

ABOVE: The attractive Nemiga district of Minsk.

LEFT: The Kormarovka indoor market, Minsk.

BELGIUM

Location:	13 F
Capital:	Brussels
Area:	11,778sq m (30518km²)
Population:	10,364,388 July 2005
Main Languages:	French, Flemish (Dutch)
Main Religions:	Roman Catholic, Protestant
Currency:	euro
Climate:	Warm summer, cool winter

A country of Western Europe, Belgium (Belgique in French, België in Flemish), has a coastline on the North Sea, but is otherwise surrounded by Netherlands, Germany, Luxembourg and France. It is characterized by the Ardennes in the south-east, and lowland plains drained by the Rivers Meuse and Scheldt.

Belgium has a long and chequered history that began when Julius Caesar conquered the Celtic tribe of the Belgae and absorbed them into the Roman Empire. The rest of its story is closely linked with that of its European neighbours, though there is more art, architecture and history within its borders than many of its larger neighbours.

Belgium became independent from the Netherlands (Low Countries), of which it had been a member since the end of the Napoleonic Wars (1815), after a national revolt in 1830, when Leopold I became king, His successor, Leopold II, encouraged industrialization and colonialism, notably in the Congo, which has remained troublesome despite becoming independent from Belgium in 1960.

Belgium was occupied by the Germans during two World Wars, when it suffered

OPPOSITE LEFT: *Brussels lace, reputed to be among the finest in the world.*

OPPOSITE RIGHT: *Brussels' Grand Square.*

RIGHT: *The well-preserved medieval city of Bruges, the centre of the Flemish textile trade until the 15th century.*

BELOW: *The Mannekin-Pis, a famous Brussels landmark.*

severe devastation. Baudouin became king in 1951, after the abdication of Leopold III.

Flemish is spoken mainly in Flanders in the north, and French and Walloon, a French dialect, in Wallonia in the south. Rivalry between the two factions led to disputes over language and calls for regional self-government in the 1970s. In 1993 a federal system of government was adopted with three parliaments, Flanders, Wallonia and Brussels, which afforded recognition and autonomy to the regions at last. That year

King Baudouin died and was succeeded by his brother, Albert II, who continues as head of state. Head of government since 1999 is Prime Minister Guy Verhofstadt.

Belgium made a rapid recovery after the Second World War and has made good economic progress ever since. It became one of the Benelux countries, with the Netherlands and Luxembourg, in 1948. This, and the geography of its position, gave it significant influence in Europe, and it became a founder member of the European

Community, with Brussels now providing the administrative headquarters of the organization.

Belgium's only significant mineral resource is coal, but it produces textiles, vehicles and chemicals among other commodities. It must therefore import raw materials and rely on export of its manufactured goods, which makes it economically dependent on the condition of world markets.

BELIZE

Location:	7 J
Capital:	Belmopan
Area:	8,867sq m (22965km²)
Population:	279,457 July 2005
Main Languages:	English, Creole, Spanish
Main Religions:	Roman Catholic 59%, Protestant 37%
Currency:	1 Belize dollar = 100 cents
Climate:	Hot all year, monsoon June–Sep

Though located in Central America, Belize has more in common with the Caribbean states than its closer neighbours, and this is reflected in its official languages, though it may eventually become a Spanish-speaking nation. Apart from a coastline on the Caribbean Sea to the east, Belize is surrounded by Mexico and Guatemala. It has a flat, swampy coastal plain, with low mountains in the south and areas of rainforest. It is subject to frequent hurricanes and coastal flooding.

The Mayan civilization flourished in the area until around AD 900. The first

Europeans began to arrive in the 16th century and the Spanish claimed the area for Spain but did not settle; instead, it was inhabited by sundry privateers and shipwrecked English sailors in 1638. As British Honduras it was a British crown colony from 1862, when sugar plantations were established using slave labour. The colony achieved internal self-government in 1964 and its name was changed to Belize in 1973; it was Britain's last colony on the American mainland. It became an independent state within the Commonwealth in 1981, and Guatemala eventually recognized its validity as an independent nation in 1992, though it still claims a part of Belize's territory in the south.

British troops established a presence in Belize in the 1970s, following border disputes with Guatemala, which has had claims to the territory since the early 19th century, based on old Spanish treaties. This dispute put an obstacle in the way of British Honduras attaining full independence, though it was eventually achieved in 1981. Even today it remains a contentious issue and from time to time mediation from the UK and the Caribbean community has been required.

Belize is a parliamentary democracy and constitutional monarchy which recognizes Queen Elizabeth II as sovereign. She has been head of state since 1952, represented since 1993 by Governor-General Sir Colville Young Sr. Head of government since 1998 is Prime Minister Said Wilbert Musa; he was re-elected in 2003.

Belize's most important source of revenue comes from tourism, followed by fish, citrus fruits, sugar, bananas, timber and clothing manufacture. However, there is a shortage of skilled labour and technical acumen, and poverty, drug trafficking and crime are problems to be addressed. Prime Minister Musa's recent austerity measures, aimed at tackling the national debt, have sparked protests, and the rights of the indigenous Mayans to land and resources remains largely unresolved.

OPPOSITE: Mayan ruins at Xunantunich.

ABOVE LEFT: Jaguars are native to Belize.

ABOVE: The Collet Canal, Belize City.

BENIN

Location:	13 J
Capital:	Porto-Novo
Area:	43,502sq m (112622km²)
Population:	7,460,025 July 2005
Main Languages:	French
Main Religions:	Traditional 70%, Christian 15%, Muslim 15%
Currency:	1 CFA franc = 100 centimes
Climate:	Hot, rains May–Jul and Sep–Dec in south: Hot Nov–Jun, cooler with rain Jul–Oct in north

Benin is located in West Africa, between Nigeria and Togo. It has a short coastline on the Bight of Benin. Known as Dahomey until 1975, it was once one of Africa's most powerful kingdoms, larger than at present, and the traditional birthplace of Voodoo. In fact, many such tribal kingdoms existed in Africa until the mid 19th century, when France assumed control of the area. It was captured by the Portuguese in the 16th century, who were expelled by the Dutch in 1642 when, as

Dahomey, it developed a flourishing slave trade, mainly with Brazil. France signed a treaty in 1851, making it a protectorate in 1863. It became a colony in 1872, becoming part of French West Africa in 1904. In 1960 it became an independent republic outside the French community. A number of military coups followed, and the country eventually adopted Marxist-Leninism in 1974, when it became Benin, though it should not be confused with the former African kingdom of that name. A multi-party democracy was established in 1991. Head of both state and government since 1996 is President Mathieu Kerekou.

Nowadays, there is little industry in Benin, but it is hoped that the architectural remnants of its glorious past as the Kingdom of Dahomey, as well as its wildlife parks, will continue to attract visitors to its shores.

ABOVE LEFT: Boukoumbe, near Natitingou.

ABOVE: A Voodoo shrine on the Route des Esclaves at Ouidah.

LEFT: A dug-out canoe on Lake Nokoume.

BERMUDA

Location:	8 H
Capital:	Hamilton
Area:	20.6sq m (53.3km²)
Population:	65,365 July 2005
Main Languages:	English
Main Religions:	Anglican 23%, Roman
	Catholic 15%,
	Protestant 18%
Currency:	Bermudian dollar
Climate:	Subtropical,
	mild, humid

Bermuda is the largest of 140 or so small islands, of which only about 20 are inhabited. It is situated in the western Atlantic, east of South Carolina in the USA. The chain of ancient volcanoes, topped by coral islands, is connected by a series of bridges and causeways, while the interior is hilly with fertile depressions.

A local curiosity is the area of sea bounded by Bermuda, Florida and Puerto Rico, known as the Bermuda Triangle. It became notorious in the 1960s for the frequency with which shipping and aircraft mysteriously and inexplicably disappeared.

Bermuda took its name from the Spanish Juan de Bermudez, who visited the islands in 1515. It was settled by shipwrecked British colonists in 1609. Since then, Bermuda has continued to be a parliamentary overseas territory of Britain, but with internal self-government. Head of state since 1952 is Queen Elizabeth II, represented locally by Governor Sir John Vereker from 2002. The head of government since 2003 is William Alexander Scott.

Bermuda has one of the highest per capita incomes in the world. Its economy is based on financial services and tourism, its visitors coming mainly from the USA. This makes it vulnerable when recent terrorist incidents have deterred Americans from travelling. Agriculture is negligible, there being little arable land, and industry is small; construction is important, however, largely of luxury houses and facilities for tourists.

ABOVE: Hamilton's Anglican cathedral.

ABOVE LEFT: The beach at Windsor.

LEFT: Moored yachts at St George.

BHUTAN

Location: 19 I
Capital: Thimphu
Area: 18,000sq m (46500km²)
Population: 2,232,291 July 2005
Main Languages: Dzongkha, English, Nepali
Main Religions: Buddhist 70%, Hindu 25%
Currency: 1 ngultrum = 100
                   chetrum
Climate: Hot, humid on plains,
                   cooler in hills,
                   June monsoon

Small and remote, the independent kingdom of Bhutan lies between China and India, on the southern slopes of the eastern Himalayas. It is mostly mountainous, with some fertile valleys and grasslands.

From 1865 Bhutan received a subsidy from Britain in exchange for ceded border areas. A monarchy was established in 1907 and Bhutan was allowed autonomy in all but foreign affairs and the ceded territory was returned. When India became independent of Britain in 1947, it continued to honour Bhutan's agreement with Britain.

There were small-scale pro-democracy demonstrations in 1990 and nothing much has happened since. However the issue of 100,000 Bhutanese refugees in Nepal remains unresolved. Head of state since 1972 is King Jigme Singye Wangchuck. Head of government since 2005 is Lyonpo Sangay Ngedup.

Bhutan has remained largely static where politics are concerned. It is a predominantly rural society, but exports a few commodities, such as talc, cement, spice, precious stones and timber.

ABOVE: A market in Thimphu.

ABOVE RIGHT: The temple at Punakha.

RIGHT: Rinchengana, a typical Himalayan village.

BOLIVIA

Location:	8 L
Capital:	La Paz/Sucre
Area:	424,165sq m (1098581km²)
Population:	8,857,870 July 2005
Main Languages:	Spanish, Quechua
Main Religions:	Roman Catholic 94%
Currency:	1 real = 100 centavos
Climate:	Mild all year, cooler in mountains, rains Nov–Feb

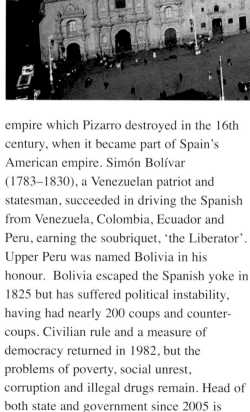

Bolivia is a landlocked republic of South America, south-west of Brazil. A range of the Andes borders its western limits, while another range lies towards the east, enclosing a great tableland 12,000ft (4200m) high, on which part of Lake Titicaca in the north, the highest navigable body of water in the world, and Lake Poopo lie. This cold *altiplano* is a region where tin is now mined, in contrast to the silver once exploited by the conquistadors, using forced native labour; wheat and maize are produced in the more temperate valleys.

The area was originally the home of the Tiahuanaco people from the 7th to the 11th centuries, who were displaced by the Inca

empire which Pizarro destroyed in the 16th century, when it became part of Spain's American empire. Simón Bolívar (1783–1830), a Venezuelan patriot and statesman, succeeded in driving the Spanish from Venezuela, Colombia, Ecuador and Peru, earning the soubriquet, 'the Liberator'. Upper Peru was named Bolivia in his honour. Bolivia escaped the Spanish yoke in 1825 but has suffered political instability, having had nearly 200 coups and counter-coups. Civilian rule and a measure of democracy returned in 1982, but the problems of poverty, social unrest, corruption and illegal drugs remain. Head of both state and government since 2005 is

President Eduardo Rodriguez Veltze.

Bolivia is one of the poorest and most highly populated of the Latin American countries, but it reformed its economy after suffering an economic crisis in the 1980s. It is a large exporter of tin, and natural gas and petroleum are present in the country, though lack of investment inhibits their exploitation. Bolivia remains dependent on foreign aid.

ABOVE: Overview of the city of La Paz.

ABOVE LEFT: Inca remains, Tiahuanaco.

LEFT: An Indian woman at Isla del Sol, Lake Titicaca.

BOSNIA-HERZEGOVINA

Location:	*14 G*
Capital:	*Sarajevo*
Area:	*19,741sq m (51129km²)*
Population:	*4,025,476 July 2005*
Main Languages:	*Serbo-Croat*
Main Religions:	*Muslim 40%,*
	Orthodox 31%
Currency:	*1 konvertibilna marka =*
	100 pfening
Climate:	*Warm summer,*
	cold winter

A country of south-eastern Europe, bordering Croatia and the Adriatic Sea, Bosnia & Herzegovina has a landscape of mountains and valleys, dominated by the Dinaric Alps bordering Croatia to the west.

In ancient times, the area was part of Roman Illyria. It was conquered by Slavs in the 7th century, becoming part of the Turkish empire from 1463. The Congress of Berlin placed Bosnia-Herzegovina under Austro-Hungarian administration from 1878, when it became a hotbed of Serb opposition to Austrian rule. Austria went a step further and annexed the country in 1908, causing Serbian nationalism to intensify. In Sarajevo in 1914, Gavrilo Princip assassinated the Archduke Franz Ferdinand, the heir to the Austrian throne, an act that precipitated the First World War.

In 1918 Bosnia-Herzegovina became part of a new Kingdom of Serbs, Croats and Slovenes, which was renamed Yugoslavia in 1929. During the Second World War it was part of the neighbouring German puppet state of Croatia, and a member of Marshal Tito's federal socialist republic after the war came to an end. The republic folded in 1991, when Croatia, Slovenia and Macedonia seceded, and fearing Serbian expansion, Croats and Muslims looked for independence. Bosnia-Herzegovina, along with Croatia and Slovenia, declared its sovereignty in 1992, but Bosnian Serbs, supported by neighbouring Serbia and Montenegro, responded with armed resistance. Their aim was to partition the republic along ethnic lines, uniting Serb-held areas to form a Greater Serbia.

In 1993, the UN declared a number of enclaves where Muslims could be protected. However, in 1994, Bosnian Serbs attacked the enclaves of Sarajevo and Goradze, prompting air strikes. This was followed by an attack on the enclave of Srebenica the following year, when 8,000 Muslims were massacred. A Muslim-Croat Federation launched a major offensive, forcing the Bosnian Serbs to negotiate. The Dayton Peace Accord (December 1995) ended the Bosnian War, with Bosnia-Herzegovina remaining a single state but divided between the Muslim-Croat Federation (51%) and the Bosnian Serbs (49%).

There are three members of the presidency, the members ruling in rotation every eight months. Head of state since June 2005 is Chairman of the Presidency Ivo Miro Jovic, a Croat, after Dragan Covic was removed. The other members are the Serb Borislav Paravac and the Bosnian Muslim Suleiman Tihic. Head of government is Adnan Terzic.

The interethnic warfare in Bosnia caused production to plummet and unemployment to soar. The country receives substantial reconstruction and humanitarian aid but a time will come when it must stand alone.

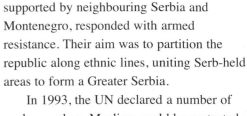

LEFT: An overview of Sarajevo.

RIGHT: The Neretva valley near Jablanica.

BOTSWANA

Location:	15 M
Capital:	Gaborone
Area:	231,803sq m (600370km²)
Population:	1,640,115 July 2005
Main Languages:	English, Setswana
Main Religions:	Traditional 50%, Christian 50%
Currency:	1 pula = 100 thebe
Climate:	Summer hot & wet, winter cooler, dry

A landlocked country of southern Africa, Botswana lies to the north of South Africa. Most of the country is covered by the Kalahari Desert, though there are areas where cattle are grazed, and much of the rest is covered by the salt pans of the Okavango Swamp in the north-west, which is the world's largest inland delta.

Inhabited by Sotho people and by nomadic bushmen in the Kalahari Desert, the San, Bechuanaland was a British protectorate from 1885. It became a republic within the Commonwealth in 1966, when it adopted the name Botswana. Politically, it has remained remarkably stable and prosperous, first under Sir Seretse Khama, then under Quett Masire, having the good fortune to be an important producer of diamonds as well as other minerals. The greatest threat to the country's stability at present is the AIDS virus. Head of both state and government since 1998 is President Festus G. Mogae.

The country has extensive game reserves and wildlife parks, which attract many tourists.

ABOVE: Traditional Kalahari dwellings.

RIGHT: Pedestrianized centre of Gaborone.

OPPOSITE: African elephants at Chobe National Park.

BRAZIL

Location:	10 L
Capital:	Brasília
Area:	3,286,473sq m
	(8511965km²)
Population:	186,112,794 July 2005
Main Languages:	Portuguese
Main Religions:	Roman Catholic 89%,
	Protestant 7%
Currency:	1 real = 100 centavos
Climate:	North hot, cooler on coast;
	centre subropical, rains
	Apr–Jul; south temperate,
	rains Nov–Mar

Located in the east of South America, Brazil has a coastline on the Atlantic Ocean. It is the largest of the South American countries and the fifth-largest in the world. It is a country of plateaux and plains, the most important of which are those of the Amazon and Paraná-Paraguay rivers. The coastal lowlands have the most concentrated areas of population in the south and south-eastern states, São Paulo being one of the most populous cities in the world. The River Amazon, the world's second-longest, is

Brazil's largest river system, carrying a fifth of the Earth's running water; but a large portion of the Río de la Plata is also within the borders, while the largest river entirely within Brazil is the São Francisco, with its huge hydro-electric plant. Brazil has the Equator passing through it in the north and the Tropic of Capricorn through the south; consequently, the dense tropical forests of the Amazon basin are always wet and steamy, and support rubber and other

valuable timbers; however, they are being destroyed at an alarming rate, causing the world's oxygen to deplete to a serious extent.

The original inhabitants of Brazil were the Tupi and Guarani people. However, many today are of Portuguese descent, Pedro Alvarez Cabral having 'discovered' the country in 1500, when it was subsequently settled by the Portuguese. However, as well as Portuguese and Amerindian, there is also

ABOVE: Rio de Janeiro.

OPPOSITE LEFT: Copacabana Beach, Rio de Janeiro.

OPPOSITE ABOVE RIGHT: The River Amazon near Porto Velho.

OPPOSITE BELOW RIGHT: A toucan, a native of Brazil.

African blood in the mix, through the importation of large numbers of slaves, brought over from West Africa to work in the sugar plantations along the northern coast.

Brazil was proclaimed an independent empire in 1822 and a republic in 1889, when the reign of Pedro II came to an end in a bloodless revolution. In order to develop the interior, the capital was transferred to Brasília in 1960. Since then, however, Brazil has had more than its share of political and economic upheaval, from the repressive military regime of 1964–79, with its torture and 'missing persons', to 1992, when President Collor de Mello was impeached for corruption. After half a century or more of military rule the military regime peacefully relinquished power to civilian rule in 1985. Having already been president since 1995, Fernando Henrique Cardosa was re-elected in 1998, in the hope of solving

Brazil's severe economic crisis, while Luíz Ignacio Lula da Silva became Brazil's first left-wing president and head of government in 2002. Both can be given credit for Brazil's successful economy.

Brazil is South America's leading economic power; its vast reserves of minerals include bauxite, iron, copper, and platinum, especially in the area of Minas Gerais. It is also a major producer of coffee, oranges, bananas, sugar, cotton, poultry, beef, and much more besides. Unequal distribution of wealth remains a problem, however.

BRUNEI

Location:	21 J
Capital:	Bandar Seri Begawan
Area:	2,226sq m (5765km²)
Population:	372,361 July 2005
Main Languages:	Malay, English
Main Religions:	Muslim 67%, Buddhist 13%, Christian 10%
Currency:	1 Brunei dollar = 100 cents
Climate:	Hot and humid all year, cooler with altitude, monsoon

A state in north-west Borneo, surrounded by Malaysia on the landward side, and bounded on the north-west by the South China Sea. It has a flat coastal plain rising to mountains in the east, with hills and lowland in the west. Much of the area is covered by virgin tropical forest.

During the 16th century, Brunei had considerably more territory, including the whole of Borneo and parts of the Philippines, but lost much of its influence over time. It was under British protection from 1888–1971, was occupied by the Japanese from 1941–45 and became independent in 1984. To this day, it still maintains close ties with Britain. Head of both state and government since 1967 is Sultan Sir Hassanal Bolkiah.

Although one of the smallest countries in the world, the Islamic sultanate is one of the richest, thanks to oil, and is famous for the astonishing wealth of its hereditary sultan and its tax-free status, free education and health services, fascinating waterways and draconian drug laws. The oil and gas fields lie offshore and are responsible for three-quarters of the country's wealth, leaving food, machinery and almost everything else to be imported. Efforts are being made to strengthen the banking and tourism sectors.

ABOVE: Stilt houses at Bandar Seri Begawan.

RIGHT and OPPOSITE: Jame asr Hassanal Bolkiah mosque, Bandar Seri Begawan.

BULGARIA

Location:	15 G
Capital:	Sofia
Area:	42,855sq m (110994km²)
Population:	7,450,349 July 2005
Main Languages:	Bulgarian
Main Religions:	Eastern Orthodox 80%, Sunni Muslim
Currency:	1 lev = 100 stotinki
Climate:	Hot, dry summer, cold, damp winter, snow

A republic of south-eastern Europe, the River Danube forms Bulgaria's northern border with Romania, while Greece and Turkey-in-Europe lie to the south. It has a coastline on the Black Sea to the east. There are lowlands in the north, which rise to the Stara Planina (Balkan Mountains) in the centre; these are separated from the Rhodope Mountains in the south by the Maritsa valley.

Bulgaria formed the province of Moesia Inferior under the Romans. It was occupied by Slavs in the 7th century, who were subjugated by the Bulgars, a Turkic tribe from Central Asia, from whom the country took its name. Bulgarian was one of the earliest of the Slavonic languages to be written down, using a modified Cyrillic character. It has close links with Russian and Serbo-Croat and has elements of Albanian, Greek and Turkish in its vocabulary.

In 865, Khan Boris adopted Eastern Orthodox Christianity, still the national religion, and Bulgaria became a major power, his son Simeon adopting the title tsar. The first Bulgarian empire was at its height when Bulgaria was annexed into the Byzantine Empire in 1018. The second Bulgarian empire was founded after the revolt of 1185 and encompassed the whole of the Balkan peninsula until 1396, when it became part of the Ottoman Empire. This persisted until the national revival of the 19th century led to the creation of an autonomous state, helped by Russia, in 1878. Bulgaria was declared an

independent monarchy by Ferdinand I in 1908.

From 1912–13 Bulgaria fought two Balkan Wars over the last European territories of the Ottoman Empire. It was successful in the first but fell into a dispute with the Allies in the second over possession of Macedonia. In 1915, Bulgaria entered the First World War on the side of the Central Powers, i.e. Germany, Austro-Hungary and Turkey, defeat causing Ferdinand to abdicate in favour of his son Boris III in 1918, who became a virtual dictator from 1934 and allied with Germany during the Second World War. Boris died in 1943, following a visit to Hitler, and was succeeded by his son Simeon II, who lost his throne in a referendum, and a People's Republic was declared in 1946. Bulgaria adopted a Communist constitution after the Russian model, and was one of the last of the socialist regimes to fall in 1996. In 2001, the former King Simeon II became prime

minister. Head of state since 2002 is President Georgi Purvanov. Head of government since August 2005 is Prime Minister Ivaylo Kalfin.

Bulgaria has grown economically stronger and more stable since the economic downturn it experienced in 1996, when the socialist government fell. Minerals (coal, copper and zinc) are industrially important, as is clothing, footwear, machinery and fuels. Cereals are the main crops and viticulture takes place in the Maritsa valley. Problems to be addressed are corruption in high places, a weak judiciary and organized crime.

OPPOSITE: The narrow streets of Nesebur.

ABOVE: Bulgarian folk dancers.

RIGHT: Ruins in the ancient Black Sea city of Nesebur.

BURKINA FASO

Location:	13 J
Capital:	Ouagadougou
Area:	105,884sq m (274240km²)
Population:	13,925,313 July 2005
Main Languages:	French
Main Religions:	Muslim 40%, Roman Catholic 12%, Traditional 40%
Currency:	1 CFA franc = 100 centimes
Climate:	Hot all year, rains May–Nov

Called Upper Volta until 1984, Burkina Faso is an inland state of West Africa, situated north of Ghana. The terrain is mostly flat, with undulating plains; hills lie in the west and south-east. There is recurrent drought.

The people belong either to the largest Voltaic group, or the Bobo. The former includes the Mossi, who originally established small kingdoms in the region around 1100, including that of Ouagadougou. Annexed by France in 1896 it became an autonomous country outside the French Community in 1960, following which there was a long period of military rule, interrupted in 1992 by the first multi-party ballots since 1978. Head of state since 1987 is President Blaise Compaore; head of government since 2000 is Prime Minister Ernest Paramanga Yonli.

Burkina Faso is a poor country with around 90 per cent of the people scratching a living from the soil. Cotton is exported, together with gold and livestock, though mineral deposits have been largely unexploited due to inadequate investment and infrastructure; the largest gold mine closed in 1999. Infant mortality is high and more than seven per cent of the population is infected by HIV. Despite hardship, Burkina Faso is a fascinating and colourful country and its people are cheerful if fatalistic. Foreign aid is received, mainly from France.

ABOVE: A communal well.

RIGHT: Burkinabe woman and child.

BURUNDI

Location:	15 K
Capital:	Bujumbura
Area:	10,751sq m (27834km²)
Population:	6,370,609 July 2005
Main Languages:	French
Main Religions:	Christian (Roman Catholic and Protestant) 78%
Currency:	1 Burundi franc = 100 centimes
Climate:	Warm all year, hotter on plateau, rains Oct–May

Burundi is a country of central Africa, lying between DR Congo and Lake Tanganyika (Tanzania); it also includes part of the Great Rift Valley. The terrain is hilly or mountainous, sloping to a high plateau in the east.

Inhabited by Bantu-speaking Hutu and Tutsi peoples, Burundi has long been divided by ancient rivalries. The area was part of German East Africa from the 1890s until the First World War, when it came under Belgian administration as Urundi. It became an independent monarchy in 1962 and a republic in 1966. Multi-party elections

in 1993 brought the Hutus to power for the first time, rather then the Tutsis, who had long been used to having the upper hand; this led to massacre and violence within a few months and the murder of the first democratically elected Hutu president in 1993. In 1996 the Tutsi army seized power and, despite sanctions and international censure, the ethnic cleansing continued. Since then, around 200,000 Burundians have perished, while hundreds of thousands more

have been displaced or have fled to neighbouring countries.

In 1998 Burundi troops briefly joined the conflict in DR Congo. In 2001 a transitional government came to power and a power-sharing agreement was signed in 2003; a provisional constitution was inaugurated in 2004. However, there have been difficulties implementing the agreement and elections have been repeatedly delayed, causing doubts that

peace can be sustained. Head of state and government since 2003, the second half of the transitional government, is the Hutu President Domitien Ndayizeye.

Burundi is one of the smallest countries in Africa. Its people rely on agriculture at subsistence level, leaving the manufacturing sector largely undeveloped. Tea and coffee are the main revenue earners, but are highly vulnerable to weather conditions and international prices.

ABOVE LEFT; Burundi landscape at sunset.

ABOVE: Burundi chief of the Gishoro drummers.

CAMBODIA

Location:	20 J
Capital:	Phnom Penh
Area:	69,898sq m (181035km²)
Population:	13,607,069 July 2005
Main Languages:	Khmer
Main Religions:	Buddhist 95%,
Currency:	one riel = 100 sen
Climate:	Hot and humid all year,
	monsoon Apr–Oct

Formerly Kampuchea, Cambodia is a country of South-East Asia, situated on the Gulf of Thailand between Thailand and South Vietnam. The vast and fertile alluvial plain that lies at its heart, and where most of the population is concentrated, is drained by the River Mekong. Lake Tonle-Sap lies to the west, which monsoon flooding greatly enlarges, so that it becomes the largest freshwater lake in Asia. From this, the River Tonle-Sap flows to link with the Mekong at Phnom Penh. To the north of the lake lie the magnificent remains of Angkor, the ancient Khmer capital and temple complex that reached its zenith between the 10th and 13th centuries.

The Cambodians are believed to be an Indonesian people with infiltrations from India. The Khmer were their most recent ancestors, whose kingdom was ultimately destroyed by Siam (Thailand). In more modern times, Cambodia was under French protection from 1863, becoming part of the French Union of Indochina in 1887, which lasted until the Japanese invasion of the Second World War in 1941. It became fully independent in 1953. Norodom Sihanouk (1922–), king from 1941, abdicated in favour of his father so that he himself could be prime minister; he proclaimed himself head of state when his father died.

During the Vietnam War (1954–75) the US bombed Communist forces in Cambodia, after which, following a civil war (1970–75), the Khmer Rouge took control, imposing their ruthless dictatorship on the people. The country was devastated and nearly two million died before the regime was toppled by the Vietnamese invasion in 1978.

Norodom Sihanouk was ousted in a US-backed coup, was briefly reinstated by the Khmer Rouge, and became king for a second time in 1993, when a coalition government was returned after UN-supervised elections. In 1991, after the Paris Peace Accords, democratic elections and a ceasefire were ordered; the ceasefire was not fully respected by the Khmer Rouge. There were UN-sponsored elections in 1993, when a semblance of normality was restored. Factional fighting ended the first coalition government in 1997 and another was established the following year, when a measure of political stability was achieved. The final elements of the Khmer Rouge surrendered in 1999. Head of state since 2004 is King Norodom Sihamoni; the prime minister since 1985 is Hun Sen.

Cambodia is a poor country, haunted by the ghosts of Pol Pot and the Khmer Rouge and decimated by war. In 1999, the first full year of peace in 30 years, the government made progress towards economic reforms, and growth has continued, driven by the expansion of the garment industry and tourism. More than 50 per cent of the population is 20 years old or less.

LEFT: Buddhist monks.

BELOW: The Buddhist Wat Ounalom (temple), Phnom Penh.

OPPOSITE: Angkor Wat.

CAMEROON

Location:	14 J
Capital:	Yaoundé
Area:	183,648sq m (475648km²)
Population:	16,380,005 July 2005
Main Languages:	French, English
Main Religions:	Christian 40%, Muslim 20%, indigenous beliefs 40%
Currency:	1 CFA franc = 100 centimes
Climate:	South hot, humid, rain Jul–Oct, north more extreme, cooler inland

A country of West Africa, located between Equatorial Guinea and Nigeria, with a coastline on the Bight of Biafra. The terrain is mixed, with a coastal plain, a dissected plateau in the centre, mountains in the west and plains in the north. Cameroon is one of the most culturally diverse nations in Africa. Bantu speakers predominate along the coast, as does the Islamic faith.

The name Cameroon comes from 15th-century Portuguese explorers, who once fished for *camerões* (prawns) along its coast. Like other African countries, it was once a centre of the slave trade, which was replaced by ivory when slavery was abolished in the 19th century. The territory was a German protectorate from 1884–1916, when it was captured by Allied forces during the First World War. It was administered post-war by France and Britain under a League of Nations mandate, before coming under the trusteeship of the UN. French Cameroun became independent within the French Community in 1960 and with part of British Cameroon merged to become the present Cameroon in 1961, the rest going to Nigeria.

Ahmadou Ahidjo was the country's president from 1960–82, followed by Paul Biya. In 1984 a failed coup led to many executions. Biya was re-elected in 1992 and

has been president ever since. The prime minister since 2004 is Ephraim Inoni.

Cameroon is one of tropical Africa's richer nations, though its wealth is unevenly distributed. The country is mostly agricultural, but it has ample oil reserves and other mineral resources, including gold and bauxite.

ABOVE: Pots for sale at Douala market.

LEFT: A northern Cameroonian woman.

RIGHT: Cameroonian landscape.

CANADA

Location:	*6 F*
Capital:	*Ottawa*
Area:	*3,855,085sq m*
	(9984670km²)
Population:	*32,805,041 July 2005*
Main Languages:	*English, French*
Main Religions:	*Roman Catholic 47%,*
	Protestant 41%
Currency:	*1 Canadian dollar =*
	100 cents
Climate:	*Warm summer, very cold*
	winter, snow, ice
	and permafrost in north

Canada, a highly prosperous and developed nation, is the second largest country in the world, after Russia. It is a federation of ten provinces and two territories in an independent union within the British Commonwealth of Nations. Apart from Alaska, which belongs to the USA, it occupies the entire northern half of North America. From north to south it extends well into the Arctic Circle and from east to west encompasses five time zones. Canada is sparsely populated, considering its great

PAGE 68: The Horseshoe Falls, Niagara, Ontario.

PAGE 69: City Hall, Toronto.

LEFT: Banff National Park, Alberta.

OPPOSITE: Vancouver's Waterfront Centre, British Columbia.

size, and much of the north is inhospitable to man; most of the land that is settled is within a few hundred miles of Canada's border with the USA.

To the north of Canada lie the bleak wastes of the Arctic, while what is referred to as the Canadian Shield or Laurentian Plateau, a vast area of ancient rocks to the centre and east, encloses the Hudson Bay and the lowlands surrounding it. It is mostly devoid of fertile soil, though it supports productive forests in parts. However, most of its productivity lies in minerals, the production of hydropower and furs. Further east of the Canadian Shield lie the provinces of Newfoundland, Nova Scotia, New Brunswick, Prince Edward Island and Québec, clustered around the Gulf of St Lawrence. Here there are productive forests and areas of fertility, while the St Lawrence Lowlands to the south, the most highly populated area of Canada, where the capital Ottawa is situated, completes the southern section of the eastern interior, together with the northern extension of the Appalachian Mountains.

The Great Plains, an extension of the prairies of the USA, extend from the edge of the Canadian Shield to the Rocky

Mountains. These are roughly located in Manitoba, Saskatchewan and Alberta, where much of the soil is deep and fertile. The Cordilleran Region in the west consists of British Columbia, the Yukon and part of Alberta, and encompasses three mountain ranges – the Rockies, the Selkirks and the Coastal Ranges. However, British Columbia possesses some fertile valleys, where fruit-

LEFT: A totem from Vancouver.

ABOVE: Moraine Lake in the Rockies, British Columbia.

OPPOSITE: St Jude's Cathedral, Baffin Island, in the North-West Territories.

growing and dairy farming take place.

Overall, the climate is variable, due to the size of the country, but predominating is the continental type, with only the coast of British Columbia enjoying a temperate climate similar to Britain.

The first people arrived from Asia, probably via the Bering Straits, around 40,000 years ago. The Inuit people, who recently acquired their own territory of Nunavut, in the North-West Territories, arrived from Asia somewhat later, while John Cabot was the first European to reach Canada in 1497; Jacques Cartier discovered the St Lawrence River in 1534. Samuel de Champlain, a French explorer, established the first French settlements in eastern Canada in the 17th century, in what are now Nova Scotia and Québec.

There was bitter rivalry from the start between the French and English colonies of New England in the south. In 1758 General Wolfe captured Louisburg, the French stronghold, and a year later the citadel of Québec. Canada was ceded to Britain by the Peace of Paris in 1763. Canada achieved dominion status in 1867 and the final step in her independence from Britain came with the signing of the Constitution Act of 1982. However, Canada remains a member of the Commonwealth. The French-speaking community is to this day largely concentrated in Québec, where the French-Canadian separatist movement is most active. This is a perennial bone of contention, as is the proximity of the USA with its economic dominance of North America.

Head of state since 1952 is Queen

Elizabeth II, represented by Governor-General Michaelle Jean since September 2005. Head of government since 2003 is Prime Minister Paul Martin.

Economically and technologically, Canada has developed in parallel with the USA, its neighbour to the south. Since the Second World War the manufacturing, mining and service industries have grown impressively and there are no fears for Canada's future prosperity. In the meantime, the task of reconciling a nation that has two official languages has been sidetracked for the moment, and the demand for separatism has somewhat cooled since Québec's referendum failed to vote for independence in 1995.

RIGHT: Montreal's downtown banks.

OPPOSITE: Gateway in Québec's old city walls.

CAPE VERDE

Location:	11 J
Capital:	Praia
Area:	1,557sq m (4033km²)
Population:	418,224 July 2005
Main Languages:	Portuguese
Main Religions:	Roman Catholic 93%,
	Protestant 7%
Currency:	1 Cape Verde escudo =
	100 centavos
Climate:	Hot and dry all year

A republic consisting of an archipelago of 15 volcanic islands in the North Atlantic Ocean, Cape Verde is strategically placed on shipping routes 350 miles (565km) west of Cape Verde in Senegal, the most westerly point in Africa. It is divided into two groupings, the Leeward and the Windward Islands, and the terrain is steep and rugged.

Previously uninhabited, the islands were settled by the Portuguese in the 15th century as a base for the slave trade, and later as an important supply stop for transatlantic shipping. They became an overseas territory of Portugal in 1951 and independent in

LEFT: A bay on the north coast of the island of São Vincente.

BELOW LEFT: Monte Verde on São Vincente.

BELOW: Local island children.

1975. Cape Verde has one of the most stable democratic governments in Africa. Since 2001 the head of state is President Pedro Pires; head of government is Prime Minister José Maria Pereira Neves.

Poor soil and lack of surface water limits agriculture, so that much of the food, apart from fish, must be exported. The people depend on foreign aid and remittances sent by relatives working abroad. Diversification is dependent on attracting more foreign investment.

CAYMAN ISLANDS

Location:	71
Capital:	George Town
Area:	100sq m (260km²)
Population:	44,270 July 2005
Main Languages:	English
Main Religions:	Various Protestant 85%
Currency:	Cayman Island dollar
Climate:	Tropical marine, warm, rainy summer, cool, relatively dry winter

Three low-lying islands in the West Indies, north-west of Jamaica. The largest is Grand Cayman (22 miles/35km long), the others being Cayman Brac and Little Cayman. The terrain has a low-lying limestone base with coral reefs.

Discovered by Christopher Columbus in 1503 and ceded to Britain in the 17th century, the islands were first settled by deserters from Cromwellian England and were the haunts of pirates in the 18th century. They were administered by Jamaica until 1962, when the islanders chose to remain a dependency of Britain. Head of state since 1952 is Queen Elizabeth II, represented since 2002 by Governor Bruce Dinwiddy. Head of government since May 2005 is Leader of Government Business, Kurt Tibbetts.

Green turtles are still farmed here, mainly to increase their population in the wild, but far more controversially for food,

while a valuable strain of coral was a source of prostaglandin, used as a hormone in medical treatment. With no direct taxation, the Caymans have become a thriving offshore financial centre and a 'tax haven' for the rich. Tourism is also an important part of the economy, enabling the islanders to enjoy one of the highest standards of living in the world.

ABOVE: Swimming with stingrays.

ABOVE LEFT: The green turtle.

LEFT: One of the Caymans' picture-book tropical beaches.

CENTRAL AFRICAN REPUBLIC

Location:	14 J
Capital:	Bangui
Area:	240,534sq m (622984m²)
Population:	3,799,897 July 2005
Main Languages:	French, Sangho
Main Religions:	Christian (various) 50%,
	indigenous beliefs 35%
Currency:	1 CFA franc = 100 centimes
Climate:	Tropical; hot, dry winter;
	mild to hot wet summer

LEFT: Making fish traps.

BELOW: Sangho tribeswomen returning from market.

rule that lasted for a decade was restored in 1993. In 1997 President Ange-Félix Patasse was faced by serious unrest, which culminated in rioting and looting after soldiers were not paid. Patasse was re-elected in 1999, beating nine other candidates, despite alleged irregularities. In 2003 he was deposed in a military coup led by François Bozize, who established a transitional government.

Subsistence agriculture, together with forestry and diamonds, form the backbone of the economy, though the people have seen little benefit from them and the country remains underdeveloped, impoverished and dependent on France for aid. Armed groups are still active in the volatile north, which has prompted thousands of Central Africans to pour into neighbouring Chad.

A republic of Central Africa, north of DR Congo, CAR consists of a rolling plateau with hills in the north-east and south-west. French is the official language, but Sangho is accepted as the lingua franca.

France established the colony of Ubangi-Shari in 1894, and with Chad, Congo and Gabon it was French Equatorial Africa from 1910. In 1958 it became a self-governing republic within the French community as the Central African Republic, and fully independent in 1960. The notorious Colonel Jean-Bédel Bokassa (1920–96) seized power in a coup in 1966 with the intention of establishing an empire for himself, styling himself Emperor Bokassa I. His brutal excesses and extravagant lifestyle led to his exile in 1979, when he was replaced by his adviser, David Dacko, and the republic was restored.

After 30 turbulent years of misrule, mostly by military governments, civilian

CHAD

Location:	14 J
Capital:	Ndjamena
Area:	496,000sq m (1284000km²)
Population:	9,826,419 July 2005
Main Languages:	French, Arabic
Main Religions:	50% Muslim,
	25% Christian, Animist 25%
Currency:	1 CFA franc =
	100 centimes
Climate:	Hot all year, rains
	May–Oct in south

A country of Central Africa, lying to the south of Libya, Chad takes its name from Lake Chad, which lies on its western border with Nigeria. A country of the Sahel, Chad has the Sahara Desert to the north, which is prone to severe drought. Uranium is present in the Aozou Strip that divides Chad from Libya; the Tibesti Mountains lie to the south of Aozou. The wetter southern lowlands allow cotton to be grown and cattle-rearing is important.

In 1908 Chad was the largest of four countries making up French Equatorial Africa. It became a separate colony of

France from 1913, an autonomy within the French community from 1958, and fully independent from 1960. The first president was the Christian Ngarta Tombalbaye. In 1969, dissatisfaction with his one-party regime led to civil war between the Muslim Arabs and Tuaregs of the north and the Christian and Animists of the south. The war was to continue for the next 30 years.

Chad had also been subjected to invasion from Libya, which led to the occupation of northern Chad by Ghadafi in 1973, and further incursions in 1983 and 1987. Libya eventually retreated, but retained the uranium-rich Aozou Strip, which was not restored to Chad until 1994.

In 1996 a new democratic consitution was adopted and Idriss Déby, who had replaced the previous leader in a coup in 1990, was re-elected in multi-party elections. He was elected again in 2001. Head of government since 2005 is Prime Minister Pascal Yoadimnadji.

In 1998 a new rebellion erupted in northern Chad, and despite two peace agreements in 2002 and 2003, bouts of fighting continue to erupt.

LEFT: A straw hut in Chad's border country with Darfur.

BELOW LEFT: Two little sisters.

BELOW: Nomads with their camels.

Chad's economy has long been impaired by its history of instability. It is primarily an agricultural country, and most of its population scratch a living from the soil. Fortunately, Chad became an oil-producing country in 2003, which augurs well for the future. Its present exports are cotton, cattle and gum arabic.

CHILE & EASTER ISLAND

Location:	8 M
Capital:	Santiago
Area:	292,258sq m (756948km)
Population:	15,980,912 July 2005
Main Languages:	Spanish
Main Religions:	Roman Catholic 80%, Protestant 6%
Currency:	1 Chilean peso = 100 centavos
Climate:	North hot, dry; centre warm summer, mild winter, rains May–Aug; south cold, wet

Chile occupies more than 2,500 miles (4000km) of the Pacific coast of South America below Peru. It can be divided into three parts: the Andes mountains, that form Chile's eastern border with Bolivia and Argentina, and which run almost the full length of the country; the central tableland; and the coastal mountain chain. This variation in terrain causes marked

differences in the climate, with drought in the Atacama Desert of the north, rain and cold in the heavily forested south and a Mediterranean-type climate in the fertile centre, which contains the largest cities and the densest population.

Before the Europeans arrived, northern Chile was part of the Inca empire, with Araucanian Indians inhabiting the rest. Magellan was the first European to see the

ABOVE: Plaza de la Constitución, Santiago.

LEFT: The Torres del Paine straddle south-eastern Chile and Patagonia.

OPPOSITE: Ranu Raraku-Moais (stone figures) on Easter Island.

country in 1520, followed by Pedro de Valdivia, the founder of Santiago in 1541. Chile then became a Spanish colony, ruled as part of Peru, until Bernardo O'Higgins (1778–1842), helped by Argentina, achieved independence for the country in 1818. In the War of the Pacific (1879–84) Chile gained mineral-rich territories from Bolivia and Peru, and her economy became rapidly industrialized in the latter part of the 19th century, though a succession of autocratic regimes hampered growth.

The Marxist democrat Salvador Allende (1908–73) was killed in a military coup in 1973, and the right-wing General Augusto Pinochet (1915–) seized power. Pinochet established a repressive dictatorship in which many who opposed his will simply disappeared (*los desaparecidos*). Patricio Aylwyn was democratically elected president in 1990, though Pinochet remained commander of the armed forces until 1997.

After this, Chile's economy and social conditions began to improve. In 1998 Pinochet was arrested by the British after the Spanish extradited him on the grounds of genocide and terrorism. In 2000, after a lengthy trial, he was released because of illness and was allowed to return to Chile, where he was deemed unfit to stand trial. In 2000 Ricardo Lagos became the first socialist president and head of government to come to power since Allende.

In spite of its troubles, Chile is a rich country by the standards of South America, being rich in copper and other minerals. It can offer a rich cultural heritage – from pre-Columbian art to the mysterious standing figures of Easter Island, which lies 2,200 miles (3500km) off Chile's western coast.

CHINA

Location:	20 H
Capital:	Beijing
Area:	3,696,100sq m
	(9572900km²)
Population:	1,306,313,812 July 2005
Main Languages:	Mandarin Chinese
Main Religions:	Taoist, Buddhist, Muslim,
	Christian
Currency:	1 yuan = 10 jiao = 100 fen
Climate:	Hot dry summer in north-east; very cold in winter in centre; hot summer, cool winter in south-east

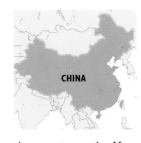

A country of eastern Asia, China is the third largest and the most populous country in the world. China has three great river systems: the Huang He (Yellow River) in the north; the Chang Jiang (Yangtze-Kiang) in the centre; and the Xi Jiang (Si-Kiang) in the south, the basins of which are separated by mountain ranges. In the north is the Mongolian plateau, that merges into the plateau of north-west China, while the south is occupied by a much-dissected, rugged plateau. In the west is the Sichuan or Red

Basin, surrounded by mountains except for the gorge where the Chang Jiang penetrates the plain of central China. To the west, beyond Sichuan, rises the great plateau of Xijang (Tibet). Such a huge and complicated geography is bound to lead to wide climatic variations; it could also explain China's relative isolation from the rest of the world.

The Chinese civilization is the oldest in existence and stretches back more than 4,000 years. The country gradually developed a stable social order and was ruled by a series of dynasties or hereditary rulers from the second millennium until the Qing or Manchu dynasty (1644–1912), responsible for greatly extending the empire, was brought to an end by revolution. Meanwhile, great things had been achieved: the Zhou dynasty (1030–221 BC) was the age

OPPOSITE: The Pudong business district, Shanghai.

LEFT: Nanjing Lu St, Shanghai.

BELOW LEFT: Temple of Heaven, Beijing.

BELOW: Yuyuan Bazar Tea House, Shanghai.

of philosophers and great writing, with Lao Tzu and Confucius; the Great Wall of China (4,000 miles long) was built under the Qin dynasty (221–206 BC), as was the tomb of its founder at Xian, with its great army of terracotta warriors; the Han dynasty (202 BC–AD 220) introduced Buddhism; the T'ang dynasty (618–907) was an age of artistic achievement; Kublai Khan founded the Yuan

dynasty (1271–1368); the Ming dynasty (1368–1644) is justly famous for its fine porcelain.

The 19th century saw more foreign involvement, with the Opium War (1939–42), when Britain occupied Hong Kong (relinquished in 1997), and the Boxer Rebellion (1900). In 1912 the infant emperor, Henry Pu Yi, was deposed and the protagonist Sun Yat-sen became President of the Republic. For a while after his death in 1925, China was torn between rival factions until after the Second World War, when the nationalist Kuomintang government of Chiang Kai-shek was overthrown by the Communists under Mao Zedong and fled to Taiwan; the People's Republic of China was declared in 1949. Dissension developed

within the Communist Party in 1957, when Mao Zedong attempted to impose a 'purer' kind of Communism. For a time, a more moderate regime prevailed when Liu Shao Chi replaced him as chairman, but he regained power and in 1964 launched the Cultural Revolution, adopted as policy in 1966 and zealously enforced by the Red Guards and others. Widespread social disturbance ensued. Mao retained the chairmanship but was joined by Chou En-lai as prime minister until the death of them both in 1976.

A struggle for power then developed between the Gang of Four and the moderate Deng Xiaoping; he was victorious, and began a process of modernization and closer links with the West from 1978. In 1989, a

pro-democracy demonstration was quashed by tanks and troops in Tiananmen Square. In 1997 Jiang Zemin succeeded Deng as leader, followed by Hu Jintao in 2003. Head of government is Wen Jiabao, also since 2003. China is now a full member of the World Trade Organization and is set to stage the 2008 Olympic games in Beijing.

Late in the 1970s, China changed from an inefficient, Soviet-type, centrally planned economy to a more market-oriented system. It also moved from a system of collectivization in agriculture to more individual responsibility, and allowed small-scale enterprises in services and light manufacturing. It also increased foreign trade and investment, which has quadrupled GDP since 1978. Agriculture employs

nearly three-quarters of the population, but there are vast mineral reserves and China also has a huge steel industry. Still to be addressed are environmental and ecological issues. In 1997 Hong Kong was returned to China and Macao two years later.

ABOVE LEFT: Army of terracotta warriors, Xian Shaanxi province.

ABOVE: Landscape near Yangshuo, Guangxi province.

OPPOSITE: The Great Wall of China, near Beijing.

COLOMBIA

Location:	8 J
Capital:	Bogotá
Area:	441,020sq m (1141748km²)
Population:	42,954,279 July 2005
Main Languages:	Spanish
Main Religions:	Roman Catholic 95%
Currency:	1 Colombian peso = 100 centavos
Climate:	Warm all year, cooler in mountains, rains May–Nov

A country in the extreme north-west of South America, Colombia has coastlines on both the Pacific Ocean and the Caribbean Sea. Traversed from north to south by three cordilleras of the Andes, vast treeless grassy plains (*llanos*) lie to the east and north, with forested plains watered by tributaries of the Amazon and Orinoco in the south. It is a tropical country, though temperature varies with altitude; the population, most of which is of mixed Spanish-Amerindian descent, usually prefer altitudes of 4–9,000ft (1200–2750m).

Not much is known of the pre-Colombian peoples of the region, though exquisite goldwork has been discovered; however, there are important archeological sites at Cuidad Perdido, San Agustín and Tierradentro.

Christopher Columbus sighted Colombia in 1499 and the Spanish conquest began in 1510. By 1538, the Spanish had founded Bogatá and established the Kingdom of New Granada in Colombia, which included Venezuela, Panama and Ecuador. Meanwhile, Simón Bolívar (1783–1830), known as the Liberator in Venezuela, where he had been tirelessly working for independence, eventually achieved, turned his attention to Colombia, defeating the Spanish in 1819 and uniting Colombia with Venezuela, Panama and Ecuador as Gran Colombia; Venezuela and Ecuador became independent in 1830. In 1885, the Republic of Colombia was formed. The rest of the 19th century saw alternate conservative (centralist) and liberal (federalist) parties holding power. Two civil wars were fought, the first from 1899–1902,

BELOW: The Plaza de la Aduana in the old Caribbean town of Cartagena.

OPPOSITE LEFT: Stone monoliths at St Agustín.

OPPOSITE RIGHT: One of Colombia's luxuriant forests.

when nearly 100,000 people were killed and Panama was lost (1903). The second was *La Violencia* of 1949–57, which saw even more casualties. In 1957 liberals and conservatives formed a National Front coalition government which lasted until 1974. Through the 1970s, however, Columbia's illegal market in cocaine was proliferating, creating powerful drug barons. In the 1980s there were frequent assassinations of politicians and others by armed cartels,

which did much to destabilize the country. A new constitution was formed in 1991 to protect human rights. In an attempt to end the guerilla warfare that had lasted for so long, Andrés Pastrano Arango, the president from 1998, sought to negotiate with the

army of anti-insurgent paramilitaries that had grown in recent years, challenging the insurgents for control of both the country and the drug trade. Alvaro Uribe Velez defeated Pastrano in 2002, promising even tougher action against terrorism.

Colombia is the most important producer of emeralds, and has gold, silver, platinum and uranium reserves, while petroleum, coffee, cotton and bananas are exported. Drugs, however, are possibly Colombia's biggest unofficial industry.

COMOROS & MAYOTTE

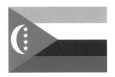

Location:	16 L
Capital:	Moroni
Area:	719sq m (1862km²)
Population:	671,247 July 2005
Main Languages:	Arabic, French
Main Religions:	Muslim 86%, Roman Catholic 14%
Currency:	1 Comorian franc = 100 centimes
Climate:	Hot and humid all year, cooler in the hills, rains Oct–Apr

Statistics apply only to Comoros

An archipelago of small volcanic islands in the Indian Ocean, lying north-west of Madagascar.

The Comoros were first visited by the British in the 16th century, when Arab influence predominated. In the middle of the 19th century, the islands were under French protection, until Grande Comore (with the capital Moroni), Anjouan and Mohéli chose independence in a referendum of 1974. In 1978, the Comoros,

OPPOSITE: Moroni harbour.

LEFT: A street in Moroni, capital of the Comoros.

BELOW: Small village huts.

apart from Mayotte, which chose to remain united with France, became the Federal and Islamic Republic of the Comoros. Coconuts, copra, vanilla, sisal and cocoa are the main products and exports of the islands.

Mayotte consists of the main island of Mahoré or Grande Terre, and the island of Pamanzi or Petite Terre. Its capital is Mamoudzou, on the island of Grande Terre. Mayotte is known as Mahoré by those who believe it should be included in the Republic of Comoros. In 2001 Mayotte's status changed to one approximating a *département* of mainland France. It has an agricultural economy, producing bananas and mangos. The total area of Mayotte is 144sq m (374km^2), and the population numbers around 178,500.

DEMOCRATIC REPUBLIC OF CONGO
(FORMERLY ZAIRE)

Location:	15 K
Capital:	Kinshasa
Area:	905,365sq m
	(2344895km²)
Population:	60,085,804 July 2005
Main Languages:	French, Lingala
Main Religions:	Roman Catholic 48%,
	Protestant 29%
Currency:	1 Congo franc =
	100 centimes
Climate:	Hot and humid all year,
	rains Mar–May, Aug–Nov
	(north), Nov–Mar (south)

A large equatorial country of Central Africa, with a short coastline on the Atlantic Ocean, DR Congo is Africa's third biggest country. Much of the northern part lies in the Congo Basin, the world's second-largest river drainage system, where tropical rainforest predominates. The great Congo or Zaïre River was developed to be a main artery of the country, while to the south and east are the beginnings of the Great Rift Valley. Lakes Albert and Edward form much of Congo's north-eastern border with Uganda, while Lake Kivu lies along its border with Rwanda. Lake Tanganyika lies along DR Congo's entire border with Tanzania.

In 1878, King Leopold II of the Belgians sponsored Henry Morton Stanley's explorations of the Congo, resulting in the formation of a Belgian colony known as the Congo Free State from 1885–1908, where the production of rubber was exploited at the

native population's expense. This was denounced by Sir Roger Casement, to which Belgium responded by establishing direct control of the colony as the Belgian Congo from 1908. Independence came in June 1960 and Patrice Lamumba took control, when civil war ensued. General Joseph Mobutu seized control in a coup in 1965 and Lamumba was imprisoned and murdered a few years later.

Mobutu declared himself president, and in 1971 changed the country's name and river to Zaïre, in a process of 'Africanization'; Zaïre became a one-party state at the same time. There was a huge influx of Hutu refugees into the country following the violence in Rwanda and Burundi in 1994. Mobutu was overthrown by Laurent Kabila in 1997, who changed the country's name again.

Civil war erupted in 1998, brought to an end by the Lusaka Peace Agreement in 1999, when UN peace-keeping forces were once again deployed, though fighting continued. Kabila was assassinated in 2001 and was succeeded by his son Joseph. In 2002 the city of Goma was devastated by an earthquake, and in 2003 an interim government under Joseph Kabila was formed with members from all rebel groups.

DR Congo is potentially a wealthy country, being a large producer of cobalt, diamonds and copper, but war has reduced output and therefore revenue, increased external debt, and led to the deaths of three-and-a-half million people from war, famine and disease

ABOVE: A mountain gorilla.

LEFT: Young Congolese girl.

REPUBLIC OF CONGO

Location:	14 K
Capital:	Brazzaville
Area:	132,046sq m (342000km²)
Population:	3,039,126 July 2005
Main Languages:	French
Main Religions:	Roman Catholic 50%, Animist 48%
Currency:	1 CFA franc = 100 centimes
Climate:	Hot all year, short rains Oct–Dec, long rains mid Jan–mid May.

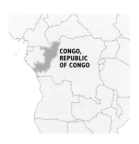

Congo is a country of west central Africa, which straddles the equator and has a short coast on the Atlantic, where the main port of Pointe Noire is situated. In the south-east, the River Congo (Zaire) and its tributary, the Oubangui, form the country's boundary with the Democratic Republic of Congo. The capitals of the two countries, Brazzaville and Kinshasa, face each other on either side of the river.

The first Europeans arrived towards the end of the 15th century and the coast became a centre for the slave trade. In 1880, Pierre Savorgnan de Brazza explored the area and it became a French protectorate. It was formerly the French colony of Middle Congo, once a part of the French Congo and later French Equatorial Africa until 1960, when it gained independence. In 1964, the country adopted Marxist-Leninism and the Congolese Workers' Party (PCT) was formed, which was the sole party until 1992.

In 1979, following a period of sporadic fighting that had lasted since independence, Colonel Denis Sassou-Nguesso seized power in a coup, only to lose it to Pascal Lissouba in 1992, in what were to be the country's first multi-party elections. During this, his first period in power, Sassou-Nguesso worked to sever his country's links with the Soviet bloc and gave French, US and other Western countries leave to pursue oil exploration and production. It was during Sassou-Nguesso's presidency that in 1990 the one-party system was at last abandoned and Marxism was renounced, the Congolese Workers' Party (PCT) having enjoyed 20 years or more as the sole party. He returned to power in 1997 after a short but bloody civil war, when he was backed by Angolan troops, and was re-elected in 2002, when a new constitution was adopted.

Congo is now one of the sub-Sahara's main oil producers and its production is the mainstay of the country's export economy, with cash crops of coffee and cocoa. Apart from these, most people manage to scrape a living working on the land, where they produce bananas, cassava, maize and rice.

ABOVE LEFT: Art exhibit from the Republic of Congo.

ABOVE: Batik cloth.

COOK ISLANDS

Location:	2 L
Capital:	Avarua
Area:	90.7sq m (235km²)
Population:	21,388 July 2005
Main Languages:	English
Main Religions:	Cook Island
	Christian Church 55.9%,
	Roman Catholic 16.6%
Currency:	NZ dollar
Climate:	Tropical, moderated by
	trade winds

A group of six main islands and a number of smaller islets in the south-west Pacific Ocean, 1,600 miles (2600km) north-east of Auckland. Lying between Tonga and French Polynesia, the islands are divided into the Northern (Manihiki) Cook Islands, and the Southern (Lower) Cook Islands. The native Cook Islanders live according to an ancient and complicated clan system, based on land divisions dating from the time the Maori arrived on the islands centuries ago.

RIGHT: A Cook Island atoll with windsurfer.

BELOW: Rorotonga beach and hotel.

The Cook Islands were discovered by Captain James Cook in 1773, were annexed by Britain in 1888 and transferred to New Zealand in 1901, becoming a self-governing territory in free association with New Zealand in 1965.

The main products are copra, bananas, pearls and citrus fruits.

COSTA RICA

Location:	7 J
Capital:	San José
Area:	19,730sq m (51100km²)
Population:	4,016,173 July 2005
Main Languages:	Spanish
Main Religions:	Roman Catholic 92%
Currency:	1 Costa Rican colón = 100 centimos
Climate:	Hot all year, rains Jun/Nov

LEFT: *View of the Gulf of Nicoya from an altitude of 3,280ft (1000m).*

BELOW: *The suburb of San Juan, San José.*

of the country, with oaks and palms along the Caribbean coast, which provide valuable timber stocks. Coffee is the most important crop, together with bananas and sugar, while cattle are raised in the far north-west. There are reserves of gold and silver and small amounts of bauxite and manganese.

Costa Rica, the 'rich coast', is a republic of Central America, lying on the Isthmus of Panama between the Caribbean Sea and Pacific Ocean. Most of the country consists of raised plateaux crossed by three mountain ranges, many of which are volcanic. The south-east has fertile, volcanic soil.

Discovered by Christopher Columbus in 1502, the country had long been inhabited by Guaymi Indians, but the Spanish arrived in 1561 and the native population was gradually subdued, so that the present population is almost entirely of Spanish stock. In 1823 independence from Spain was achieved and Costa Rica emerged as a

separate country in 1838 after 14 years within the Central American Federation.

There was a brief period when democracy failed, under the dictatorship of General Tinoco from 1917–19, and there were disputes over boundaries with neighbouring countries in the late 19th and early 20th centuries, but since the civil war of 1948–49, Costa Rica has had no army of its own and the country has been remarkably stable, compared with many of its neighbours. José Figueres Ferrer was president from 1953–58 and again from 1970–74. In 1987, President Oscar Arias Sánchez received the Nobel Peace Prize for his attempts at ending the civil wars in Central America, while Abel Pancho has been president since 2002.

Costa Rica is one of the most prosperous countries in Central America. Forests of evergreen trees cover around half

CÔTE D'IVOIRE

COTE D'IVOIRE

Location:	13 J
Capital:	Yamoussoukro
Area:	124,504sq m (322465km²)
Population:	17,298,040 July 2005
Main Languages:	French
Main Religions:	Traditional beliefs 44%, Christian 32%, Muslim 24%
Currency:	1 CFA franc = 100 centimes
Climate:	Hot all year, short rains Oct–Nov, long rains May–Jul; more extreme in north, rains Jun–Sep

A republic of West Africa on the Gulf of Guinea, Côte d'Ivoire has borders with Liberia, Guinea, Mali, Burkina Faso and Ghana. The heavily-forested coastal plain ascends steeply to a central plateau and mountains in the north-west, an extension of the Guinea Highlands. The south-east coast is an area of enclosed lagoons, on one of which stands the former capital of Abidjan,

which is also the chief port, while further along, rocky cliffs line the south-west coast.

Portuguese explorers visited the area in the late 15th century, but various European traders, in search of slaves and ivory, wrangled over its possession. It became a French protectorate, however, when France secured trading rights on the coast in 1842, and occupied the interior from 1882. It became part of French West Africa in 1904.

Ivory Coast gained full independence in 1960, though French is still the official language to this day. Her first president, Félix Houphoët-Boigny, was Africa's longest-serving leader, having held the post for 33 years until his death in 1993. He was succeeded by Henri Konan Bédié, who was deposed in a military coup led by General Robert Guei. Laurent Ghagbo became president in 2000, though the result of the

LEFT: Women buying and selling produce.

BELOW: A spitting cobra.

RIGHT: Yamoussoukro's Basilica de Notre Dame de la Paix.

election was disputed and civil unrest followed in its wake.

Agriculture employs two-thirds of the population and accounts for 50 per cent of Ivory Coast's exports. It is the world's largest exporter of cocoa beans and the fourth-largest producer of coffee in the world. Other exports include bananas, pineapples, cotton, hardwoods and palm oil, while cassava, rice and yams are local food crops.

CROATIA

Location: 14 G
Capital: Zagreb
Area: 20,812sq m (56538km²)
Population: 4,495,904 July 2005
Main Languages: Serbo-Croat
Main Religions: Roman Catholic 77%,
Serbian Orthodox 11%
Currency: 1 kuna = 100 lipa
Climate: Warm summer, cold
winter, snow

Formerly a constituent republic of Yugoslavia, Croatia is located on the Balkan peninsula of southeast Europe, occupying a narrow strip along the Adriatic Sea and curving inland towards Hungary in the north. The Dalmatian coast borders the Adriatic, dominated on the landward side by the Dinaric Alps. Dalmatia is studded with numerous islands, while along the coast the major port of Split and the peerless walled city of Dubrovnik, built by the Venetians, look out to sea. Sadly, Croatia also sustained some of the worst damage since the break-up of Yugoslavia began in 1991. The River Drava marks most of Croatia's border with Hungary, while the capital, Zagreb, lies on the River Sava. Most of the country consists of farmland, sparsely forested, and with scrub along the coast.

Apart from a period when part of Croatia fell to the Ottoman Empire in the 16th and 17th centuries, Croatia has had more in common with Hungary than its other neighbours, having been a member of the Austro-Hungarian Empire until the end of the First World War. In 1918 it became part of the Kingdom of the Serbs, Croats and Slovenes (known as Yugoslavia after 1929 and now Serbia & Montenegro), of which it was a part until independence in 1991.

After a period as a puppet state of the Nazis from 1941to 1945, Croatia reverted to being a part of Yugoslavia. After the Second World War, it became an independent

Communist state under Marshal Josip Broz Tito, who was able to hold the country together until his death in 1980. Ethnic and economic problems followed and relations between Croatia and Serbia deteriorated, threatening the country's stability in the process.

In 1990, after Franjo Tudjman won the first democratic election, a referendum voted for Croatia to become an independent republic, though Serb-dominated areas were prepared to fight for the status quo. War between Croatia and Serbia erupted and there were four years of bitter fighting before occupying Serb armies could be removed from Croatian territory. Under UN supervision, the last Serb-held enclave of Krajina was returned to Croatia in 1998. In 2000, following Tudjman's death, Stjepan Mesic became president. In 2001, the former Yugoslav president, Slobodan Milosevic, was indicted for war crimes during the war with Croatia.

Before its dissolution, Croatia, after Slovenia, had been the most prosperous and industrialized region of Yugoslavia, but tourism and public investment have gone far to help recovery, following the disruption caused by war. Croatia has a wide range of manufacturing industries, such as steel, chemicals and oil refining, though agriculture remains predominant.

OPPOSITE LEFT: Waterfall at Plitvicka.

OPPOSITE RIGHT: Dubrovnik.

RIGHT: Split Harbour.

CUBA

Location:	7 I
Capital:	Havana
Area:	44,237sq m (114574km²)
Population:	11,346,670 July 2005
Main Languages:	Spanish
Main Religions:	Roman Catholic 60%,
	Protestant 4%
Currency:	1 Cuban peso =
	100 centavos
Climate:	Hot all year, rains May–Oct,
	hurricanes Aug–Nov

The largest and most westerly of the islands of the West Indies, Cuba lies at the mouth of the Gulf of Mexico. It comprises the main island of Cuba, the smaller *Isla de la Juventud* (Isle of Youth), and many islets. The mountains of the Sierra Maestra lie in Cuba's south-east, culminating in Pico Turquino at 6,562ft (2000m). The rest is rolling hills and fertile plains, where tobacco, sugar and other tropical crops are grown. There is also valuable timber, and iron, copper and nickel workings, first developed by American companies, are controlled by the state.

Discovered by Columbus in 1492, Cuba was conquered by the Spanish about 20 years later. The importation of slaves from Africa began in 1523, and continued until abolition in 1886. In 1868 civil war erupted after a long period of corrupt government; this led to a second war of independence in 1895. The sinking of the USS *Maine* in Havana harbour in 1898 sparked the Spanish-American War, which Spain lost, and American military rule prevailed for a time. The US withdrew in 1901, and the country became an independent republic, with its first president, in 1902.

Since the Communist revolution of

1959, when the right-wing dictator, Fulgencio Batista y Zaldivar, was overthrown by Fidel Castro, supported by Che Guevara, Cuba has been firmly under Castro's control. In 1961, the US broke off diplomatic relations and imposed a trade embargo. This was followed by the disastrous incident of the Bay of Pigs, when the US attempted to invade Cuba and overthrow Castro's regime, with its violent anti-American policies. In 1962, the siting of Soviet missiles triggered the potentially catastrophic Cuban Missile Crisis, which was thankfully averted. Nevertheless, Cuba is of great strategic importance and the US has had a base at Guantánamo Bay since 1934, recently used to intern suspected terrorists. Many disaffected Cubans went into voluntary exile in the 1960s and '70s

and many more in the 1980s when emigration was made legal.

The US embargo continues to take its toll on Cuba's economy, despite calls for its removal. Cuba was particularly devastated by the collapse of the Soviet Union, when trade with the Eastern bloc countries was lost. Cuba's most important export is sugar, but nickel, cigars and rum are good revenue earners.

LEFT: Cuban women in traditional dress.

ABOVE: The Cathedral of San Cristobal, Havana.

OPPOSITE: Playa Ancon beach in the province of Sancto Spiritus.

CYPRUS

Location:	15 H
Capital:	Nicosia
Area:	3,572sq m (9251km²)
Population:	780,133 July 2005
Main Languages:	Greek, Turkish
Main Religions:	Greek Orthodox 76%,
	Muslim 23%
Currency:	1 Cyprus pound =
	100 cents
Climate:	Hot dry summer, mild
	winter

Cyprus is a strategically placed island lying in the eastern Mediterranean about 50 miles (80km) from the coast of Turkey in Asia. The name Cyprus is an allusion to the copper once found there, though little remains today. Between the Kyrenia range of mountains in the north-east and the Troödos in the south-east lies the broad, fertile plain of Messaoria and the capital, Nicosia.

In antiquity, Cyprus was colonized by Greece, then by a succession of invaders from the mainland, including Assyrians, Babylonians, Egyptians and Persians and it

OPPOSITE: A Cypriot fishing village.

RIGHT: Ruins of a Byzantine castle at Paphos.

BELOW: Men outside a taverna at Lefkara.

was seized by Rome in 58 BC. The Lusignan family ruled the island from the end of the 12th century until the Venetians captured it in 1489. It was held by the Turks from 1571 until 1878, when it was surrendered to British administration.

Cyprus was annexed by Britain in 1914, and it was declared a colony in 1925. In the 1950s, the Greek Cypriots, by far the greater majority, began to press for union with Greece (*enosis*). They were supported by a Greek Orthodox archbishop, Makarios, who

was exiled by the British from 1956–59 for allegedly supporting the EOKA terrorists who were attacking the British. Meanwhile, the Turkish were beginning to press for partition. In 1960 Cyprus became an independent republic, following years of resistance to British rule. It was admitted to the Commonwealth in 1961, when Archbishop Makarios became Cyprus's first president.

Despite the presence of UN peace-keepers, sporadic intercommunal violence continued, forcing Turkish Cypriots into enclaves throughout the island, while Britain kept three military bases in the south. Makarios was eventually overthrown in a military coup supported by Greece in 1974, whereupon Turkish forces seized about 40 per cent of the northern part of the island, displacing 200,000 Greek Cypriots who fled to the south. In 1983 the north proclaimed itself the Turkish Republic of Northern Cyprus, though it is only recognized by Turkey itself; the UN regards Cyprus as a single nation under the Greek Cypriot government. There are still border clashes between the two communities, despite the UN-brokered peace negotiations of 1997. The latest round of talks, seeking to reunite the island ended when the Greek Cypriots rejected the UN resettlement plan in an April 2004 referendum. Only the Greek Cypriot Republic of Cyprus was able to join the EU on 1 May 2004.

Manufacture includes footwear, cement, tiles and wine, though by far the most lucrative industry is tourism. Not surprisingly, the economy of the Turkish north lags behind that of the Greek south.

CZECH REPUBLIC

Location:	14 G
Capital:	Prague
Area:	30,449sq m (78863km²)
Population:	10,241,138 July 2005
Main Languages:	Czech
Main Religions:	Roman Catholic
Currency:	1 koruna = 100 haler
Climate:	Mild summer, cold winter

On 1 January 1993, Czechoslovakia was divided into two entities – the Czech Republic and the Republic of Slovakia. The Czech Republic now occupies about two-thirds of the area that was once Czechoslovakia, and consists of the Bohemian plateau in the east and the Moravian lowlands in the west. Mountains form most of the republic's northern border with Germany and Poland

Czechoslovakia came into being at the end of the First World War, after the break-up of the Austro-Hungarian Empire, of which it had been a part since 1526. Then, the area that had been absorbed into Austria-Hungary consisted not only of today's Czech Republic and Slovakia, but also of the part of Hungary occupied by the Slavonic peoples, to which had been added part of Ruthenia.

Czechoslovakia was occupied by Germany during the Second World War, but the Communists emerged as the strongest party in 1946 and by 1948 their grip on the country had tightened. However, there was a brief period of liberalization (the Prague

ABOVE: The famous astronomical clock, Prague.

RIGHT: St Vitus' Cathedral, Prague.

OPPOSITE: Prague and the River Vltava.

Spring) in 1968, during which a programme of political, economic and cultural reforms was initiated, while the 'Velvet Revolution' of 1989 ensured a relatively painless transition towards a non-Communist government. In 1992 the government agreed to the partition of Czechoslovakia and the Czech and Slovak Republics were born the following year. Since their separation, that was remarkably amicable, Czechs and Slovaks have continued to maintain economic ties .

Václav Havel, the Czech dramatist, was elected president of the new Czech Republic. He was re-elected in 1998, when talks began on the Czech Republic's entry into the EU. In 1999 the country became a NATO member, and in 2003 Havel resigned and Václav Klaus became president.

Under Communism, the old Czechoslovakia had been one of the most highly industrialized areas of Eastern Europe. Private ownership of the land in the Czech Republic has gradually increased, and crops including hops, grains and fruits are grown. There are reserves of coal, uranium, iron ore and other minerals, and machinery and vehicles are produced for export.

DENMARK

Location:	14 F
Capital:	Copenhagen
Area:	16,631sq m (43074km²)
Population:	5,432,335 July 2005 E
Main Languages:	Danish
Main Religions:	Lutheran 85%
Currency:	1 Danish krone = 100 øre
Climate:	Mild summer, cold winter

Strategically located at the entrance to the Baltic, Denmark is a kingdom of north-west Europe bordering the North and Baltic Seas. It occupies the northern two-thirds of the Jutland peninsula, together with the islands lying between the peninsula and Sweden. The most densely populated of the islands is Sjaelland (Zealand), which lies close to the coast of Sweden and on which the capital Copenhagen stands. Denmark is a flat, low-lying country, the highest point being Yding Skovhöj in eastern Jutland at only 568ft (173m), while the west of the peninsula is an area of sandy soil, with dunes along the coast and lagoons behind.

Originally from southern Sweden, the Danes migrated east in the 5th and 6th

LEFT: Hans Christian Andersen's Little Mermaid, Denmark's national symbol.

OPPOSITE LEFT: Rosenberg Castle, Copenhagen.

OPPOSITE RIGHT: Nyhavn, Copenhagen.

centuries. In the following centuries, Viking raiders subdued much of Western Europe, and the Danish conquered parts of England. Harald Bluetooth (940–85) unified Denmark and introduced Christianity, while Canute (1014–35) was the founder of an empire that included Denmark, England and Norway, but which disintegrated upon his death.

Denmark acquired power in the Baltic under a succession of rulers, but domestic troubles led to chaos until Valdemar IV (1340–75) eventually restored order. Denmark, Norway and Sweden were united under one sovereign in 1397, but Sweden broke away in 1449 and was declared independent after a long struggle in 1523. In the 15th century, Christian I (1448–81) secured the duchies of Schleswig-Holstein, vassals of the Holy Roman Empire, which were held by his descendants until 1863. They were seized by Prussia after a short war, though northern Schleswig was not recovered until 1920.

During the Second World War, Denmark was invaded by Germany, but offered strong resistance throughout the occupation. Denmark joined NATO in 1949 and in 1973, together with Britain, entered the EU, while opting out of certain elements of the Maastricht Treaty. These included full monetary union, issues of European defence,

and certain aspects of justice and home affairs. (Both recently decided again not to adopt the euro as currency.) Together with the other Scandinavian countries, Denmark is a member of the Nordic Council. Queen Margarethe II has been head of state since 1972, her heir being her eldest son, Crown Prince Frederik; Anders Fogh Rasmussen has been head of government since November 2001.

Today, Denmark is a prosperous, progressive and thoroughly modern country with an enviable social-welfare system. Industries include dairy products, cereals, sugar beet, fish, iron, steel, chemicals, electronics, wooden products and furniture, and shipbuilding.

The Faröes, a group of islands in the North Atlantic between Iceland and the Shetland Islands, also belong to Denmark, though they have been partly autonomous since 1948.

DJIBOUTI

Location:	16 J
Capital:	Djibouti
Area:	8,978sq m (23253km²)
Population:	476,703 July 2005
Main Languages:	French, Arabic
Main Religions:	Muslim 96%, Roman Catholic
Currency:	1 Djibouti franc = 100 centimes
Climate:	Very hot, dry, cooler Oct–Apr

Djibouti is strategically linked by rail with Addis Ababa, and is Ethiopia's main outlet for overseas trade. Indeed, much of Djibouti's economy is based on this fact, as well as her status as a free trade zone in north-east Africa.

The country is a seductive mix of African, Indian, European and Arab influences. Formerly French Somaliland from 1892–1967 and the French Territory of the Afars and the Issas (the two main ethnic groups) from 1967–77, the republic is situated in the Afro-Asian rift valley system on the Gulf of Tadjoura, where the Red Sea and the Gulf of Aden meet. Part of the country is below sea level, with Lake Assal at -508ft (-155m) the lowest point in Africa. Much of the remainder of the country is an arid, unproductive plain, apart from the Mabla Mountains that back the coastal plain, with Mount Moussa Ali rising to 6,653ft (2,028m) in the north.

Islam arrived in the 9th century and is still the predominant religion. The conversion of the Afars brought them into conflict with the Christian Ethiopians who occupied the interior. By the 19th century, Somalian Issas had moved north and occupied most of the Afars' traditional grazing lands. The Afars are in the minority to this day and are still in sporadic conflict with the Issas; a civil war between the two

ended in 2001. On full independence in 1977, Hassan Gouled Aptidon, of the Popular Rally for Progress, initiated a one-party state. He served as president until 1999, when Djibouti's first multi-party elections gave Ismail Omar Guellah the presidential seat.

Two-thirds of the inhabitants live in the capital, Djibouti, the remainder being mostly nomadic herders. Extreme heat and scanty rainfall mean that little can be grown and most food must be imported. With little industry and few natural resources the country is heavily reliant on foreign aid to support its balance of payments and finance its development. Djibouti still has political

ties with Somaliland, though most of the 26,000 Somalis who sought refuge during the civil unrest of the 1990s have since returned home. France still maintains a military presence in Djibouti and currently hosts the only US military base in sub-Saharan Africa, a useful tool in the current fight against terrorism.

OPPOSITE: Very little can be grown locally, so fruit and vegetables tend to be expensive.

ABOVE: Food aid being unloaded.

RIGHT: Djibouti's streets are teeming with activity.

DOMINICA

Location:	9 J
Capital:	Roseau
Area:	290sq m (751km²)
Population:	69,029 July 2005
Main Languages:	English
Main Religions:	Roman Catholic 77%
Currency:	1 East Caribbean dollar = 100 cents
Climate:	Hot all year, rains Jun–Oct

Named by Christopher Columbus, who discovered it on the Lord's Day (a Sunday) in 1493, the Caribbean island of Dominica is the highest, most mountainous of the Lesser Antilles and the northernmost and largest of the Windward Islands group. Its volcanic peaks are scattered with lava craters and include Boiling Lake, the second-largest thermally-active lake in the world.

Long defended by fierce native Caribs, Dominica was the last of the Caribbean islands to be colonized by Europeans. In fact, 3,000 Caribs are still living in Dominica and they are the only pre-Columbian

population remaining in the eastern Caribbean. The majority of the present population are descendants of African slaves.

Dominica came into British possession in 1763, having been ceded to Britain by the French. It became a British colony in 1805 and was a member of the Federation of the West Indies from 1958–62. It became an independent republic within the Commonwealth in 1978.

In 1980, the existing corrupt government was replaced by that of Mary Eugenia Charles, the Caribbean's first female prime minister, who held the office for 15 years. Head of state since 2003 is Nicholas Liverpool, while head of government since 2004 is Roosevelt Skerrit. The unicameral parliament consists of a 30-member House of Assembly of 21 elected members and nine senators.

Dominica, a land of lush rainforest and

LEFT: View of Roseau.

BELOW LEFT: The Emerald Pool at Trois Pitons National Park.

BELOW: A Carib dancer.

ample fresh water, is known as 'The Nature Island of the Caribbean', due to its relatively unspoiled natural beauty and the diversity and flamboyance of its flora and fauna, some of which are extinct elsewhere. Now they are preserved within an extensive system of national parks. Efforts are being made to promote the country as a destination for ecotourists, though this is difficult due to the rugged coastline, lack of beaches and absence of an international airport. Instead, the economy relies mostly on agriculture (primarily bananas, which are highly subject to the vagaries of the weather), which has suffered as a result of the government's concentration on tourism.

DOMINICAN REPUBLIC

Location:	81
Capital:	Santo Domingo
Area:	18,700sq m (48433km²)
Population:	8,950,034 July 2005
Main Languages:	Spanish
Main Religions:	Roman Catholic 93%
Currency:	1 peso oro = 100 centavos
Climate:	Hot and humid all year, cooler in highlands

Occupying the eastern two-thirds of the island of Hispaniola in the West Indies, the Dominican Republic was a springboard for the Spanish conquest of the Caribbean and the American mainland, being the oldest European-founded settlement in the vicinity. The terrain is mostly mountainous, rising to a central range of around 10,300ft (3140m); the most densely populated area, and the place where most of the sugar plantations are situated, is the long east-west valley between the central and northern ranges. The Dominican

Republic lies to the centre of a hurricane belt and is subject to severe onslaughts from June to October, as well as frequent floods, interspersed by periods of drought. There was severe hurricane damage to crops in 1979 and 1980.

Christopher Columbus discovered the island and claimed it in 1492, naming it Hispaniola, or 'little Spain'. In 1697, Spain ceded the western third of the island to France, which in 1804 became Haiti, while the remainder of the island was known as Santo Domingo. It achieved its own independence from Spain in 1821, but was conquered and ruled by Haiti until 1844, when it finally received autonomy as the Dominican Republic. It voluntarily returned to Spain in 1861 but fought to restore its independence in 1865.

The Dominican Republic was occupied by the USA from 1916–24 and from 1930 acquired stability at the price of democracy under the notorious Rafael Trujillo. After he was assassinated in 1961, conflict arose between rival factions, and US troops intervened in 1965. A new constitution was adopted and Joaquín Balaguer became president in free elections held the following year; land reforms were effected from 1970. Balaguer kept his hold on power for many years, until international reaction to election rigging led to his removal in 1996, since when normal transference of power has become the norm. Hipóliti Mejía became president in 2000 and was superseded by Leonel Fernandez Reyna in 2004; Rafael Albuquerque de Castro is his deputy.

The Dominican Republic is traditionally an exporter of sugar, coffee and tobacco, but these have recently been overtaken by tourism and the introduction of free trade zones. Exports of minerals are becoming increasingly important and include bauxite, nickel, gold and silver. Even so, the distribution of wealth is unequal and increasing numbers of illegal immigrants are making the crossing to Puerto Rico in search of work.

ABOVE LEFT: La Bahia de las Fleches (Bay of Arrows).

LEFT: A family stall at Samana market.

ECUADOR & THE GALAPAGOS ISLANDS

Location:	8 K
Capital:	Quito
Area:	104,551sq m (270787km²)
Population:	13,363,593 July 2005
Main Languages:	Spanish
Main Religions:	Roman Catholic 90%,
	Protestant 6%
Currency:	1 US dollar = 100 cents
Climate:	Warm all year, cooler in
	mountains

ECUADOR AND THE GALAPAGOS ISLANDS

Ecuador straddles the equator and is how it got its name. It is situated on the western coast of South America, bounded by Colombia and Peru. The country can be divided into the tropical coastal plain, where coffee, cocoa, sugar and bananas are grown for export; the central Andean highlands or sierra, which includes Mount Chimborazo (20,561ft/6,267m) and Cotopaxi, the world's

LEFT: A blue-footed boobie on Genevesa, one of the Galapagos Islands.

OPPOSITE LEFT: The southern highlands of Ecuador.

OPPOSITE RIGHT: The Catedral Nueva, Cuenca.

highest active volcano at 19,344ft (5896m), and the valleys in between. This is where most of the agricultural produce for domestic consumption is grown; the Oriente or eastern area of rolling jungle, stretching from the Andes to the Amazon basin, where valuable unexploited timber, oil and natural gas are to be found; the archipelago of Colón and the Galápagos Islands, a province of Ecuador in the Pacific Ocean, 650 miles (1050km) off the coast.

Ecuador, then the kingdom of Quito, was conquered by the Incas shortly before the Spanish arrived in the 16th century; the Spanish then defeated the Incas, taking Quito for Spain. Ecuador became part of Bolívar's Gran Colombia in 1822, and achieved independence, along with Colombia and Venezuela, following Gran Colombia's collapse in 1830.

The army dominated the political scene in the first half of the 20th century and Ecuador lost territories in a series of conflicts with neighbouring countries. Steps were taken in 1967 to prevent a return to military rule; nevertheless, José Maria Velasco Ibarra (1893–1979), who had been president twice since 1944, established a dictatorship in 1972, but was overthrown in a coup, and a military junta was imposed instead. Under a new constitution, Jaime Roldós Aguilero became president in 1979, and León Fébres Cordero's presidency in 1984 was followed by continuous political unrest. The presidency of Durán Ballen from 1992–96 saw more of the same and there have been seven more presidents since then. A border war with Peru began in 1995, which was resolved in 1999, when a demilitarized zone was established. Head of state since May 2005 is Alfredo Palacio.

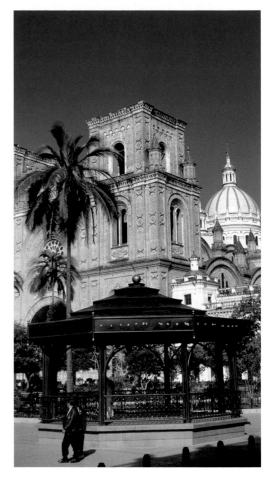

In 2000 the US dollar became the national currency in an attempt to stabilize the economy and control inflation. Ecuador is an important producer of bananas and has substantial reserves of petroleum, which in recent years accounted for nearly half the country's export earnings and a quarter of government revenues, though fluctuations in world market prices can have a substantial domestic impact. Fortunately, Ecuador has benefited from higher oil prices in the last two years, though economic reforms have yet to be implemented to reduce its vulnerability.

EGYPT

Location:	15 I
Capital:	Cairo
Area:	386,900sq m (1002071km²)
Population:	77,505,756 July 2005
Main Languages:	Arabic
Main Religions:	Muslim 94%
Currency:	1 Egyptian pound = 100 piastres
Climate:	Summer very hot, winter mild

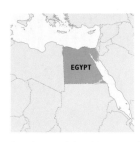

A country in north-east Africa, bordered by the Mediterranean Sea to the north and the Red Sea to the east. Egypt has land borders with Libya to the west, the Gaza Strip to the north-east, and Sudan to the south. It also includes the Sinai Peninsula. Egypt's population is concentrated chiefly along the valley of the River Nile, which flows from south to north towards the sea, depositing alluvium and forming a narrow fertile strip along each bank. The rest of the country is mostly desert, with the Eastern or Arabian Desert in the east and the Western and Libyan Deserts in the west. Where the Nile flows into the Mediterranean, a triangular delta has formed that is 150 miles (240km) across at the seaward end. To counter the almost total lack of rainfall, irrigation is used and the annual floodwaters of the Nile were conserved by construction of the Aswan Dam in 1971. However, the result is Lake Nasser, which has substantially altered the Nile's place in the agriculture and ecology of Egypt, which it has occupied since time immemorial. The Nile is also under threat due to the rapid growth in population.

Egypt's history spans 5,000 years, but a more unified society arose around 3200 BC. The ancient kingdoms of Upper and Lower Nile were ruled successively by 31 dynasties, and can be divided into those of the Old Kingdom, during which the great pyramids of Giza were built in the 26th century BC; the Middle Kingdom (c.22nd–18th centuries BC), when Luxor was built; the New Kingdom, which began in 1580 BC with the expulsion of the Semitic Hyksos from Egypt and ended in 1370 BC.

Egypt became a centre of Hellenistic culture after Alexander the Great conquered Egypt in 332 BC and founded a new capital at Alexandria, now Egypt's principal port. On the division of his empire, Alexander was followed by the Ptolemys, the Greek influence ending with Cleopatra's tragic liaison with Mark Antony and her death in

30 BC. Egypt was conquered by Augustus in 30 BC and became a province of Rome and later Byzantium.

The Arab conquest of 641 saw Egypt's conversion to Islam and the introduction of the Arabic language. The Sultan Saladin attempted to recover the Holy Land, but was defeated by Richard the Lionheart at Arsuf in 1191. The Mamelukes, a soldier caste and descendants of Turkish, Mongol and Circassian slaves, gained control of Egypt in 1250, and ruled Syria almost simultaneously. In 1517 Egypt was conquered by the Turks and became part of the Ottoman Empire, still under the control of the Mamelukes, which ended with the massacre of the Mamelukes in 1811.

Contact with Europe began with Napoleon's invasion and the French occupation of Egypt in 1798–1801. Muhammad Ali expelled the French and in 1805 was appointed viceroy and pasha, an hereditary title; his dynasty lasted until 1952. He died in 1849 and is regarded as the founder of modern Egypt. Under his successors, British and French investment was made in Egypt and the building of the Suez Canal in 1869 made Egypt strategically important. British influence was uppermost after 1882, though nominal allegiance to the Ottoman Empire continued until 1914, when Egypt became a British protectorate. Britain maintained a military presence from 1914 until Egypt achieved independence and established a monarchy in 1922.

The creation of Israel in 1948 saw the involvement of Egypt in the first of the Arab-Israeli Wars. In 1952, the corrupt King Farouk was toppled by the army and escaped into exile. Muhammad Neguib pronounced Egypt a republic, with himself as president, but was usurped by his prime minister, Gamal Abdel Nasser (1918–70) in 1954; Nasser nationalized the Suez Canal to protests from Israel, Britain and France. Following border clashes later that year, Israel invaded Egypt. Franco-British troops again intervened to protect the canal, which Nasser immediately blocked until it was cleared three weeks later on intervention by the UN. Egypt united with Syria in 1958 to form the United Arab Republic. Syria withdrew in 1961 but Egypt kept the title until 1971, when the style Arab Republic of Egypt was adopted. Nasser was succeeded in 1970 by Anwar Sadat.

Meanwhile, further wars with Israel had been fought in 1967 (the Six Day War) and 1973 (the Yom Kippur or October War), and the Suez Canal had again been blocked. Peace with Israel was restored by the Camp David Agreements of 1979 and Israel relinquished Sinai in 1982; however, an answer has yet to be found to the problem of the Israeli occupation of Palestine. Egypt was expelled from the Arab League and Sadat was assassinated in an Islamic *jihad* in 1981. Hosni Mubarak succeeded him as president, but by now the spread of Islamic fundamentalism was gathering speed. Mubarak effected Egypt's return to the Arab League in 1989 and greatly improved relations with the West.

Egypt's tourist industry was damaged when 58 tourists were massacred by terrorists in Luxor in 1997. Textiles are the second most valuable export after oil, while other resources are natural gas, iron ore, phosphates, manganese, limestone, gypsum, talc, asbestos, lead and zinc.

OPPOSITE LEFT: The pyramids at Giza.

OPPOSITE RIGHT: Spices for sale at Luxor.

LEFT: The banks of the Nile, with the Dendera mosque in the background.

EL SALVADOR

Location: 7 J
Capital: San Salvador
Area: 8,124sq m (21041km²)
Population: 6,704,932 July 2005
Main Languages: Spanish
Main Religions: Roman Catholic 90%
Currency: US dollar
Climate: Hot all year, rains
                   May–Oct, cooler inland

EL SALVADOR

The smallest and most densely populated of the Central American republics, and the only one lacking a coastline on the Caribbean Sea, El Salvador is bounded by Guatemala to the north-west, Honduras to the north-east and by the Pacific Ocean to the south. The narrow coastal plain rises to a mountainous region of active and extinct volcanoes and crater lakes that overlook a central plateau; this is where most of the population is concentrated. Known as the Land of Volcanoes, El Salvador experiences frequent eruptions; it is also subject to hurricanes and earthquakes. In 2001 a massive earthquake killed around 1,200 people and left a million homeless.

RIGHT: Shoeshine boys ply their trade outside the Cathedral of El Salvador, San Salvador.

OPPOSITE LEFT: The Cathedral of El Salvador.

OPPOSITE RIGHT: An unusually decorated country veterinary clinic and pharmacy.

The indigenous people of the territory were conquered by the Spanish in 1524, when what is now El Salvador became a part of Spanish Guatemala. It achieved independence from Spain in 1821, and eventually joined the Central American Federation, which came to an end in 1839. Though by now fully independent, El Salvador continued to receive interference from its neighbours, especially Guatemala, but began to develop its coffee plantations in the latter part of the 19th century. In 1931, following the collapse of the world coffee market, Maximiliano Hernández Martínez seized power in a coup and began a period of repressive dictatorship. In the 1960s, a military junta, headed by Julio Adalberto Rivera, came to an end when Fidel Sánchez Hernández seized power, which he maintained until 1972.

Tensions had long existed between El Salvador and its more sparsely-populated neighbour, Honduras, over the number of Salvadoreans that were arriving across the Honduran border. In 1969, following a football match between the two, in which El Salvador was victorious, open warfare was declared, which lasted for weeks, with

the state and the unicameral Legislative Assembly from June 2004 is President Elias Antonio Saca Gonzalez.

Salvador's GDP is roughly half that of Brazil, Argentina and Chile and distribution of income is highly unequal. Many poor households have been sustained by US dollars sent home by relatives who have emigrated to the USA, and the currency has long been used by commerce and business in El Savador. With the adoption of the US dollar as its currency in 2001, El Salvador is the second Latin American country to have followed this path, Ecuador having

been the first. El Salvador may have lost control over its monetary policy but it can now concentrate on developing a disciplined fiscal policy.

Coffee, sugar, corn, rice, beans, oilseed, cotton, sorghum, fish, beef and dairy products are produced in El Salvador, with coffee accounting for over half its export revenue. Industries include food processing, beverages, petroleum, chemicals, fertilizers, furniture, textiles and light metals. Current environmental issues are deforestation, soil erosion, and water and soil pollution.

many people injured. Further fighting followed in 1970 which lasted until a peace treaty was signed ten years later.

José Napoleon Duarte was elected president in 1972, but was overthrown in a coup and exiled – all in the same year. He made a comeback after another coup in 1979, with the firm commitment to restore democracy. He was re-elected in 1985. From 1980 the country was devastated by a

brutal civil war between US-backed government forces and the Farabundo Marti Liberation Front, leaving at least 75,000 people dead or homeless. After intervention by the UN, a peace accord was agreed in 1992 that provided for military and political reforms; even so, chaos remains.

Armando Calderón Sol, of the ARENA party, became president in 1994, succeeded in 1999 by Francisco Flores. Head of both

ENGLAND

Location:	13 F
Capital:	London
Area:	50,288sq m (130246km²)
Population:	49,138,831 2001
Main Languages:	English
Main Religions:	Anglican, Roman Catholic
Currency:	1 pound = 100 pence
Climate:	Mild summer, cool winter

A country of Western Europe, England is part of the United Kingdom of Great Britain and Northern Ireland and occupies the greater part of the British Isles. Britain's capital, London, is located in south-east England and lies on the River Thames. England is bordered by Scotland in the north and Wales in the west. Its east coast is on the North Sea, while to the south lies the English Channel and France; the Irish Sea, Ireland and the Atlantic Ocean lie

RIGHT: London's Docklands: Canary Wharf (centre) is flanked on the left and right by the Citygroup and HSBC buildings.

OPPOSITE: Tower Bridge, which crosses the River Thames.

to the west. The landscape is varied and complex. The south of England consists of lowlands and downs, with fenland in the east. The terrain rises towards the north and includes the north-central Pennines, the Cheviot Hills that border Scotland in the far north, and the Cumbrian Mountains. The latter dominate the scenic Lake District in the north-west.

As an island nation, Britain, despite its proximity to the rest of Europe, has a long tradition of independence from its neighbours. Its people are of mixed stock, the result of invasion and immigration by a multitude of races from all over the world. Its beginnings lie in prehistory: the megalithic monument of Stonehenge was completed c.2950 BC, and stands to this day. Britain was conquered by the Romans in the 1st century AD, when England was inhabited by Celtic peoples, who had been in the area since at least 400 BC.

Britain was a Roman province until the early 5th century. Following the departure of the Romans in 407, Germanic tribes (Angles, Saxons and Jutes) arrived from Europe and overran much of England, forcing the Celts to retreat to the west. Christianity arrived in the 6th century from Rome and a number of independent

OPPOSITE: Buckingham Palace, London.

RIGHT: All Souls' College, Oxford University.

PAGE 120: The Royal Horticultural Society's museum at Kew.

PAGE 121: The Poultney Bridge and weir, Bath, Avon.

kingdoms were established, that fought for supremacy among themselves. Then came the invasion of the Vikings from Scandinavia, with Alfred the Great uniting the English to fight the Danes. However, a second invasion culminated in rule by Danish kings from 1016–42, after which Edward the Confessor was restored as the first of the West Saxon Kings. However, just as England was beginning to develop an identity of its own, under Harold II, it was invaded and conquered by William, Duke of Normandy in 1066.

The Normans consolidated their conquest during the next 100 years by introducing a feudal system and establishing a more orderly society. In 1215 the Plantagenet King John was forced to agree to Magna Carta, a charter for liberty and political rights, which is regarded as seminal to the development of the Parliamentary system as it is today. It was in this century that one of the two great legal systems developed (the other being Roman Law), which have been adopted throughout the anglophone world.

Wales became a principality in 1284, and became more politically connected with England once the Welsh Tudors had ascended the English throne in 1485.

Following the Norman kings, several dynasties of monarchs ruled in England and continue to this day. They include: the Plantagenets (1154–1377) – when territories in France were obtained; the House of Lancaster (1399–1422); the House of York (1461–1483); the Tudors (1485–1603) – an age of exploration, colonial expansion and religious reformation; the Stuarts (1603–1648) – when the crowns of England

LEFT: *St Ives, Cornwall.*

OPPOSITE: *Brighton Pier, Sussex.*

and Scotland merged; the Stuarts (restored) 1660–1714; the House of Hanover (1714–1901); the House of Saxe-Coburg (1901–1910); the House of Windsor (1910–). Since the middle of the 12th century, therefore, the rule of the monarchy has been interrupted only once. This was during the period 1649–1660, when the Commonwealth, a period of republican government, was established by Oliver Cromwell, following the execution of Charles I in 1649 and ending with the restoration of Charles II in 1660.

The foundations of the British Empire were laid in the 17th century with the colonization of North America and India. Expansion continued into the mid 19th century, though most dependencies had seceded from Britain by the end of the Second World War. The 18th century saw the ascendency of British sea power, parliamentary union with Ireland, and the beginning of the Industrial Revolution, while the 19th century was characterized by more empire-building and the peace and prosperity of the Victorian age. The 20th and 21st centuries were dominated by two World Wars (1914–18 and 1939–45), the birth of the National Health Service, the return of a Labour government, the accession of Queen Elizabeth II, devolution in Wales and Scotland, entry to the EU, Britain's first woman prime minister, Margaret Thatcher, Tony Blair's New Labour government, the beginning of the 'war on terror' in

Afghanistan and the removal of Saddam Hussein and the continuing democratization of Iraq. The summer of 2005 saw new developments in terrorist activity, when terrorist bombings spread to the transport system in London.

Britain is a major industrial and trading nation, though some industries, such as coal, steel, ship- and car-building, once important, have declined in recent times. Emphasis has now shifted towards the service industry, high-technology, scientific research and financial services. Agriculture is still extensive and livestock, wool and dairy products are important, as is oil from the North Sea, natural gas and tourism.

OPPOSITE: Liverpool's Anglican Cathedral.

RIGHT: An Exmoor farm in Somerset, England.

PAGE 126: Bridge over the River Tyne, Newcastle.

PAGE 127: Bamburgh Castle, Northumberland.

EQUATORIAL GUINEA

Location:	14 K
Capital:	Malabo
Area:	1,0831sq m (28052km²)
Population:	535,881 July 2005
Main Languages:	Spanish
Main Religions:	Roman Catholic 89%
Currency:	1 CFA franc =
	100 centimes
Climate:	Hot, wet all year

A tiny country on West Africa's Gulf of Guinea, Equatorial Guinea consists of several offshore islands, most of which are uninhabited, and a portion of the coast (Mbini) between Cameroon and Gabon. The capital is Malabo, on the largest island of Bioko (Fernando Póo). Bioko is volcanic and mountainous, with fertile soil and heavy rainfall. Mbini (Río Muni), which makes up the bulk of the republic, is an area of hills and plateaux behind a coastal plain; it has a similar climate to that of Bioko, though with less rainfall inland. It is covered in dense rainforest.

The Portuguese navigator, Fernando Póo, first saw Bioko in 1472. In 1778 Portugal ceded the islands and mainland areas to Spain, when it became known as Spanish Guinea. In the early 19th century, Britain, with Spain's permission, settled freed slaves on Bioko, and some of their descendants still survive here to this day. Bioko and Mbini became fully independent of Spain in 1968.

President Obiang Nguema Mbasogo has ruled the country for over 25 years, having seized power from his uncle, Francisco Mácias Nguema, in a coup in 1979; during Mácias' dictatorship more than 40,000 people were killed. Although the country has nominally been a constitutional multi-party democracy since 1991, the 1996 and 2002 presidential elections, as well as the 1999 legislative elections, were widely seen as flawed, though Obiang claimed almost the entire vote. The president controls most opposition parties through the judicious use of patronage, with businesses, in the main, owned by government officials and their families. The present prime minister is Miguel Abia Biteo Borico.

Despite the country's oil reserves, which yielded a record increase in government revenue in recent years, there have been few benefits to the people or their standard of living. There is no clean water and waterborne diseases are endemic. Other industries and resources are farming, fishing, forestry, natural gas, gold, bauxite, diamonds, tantalum, sand, gravel and clay, though some of these remain to be developed.

ERITREA

Location:	16 J
Capital:	Asmara
Area:	3,6171sq m (93683km²)
Population:	4,561,599 July 2005
Main Languages:	Tigrinya, English, Arabic
Main Religions:	Muslim 50%,
	Christian 50%
Currency:	nakfa
Climate:	Hot & dry along coast,
	cooler and wetter in
	highlands, semi-arid
	elsewhere

An independent state in north-east Africa, Eritrea is bordered by Ethiopia, Djibouti and Sudan, and has a strategically important 715-mile (1150-km) coastline on the Red Sea. There is a hot, dry, desert strip along the Red Sea coast, with an area of highland in the centre and north-west (a continuation of the high Ethiopian plateau), while flat to rolling semi-arid plains cover the south-west. There are frequent droughts, but irrigation allows a few crops to be grown.

Eritrea was under Egyptian rule in earlier times, when it was described as the legendary Land of Punt. It was a dependency of Ethiopia until the 16th century, when it fell to the Ottoman Empire. From 1890 to 1941 Eritrea was an Italian colony, created from Ottoman territory and coastal areas of Ethiopia. In 1935 Italy used Eritrea as a base from which to pursue its conquest of Ethiopia, which became part of Italian East Africa in 1936. In 1941 Eritrea was made a protectorate of Britain, following Italy's removal from East Africa. After this, it was taken into British administration until 1952, and was made an autonomous region in federation with Ethiopia. In 1962, it was annexed by Ethiopia and harshly subjugated. Ethiopia was particularly loath to relinquish its hold on Eritrea, being reliant on the Eritrean ports of Aseb and Massawa, the latter one of the largest ports in East Africa, as its only outlets to the sea.

A 30-year struggle for independence ensued, fought as guerilla warfare by the Eritrean People's Liberation Front (EPLF); during this time 150,000 were killed and 700,000 refugees fled to Sudan. By 1978 the EPLF had succeeded in driving all Ethiopian forces from Eritrean territory, but the situation was reversed when the Soviets intervened and backed Colonel Mengistu's Marxist regime. There was severe famine in Eritrea in the 1980s, followed by a refugee crisis due to Ethiopia's policy of forcible resettlement.

After the fall of Mengistu's Ethiopian government in 1991, Eritrea became internally self-governing. It became fully independent in May 1993, when thousands of Eritrean refugees began to return home.

In 1998 a border dispute between Eritrea and Ethiopia erupted, with bombing by both sides, which soon escalated into war. War ended in 2000 after the intervention of the UN; since then, a security zone on the border has been monitored by a UN peacekeeping operation. Despite an international commission in 2002, designed to settle the dispute once and for all, the matter remains to be fully resolved.

Head of state and leader of the EPLF government since independence in 1993 is Isaias Afwerki, who presides over a unicameral National Assembly of 150 seats.

Since independence, Eritrea, a desperately poor country, has had many problems to face, especially in the aftermath of the Ethiopian-Eritrean war of 1998–2000, when property, livestock and homes were destroyed and the planting of crops was prevented. Most of the population relies on agriculture at subsistence level, but are at the mercy of erratic rainfall; however, herding and fishing also take place. There are gold, potash, zinc, copper and salt present, with the potential for oil and natural gas. Exports are livestock, sorghum and textiles. Together with its other problems, Eritrea's economic future is dependent on overcoming its many social problems, which include illiteracy, poor levels of skills and unemployment.

An Eritrean desert landscape.

ESTONIA

Location:	15 F
Capital:	Tallinn
Area:	17,300sq m (44800km²)
Population:	1,332,893 July 2005
Main Languages:	Estonian
Main Religions:	Christian (Lutheran & Orthodox)
Currency:	1 kroon = 100 senti
Climate:	Warm summer, cold winter

Bordered by Latvia and Russia, Estonia is the smallest of the three Baltic states, the others being Latvia and Lithuania. It is located on the southern shores of the Gulf of Finland, with the Baltic Sea to the west. The territory also includes hundreds of islands in the Baltic Sea, of which the largest are Hiumaa and Saaremaa. Geographically it is an extension of the Russian Plain, consisting of marsh and glaciated lowland, much of which has been drained; the land is strewn with moraine and interspersed with over 1,500 lakes.

The German order of the Brothers of the Sword captured southern Estonia, or Livonia, in the early 13th century. By the middle of the 14th century it was under the control of the Teutonic Knights, a German military and religious order founded in the early 12th century, with most of the land in the hands of German noblemen by the 16th century. In 1561 Sweden annexed the north and Poland the south. It was ceded to Russia in 1721, becoming independent, after a struggle, in 1918, following the Russian Revolution. However, it was again occupied by the Soviet Union, and was annexed in 1940, when more than 60,000 Estonians were killed or deported in the first year of Soviet rule. The country was overrun by the Germans during the Second World War, who were eventually expelled in 1944, when Estonia became one of the 15 socialist republics of the Soviet Union. In the 1970s, large numbers of Russians migrated to Estonia and attempts were made to suppress the Estonian language, which led to anti-Russian demonstrations. Estonia eventually gained its independence, along with the other two Baltic states, on the break-up of the Soviet Union in 1991.

Since the departure of the last Russian troops in 1994, Estonia has been free to develop economic and political ties with Western Europe. It joined both NATO and the EU in 2004 and its currency is now pegged to the euro. As well as timber, which is Estonia's most important export, oil shale, peat, phosphorite, clay, limestone, sand and dolomite are present. It also benefits from strong electronics and telecommunications sectors, with Internet available throughout the country. It is greatly influenced by developments in Sweden, Finland and Germany, three of its major trading partners. Exports are wood and paper, machinery, textiles, food products, furniture, metals and chemicals. A healthy surplus in Estonia's balance of payments was achieved in 2003.

The president of the unicameral Parliament or *Riigikogu* since 2001 is Arnold Ruutel and the prime minister is Andrus Ansip, since April 2005.

LEFT: The brown bear, a native of Estonia.

RIGHT: Overview of Tallinn.

ETHIOPIA

Location:	16 J
Capital:	Addis Ababa
Area:	437,794sq m (1133886km²)
Population:	73,053,286 July 2005
Main Languages:	Amharic
Main Religions:	Coptic Christian 53%, Muslim 30%
Currency:	1 Ethiopian birr = 100 cents
Climate:	Hot & humid all year, warm in highlands, rains Jun–Sep

Geographically, Ethiopia's most dominant feature is the massive range of volcanic mountains that rise at Ras Dashen in the north to over 15,000ft (4575m). It is divided by the Great Rift Valley into the Eastern and Western Highlands, the latter being the source of the Blue Nile. To the north-east is the Denakil Desert, forming Ethiopia's border with Eritrea, while the Ogaden Desert lies to the south-east and borders Somalia.

Ethiopia (previously Abyssinia) has a longer history than any other African country, in that it dates from the 2nd millennium BC. According to legend, it was founded in around 1000 BC by Menelek I, son of King Solomon and the Queen of Sheba. Ethiopia is also claimed to be the final resting place of the Ark of the Covenant, once kept in the Temple of Solomon in Jerusalem, which held the tablets of the law given by God to Moses, and which was carried by the Israelites during their wanderings in the wilderness.

Situated in Tigray, in northern Ethiopia, is Aksum (Axum), once the capital of a powerful ancient kingdom, though it later fragmented. It was here that Coptic Christianity, introduced from Egypt in the 4th century and still the predominant religion, flourished. The Arab conquests of the 7th century isolated Axum from the rest

BELOW: Tississat Falls, Bahir Dar.

OPPOSITE LEFT: Gondar landscape.

OPPOSITE RIGHT: Debre Birhan Selassie church, Gondar.

of Christendom. Today, the dominant Amhara and related peoples are of mixed Hamitic and Semitic origins and are Coptic Christians, while the second largest group, the Muslims, are chiefly centred in Harar. There is a Jewish minority, the Falashas, living in the area north of Lake Tana, 10,000 of whom, during the famine of 1984–85, were airlifted to Israel.

Contact with Europe was established in the 16th century by the Portuguese and was renewed when the Scottish explorer, James Bruce, found the source of the Blue Nile in 1770. In the late 19th century, Menelek II (1889–1913) expanded the empire and established Addis Ababa as his capital. Between 1897 and 1908, Abyssinia was a colonial power, encompassing Somali and

other peoples within its feudal empire. In 1930, Menelek's son, Ras Tafari, became emperor as Haile Selassie I (the 'Lion of Judah'), but was deposed and exiled in Britain when Italy invaded in 1935. Italy combined the country with Eritrea and Somalia to form Italian East Africa. Haile Selassie was restored to power in 1941 by the British, during the Second World War, when the Italians were ejected, and continued to rule until he was overthrown by a Marxist military junta in 1974, when a one-party state was established.

The 1960s were characterized by violent conflict with Eritrea, which had been federated with Ethiopia since 1952, but now demanded independence. Ethiopia responded

by annexing Eritrea in 1962. Following a period of famine in northern Ethiopia, Haile Selassie was killed in 1974, the monarchy was abolished, and military rule followed by civil war prevailed. Haile Selassie continues to be revered by the Rastafarians, a sect that regards him as their messiah.

Mengistu Haile Mariam assumed power in 1977, and initiated a reign of terror in which thousands of people died. Mengistu proceeded to recapture territories in Eritrea and the Ogaden with Soviet assistance. There was widespread famine in 1984–85. In 1991, a coalition of rebel forces, the EPRDF (Ethiopian People's Revolutionary Democratic Front) and the EPLF (Eritrean People's Liberation Front) overthrew

Mengistu, while 1995 saw the creation of the Federal Democratic Republic of Ethiopia. Girma Woldegiorgis was elected president and Meles Zenawi became prime minister of a multi-party system of government. In 1999, more than 40,000 people perished in a border war with Eritrea. The war ended in December 2000, though demarcation is still being disputed.

One of the world's most impoverished countries, the population survives on subsistence agriculture, which is often affected by severe drought. Coffee is critical to Ethiopia's economy and it remains heavily dependent on foreign food subsidies and financial aid. There are small reserves of precious metals, minerals and natural gas.

FALKLAND ISLANDS

Location:	9 0
Capital:	Stanley
Area:	4,709sq m (12196km²)
Population:	2,967 July 2005
Main Languages:	English
Main Religions:	Christian
Currency:	Falkland pound
Climate:	Cold, marine

FALKLAND ISLANDS

A British crown colony consisting of the two main islands of East Falkland (with the capital, Stanley) and West Falkland, and hundreds of smaller islands. They are situated in the South Atlantic, about 300 miles (500km) off the coast of South America, east of the Strait of Magellan.

The islands are mostly hilly and bare of vegetation. The uplands are covered with scree, eroded peaty moorland and tussocky grass on which sheep are grazed.

The islands, later named after Lord Falkland, were discovered by an Englishman, John Davis, in 1592 and were settled by the British in 1765. The following

RIGHT: The Globe Hotel, Port Stanley.

BELOW: Whalebone arch, Port Stanley.

BELOW RIGHT: Magellanic penguins, Gypsy Cove.

year the Spanish acquired an area occupied by French settlers and ejected the British four years later, which almost sparked an Anglo-Spanish war. The islands were colonized by the British in 1831–33, following the expulsion of an Argentinian garrison.

In the Battle of the Falkland Islands (1914), during the First World War, British forces destroyed nearly an entire German squadron that had recently been successful in the Battle of Coronel, fought off Chile under Admiral von Spee.

Even though the islands were left unpopulated at times, British sovereignty was

never relinquished. Argentina refuses to recognize British sovereignty and still refers to the Falklands as the Malvinas, their old Spanish name.

In 1982, on the eve of General Leopoldo Galtieri's military junta, Argentinian forces invaded the Falklands in support of their own claim to sovereignty. Under the premiership of Margaret Thatcher, Britain responded by sending ships and aircraft, forcing the surrender of Argentina six weeks later.

The main activity of the islanders is sheep farming and wool and hides are exported.

FIJI

Location:	25 L
Capital:	Suva
Area:	7,078sq m (18332km²)
Population:	893,354 July 2005
Main Languages:	English
Main Religions:	Christian 52%, Hindu 40%, Muslim 8%
Currency:	1 Fijian dollar = 100 cents
Climate:	Hot all year, rains Dec–Apr

Fiji consists of a group of many hundreds of South Pacific islands in the Melanisian archipelago, of which a 100 or so are inhabited. The larger islands are volcanic, mountainous and surrounded by coral reefs, the rest are low-lying coral atolls. The south-east trade winds blow all year round, bringing rain to the islands 200 days a year. The largest islands are Viti and Vanu Levu, where Suva, the capital, is situated.

Fiji was discovered by Abel Tasman in 1643 and was ceded to Britain in 1874, when Indian labour was imported to work the sugar plantations. There has been little

intermarriage and by the 1950s the Indians had outnumbered the native Fijians, which causes racial tensions.

Fiji became an independent Commonwealth state in 1970, but a military coup in 1987, following the election of an Indian-majority government, led to its withdrawal from the Commonwealth, when it was declared a republic. In 1992 a military coup was led by Colonel Sitiveni Rabuka, who became prime minister. In 1997 a multi-racial constitution was approved and Fiji rejoined the Commonwealth. Mahendra Chaudhry, an ethnic Indian, defeated Rabuka in the 1999 elections. In 2000 George Speight led a coup, holding the entire cabinet hostage. Chaudhry was dismissed and martial law declared, causing Fiji's suspension from the Commonwealth. Ratu Iloilo became president and Laisenia Qarase prime minister in 2001, when Fiji was readmitted to the Commonwealth. In 2002 Speight was sentenced to death for treason, but the sentence was eventually commuted to life imprisonment.

Being heavily reliant on tourism and foreign aid, political instability has devastated Fiji's economy. However, it continues to grow copra, sugar and rice, and silver and gold are mined.

ABOVE LEFT: Wakaya Island resort, a favourite venue for weddings and honeymoons.

LEFT: A Bure house, the traditional, classic dwelling of a Fijian chief.

FINLAND

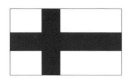

Location:	15 E
Capital:	Helsinki
Area:	130,559sq m (338148km²)
Population:	5,223,442 July 2005
Main Languages:	Finnish, Swedish
Main Religions:	Lutheran 85%
Currency:	euro
Climate:	Warm summer, very cold winter

A country of Northern Europe bounded by the Baltic Sea, the Gulf of Bothnia and the Gulf of Finland, and lying between Sweden and Russia. Finnish territory also includes the Aland Island in the Gulf of Bothnia. The northern third of the country lies within the Arctic Circle and is called Lappland, 'the land of the midnight sun'. Finland consists of a central plateau of ancient crystalline rock, surrounded by lowland created by glacial deposits. Much of the land is covered in birch and conifer forests, with frozen tundra in the north. There are many narrow, shallow lakes, that freeze over during the long, severe winters; these are a principal means of

RIGHT: Nelim Orthodox Church, Lappland.

OPPOSITE: Museum of Contemporary Art, Helsinki.

BELOW: A reindeer sledge in Lappland.

communication, even in winter. Summers are short but warm. In 1968 the Saimaa Canal in the south-east, linking the Saimaa lake area to the Gulf of Finland, and with half its length in Russia, was modernized, and is now Europe's largest inland water system.

The present-day Lapps are descendants of Finland's indigenous people, though migrants from Asia began to arrive in the 7th and 8th centuries. In the 13th century Sweden conquered Finland, and attempted to convert the Finns from paganism to

Christianity, though it took another 150 years for this to occur, and Finland remained part of the Swedish kingdom for 600 years. In 1809, after contention between Sweden and Russia, Finland became a grand duchy of Russia, but with almost full autonomy. In 1863 a national campaign succeeded in making the official language Finnish rather than Swedish, though both are now official. Later, Russia tried to restrict Finnish liberties and make Finland more Russian, which was fiercely resisted. Finland proclaimed itself an independent republic in 1918 following the Russian Revolution.

During the Second World War, Finland resisted invasions by the Soviet Union, though it did lose some of its territory, including an area on the Arctic coast that gave Russia a border with Norway – also a part of Karelia. Finland joined the EU in 1995 and was the only Scandinavian state to adopt the euro for financial institutions in January 1999, using it for all transactions from 2002.

Tarja Halonen is Finland's first woman president (since 2000), with Matti Vanhanen the head of government since 2003, when the previous prime minister resigned.

Since the war, Finland has made a remarkable transition from a land-based economy to one that is diverse, modern and industrial, with an income similar to the rest of Western Europe. Industry is based principally on wood and wooden products, metals, engineering, telecommunications and electronics, with exports acounting for two-fifths of GDP. Agriculture is at the level of self-sufficiency, due to the climate, while forestry and timber are of primary importance.

FRANCE

Location:	*13 G*
Capital:	*Paris*
Area:	*210,033sq m (543985km²)*
Population:	*60,656,178 July 2005*
Main Languages:	*French*
Main Religions:	*Roman Catholic 76%*
Currency:	*1 euro = 100 cents*
Climate:	*Warm summer, cool winter in north; hot summer, mild winter in south, with snow in mountains*

France, which has land borders with Spain in the southwest and with Italy, Switzerland, Germany, Belgium and Luxembourg to the east, is Europe's third-largest country after Russia and the Ukraine. The remainder of France is bordered by 3,440 miles (5500km) of coastline, with the English Channel (called La Manche by the French) to the north, the Bay of Biscay/Atlantic Ocean to the west and the Mediterranean Sea to the south; French territory also includes the Mediterranean island of Corsica and there are a number of dependencies overseas. Principal areas of lowland are the

OPPOSITE: I M Pei pyramid at the Louvre.

ABOVE LEFT: The Pompidou Centre, Paris.

LEFT: An entrance to the Paris Métro.

ABOVE: The Eiffel Tower.

PAGE 140: The western ramparts of the Château Comtal, Carcassonne.

PAGE 141: Nice, with a view of the port.

140

The Château de Tarascon, a 13th-century castle on the River Rhône in Provence.

Paris basin, drained by the River Seine; the Aquitaine basin, drained by the River Garonne; and the valley of the Loire, drained by the River Loire. The region drained by the Rhône-Saône rivers is dominated by the Alps to the east, while to their north the Jura Mountains skirt the Rhine at Basle, with the Vosges to their west. North of the Vosges are the Ardennes, which abut a further area of lowland and stretch to the North Sea. The Pyrenees in the south-west form a natural border with Spain, sandwiched between the Mediterranean and the Atlantic Oceans, while the ancient massif of Brittany is in the north-west; the Massif Central dominates the centre, stretching towards the south.

Julius Caesar completed the conquest of

142

LEFT: A field of sunflowers at Montpélier.

ABOVE: A vineyard in the St-Émilion wine region.

Gaul, the ancient region of Europe that corresponds to modern France, in 51 BC, but by the 3rd century AD the Roman Empire had begun to decline. Clovis I, King of the Franks (481–511), established the Merovingian dynasty in Gaul in 486, followed by that of the Carolingians. The most notable member of this dynasty was Charlemagne (Charles the Great), who was King of the Franks (768–814) and the first Holy Roman Emperor from 800.

Hugh Capet founded the Capetian dynasty, which lasted from 987 to 1328; he is regarded by many as the first king of France. The Norman Conquest of England marked the beginning of Anglo-French rivalry in 1066, while Normandy, Anjou and Poitiers, lost to the English through a dowry, were recovered by the French in 1204–05. The Valois dynasty began with Philip VI in 1328 and ended on the death of Henry III in 1589. The Hundred Years' War (1337–1453) was a series of conflicts between France and successive English kings for control of French territory, most of which had been captured by the English by 1422. However, with the help of Jeanne d'Arc at Orléans in 1429, the English were eventually expelled in 1453. In the meantime, however, she was captured by the English and burnt at the stake in 1431.

France became a major power under the Valois and Bourbon in the 16th to 18th centuries. After the French Revolution (1789–99) the monarchy was overthrown and France under Napoleon gained brief domination of Europe. The defeat of Napoleon III in the Franco-Prussian War (1870–71) led to the formation of the Third Republic (1870–1940). France suffered widespread devastation and loss of life during the First World War and was occupied by the Germans, who established a Vichy government during the Second World War, at the end of which the Fourth Republic was established. Charles de Gaulle became president of France in 1958, establishing the Fifth Republic, followed by Georges Pompidou and Valéry Giscard d'Estaing. The presidency of François Mitterand brought nationalization, centralization, civil rebuilding and support for the EU. After Mitterand's death in 1995, Jacques Chirac became president, though unemployment and strikes led to the election of a socialist prime minister, Lionel Jospin. In 2002 there was a swing to the right and Chirac was re-elected. Dominique Devillepin became prime minister in May 2005.

Today France is one of the most modern countries in the world and a leader of Europe, having achieved a degree of reconciliation and co-operation with Germany that is central to the economic integration of Europe, including a common currency in 1999. It is instrumental in developing the EU's military capabilities and progress towards an EU foreign policy. Industries include car manufacture, chemicals and steel. France is a leading producer of farm products in Europe, and livestock and dairy products are of particular importance, as is wine. Tourism is a major industry.

OPPOSITE: The Roman theatre at Lyon dates from the 1st century BC.

LEFT: The horses of the Camargue.

PAGE 146: The great vineyards of Château de Corton-André, Aloxe-Corton, Côte de Beaune.

FRENCH GUIANA

Location:	9 K
Capital:	Cayenne
Area:	33,016sq m (85511km²)
Population:	195,506 July 2005
Main Languages:	French
Main Religions:	Roman Catholic
Currency:	euro
Climate:	Tropical, hot, humid

An overseas department of France in northern South America, French Guiana has a coastline on the North Atlantic Ocean, and lies between Suriname and Brazil. It is the smallest country in South America. It has a narrow coastal plain, partly covered by marshes and mangrove swamps, and the remainder is rainforest.

Inhabited by indigenous peoples, French settlement was established in 1604, though French Guiana did not become a French colony until later in the century. The imported workforce consisted of African slaves, until slavery was abolished in 1848 and Asians were brought in from Laos to

work the land. From 1852 to 1939, the notorious Devil's Island, one of the offshore Îles de Salut, was used as a French penal colony and was finally closed in 1945.

The economy is closely tied to that of France, and French Guiana is largely dependent on the mother country for food and manufactured goods. Only a small area of the coast, particularly around the capital, Cayenne, is cultivated, which is where most of the population is concentrated. But there are rich timber forests with large reserves of tropical hardwoods that have not yet been

ABOVE: One of the Îles de Salut (Salvation), viewed from Royal Island.

RIGHT: An island hospital and lighthouse.

FAR RIGHT: Royal Island.

fully exploited. Gold is mined, there is commercial fishing, and rice and manioc are major crops. Tourism is gaining in importance. The European Space Agency has been launching its communications satellites from Kourou on the coast since 1968, which accounts for a quarter of GDP. Head of state since 1995 is President Jacques Chirac of France, represented by Ange Mancini since 2002.

GABON

Location:	14 K
Capital:	Libreville
Area:	103,391sq m (267783km²)
Population:	1,389,201 July 2005
Main Languages:	French
Main Religions:	Roman Catholic 65%
Currency:	1 CFA franc =
	100 centimes
Climate:	Hot, wet, humid all year,
	monsoon Oct–Dec

A country on the Atlantic coast of West Africa, Gabon lies between Equatorial Guinea and Cameroon in the north and the Republic of Congo; Congo almost totally envelops Gabon to the east and south. The country straddles the equator and has a broad coastal plain, rising to mountains dissected by deep valleys. Three-quarters of the country consists of unpolluted rainforest teeming with wildlife.

Portuguese explorers reached Gabon in the 15th century and probably gave the country its name, but it was not until 1839 that the first European settlement was established. Gabon became French territory in 1888, and part of French Equatorial Africa from 1910, becoming an independent republic in 1960. The capital, Libreville, was founded by the French in 1849 as a place where freed slaves could live in peace.

President Omar Bongo Ondimba has dominated Gabonese politics for almost 40 years; in fact, there has been only one other president since independence, the other being Léon Mba from 1960 to 1967. A one-party state from 1968, Bongo introduced a nominal multi-party system and new constitution in 1990, though allegations of corruption and electoral fraud in the 2002–03 elections, together with a low turnout, cast doubts as to his political integrity.

Gabon has an abundance of natural resources, which include petroleum, natural gas, diamonds, uranium, gold, timber and manganese, making it one of the most stable and prosperous countries in Africa, with four times the per capita income of most sub-Saharan nations. Nevertheless, it has political weaknesses, and poverty does exist, due to an unequal distribution of wealth.

Timber was previously Gabon's most important export, but the opening of new national parks to encourage ecotourism means that this is no longer the case, and oil now provides the bulk of export earnings.

A reliquary figure from Gabon, designed to perpetuate the memory of an ancestor through family or community worship.

GAMBIA

Location: 12 J
Capital: Banjul
Area: 4,363sq m (11300km²)
Population: 1,593,256 July 2005
Main Languages: English
Main Religions: Muslim 90%
Currency: 1 dalasi = 100 butut
Climate: Hot all year, hotter inland, rains Jun–Oct

A country on the coast of West Africa, and the smallest in Africa, Gambia consists of a narrow strip of territory 20 miles (32km) wide and extending 200 miles (320km) inland on both sides of the River Gambia. Apart from its coastline, it is totally encompassed by Senegal. The river is bordered by swamps, rising to bush country, much of which has been cleared for agriculture.

Portuguese ships visited Gambia in the 15th century, but British traders first settled the area nearly 100 years later, when a settlement was established. It was created a British colony in 1843, became an independent member of the Commonwealth in 1965, when Dawda Jawara became prime minister, and achieved full independence in 1970. From 1982, Gambia, with Senegal, formed the federation of Senegambia, which lasted only until 1989, when Gambia declined further integration. In 1992 Jawara was re-elected for a fifth term and in 1994 was overthrown in a military coup, led by Yahya Jammeh, chairman of the junta from 1994–96. Jammeh was elected president in 1996, but his regime was accused of political repression. However, there was a nominal return to civilian rule in 1997. In 2001, Jammeh lifted the ban on opposition

ABOVE: The Gambia coastline.

RIGHT: Crocodiles are indigenous.

ABOVE RIGHT: A Gambian woman.

parties and was subsequently re-elected.

Gambia has no significant mineral resources and has a limited agricultural base, most of the population relying on their own crops and livestock for subsistance. The processing of peanuts for export, fish and hides is carried out in a limited way, but tourism is becoming increasingly important.

GEORGIA

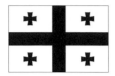

Location:	16 G
Capital:	Tbilisi
Area:	26,900sq m (69700km²)
Population:	4,677,401 July 2005
Main Languages:	Georgian
Main Religions:	Georgian Orthodox 83%, Muslim 11%
Currency:	1 lari = 100 tetri
Climate:	Warm summer, cold winter

Georgia is a country of southeastern Europe, occupying the centre and west of the Transcaucasian region. It includes the autonomous states of Abkhazia and Ajaria and the province of South Ossetia (Tskhinvali). Georgia has borders with Russia in the north and with Azerbaijan, Armenia and Turkey (marked by the Pontine Mountains) in the east and south. To the west are the eastern shores of the Black Sea, known as the Euxine in ancient times, the coastline of which forms a fertile plain, where tea, cereals, mulberries, hazelnuts and citrus fruit are produced. The rest is mountain and highland covered with forests.

The mountain ranges of north and south are separated by the Kura Valley, with a plateau to the east extending into Azerbaijan, which is famous for its vineyards.

Georgians are an ancient people and their language does not belong to the Indo-European group; they have proudly preserved their language for more than 2,000 years.

What is now Georgia was once the site of the ancient kingdoms of Kartli-Iberia, founded in the 4th century BC, and Colchis, the legendary home of Medea and the focus of Jason's expedition to find the Golden Fleece. Georgia came under Roman influence in the 1st century AD and was Christianized in the 330s. It was dominated in turn by Persians, Arabs and Turks until

the 11th century, when it gained independence from the Turkish Seljuk Empire. The 12th century was Georgia's golden age, marked by a period of cultural, economic and military expansion. Thereafter, it became the object of a power struggle between Persia and Turkey until Georgia became divided in the middle of the 16th century, the west going to Persia, the east to Turkey.

The whole of Georgia became part of the Russian Empire in the 19th century, enjoying brief independence after the Russian Revolution before it was absorbed into the Soviet Union; it was combined with Azerbaijan and Armenia into the republic of Transcaucasia, which was dissolved in 1936, when Georgia again became a separate

LEFT: Tbilisi's old town, with the Narikala Fortress.

OPPOSITE: View of the High Caucasus near Gudauri.

Soviet republic. On the break-up of the USSR in 1991, Georgia declared its independence. This was followed by civil war, which ended the following year, when the authoritarian regime of President Gamsakhurdia was overthrown and Eduard Shevardnadze emerged as leader. This was followed by more conflict from Gamsakhurdia's supporters and secessionists in Abkhazia and South Ossetia, when Russian troops were summoned; in return for this, Georgia joined the Commonwealth of Independent States (CIS).

Shevardnadze became president in 1995 and was re-elected five years later. Meanwhile, calls for secession continued, culminating in autonomy for South Ossetia (renamed Tskhinvali) and Abkhazia. By 2002, Georgian special forces were being trained by the US military for combat with Chechen and al-Quaeda fighters in the Pankisi Gorge. In 2003 protests that elections had been rigged led to the resignation of Eduard Shevardnadze. In new elections in 2004, Mikheil Saakashvili was swept to power, along with his National Movement Party; he is now both head of state and head of government.

Manganese is the chief resource, though other minerals have been left largely unexploited, and metals, machinery, wood products, wine and chemicals are produced.

Most of Georgia's power – natural gas and oil products – has to be exported, though it does produce hydro-electricity. Georgia's economy has suffered severe damage, due to the break-up of the Soviet Union, civil strife, corruption and failure to collect taxes. However, it is currently receiving help from the IMF and World Bank and has made substantial progress since 1995, while the construction of the Baku-Tblisi-Ceyhan and Baku-Tbilisi-Erzerum pipelines have attracted investment and created jobs.

GERMANY

Location:	14 F
Capital:	Berlin
Area:	137,849sq m (357029km²)
Population:	82,431,390 July 2005
Main Languages:	German
Main Religions:	Protestant 45%,
	Roman Catholic 37%,
	Muslim 2%
Currency:	euro
Climate:	Warm summer,
	cold winter

Germany, in the heart of Europe, stretches from the North Sea and Baltic coasts in the north to the Alps in the south and has land borders with nine countries – Austria, Belgium, Czech Republic, Denmark, France, Luxembourg, Netherlands, Poland and Switzerland. The fertile farmland of the north German plain is dotted with lagoons along the Baltic coast and is drained by the Elbe, Wesel and part of the Oder river systems. It is also where the industrial cities of Hamburg, Breman, Hannover and Kiel are situated. In the east is the capital, Berlin, while to the north-west lies the industrial

LEFT: *Römerberg Square, Frankfurt.*

OPPOSITE: Neuschwanstein, King Ludwig's castle in Bavaria.

heartland of the Rhine, Ruhr and Saar valleys. The central belt of forested highlands and plateaux stretch from the Eifel region in the west to the range of the Erzgebirge on the border of the Czech Republic. Further south, the land rises to the Swabian Alps, with the Black Forest in the south-west. In the far south, the Bavarian Alps with the Zugspitze (9,721ft/2963m), Germany's highest peak, form Germany's border with Austria.

Around 200 BC, German tribes began to displace the pre-existing Celts, conquering much of the western Roman Empire in the 5th century AD. In 486 the Merovingian king, Clovis I, conquered southern and western Germany, together with Thuringia, and Charlemagne extended the territory to the Elbe, becoming emperor in 800, when the Holy Roman Empire was established. The name was also applied to the German Empire or First Reich from 962–1806, both being regarded as revivals of the Roman Empire. On Charlemagne's death, Germany separated from France, adopting a feudal system of powerful duchies, to be replaced by a dynasty of Saxon kings from 918–1002.

Otto I revived the title emperor in 962 and began the colonization of the Slavonic lands east of the Elbe. This was followed by a feud between emperors and popes (1075–1250), a temporary revival of imperial power under Maximilian I

OPPOSITE: Esslingen old town.

ABOVE: The Schlossplatz and the Königsbau fountain, Stuttgart.

RIGHT: Television tower, Stuttgart.

PAGE 156: Dresden Castle, Cathedral and Opera House.

PAGE 157: An Esslingen vineyard.

(1493–1519) – whose dynastic ambitions outside Germany, together with those of his son, Charles V, led to conflict with France – and the Reformation and the Thirty Years' War (1618–48), which effectively weakened the empire and destroyed Germany's cultural and economic life.

The rise of Brandenburg-Prussia as a military power began in the 17th century, though Germany's regeneration was largely due to Napoleon, who unified western Germany and introduced the ideals and reforms of the French Revolution. The

empire was abolished in 1806 and had become a loose federation by 1815, following the Congress of Vienna. By this time unity had become ever more necessary due to the growth of industry from 1850. In 1871, following the Franco-Prussian War, Bismarck created a second German empire (the Second Reich), which united 25 German states under the Hohenzollern king of Prussia, William I, when an alliance with Austria-Hungary was formed.

There followed a period of colonial expansion in Africa, China and the Far East, while Germany became the greatest industrial power in Europe. Tensions arising between Germany and other colonial powers led to Germany's defeat in the First World War, the collapse of the empire, and the creation of the Weimar Republic (1919–33), which was obliged to make not only crippling reparations, following the Treaty of Versailles, but was also left to deal with

ABOVE: Schauspielhaus, Düsseldorf.

RIGHT: The Reichstag, Berlin.

OPPOSITE, The Brandenberg Gate, Berlin

158

soaring inflation and high unemployment. The rise to power of a Nazi dictatorship in the 1930s, led to a policy of expansionism and the country's eventual humiliation in the Second World War, after which it was occupied by the victorious Allies and partitioned. The western part, including West Berlin, which was occupied by the US, Britain and France, became the Federal Republic of Germany or West Germany, with its capital at Bonn. The eastern part, occupied by the Soviet Union, became the German Democratic Republic or East Germany, with its capital in East Berlin.

West Germany eventually emerged as a major European power and a founder member of the EEC, now the European Union, while the east remained under the dominance of the Soviet Union. After the general collapse of Communism in Eastern Europe, East and West Germany reunited on 3 October 1990, when all four occupying powers relinquished their rights. On 1 January 1999, Germany, together with ten other EU countries, introduced the euro as its exchange currency; this was adopted as the sole currency for everyday transactions from 1 January 2002.

Horst Koehler has been president of Germany since July 2004. Head of government since October 1998 was Chancellor Gerhard Schroeder, with Vice Chancellor Joschka Fischer as his deputy. General elections in September 2005 resulted in Angela Merkel becoming Germany's first female chancellor. However, the results of the elections were very close, and Gerhard Schroeder was reluctant to admit defeat. Eventually, however, it was agreed that Merkel should be chancellor in a grand coalition, involving Merkel's Christian Democrats (CDU), their CSU allies and Schroeder's Social Democrat Party (SPD).

From its position as the fifth-largest economy in the world, Germany has been reduced to one of the slowest-growing in the euro zone. Germany's ageing population and high unemployment has severely strained the resources of the social security system, to the extent that expenditure now exceeds contributions made by the working population. However, corporate restructuring, a relaxation of regulations regarding labour, and growing capital markets, should eventually see Germany fulfil its goals. It is one of the world's largest and most technically-advanced producers of iron, steel, coal, cement, chemicals, machinery, vehicles, machine tools, electronics, food, shipbuilding and textiles.

LEFT: Kaiser Wilhelm Gedächtniskirche (Memorial Church), Berlin.

OPPOSITE: The Kurfürstendamm, Berlin.

GHANA

Location:	13 J
Capital:	Accra
Area:	92,456sq m (239461km²)
Population:	21,029,853 July 2005
Main Languages:	English
Main Religions:	Traditional 38%,
	Muslim 30%, Christian 24%
Currency:	1 cedi = 100 pesewas
Climate:	Hot all year, rains Apr–Jul

A country of West Africa, Ghana has land borders with Côte d'Ivoire in the west, Burkina Faso in the north and Togo in the east, with a coastline bordering the Gulf of Guinea and the Atlantic Ocean. It is a mostly low-lying country, parts of which are irrigated to make them more productive, with a dissected forested plateau occupying the centre and extending to the south. To the east and south lies Lake Volta, the largest artificial lake in the world, created in 1964 by damming the River Volta, and which runs north to south. In the north, recurrent drought has a serious effect on agriculture, which in any case is mostly at a domestic subsistence level throughout the country.

Various African kingdoms existed in the area before the Portuguese arrived in the 15th century and called it the Gold Coast, on account of its mineral wealth. It came under Dutch occupation in the 17th century and a centre of the slave trade, which was eventually abolished when the Europeans retreated, leaving the Ashanti people to reclaim their land. The Gold Coast became a British colony in 1874, but it was not until 1901 that the war-like Ashanti lost their kingdom to the British. In 1957, Ghana, as it was called by now, was formed through the merger of the Gold Coast with the trust territory of Togoland, making it the first sub-Saharan country to gain independence as a member of the Commonwealth.

Dr Kwame Nkrumah, a prominent commentator on Third World affairs and pioneer of Pan-African socialism, first came to power as prime minister in 1951, becoming president in 1960. However, as time went on he became increasingly dictatorial, and by 1964 the country had become a one-party state. His colourful reign was brought to a end by a military coup in 1966. A long series of coups resulted in the suspension of Ghana's 1979 constitution, when political parties were banned, though a new constitution restoring multi-party politics was approved in 1992. Lt Jerry Rawlings, head of state since 1981, won presidential elections in 1992 and 1996, but was prevented under the constitution from running for a third term in 2000. He was succeeded by John Agyekum Kufuor, who defeated Vice President John Atta Mills in a free and fair election.

LEFT: Akosombo Dam, Lake Volta.

BELOW: Kejetia market, Kumasi.

Ghana is well endowed with natural resources, that include gold, cocoa and timber (the main sources of foreign exchange), silver, industrial diamonds, bauxite, manganese, fish, rubber, hydro-electricity, petroleum, salt and limestone. Even so, it remains dependent on outside aid and technical assistance. Industries include mining, forestry, light manufacturing, aluminium smelting, food processing and, in a small way, shipbuilding.

GIBRALTAR

Location:	13 H
Capital:	Gibraltar
Area:	2.5sq m (6.5km²)
Population:	27,884 July 2005
Main Languages:	English
Main Religions:	Roman Catholic 78%,
	Anglican 7%
Currency:	Gibraltar pound
Climate:	Mediterranean, with mild
	winters and warm summers

Gibraltar is a British dependency occupying a rocky monolith near the southern tip of the Iberian peninsula. It lies at the north-eastern end of the Strait of Gibraltar that divides Europe from North Africa. The strait is the only point of access to the Mediterranean by sea, a fact that gives Gibraltar its great strategic importance and which has shaped its history. It consists of a fortified town and military base at the foot of the Rock of Gibraltar, which is inhabited by a colony of Barbary apes that originated in Africa.

From the beginning of the Muslim conquest of Spain in 711 until 1462,

Gibraltar remained in the hands of the Moors. The British captured it during the War of the Spanish Succession in 1704 and it was ceded to Britain under the Treaty of Utrecht, which ended the war in 1713. Attempts were made by the Spanish to repossess the Rock in the siege of 1779–83 and a blockade imposed by General Franco in 1969, when the border with Spain was closed, was not lifted until 1980. There was a referendum in 1967, when government by Spain was rejected, and another in 2002, when the proposal that there be joint Anglo-Spanish sovereignty failed to be approved by the people. Peter Caruana, QC, of the

Gibraltar Social Democrats, is Gibraltar's Chief Minister, having been re-elected three times since 1996.

For obvious reasons, Gibraltar has no agriculture of its own. Instead, its revenue comes from tourism, finance and its military air bases.

ABOVE LEFT: One of Gibraltar's famous Barbary apes.

ABOVE: The Changing of the Guard.

FAR LEFT: The Rock of Gibraltar.

LEFT: Yacht harbour with the Rock in the background.

GREECE

Location:	15 H
Capital:	Athens
Area:	50,949sq m (131958km²)
Population:	10,668,354 July 2005
Main Languages:	Greek
Main Religions:	Greek Orthodox 98%
Currency:	euro
Climate:	Hot, dry summer, mild winter, colder in north

A European country in the southern Balkans, Greece is a complicated series of mountain ridges and enclosed valleys, forming a deeply indented peninsula that extends down into the Mediterranean Sea. To the west is the Ionian Sea; the Aegean Sea to the east divides Greece from Turkey-in-Asia. The Pindus Mountains dominate the peninsula, extending south-eastwards from the Albanian border. Greece is famous for the clarity of its light and no place is very far from the sea. Scores of islands, some of then forming named groups, most of then uninhabited, make up a fifth or so of the country, the largest of which, Crete, acquired by Greece in 1913, lies in the Mediterranean Sea.

OPPOSITE: *The fortress of Ayios Nikolaos on the island of Rhodes.*

LEFT: *The harbour at Samos.*

BELOW: *A Greek fisherman on Samos.*

though the Greek economy has recently benefited from increased investment attracted by the 2004 Athens Olympic Games, which were something of a triumph. Industries include tourism and shipping, which are of major importance, food and tobacco processing, textiles, chemicals, metal products, mining and petroleum. Crops include tobacco, olives, grapes, cotton, beef and dairy products.

Athens and Sparta were the most important of the city states (*polis*) of classical times that evolved into what is now modern Greece. They reached their zenith in the 5th century BC, when the concept of democracy was invented; this is the time most people imagine when they think of Ancient Greece. After this, Greece fell to Macedonia and eventually became part of the Roman and Byzantine Empires. It was conquered by the Turks in 1456 and remained under Turkish rule until the War of Independence (1821–29), after which it became a kingdom. Greece entered the First World War on the side of the Allies in 1917. During the Second World War it was invaded by Italy in 1940, and was occupied by the Germans from 1941–44. After the war there was protracted civil war between royalist supporters of the king and Communist rebels, which lasted until 1949. Greece joined NATO in 1952.

A military coup in 1967 brought the oppressive regime of the 'colonels' to power and lasted for seven years, during which time the king was forced into exile. Following democratic elections and a referendum, a civilian parliamentary republic was established in 1974, headed by Konstandinos Karamanlis, and the monarchy was abolished. Andreas Papandreou became Greece's first socialist prime minister in 1981, following which Greece joined the EU, becoming the 12th member of the community in 2001.

In 1990, Karamanlis was returned as president, followed by Konstandinos Stephanopoulos in 1995. Kostas Simitis, of the Panhellenic Socialist Party, won the 1996 election, and again in 2000, followed by Karamanlis' New Democracy party in 2004. Head of state since March 2005 is President Karolos Papoulios.

Greece is one of the poorest members of the EU and one of its major beneficiaries,

GREENLAND

Location:	10 C
Capital:	Nuuk
Area:	840,000sq m (2175600km²)
Population:	56,375 July 2005
Main Languages:	Greenlandic, Danish, English
Main Religions:	Evangelical Lutheran
Currency:	Danish krone
Climate:	Arctic to sub-arctic, cool summers, cold winters

The world's largest island, Greenland lies in the North Atlantic Ocean to the north-east of Canada and mostly within the Arctic Circle. The northern two-thirds of the land always has a covering of permafrost 5,000ft (1500m) thick, but where it is free from ice there are sandy plains. Settlement is mostly confined to the narrow, rocky south-western coastal area and to the capital, Nuuk. Only about 5 per cent of Greenland is habitable, the population being largely Inuit and Greenland-born whites.

Greenland was discovered in about 982 by Eric the Red, a Norse explorer, who founded colonies on the west coast in 986.

Christianity came to the island in c.1000. In 1261, the colonies accepted the sovereignty of Norway, but by the beginning of the 15th century all communications with Europe ceased; by the time Greenland was visited in the next century, the colonies had disappeared. Colonization by Denmark began in the 18th century, and Greenland became a dependency of Denmark in 1953, gaining autonomy from 1979; however,

Denmark is responsible for defence, and also controls Greenland's foreign affairs, though with some participation from Greenland itself. Greenland joined the EC (now EU) with Denmark in 1973, but resigned in 1985 following a dispute over fishing quotas.

Head of state is Queen Margarethe II of Denmark, represented in Greenland by High Commissioner Peter Lauriteen. Prime minister since 2002 is Hans Enoksen.

LEFT: Tundra landscape with Arctic poppies, Kurdlissat.

BELOW LEFT: Ilulissat fjord with icebergs.

BELOW: Girl in national costume.

Greenland's economy is critically dependent on fishing and its by-products, as well as on the substantial aid it receives from Denmark. Other natural resources include coal, iron ore, lead, zinc, molybdenum, gold, platinum, uranium and hydro-electricity; oil and natural gas are probably present. Tourism exists, but is limited by the shortness of the season.

GRENADA

Location:	9 J
Capital:	St George's
Area:	133sq m (344km²)
Population:	89,502 July 2005
Main Languages:	English
Main Religions:	Roman Catholic 53%,
	Protestant 30%
Currency:	1 East Caribbean
	dollar = 100 cents
Climate:	Hot all year, rains Jun–Dec

A country in the Caribbean Sea consisting of the island of Grenada – the most southerly of the Windward Islands – and the southern Grenadine Islands to the north. The islands are of volcanic origin, and there is a volcanic ridge running from north to south.

Christopher Columbus first sighted Grenada in 1498, when it was inhabited by Carib Indians. Later, it was colonized by the French, was ceded to Britain in 1763, was recaptured by the French, and was restored to Britain in 1783. It became an independent Commonwealth state in 1974. In 1979, Eric Gairy's autocratic regime was overthrown by Maurice Bishop of the left-wing New Jewel movement, when links with Cuba were established. However, his overthrow and execution in 1983 by a left-wing military junta, prompted intervention by US forces and six other Caribbean countries, which captured the ringleaders and their Cuban advisers. They withdrew in 1985 after democracy had been restored and free elections were reinstated the following year. Head of state since 1952 is Queen Elizabeth II, represented by Governor-General Daniel Williams since 1996. Head of government is Keith Mitchell since 1995.

Natural resources include timber, spices,

tropical fruit and deep harbours, though tourism has recently become the main source of revenue since an international airport was opened in 1985. Grenada also has a strong construction and manufacturing base and an offshore financial industry has contributed to its growth.

ABOVE: A spice stall at St George's.

LEFT: Grenada's capital, St George's.

GUADELOUPE

Location:	9 I
Capital:	Basse-Terre
Area:	658sq m (1705km²)
Population:	448,713 July 2005
Main Languages:	French
Main Religions:	Roman Catholic 95%
Currency:	euro
Climate:	Subtropical, tempered by trade winds

A group of Caribbean islands in the Lesser Antilles, south-east of Puerto Rico. Guadeloupe is an overseas department of France, having been a French possession since 1635. The narrow Rivière Salée channel divides Guadeloupe proper into two islands, the larger, western Basse-Terre, with its interior volcanic mountains, and the low-lying limestone Grande-Terre to the east. Most of the other islands, including Saint-Martin and Saint-Barthélemy to the north-west, are also volcanic. The island of Saint-Martin is shared with the Netherlands, its southern portion (Saint Maarten) belonging to the Netherlands Antilles and the north (Saint-Martin) to Guadeloupe.

RIGHT: Pointe-à-Pitre, with the cruise ship Zenith.

BELOW: A market in Pointe-à-Pitre.

Discovered in 1493 by Columbus, the French were the earliest settlers of Guadeloupe in the 17th century. It was briefly held by Britain and Sweden before it was returned to France in 1816. Head of state since 1995 is President Jacques Chirac of France, represented by Prefect Paul Girot de Langlade since 2004. Head of government is President of the General Council Jacques Gillot since 2001.

Guadeloupe's economy is dependent on tourism (the most important), agriculture (bananas, sugar), light industry (sugar and rum production) and services – also on France for subsidies and imports. Crops are devastated by hurricanes from time to time.

GUAM & NORTH MARIANA ISLANDS

Location: Guam 23 J
Capital: Hagatna
Area: 212sq m (549km²)
Population: 168,564 July 2005
Main Languages: English, Chamorro,
                   Philippine languages
Main Religions: Roman Catholic 85%
Currency: US dollar
Climate: Tropical marine,
                   moderated by north-east
                   trade winds

The Marianas are islands of Oceania, lying in the Pacific Ocean, and situated north-east of Australia and east of the Philippines. They are the northernmost of the larger Micronesian group of islands, having been formed from the summits of 15 submerged volcanic mountains, in a range that extends from Guam almost to Japan. The islands to the south are limestone plateaux fringed by coral reefs. To the south-east of the islands lies the Mariana Trench, the greatest known ocean depth, which measures 36,201ft (11034m) at the Challenger Deep.

Ferdinand Magellan discovered the islands in 1521. In 1667 they were formally claimed by Spain and were named in honour of the Spanish Queen, the widow of Philip IV, Maria Anna of Austria. Following the Spanish-American War of 1898, Spain ceded the southern part of the group to the USA. The remaining islands in the north went to Germany until the First World War, after which the League of Nations placed them under the control of Japan. In the Second World War, Guam was captured by the Japanese in 1941, who recognized its strategic position in the Pacific, though it was recaptured by the US three years later.

Guam is the largest and southernmost of the islands. It is administered as an unincorporated territory of the USA, while the rest of the Marianas make up a self-governing commonwealth in union with the United States, which was effective from 1978.

The economy of Guam revolves around its US military bases and the spending generated by them; it also benefits from duty-free shopping and generous US grants. Tourism is something of a growth industry on the island, prompting a boom in hotel-

BELOW: Tuman Bay, Guam.

building, while fishing, publishing, printing, and handicrafts, are of similar importance.

The North Marianas benefit substantially from US finance, though local generation of revenue has recently increased. Tourism is important, as is garment-production, mostly by Chinese workers, while small farms produce coconuts, breadfruit, melons, tomatoes and cattle.

GUATEMALA

Location:	7 J
Capital:	Guatemala City
Area:	42,042sq m (108889km²)
Population:	14,655,189 July 2005
Main Languages:	Spanish
Main Religions:	Roman Catholic 75%,
	Protestant 23%
Currency:	1 quetzal = 100 centavos
Climate:	Hot all year, cool in
	highlands, rains Jun/Oct

A country in Central America bordering the Pacific Ocean to the west, and with a coastline on the Caribbean Sea to the east. Guatemala has land borders with Mexico, Belize, Honduras and El Salvador. Apart from the southern coastal region and the vast limestone plateau of the Petén, with its vast rainforests lying in the north, Guatemala is mountainous, with many active volcanoes. The large Lago de Izabal lies close to the Caribbean coast, where it drains into the sea. All the major cities are situated in the south. Being the largest and most populous country in Central America, Guadeloupe was fortunate in escaping the full onslaught of

Hurricane Mitch in 1998, though its neighbours were less fortunate.

Guatemala was a centre of Mayan culture until the 10th century and much of the influence of the Mayans is still in evidence, from the way the people live today to the ruins of the great temple pyramid at Tikal. The Spanish conquistador, Pedro de Alvarado, conquered the native tribes in 1523–24. After its independence from Spain in 1821, Guatemala was a part of the Central American Federation from 1828–38, before again becoming an independent republic in its own right.

There were many different political regimes during the latter part of the 20th century and a guerilla war was fought that lasted for 36 years. This came to an end in 1996, leaving more than a million dead; it created as many refugees, many of them now living in the rainforests of Belize.

In 1985, the first civilian president for 15 years was elected. Alvaro Arzú Irigoyen was elected from 1996 and Alfonso Portillo from 1999, in spite of criminal allegations. Chief of state and head of the unicameral Congress of the Republic since 2004 is President Oscar Berger Perdomo.

Half the labour force of Guatemala is engaged in agriculture, producing two-thirds of the country's exports and a quarter of its revenue from coffee, bananas, sugar and beef. Rubber, valuable hardwoods, cotton and textiles are also produced. What wealth there is is unequally distributed, however,

LEFT: The temple-pyramid of the Grand Jaguar, Tikal, Petén.

BELOW: Indian women, Chichicastenango.

OPPOSITE: Church of San Francisco, Antigua.

and most live below the poverty line, while trafficking in heroin and cocaine is an ongoing problem. The end of war in 1996 should have seen an increase in foreign investment, but political unrest, scandals and corruption have done little to restore confidence abroad.

GUINEA

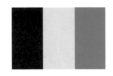

Location:	12 J
Capital:	Conakry
Area:	94,926sq m (245858km²)
Population:	9,467,866 July 2005
Main Languages:	French
Main Religions:	Muslim 85%
Currency:	1 Guinean franc =
	100 cauris (cents)
Climate:	Hot and humid all year,
	rains May–Oct

A country in West Africa, bordering the Atlantic Ocean, the Republic of Guinea has land borders with Guinea-Bissau, Senegal and Mali to the north and north-east, the Côte d'Ivoire to the south-east, Liberia to the south, and Sierra Leone to the west. There are mangrove swamps along part of the alluvial coastal plain, which includes the capital, Conakry. This rises to the dense forests of Fouta Djalon in the north-west. In the north-east is an area of tropical savannah, while to the south the Guinea highlands rise to a height of 5,748ft (1752m) at Mount Nimba.

Guinea was the site of African empires

that reached their zenith and then fell; this included the great Mali Empire in the 12th century. The Portuguese developed a trade in slaves centred on Guinea in the 16th century. Fulani Arabs established a Muslim state from 1735 until, following a series of wars, France gained control from 1849, the colony becoming French Guinea in 1890. Guinea gained independence from France in 1958, when it turned to the Soviet Union, since when there have been only two presidents.

The first president, Ahmed Sékou Touré, headed a repressive regime, crushing all political opposition in his path. As a result, thousands were tortured, killed or disappeared. A military coup followed Touré's death in 1984, when power was seized by Lansana Conté, who abandoned socialism, released political prisoners and encouraged exiles to return. However, democratic elections did not take place in Guinea until 1993, when Conté, who had

been head of the previous military regime, again came to power, despite accusations of ballot fraud. He was re-elected in 1998 and again in 2003. Head of government since 2004 is Cellou Dalein Diallo.

Strong-arm government, from the only two presidents Guinea has ever had, has nevertheless made Guinea relatively stable, despite economic mismanagement. During the last decade, however, wars in neighbouring Liberia and Sierra Leone have had their effect, causing an influx of refugees into the country and putting a strain on resources.

The people of Guinea are some of the poorest in West Africa, even though the country is potentially rich in minerals.

LEFT and BELOW: Children around a water pump, Kissidougou.

Agriculture, in which about 80 per cent of the population is employed, is mainly at subsistence level and bananas, pineapples, cassava, rice and coffee are produced, while cattle and other livestock are raised in highland areas. Natural resources include bauxite (the most important export), iron ore, diamonds, gold, uranium, hydo-electricity, fish and salt.

GUINEA-BISSAU

Location: 12 J
Capital: Bissau
Area: 13,948sq m (36125km²)
Population: 1,416,027 July 2005
Main Languages: Portuguese
Main Religions: Traditional 65%,
Muslim 30%, Christian 5%
Currency: 1 Guinea-Bissau peso =
100 centavos
Climate: Hot all year, cooler on coast
and in hills, rains May–Nov

The small republic on the coast of West Africa, lies between Senegal and Guinea. Guinea-Bissau is swampy, with many inland waterways and rainforests along its indented coast; it has low-lying savannah elsewhere. Offshore, the islands of the Bijagós archipelago have a culture all their own and a diverse animal and marine wildlife.

The Portuguese explored the area in the 15th century, when it became a centre of the slave trade. Formerly Portuguese Guinea, it became a colony in 1879, winning independence from Portugal in 1974 after there had been guerilla warfare involving the PAIGC – the African Party for the Independence of Guinea and Cape Verde – for over ten years. The first government, under Luis Cabral, was a single-party system with a planned economy. In 1980 there was a military coup in which Joao Vieira came to power, beginning the trend towards a muti-party system and a market economy.

Throughout the 1980s and early '90s, Vieira survived several abortive coups and in 1994 became president in the country's first free elections. However, his dismissal of his army chief triggered a crippling civil war and his overthrow in 1999. After an interim government, opposition leader Kumba Yalá became president in 2000, but was removed

LEFT: Market stalls at Cachungoi.

BELOW: A dragon sculpture from Guinea-Bissau.

in a bloodless coup in 2003, when Henrique Rosa became interim president. Head of government from 2004 is Carlos Gomes, Jr.

One of the ten poorest countries in the world, and one where income is most unequally distributed, Guinea-Bissau is dependent on farming and fishing for its survival, with cashews and rice its most important exports. Peanuts, coconuts, pine nuts and timber are also produced. There are reserves of unexploited oil still lying offshore, which could well transform the country's economy, relying as it does on support from the IMF and World Bank.

173

GUYANA

Location: 9 J
Capital: Georgetown
Area: 83,000sq m (214970km²)
Population: 765,283 July 2005
Main Languages: English
Main Religions: Christian 57%,
Hindu 33%, Muslim 9%
Currency: 1 Guyana dollar =
100 cents
Climate: Hot all year, cooler on
coast, rains Nov–Jan

A country on the north-eastern coast of South America, the Co-Operative Republic of Guyana is bordered by Venezuela to the north-east, Brazil to the south and west and by Suriname to the east. The border of Venezuela and the most southerly part of Guyana's border with Suriname are areas still under dispute. The coastal plain of this 'Land of Many Waters', where the majority of the population is centred, has been mostly reclaimed from marshes and swamps. A little further inland is a sandy belt, where rainforest and mineral deposits are to be found, while the interior is mostly upland, with densely-forested plateaux, wooded savannah, and the valleys of the Essequibo, and the Pakaraima Mountains on the Venezuela-Brazil border.

At the time that Spanish explorers came to the area in 1499, Guyana was inhabited by Amerindian tribes. Then came the Dutch, who established three different colonies in the 17th century, and it was occupied by the British from 1796. It was formally ceded to Britain by the Dutch in 1814, becoming the single colony of British Guiana in 1831 and an independent Commonwealth state from 1966.

The abolition of slavery in the 1830s led to black settlement of the area and the importation of indentured labour from India, China and Portugal to work the sugar plantations. This resulted in the explosive ethnic mix that causes political unrest even to this day. Until the 1990s, Guyana had mostly socialist-oriented governments. In 1992, Cheddi Jagan, whose first presidency was in the 1950s, came to power in what is considered to be Guyana's first free elections since independence. When he died, he was succeeded by his wife, Janet, who resigned in 1999 because of poor health. Her successor was Bharrat Jagdeo, who was re-elected in 2001.

The economy of Guyana has seen moderate growth since 1999, due to increased mining and agriculture, a more favourable business atmosphere, lowish inflation and financial support from abroad. Principal exports are bauxite, sugar and rice and diamond and gold mining are important, while fishing, forestry and ecotourism are expanding. However, Guyana is hampered by a shortage of skilled labour and a deficient infrastructure, while continual emigration has led to fears of depopulation.

Meanwhile, Guyana continues its bid to be declared a World Heritage Site, with various nominations that include the Kaietur National Park, the Iwokrama Rain Forest Reserve and the Kanuku Mountains.

BELOW: The Guyanan coast.

HAITI

Location:	8 I
Capital:	Port-au-Prince
Area:	10,714sq m (27750km²)
Population:	8,121,622 July 2005
Main Languages:	French, Creole
Main Religions:	Roman Catholic 90%
Currency:	1 gourde =
	100 centimes
Climate:	Hot all year, cooler in hills

Occupying a portion of Hispaniola, the Caribbean's second largest island, Haiti is predominantly a rough mountainous country with a long indented coastline. There are small coastal plains, while in the east and centre is a large elevated plateau. It also includes several smaller offshore islands, including Tortuga and Gonâve. Its neighbour to the east, the Dominican Republic, occupies the remaining two-thirds of Hispaniola. Haiti is at the centre of a hurricane belt and is subject to severe storms from June to October, while flooding, earthquakes and periods of drought are not uncommon.

Although the majority of the people are

Overview of Port-au-Prince.

of African descent and profess Roman Catholicism, almost half practise Voodoo, a combination of Catholic ritual and African magic, which involves communication with the dead. This differs from the version practised in New Orleans, which relies heavily on charms and talismans.

Hispaniola was inhabited by Arawak Amerindians when Columbus discovered Hispaniola in 1492, but they were wiped out by Spanish settlers in the east within a century. Then the French arrived and the western third of the island was ceded to them by Spain in 1697, where they developed thriving forestry and sugar industries. However, this was achieved by using slaves imported from West Africa to work the plantations, who soon formed the majority of the population. In 1791 almost half a million slaves rebelled under the leadership of Toussaint l'Ouverture, and after a prolonged struggle, Haiti was proclaimed

independent of Napoleonic France in 1804.

A series of assassinations, dictatorships and revolutions plagued Haiti in the 19th century. From 1915, following a series of corrupt dictatorships, it was administered by the US for a period lasting 19 years, when government of the country was virtually by the US Marines. From the very start of the American occupation there had been fierce opposition from rebel forces, which the US firmly suppressed. Philippe Sudré Dartiguenave accepted the presidency of Haiti in the absence of any other volunteers, and the US declared martial law, which lasted until 1929.

François Duvallier, also known as 'Papa Doc', a black doctor unable to practise medicine because of his race, became president of Haiti in 1957; but his regime soon degenerated into an oppressive, corrupt and brutal dictatorship, that lasted for 29 years, and was continued by his son.

Duvallier was famous for his army of sunglass-wearing volunteers – the Tonton Macoute. He died suddenly in 1971 and was superseded by his son, Jean-Claude ('Baby Doc'), who was then only 19 years old. General social unrest caused the Duvalliers to flee to the south of France in 1986, where Baby Doc and his wife lived in considerable luxury until his wife left him, taking the children and most of their cash with her. In the meantime, the US had installed a military regime with the task of formulating a new democratic constitution within two years. However, Haiti's first democratically elected president, Jean-Bertrand Aristide, did not take office until 1990, and was overthrown by a military coup the following year. But democracy was restored in 1994, when Aristide was able to return. Rioting forced him to resign the presidency in February 2004, when Boniface Alexandre became interim head of state.

Such a long history of political turbulence, along with frequent natural catastrophes, goes a long way to explain why Haiti is the poorest country in the Western hemisphere. The majority of the population scrapes an existence from farming, and to add to their troubles almost all foreign aid was suspended after irregular elections in 2002, though it was restored after Haiti paid off arrears of its debt to the World Bank in 2005. Coffee, mangos, sugar, rice, corn and sorghum are grown, while natural resources include bauxite, copper, calcium carbonate, gold, marble, hydropower and wood.

HONDURAS

Location:	7 J
Capital City:	Tegucigalpa
Area:	43,433sq m (112491km²)
Population:	6,975,204 July 2005
Main Languages:	Spanish
Main Religions:	Roman Catholic 97%
Currency:	1 lempira = 100 centavos
Climate:	Hot all year, cooler in mountains

A country of Central America, bordering the Caribbean Sea and with a short coastline on the Pacific, Honduras has land borders with Guatemala and El Salvador to the west and Nicaragua to the south. Honduras, not to be confused with British Honduras, which is now Belize, has narrow coastal plains with an largely undeveloped lowland jungle in the north-east – sometimes referred to, along with the Nicaraguan Caribbean coast, as the 'Mosquito Coast', while the populous San Pedro Sula valley lies to the north-west. There is an area of rainforest in La Mosquita, which is home to Honduras' rich

and varied wildlife, also a feature of the rest of Mesoamerica; it is so important that it was made a World Heritage Site in 1982. Elsewhere, the country is predominently mountainous, the highest range being the Montañas de Selaque, which rise to over 7,000ft (2100m). Almost half the country is covered by great forests, which provide mahogany and other valuable hardwoods, though some deforestation has occurred due to the expanding population.

Honduras once marked the southern limit of the Mayan empire, which flourished from 400 to 900, of which spectacular remains survive in what was the Pre-Columbian city-state of Copán. Columbus sighted Honduras in 1502 and it was colonized by the Spanish, attracted by the promise of gold, in 1523. In 1821 it became an independent republic and was part of the Central American Federation between 1823 and 1838. For the rest of the 19th century, Honduras was subjected to continuous

political interference from its neighbour, Guatemala. In the 1890s, the US developed the banana plantations, from which the description 'banana republic' possibly originates.

General Oswaldo López Arellano seized power in a military coup in 1963 and led Honduras in the 'Football War' of 1969, sparked when Honduras was defeated in a World Cup qualifying match by El Salvador. A freely elected government came to power in 1982, after nearly three decades of

LEFT: A tourist guide at the Mayan ruins of Copán.

BELOW: Honduras' luxuriant vegetation.

OPPOSITE: The Mayan Great Plaza at Copán.

military rule. During the 1980s, Honduras was host to US-backed Nicaraguan Contra rebels fighting the Marxist Sandanista government, which had ousted the

Nicaraguan Somozo regime in 1979. This led to a state of emergency, following popular opposition to the Contras, in 1988. Conflict in Nicaragua ended in 1990. Chief of state and head of the unicameral government since 2002, though not without controversy, is President Ricardo Maduro.

Hondurans suffer, not only from an unequal distribution of wealth and widespread unemployment, but also live in a country that is one of the poorest in the Western hemisphere, and where crime is endemic. (It is estimated that 'death squads' killed over 1,000 street children in 2000.)

It is the least industrialized country in Central America, but there are important mineral reserves that remain to be exploited, such as gold, silver, iron, lead, coal and zinc, while bananas, coffee, cotton, maize, tobacco, sugar and fruit are grown on the coastal plains. Timber, wood products and

fishing are also important. The country was devastated by Hurricane Mitch in 1998, which killed nearly 6,000 people and wrecked the economy. Honduras has recently been classified as one of the Heavily Indebted Poor Countries (HIPC) now eligible for debt relief.

HONG KONG

Location:	21 I
Capital:	Hong Kong
Area:	402sq m (1041km²)
Population:	6,898,686 July 2005
Main Languages:	Cantonese, English
Main Religions:	Local religions (Buddhism, Taoism, Confucianism) 90%
Currency:	Hong Kong dollar
Climate:	Tropical monsoon; cool, humid winter; hot, rainy summer

Formerly a dependency of Britain on the south-east coast of China, Hong Kong was peacefully returned to China on 1 July 1997. Bordering the South China Sea, it comprises Hong Kong island, ceded to Britain in 1842, the Kowloon peninsula, ceded in 1860, and the New Territories, additional areas of the mainland that were leased to Britain for 99 years in 1898. A number of smaller islands in the South China Sea were also included.

When it was returned in 1997, China promised it would not impose its socialist economic system on Hong Kong. It would

also remain largely autonomous, apart from matters of defence and foreign affairs, for the next 50 years.

The last governor of Hong Kong was Chris Patten from 1992, who relinquished his position in 1997, when Tung Chee-hwa became chief executive and a provisional legislative council was appointed. Head of state since 2003 is Hu Jintao, and prime minister since June 2005 is Donald Tsang.

Hong Kong has few natural resources and is highly dependent on international trade and manufacturing, even though it has always maintained its links with China, as far as

BELOW:
A Hong Kong fish market.

OPPOSITE: Traditional boats in Aberdeen's harbour.

trade and investment are concerned. It is also benefiting from China's increasing openness to the rest of the world and the fact that the cost of manufacture is cheaper in China than elsewhere. It has also kept its free-market

OPPOSITE
Painted statues in Repulse Bay.

ABOVE AND RIGHT: Kowloon's theatre.

economy and is an important financial and manufacturing centre, with the largest container port in the world. Its economy can be compared with those of the four largest in Western Europe, though Hong Kong did suffer two recessions in recent years, in the Asian financial crisis of 1998 (when the Hang Seng index lost half its value) and the global downturn of 2001–02; moreover, the outbreak of Severe Acute Respiratory Syndrome (SARS) in 2003, a relatively new phenomenon, also took its toll. However, the effects of these setbacks have been lessened by more tourists coming from the Chinese mainland and increased exports in 2003/04. Manufacturing industries include textiles, electronics, cameras, toys, plastic goods and printing.

HUNGARY

Location:	14 G
Capital:	Budapest
Area:	35,911sq m (93009km²)
Population:	10,006,835 July 2005
Main Languages:	Hungarian
Main Religions:	Roman Catholic 68%, Protestant 25%
Currency:	1 forint = 100 fillér
Climate:	Very warm summer, cold winter, snow

A landlocked country of Central Europe, largely occupying the plains of the middle Danube, that bisects Hungary from north to south. Hungary has borders with the Slovak Republic, Ukraine, Romania, Serbia & Montenegro, Croatia, Slovenia and Austria. The Great Hungarian Plain, watered by the River Tisza, lies to the east and parallel with the Danube as it makes its way to the Black Sea; the Danube is Europe's second longest river and flows through the capital, Budapest. The hills and low mountains of the Bákony forest line the Slovakian border, while the Little Plain lies to the north-west. To the west lies

cyanide plant contaminated the River Tisza. Head of state since 2000 is Ferenc Madl; Ferenc Gyurcsany has been head of government since 2004.

Hungary has completed its transition to a market economy and now has half the per capita income of Europe's Big Four. It has some of the most fertile agricultural land in Europe, growing wheat, corn, grapes, sunflowers, potatoes and sugar beet and raises cattle and poultry. It has important timber, dairy, mining and metallurgy industries and produces construction materials, processed foods, textiles, chemicals, pharmaceuticals and motor vehicles. Tourism is fast becoming an important sector.

OPPOSITE: The Gresham Palace, now a hotel, Budapest.

LEFT: Vajdahunyad Castle, Budapest.

BELOW: A Csikos horseman, Bugac.

Balaton, the largest lake in central Europe.

Originally inhabited by Celts and Slavonic tribes, part of Hungary was later occupied by the Romans, who were superseded by Avars and Huns once the Romans had withdrawn. The Hungarian state was founded by the Magyars, a Finno-Ugric tribe under the chieftain Arpád. St Stephen (997–1038) brought Christianity to Hungary, taking the title of king, conquering Transylvania, and making it part of Hungary. The Ottoman Turks annihilated the Hungarian army at the Battle of Mohács in 1526, and Transylvania came under Turkish suzerainty when the Turks were expelled by the Habsburgs in the 17th century.

Hungary became an equal partner in the Austro-Hungarian Empire in 1867, becoming an idependent kingdom following the collapse of the empire in 1918. After

participating in the Second World War on the side of the Axis, it was occupied by the USSR and became a Communist state. Imre Nagy was prime minister from 1953 and again from 1956, when he withdrew Hungary from the Warsaw Pact (a treaty of co-operation between the Communist states of Europe, formulated the previous year) so that Hungary could adopt a more neutral stance. Nagy was executed and 200,000 people fled after Soviet troops brutally crushed the uprising later that year.

Hungary began to liberalize its economy under the leadership of Janos Kadár in 1968. The Communist system was abandoned in 1989, reforming itself into the Hungarian Socialist Party. In 1990 Hungary held its first multi-party elections and initiated a free market economy, joining NATO in 1999 and the EU in 2004. In 2000 a leak from a

ICELAND

Location:	12 E
Capital City:	Reykjavic
Area:	39,768sq m (103000km²)
Population:	296,737 July 2005
Main Languages:	Icelandic
Main Religions:	Lutheran 88%
Currency:	1 kóna = 100 aurar
Climate:	Mild summer,
	cold winter, snow

ICELAND

A European island nation in the North Atlantic Ocean, Iceland lies just south of the Arctic Circle. In places, the coastline is heavily indented by fjords, which is where most towns are situated. This is because the central area is uninhabitable, and some of it is covered in glaciers. Tectonically vulnerable because of its location at the northern end of the Mid-Atlantic Ridge, Iceland is a still-active volcanic plateau, and being active generates geysers and underground hot water. This geothermal power, together with the abundant hydro-electricity generated by Iceland's many rivers and waterfalls, means that energy is cheap. The most famous volcano is Hekla – the legendary gateway to

Hell – while another eruption caused the new island of Surtsey to appear off the south coast in 1963.

Iceland was an empty wilderness before Norse and Celtic settlers arrived in the 9th century, though Vikings may have seen it earlier. In 930 the world's first general assembly or parliament (*Althing*) declared Iceland a republic and Christianity was adopted 70 years later. Iceland was under Norwegian rule from 1262 to 1380, when, together with Norway, it passed to Denmark. Iceland remained attached to Denmark even after Norway became independent in 1814, but was granted internal self-government in 1874. Denmark was occupied by the Germans during the Second World War and it was left to the Allies to protect Iceland from similar invasion. In the absence of Danish authority, Iceland became an independent

republic in 1944, and a member of NATO in 1949. The US continues to operate a military base at Keflavík, based on a treaty of 1950 in which it undertook the defence of Iceland, which has no military forces of its own.

Iceland is an admirable country, being highly literate, long-lived and with a stable society. Cement is the only natural resource and fishing is the main activity of the

ABOVE: Barnafoss waterfall.

LEFT: A native Icelandic pony at Myvatyn.

OPPOSITE LEFT: The fishing village of Husavik.

OPPOSITE RIGHT: The Strokkur geyser.

islanders, with herring the most important export. Therefore, although Iceland is a prosperous country with few unemployed, it is vulnerable to fluctuating supplies and prices. Other nations, including Britain, have long been used to fishing the same waters. This led to disputes over fishing limits, known as the Cod Wars, which erupted in the mid 1950s, re-emerging on two occasions in the 1970s. In recent times, however, there has been investment in heavy industry, such as aluminium smelting, and biotechnology, software production and financial services are under development. Iceland also has four national parks that attract ecotourists, and whale-watching is popular. Iceland belongs to the European common market, but remains opposed to full membership of the EU.

Olafur Ragnar Grimsson has been President of Iceland since 1996; Prime Minister Halldor Asgrimsson has been head of government since 2004.

INDIA

Location:	18 I
Capital:	New Dehli
Area:	1,222,238sq m
	(3165596km²)
Population:	1,080,264,388 July 2005
Main Languages:	Hindi, English, etc.
Main Religions:	Hindu 82%, Muslim 12%,
	Christian 2%, Sikh 2%
Currency:	1 rupee = 100 paisa
Climate:	Hot dry summer;
	sunny dry winter; cooler in
	hills, monsoons Jun–Sep
	(SW), Oct–Dec (SE)

A country of southern Asia, India occupies the greater part of the Indian subcontinent in a triangular shape that extends into the Indian Ocean between the Arabian Sea and the Bay of Bengal. It is the most populous country in the world after China, and has common land borders with Pakistan, China (Tibet), Nepal, Bhutan, Bangladesh and Myanmar/Burma. The north-east is dominated by the great range of the Himalayas, together with parts of the ranges of the Karakoram and Hindu Kush. The Himalayas have some of the highest mountains in the world, the largest in India being Kanchenjunga at 28,208ft (8598m). The widest part of the country consists of fertile, alluvial plains, watered by the Ganges, Indus and Brahmaputra rivers that rise in the Himalayas: this is the most highly populated and intensively farmed area in India and is where the capital, New Delhi, lies (though Mumbai (Bombay) is India's largest city). In the west is the Thar or Indian Desert, bordering Pakistan, which is located in India's largest state of Rajasthan. To the south, and covering the greater part of the country, stretches the Deccan plateau, flanked along each coastline by the heavily forested Eastern and Western Ghats and by the range of the Vindya to the north.

India has a rich and unique cultural heritage. The civilization that developed in the Indus Valley is one of the oldest in the world, having reached its apogee from c.2600–1760 BC. In about 1500 BC, the India was invaded by Aryan tribes from Persia,

ABOVE: Mumbai skyline and waterfront.

OPPOSITE LEFT: The Flora Fountain and the Fort Mumbai area.

OPPOSITE RIGHT: The Taj Mahal, Agra.

who merged with the earlier Dravidian inhabitants, and from whose Vedic beliefs the origins of Hinduism, Brahmanism and the caste system eventually emerged. Buddhism was established in the 3rd century BC, and Alexander the Great extended his empire to its furthest limits when he conquered parts of north-west India from 327–25 BC. Independent kingdoms had begun to proliferate from about 500 BC, culminating in the great dynasties and the development of mathematics, philosophy and religion under the Guptas in the 4th and 5th centuries AD.

In 1192, much of India was united under a Muslim sultanate, centred on Delhi, which was incorporated into the Mogul Empire in 1526; this led to the flowering of Muslim art and architecture in India. Meanwhile, traders from Europe had begun to arrive, and colonial expansion, especially by the British, began in the 1600s. In 1757, Robert Clive established the British Empire in India, the East India Company acquiring the right to administer Bengal in 1765. In 1858, after the Indian Mutiny, the crown assumed the company's authority and Queen Victoria was proclaimed Empress of India in 1876.

Following the First World War, a campaign of non-violent resistance to colonization was led by Mahatma Gandhi and Jawaharlal Nehru. Nationalism intensified following the massacre at Amritsar in 1919 and independence was eventually won in 1947. India was partitioned into the secular state of India and

OPPOSITE: *The Golden Temple of Amritsar.*

RIGHT: *Boat on the backwaters of Kerala.*

BELOW: *The Red Fort, Delhi.*

BELOW RIGHT: *Harvesting rice in Kerala.*

the Muslim state of Pakistan was established in the north-east and north-west of India; East Pakistan later became the independent state of Bangladesh after a civil war. The unresolved dispute between India and Pakistan over Jammu and Kashmir began in 1948 and continues to this day.

Thus began India's progression to its position as the world's largest democracy. Nehru became India's first prime minister, followed in the office by his daughter, Indira in 1965. In 1984 Sikh demands for independence resulted in troops storming the Golden Temple of Amritsar and the later assassination of Indira Gandhi by Sikh bodyguards. She was succeeded by her son, Rajiv, who was assassinated during the 1990 election campaign. Head of state since 2002 is President A J P Abdul Kalam. Prime minister since 2004 is Manmohan Singh.

India is no stranger to natural disasters and the effect they have on its resources: as recently as 1999, more than 10,000 people lost their lives when a cyclone hit Orissa. In late December 2004, a major tsunami took at least 60,000 lives, causing massive destruction of property and severe damage to

fishing. Economically, however, India has made great strides since independence, though massive population, extensive poverty, environmental degradation and ethnic and religious strife are perennial problems.

The economy of India is extremely diverse, ranging from the traditional farming of the villages to agriculture on a more modern scale, and employs two-thirds of the population. Rice, wheat, oilseed, jute, tea, sugar and potatoes are grown and cattle, water buffalo and poultry are raised. There is also a wide range of industrial activity, including textiles, cinema (Bollywood), chemicals, steel, vehicles, mining and petroleum. However, services are now the main area of growth. India has large numbers of well-educated people, skilled in the English language, which has enabled it to become a major exporter of information technology, software and business outsourcing services.

INDONESIA

Location:	21 K
Capital:	Jakarta
Area:	740,356sq m (1917522km²)
Population:	241,973,879 July 2005
Main Languages:	Bahasa Indonesian
Main Religions:	Muslim 87%,
	Christian 10%, Hindu 2%
Currency:	1 rupiah = 100 sen
Climate:	Hot and humid all year,
	cooler in the hills, monsoon
	Dec–Mar

Formerly the Dutch East Indies, Indonesia is a country of South-East Asia spread over many islands of the Malay Archipelago: these lie in the Indian and Pacific Oceans, between Indo-China and Australia. Indonesian territory covers Java, Sumatra, southern Borneo, western New Guinea, the Moluccas and Sulawesi. All the islands are mountainous and have more active volcanos than anywhere else in the world: the eruption on Krakatoa killed 30,000 people, and destroyed much of the island in 1883. Tropical rainforest covers the coastal lowlands, much of which has been cleared to allow cultivation of other crops.

Arab traders brought Islam to Indonesia, after the collapse of Hindu and Buddhist kingdoms that had existed since the 7th century: today, more Muslims live in Indonesia than anywhere else in the world. The Dutch established control over the area from the 17th century. It was occupied by Japan during the Second World War, during which time freedom movements began to proliferate: after four years of negotiations, hostilities and UN mediation, the Netherlands reluctantly relinquished its colony in 1949. Achmad Sukarno became Indonesia's first president, but lost power after he was implicated in an abortive Communist coup in 1965. General Suharto became president in 1967, but was forced to relinquish power when his own corruption and a faltering economy caused the Indonesian Revolution of 1998. East Timor was forcibly annexed in 1976; however, the

LEFT: Tapping for rubber.

BELOW LEFT: Borobudur Temple, Java.

OPPOSITE: Lake Toba, Sumatra.

end of the 20th century saw the introduction of democratic elections and the granting of full independence for East Timor. Head of the state of Indonesia since 2004 is President Susilo Bambang Yudhoyono: he is also head of government.

Although progress has been made, Indonesia has many problems to overcome before it can achieve full economic stability: these include widespread poverty and unequal distribution of wealth, issues of human rights, terrorism, endemic corruption and a fragile banking system. Moreover, it has not fully recovered from the Asian financial crisis of the late 1990s, and the transition from 40 years of authoritarianism to a more democratic form of government also remains to be achieved. Indonesia has always been prone to natural disasters: in December 2004, a tsunami stretching as far as Thailand and India, killed 237,000 Indonesians and caused massive destruction to property, particularly in Aceh.

Natural resources include petroleum – not fully exploited through lack of investment – natural gas (of which Indonesia is a large exporter), tin, copper and gold. Soil is generally fertile and major crops are rice, tea, coffee, spices and rubber. Industries include textiles, clothing, footwear, mining, cement, chemical fertilizers, plywood, rubber and tourism.

IRAN

Location:	17 H
Capital:	Tehran
Area:	634,293sq m (1642819km²)
Population:	68,017,860 July 2005
Main Languages:	Farsi
Main Religions:	Muslim: Shi'a 89%, Sunni 10%
Currency:	rial
Climate:	Very hot, dry summer; mild to cold winter

A country in the Middle East, lying between the Caspian Sea in the north and the Gulf of Oman and the Persian Gulf in the south. Iran has land borders with Iraq, Armenia, Azerbaijan, Turkmenistan, Afghanistan, Pakistan and Turkey. The terrain consists of a central plateau, crossed by mountain ranges and deserts, with flatter areas along the coasts. It is subject to earthquakes and periods of prolonged drought.

Previously Persia, the country was known as Iran from 1935, the name taken from the Aryan tribes that settled in Persia around 2000 BC, and from whom modern Persians claim descent. The Medes were an Indo-European people who had established an empire in Azerbaijan and north-eastern Iraq, extending to the south-west of the Caspian Sea. Cyrus the Great conquered the Medes in 550 BC, establishing the Achaemenid dynasty and Iran's first empire. This expanded to include much of Asia Minor, and Egypt, Thrace and Macedonia were added later. The Persian Empire survived the Persian Wars (499–449 BC) against the Greeks, but fell to Alexander the Great in 331 BC. Persia then passed to Seleucids, Parthians and eventually to the Sassanid dynasty, which restored Persian rule in AD 224.

Arabs conquered Iran in the 7th century, replacing Zoroastrianism with Islam. The rule of the Seljuk Turks began in the 12th century, until Persia became part of the empire of Tamerlane (the ancestor of the

Mogul dynasty in India) in the 1380s. Safavid and Qajar dynasties then ruled Persia, the Qajars transferring the capital from Isfahan to Teheran.

In the 19th century, tsarist Russia became increasingly influential in the north and the British in the south: Britain fought a war from 1856–57 over Persia's claims to Herat in Afghanistan. In 1907, the discovery of oil led to Persia's occupation by Russian and British forces and Persia was virtually a British protectorate by 1917. In 1921, Reza Khan, an army officer, seized power in a military coup, becoming Shah of Persia in 1925, when he established the Pahlavi dynasty. Alarmed by his Axist sympathies, Iran was occupied by British and Soviet forces in 1941. Reza Pahlavi abdicated in favour of his son, Mohammad Reza Pahlavi, that year, who began a pro-Western social and economic programme of modernization that increasingly alienated leftist and fundamentalist Muslim elements. He became increasingly dictatorial, and violations of human rights led to revolution, forcing him into exile in 1979.

The exiled religious leader, Ayatollah Khomeini, returned to a position of power as Supreme Leader of the Islamic Republic of Iran, which by now had a theocratic form of government, overseen by Shi'a ayatollohs. This did nothing to help relations with the US, which had supported the shah, and tensions increased further when US embassy staff in Tehran were taken hostage. From 1980 to 1988, Iran fought a bloody war with its neighbour, Iraq, with Ayatollah Khomeini encouraging Iraqi Shi'as to revolt against their government. This spread to the Persian

OPPOSITE: Argh-e Bam Citadel, Bam.

LEFT: The Hazrat e Masumeh shrine at Qom.

Gulf and culminated in military involvement with the US Navy. Ayatollah Khomeini died in 1989, but not before he had placed a *fatwa* for blasphemy on the British writer Salman Rushdie. Hashemi Rafsanjani became head of government that year, when relations with the West slightly improved. However, allegations that Iran was supporting international terrorism and developing a nuclear capability led the US to impose economic sanctions and export controls in 1995; concerns about these activities persist to this day. In 1997, Muhammad Khatami succeeded Rafsanjani, who continued his reforms when re-elected in 2001. In 2003, the town of Bam was decimated by an earthquake in which 40,000 people lost their lives. Head of government since August 2005 is President Mahmud Ahmadi-Nejad.

Only about ten per cent of Iran is fertile, but rice, tobacco, sugar-beet, cotton and tea are grown. Caviar is produced from the Caspian sturgeon and sheep are raised; these produce wool for the exquisite carpets for which Iran is justly famous. However, its most important attribute and chief export is oil, first developed by British enterprise. There is still an overreliance on oil, but there are also reserves of natural gas, coal, chromium, copper, iron ore, lead, manganese and sulphur. There is much to attract visitors to Iran, and tourism is still being developed. Industries include petrochemicals, armaments, sugar refining and textiles.

IRAQ

Location:	16 H
Capital:	Baghdad
Area:	169,247sq m (438350km²)
Population:	26,074,906 July 2005
Main Languages:	Arabic
Main Religions:	Muslim: Shi'a 54%, Sunni 42%
Currency:	1 Iraqi dinar = 1,000 fils
Climate:	Very hot, dry summer: warm winter, cooler in north

A Middle Eastern country of south-western Asia, with a short coastline at Umm Qasr on the Persian Gulf, Iraq has land borders with Jordan, Syria, Turkey, Iran, Kuwait and Saudi Arabia. Southern Kurdistan is also included in the territory. The western part of Iraq is an extension of the Syrian Desert, and there are mountains along the Turkish and Iranian borders. To the south of Iraq's border with Iran is a marshy area, covered in reeds and subject to flooding. This was the province of the Marsh Arabs for thousands of years, until deliberate diversion of the feeder streams dried up the area and caused destruction of the habitat, displacing the people and threatening wildlife.

The area between the two great rivers that traverse Iraq, the Tigris and the Euphrates, was the site of the ancient civilizations of Mesopotamia and approximates to the area of modern Iraq. It was conquered by Arabia in the 7th century and from 1534 formed part of the Ottoman Empire. A Hashemite kingdom was installed by the British after the First World War, though the country remained under British administration until 1932. A republic was declared in 1958, which was in reality ruled by a series of military despots, of which the latest was Saddam Hussein: Saddam became president in 1979, disposing of many of his opponents in the process. His absolute and bloody rule saw territorial disputes that led to war with Iran from 1980 to 1988, causing great hardship and loss of life on both sides but resolving nothing. In 1990 Iraq seized Kuwait, but was expelled by an international coalition of forces in the Gulf War of 1991.

BELOW: Ukhaider Castle, c.645 AD, near Karbala.

OPPOSITE LEFT: Ali El Hadi Mosque in Samarra. It contains the tombs of the 10th, 11th and 12th Imans.

OPPOSITE RIGHT
An Iraqi Marsh Arab.

Following this, a UN resolution was passed that Iraq should produce no further weapons of mass destruction or long-range missiles, and that it should submit to long-term inspections to verify its compliance. However, perceived non-compliance led to invasion by US- and UK-led forces in 2003, when Saddam Hussein and his Ba'ath Party were deprived of power. Coalition forces remain in Iraq to help restore the damaged infrastructure of the country, establish a freely-elected government and subdue insurgency, principally by Sunni Muslims. Transfer of power went from the coalition to an interim Iraqi government in June 2004.

In January 2005, Iraqis elected a transitional National Assembly, which radically changed the balance of power previously held by the Sunni minority. Its task will be to draft a new constitution, with a view to holding new national elections at the end of the year. In the meantime, President Jalal Talabani, a prominent Kurdish leader, is interim head of state, while Ibrahim al-Jafari, a Shi'a, is prime minister, heading a coalition government of Kurds, Sunnis and Shi'as. Meanwhile, Saddam Hussein, and other war criminals from his regime, will get a fair and open trial, subject to the scrutiny of a free press.

Natural resources are petroleum, natural gas, phosphates and sulphur. Iraq's economy was long dominated by oil production, which provided practically all its income. However, subsequent sanctions, warfare and sabotage have seriously damaged the economy and industries and much needs to be done before normality is restored.

IRELAND
(THE REPUBLIC of IRELAND & NORTHERN IRELAND)

Location:	Republic of Ireland 12 F
Capital:	Dublin
Area:	27,148sq m (70313km²)
Population:	4,015,676 July 2005
Main Languages:	Irish, English
Main Religions:	Roman Catholic 93%,
	Protestant 3%
Currency:	euro
Climate:	Mild summer, cool winter

The island of Ireland lies to the west of England and Wales and faces them across the Irish Sea. To the far west lies the Atlantic Ocean and to the north-east the North Channel. To the south-west, the Irish Sea flows into the Atlantic via St George's Channel and the Celtic Sea. About 80 per cent of the total area of the island is occupied by the Republic of Ireland (usually referred to simply as Ireland), which is divided into 26 counties. Ireland as a whole is divided into four provinces: Ulster (in which the British province of Northern Ireland occupies six counties in the north-east), Leinster, Munster and Connaught. The territory as a whole consists of a central lowland area traversed by rivers, such as the Shannon, and with large areas of peat bog, an important source of fuel. The bogs are interspersed by areas of fertile limestone, where mostly dairy farming is carried out. The perimeter of the island has cliffs, hills and low mountains, the coastline to the west and north being heavily indented with bays and estuaries, while there are many *loughs* where rivers widen into lakes.

There were several invasions from Europe during prehistoric times, the most important being that of the Gaels in the 3rd century BC, when Ireland was divided into separate kingdoms. Christianity was brought to the island by St Patrick in AD 432, after which Ireland became a highly developed civilization, described as the 'land of saints and scholars'. Danish Vikings began their raids around 800, but later colonized the island, founding Dublin among other coastal towns; they were decisively repelled by Brian Boru in 1014.

By the Middle Ages, English rule had been confined to the Pale, the area surrounding Dublin. It was not wholly conquered until Tudor times, when Irish land

RIGHT: A Celtic Cross in County Meath.

OPPOSITE: Derry's northern coast, Northern Ireland, where the Giant's Causeway is located.

was confiscated and English settlers were installed, the most important plantation being that of Ulster in 1610. An Irish rebellion was crushed by Cromwell in 1649, when rebel land was confiscated. After an unsuccessful rebellion in 1798, union of Britain and Ireland followed in 1801. Increased prosperity was experienced in Protestant Ulster, though not in the rest of Ireland, and after the failure of the potato crop in the 1840s, thousands died from famine and many more emigrated.

From 1880, under Parnell, the move towards Home Rule for Ireland accelerated. In 1921, Ireland was partitioned by the Anglo-Irish Treaty. This gave the southern part of Ireland dominion status as the Irish Free State. The treaty was followed by the Irish Civil War between the Free State government and republicans, led by Eamon de Valera, who rejected partition; the war

ended in victory for the government in 1923. A new constitution as a sovereign state (Eire) was adopted in 1937, with Eire remaining neutral during the Second World War. In 1949 it left the Commonwealth and became fully independent as the Republic of Ireland, joining the EC in 1973. Bertie Ahern (b.1951) has been Ireland's Taoiseach (prime minister) since 1997.

The Irish Republican Army (IRA) was formed during Ireland's struggle for independence from Britain in 1916–21. In 1969 it split into Official and Provisional, the Official IRA becoming virtually inactive, while the Provisional IRA increased its level of violence against military and civilian targets in Northern Ireland, Britain and Europe. It declared a ceasefire in 1994 and another in 1997. In 2001 and 2002, the decommissioning of some IRA weapons raised hopes of future peace. In July 2005, the IRA announced its intention to relinquish weapons and use only peaceful political means to further its cause. Hope remains.

Northern Ireland was established as a self-governing province of Great Britain in 1920. It is dominated by a Protestant majority, though much of the Roman Catholic minority would prefer union with the Catholic Republic of Ireland in the south. From 1969, discrimination against the Catholic minority led to violent conflict and the continuing presence of the British Army in Northern Ireland, sent there to protect the Catholics. Terrorism and sectarian violence by the Provisional IRA and other paramilitary

OPPOSITE ABOVE LEFT: The Half Penny Bridge across the River Liffey, Dublin.

OPPOSITE ABOVE RIGHT: One of Dublin's famous pubs.

OPPOSITE BELOW: The ancient burial mound of Newgrange, County Meath.

BELOW: The site of the Battle of the Boyne in 1690, when William of Orange (William III) defeated the Catholic army of James II.

groups, both Republican and Loyalist, led to 'Bloody Sunday' in 1972, when civil rights demonstrators were shot by British troops. Northern Ireland's Stormont government in Belfast, the capital, was suspended and direct rule from Westminster was established. Extensive multi-party talks began in 1996, with the intention of resolving the situation, which led to the Good Friday Agreement two years later. In 1999 a devolved parliament was established in Northern Ireland, with representatives taken from both Unionist and Nationalist groups.

The Republic of Ireland has benefited greatly from its membership of the EU, receiving generous agricultural grants that have aided modernization. It made great strides towards developing a robust economy from 1995–2000, when it was referred to as the Celtic Tiger, and has continued to prosper in spite of the global economic slow-down of 2001. Agriculture has traditionally been Ireland's most important occupation, but it has been superseded by high-tech industries and services, which also supplement the more traditional brewing, fishing and textile industries.

ISRAEL

Location:	15 H
Capital:	Jerusalem
Area:	8,473sq m (21945km²)
Population:	6,276,883 July 2005
Main Languages:	Hebrew, Arabic
Main Religions:	Jewish 82%,
	Muslim 14%, Christian 2%
Currency:	1 shekel = 100 agorot
Climate:	Hot, dry summer;
	mild winter, cooler in hills

A country of the Middle East on the eastern shore of the Mediterranean Sea, between Egypt and Lebanon. Israel has a narrow, fertile plain running along the coast, with the Negev Desert, some of it irrigated, occupying half the land in the south and extending to Eilat on the Gulf of Aqaba. To the east lie the Jordanian Great Rift Valley, the Sea of Galilee, the River Jordan and the Dead Sea, which is the lowest point on earth. Israeli territory also includes the Gaza Strip, the West Bank of the Jordan, taken from Jordan in the Six-Day War, and the Golan Heights, annexed from Syria.

In 1948, following the Second World War, the modern state of Israel was established by the UN as a home for the Jewish people. The new state was in Palestinian territory, that had previously been mandated to Britain. After centuries of exile, the Israelis regarded this as coming home to the land that was rightly theirs, it being the place where Jewish tribes established Biblical Israel after the death of Solomon. This point of view was not shared by the Palestinian Arabs, however, and hundreds of thousands of Palestinians fled the area. Israel was accepted as a UN member soon after and attacks began by surrounding Arab states, including Syria, Lebanon, Jordan and Egypt. Thus began the Arab-Israeli Wars, the first of which ended in victory for Israel and the enlargement of the territory originally allotted to Israel by the UN. These acquisitions included Galilee in the north, the coastal plain along the Mediterranean, and the Negev Desert in the south. There were subsequent Arab-Israeli Wars in 1956, 1967 and 1973 (see also Egypt), that were followed by Israeli gains in eastern Jerusalem, the West Bank, the Gaza Strip, the Golan Heights and the Sinai Peninsula. Sinai, however, was restored to Egypt in 1982 after the Camp David Agreements of 1979. In the meantime, Israel

BELOW: An overview of Jerusalem.

OPPOSITE ABOVE LEFT: Gathering olives on a kibbutz.

OPPOSITE ABOVE RIGHT: Galilee, long associated with the ministry of Jesus.

OPPOSITE BELOW LEFT: The Wailing Wall, Jerusalem.

declared Jerusalem its capital, a city of equal holiness to Muslims and Christians.

From 1989, the Israeli population began

to increase, following transportations of Falashas from Ethiopia and influxes of Soviet Jews. This led to more Israeli settlement of Palestinian territory, which has led to tensions, intermittant terrorism and military activity ever since.

In 1993 the Israeli prime minister, Yitzhak Rabin, with Shimon Peres, negotiated an accord with Yasser Arafat and the Palestine Liberation Organization (PLO), whereby limited Palestinian autonomy would be granted in the West Bank and Gaza Strip: Arafat became head of the autonomous Palestinian authority the following year. A Nobel Peace Prize was awarded as a result of this, which was shared by Rabin, Peres and Arafat. In 1995 Rabin was assassinated by an Israeli opponent of the peace accord that Rabin had

negotiated with Jordan the previous year. In 2000 Israel withdrew from southern Lebanon, which it had occupied since 1982. In keeping with the proposals of the Madrid Conference of 1991, negotiations began between Israel, Syria and the Palestinians with a view to establish a permanent Palestinian state. This developed into the drawing up of a 'road map' by the American president, George Bush, in 2002, whereby Israeli-Palestinian conflict would be resolved once and for all. This has again been undermined by violence on both sides.

Yasser Arafat died in 2004 and was succeeded as leader by Mahmud Abbas, since when there have been hopeful signs that the conflict will be finally resolved. In August 2005, certain Israeli settlements of Palestinian territory in the Gaza Strip and West Bank were officially disbanded.

Despite compensation awarded by the Israeli government, to enable the settlers to establish new homes elsewhere, many understandably resisted, but were forcibly removed. Moshe Katzov has been president of Israel since 2003, with Prime Minister Ariel Sharon the head of government since 2001.

Despite limited natural resources, Israel has intensively developed its industrial and agricultural sectors. Apart from wheat, which it imports, it is largely self-sufficient in other agricultural products. Two-thirds of its workforce is employed in service industries and tourism is also important. Israel's main exports are cut diamonds, high-tech equipment and fruit and vegetables. Its economy is helped by payments from abroad, notably the US, as well as foreign loans.

ITALY

Location:	14 H
Capital:	Rome
Area:	116,332sq m (301300km²)
Population:	58,103,033 July 2005
Main Languages:	Italian
Main Religions:	Roman Catholic 83%
Currency:	euro
Climate:	Hot summer, warm winter in south, cold in north, snow in mountains

A country of southern Europe, Italy borders France to the west, Switzerland, Liechtenstein and Austria to the north, and Slovenia to the north-east. It consists of an elongated peninsula extending south into the Mediterranean, with the Ligurian and Tyrrhenian Seas to the west, and the Adriatic and Ionian Seas to the east and south. To the north lie the Alps, with Garda, Italy's largest lake, dominated by the Dolomites in the north-east. Moving southwards, the Alps give way to the vast fertile plain of Lombardy, drained by the River Po, and Italy's most important industrial and agricultural region. The range of the Apennines extends from the

LEFT: *Temple of Castor and Pollux in the Roman Forum.*

OPPOSITE: *Florence.*

Alps and forms the backbone of the peninsula, stretching down to the very tip of Italy, while narrow coastal lowlands lie to either side. Within Italy lie the enclaves of San Marino and Vatican City.

Italy has always been the driving force behind the cultural and social life of the Mediterranean, having been exposed to some of its most important civilizations. According to legend, Italy was founded by Romulus and Remus in 753 BC. The southern cities were later colonized by Greeks from Sparta and Euboea, and became part of Magna Graecia. Then came the Etruscans, who in turn influenced the Romans: however, the Romans eventually expelled the Etruscans and established a republic in 505 BC, uniting Italy until the collapse of the Roman Empire in AD 476.

Italy was central to the development of science, philosophy and the arts in the Middle Ages. At this time, Italy was not as we know it today, but a collection of papal and city states. Florence and Milan were two such states, ruled by the Medici and Sforza, powerful families and great patrons of the arts. The Renaissance was a time when European art and literature were revived, influenced by classical models; Leonardo, Michelangelo and other luminaries were at the height of their powers in the 15th and 16th centuries.

A movement led by Garibaldi in the 19th century created the modern Italian state, which included Sicily and Sardinia: Victor

Emmanuel II became king of Italy in 1861. Italy entered the First World War on the side of the Allies in 1915. From 1922 the country was dominated by the fascist dictator, Benito Mussolini; but his disastrous alliance with Nazi Germany in the Second World War led to Italy's defeat and his own execution. After the war, Italy abandoned the monarchy and became a republic in 1946; this was followed by a period of economic revival. Italy was a charter member of NATO and the EC, joining the Economic and Monetary Union in 1999. Head of state since 1999 is President Carlo Azeglio, while Silvio Berlusconi has been head of government since 2001.

Italy has its problems, however, namely the gap between the prosperous industrial north and the poorer agricultural Mezzogiorno to the south. There have also been the activities of the Lega Nord

(Northern League), a separatist organization since 1993 to contend with, together with organized crime, corruption, high unemployment and illegal immigration from south-eastern Europe and North Africa – all of which have hampered growth. However, Italy has a diverse industrial economy, with almost the same per capita output as France and the UK. It is also the largest producer of wine in the world and has more than enough to interest tourists. It is a large producer of olive oil, steel and motor vehicles.

ABOVE LEFT: San Gimignano, Tuscany.

ABOVE: The island of Capri, off Naples.

LEFT: The Piazza Navona and Fountain of Neptune, Rome.

OPPOSITE: San Giorgio Maggiore, Venice.

JAMAICA

Location:	8 I
Capital:	Kingston
Area:	4,411sq m (11425km²)
Population:	2,731,832 July 2005
Main Languages:	English
Main Religions:	Protestant 70%, Roman Catholic 8%
Currency:	1 Jamaican dollar = 100 cents
Climate:	Hot all year, cooler in hills, rains May–Oct

An island nation of the Greater Antilles, Jamaica is the third-largest island in the Caribbean Sea and lies 90 miles (145km) south-east of Cuba. It has great natural beauty, having an elevated, well-watered plain crossed by the Blue Mountains, which run east to west and rise to 7,400ft (2255m). Jamaica has a narrow coastal plain where most of the population is concentrated. A former capital of Jamaica was Port-Royal, the haunt of Captain Morgan, which was buried in an earthquake in 1692. Attempts to excavate it began in 1965.

Discovered by Columbus in 1494, Jamaica was colonized by the Spanish, who enslaved or killed the native Arawak or Taino inhabitants, making them virtually extinct. The natives called the island *Xaymaca* ('Land of wood and water'), from which the name Jamaica evolved. Both the Spanish and the British, who forcefully took the island in 1655, imported great numbers of slaves from Africa to work the sugar plantations, with the result that by the beginning of the 19th century, blacks far outnumbered whites, thereby increasing the likelihood of revolt. Inevitably a series of rebellions followed, and slavery was abolished in 1834; there was full emancipation in 1838, following which the economy began to decline. Most of the population is therefore descended from these slaves; the patois in everyday use combines elements of old and new English, Spanish,

BELOW: Montego Bay.

OPPOSITE LEFT: Jamaica's scenic Blue Mountains.

OPPOSITE RIGHT: Vale Royal, the official residence of the Jamaican prime minister.

French and African dialects. Self-government was achieved in 1944 and Jamaica became an independent country within the Commonwealth of Nations, with full independence from 1962.

Since the mid-20th century there has been widespread emigration from Jamaica, mostly to America but also to Canada and the UK, which is referred to as the Jamaican diaspora. Jamaica is the home of Rastafarianism, a religious movement popularized by Bob Marley, whose followers believe Emperor Haile Selassie of Ethiopia to be their messiah; they also believe they are a chosen people who will eventually return to their promised land.

Head of state is Queen Elizabeth II, her representative in Jamaica being the Governor-General. The head of government is currently Prime Minister P J. Patterson, who has held office since the resignation of Michael Manley in 1992, having been re-elected three more times since then.

Jamaica was the world's largest exporter of sugar in the 1820s. However, sugar is no longer the main industry, but has been replaced by bauxite production and tourism. Agriculture is still important, though the worst drought for 70 years in 1997 drastically reduced production.

JAPAN

Location:	23 H
Capital:	Tokyo
Area:	145,840sq m (377726km²)
Population:	127,417,244 July 2005
Main Languages:	Japanese
Main Religions:	Shinto 50%, Buddhist 45%
Currency:	1 yen = 100 sen
Climate:	Mild, rains mid Jan–mid Jul, snow in winter in north

A sovereign state of eastern Asia, Japan occupies a chain of hundreds of islands lying in the Northern Pacific. It is separated from Russia, North and South Korea and the rest of Asia by the Sea of Japan, the Sea of Okhotsk lying to the north. The principal islands are Hokkaido, Honshu (on which the capital, Tokyo, stands), Shikoku and Kyushu. The islands are mostly mountainous, with flatter areas in between, the highest spot being Mount Fujiyama on Honshu at 12,390ft (3776m). Woodland covers nearly three-quarters of the terrain. Around the coastlines are densely populated areas of flatter fertile land, that includes the

LEFT: Kimonos in Kyoto.

OPPOSITE ABOVE : The moat of the Imperial Palace, Tokyo.

OPPOSITE BELOW: Lake Kawaguchi, dominated by sacred Mount Fujiyama, Honshu.

Kanto plain, that extends from southern Honshu into northern Kyushu and is Japan's industrial heartland. There are many active volcanoes, which have been instrumental in shaping Japan's unique and varied landscape; there are frequent earthquakes and tsunamis. (An earthquake in 1923 killed 123,000 people, devastating Tokyo and Yokohama and disrupting Japan's economy.) Japan also encompasses the Ryukyu archipelago, of which Okinawa is a part.

The Japanese are a possible fusion of peoples from Malaya, Polynesia and Asia, who largely displaced the original Ainu inhabitants, some of whom still survive in Hokkaido today. Much of Japan's early history is the stuff of legends, until the 5th century AD, when writing was introduced from Korea, and whence Buddhism came in the 6th century. China was instrumental in shaping Japan's society and culture during the following centuries, when Japan was ruled by feudal dynasties. Eventually, emperors were the nominal rulers, but the real power lay in the hands of the military shoguns, which persisted until Japan began to modernize itself in the 19th century.

Contact with Europeans began in the 16th century, when Portuguese, Spanish and Dutch traders arrived, as did Christianity,

died in 1989 and was succeeded by his son, Akhito.

The Liberal Democratic Government held power since 1948, only splitting in 1993 after a series of corruption charges had been levelled against it. During this time US bases were established in Japan, which led to demonstrations in the 1960s and 70s against US interference. The present head of state is the Emperor Akihito, while head of government since 2001 is Junichiro Koizumi.

Being predominantly mountainous, Japan has less than a quarter of cultivable land with which to support one of the largest populations in the world. Rice, silk and fishing, for long the traditional industries,

began to decline in the 1960s; Japan compensated for this by becoming a highly industrialized country, second only to the USA in economic power. This was achieved despite an economic slowdown in the 1990s, culminating in the spread of the economic crisis in South-East Asia to Japan in 1998. Japan's success is due to the strong work ethic of the Japanese and their mastery of technology. Today, services and banking are Japan's most important industries and machinery and transport form the bulk of its exports; Japan is also a leading manufacturer of cars, ships, steel, iron and cement, electronic and electrical equipment, chemicals and textiles, while its fishing industry is second only to that of China.

introduced by St Francis Xavier in 1549. However, the fear that conversion might be a prelude to conquest led to the expulsion of the Spanish and Portuguese and the persecution of the Christians. Only the Dutch were allowed to trade, though in a restricted form, and the Japanese people were forbidden to travel abroad. Isolation from the rest of the world continued until 1853, when trade with Japan was enforced by the USA. The year 1867 saw the last of the shoguns, when power was restored at last to the emperor.

The first of the Sino-Japanese Wars was fought from 1894–95, when Japan secured Formosa (Taiwan), southern Manchuria and Korea, which it annexed in 1910. Japan also acquired half of Sakhalin in a war with

Russia from 1904–05. In 1930 Japan invaded Manchuria, setting up a puppet state. It invaded China in 1937, precipitating the second Sino-Japanese War. Japan supported the Allies during the First World War, but switched its allegiance to the Axis in the Second, making a surprise attack on Pearl Harbor in 1941. Japan surrendered in 1945 after the US dropped atomic bombs on Hiroshima and Nagasaki, in the hope of bringing a swift conclusion to the war.

Japan was occupied by the US from 1945–52, under the command of Douglas MacArthur, when a move away from militarization and towards a democratic constitution was made; following this, the Emperor Hirohito became a constitutional monarch and proclaimed himself divine. He

JORDAN

Location:	16 H
Capital:	Amman
Area:	34,443sq m (89207km²)
Population:	5,759,732 July 2005
Main Languages:	Arabic
Main Religions:	Sunni Muslim 96%, Christian 4%
Currency:	1 Jordanian dinar = 1,000 fils
Climate:	Transitional Mediterranean–desert-type

A kingdom in the Middle East, east of the Jordan – a river that flows from the Anti-Lebanon Mountains, through the Sea of Galilee and into the Dead Sea, which Jordan shares with Israel to the west. Jordan also has common borders with Syria to the north, Iraq to the east, and with Saudi Arabia to the east and south. Jordan has a short coastline on the Gulf of Aqaba, to the east of which, near Jabal Ram (Jordan's highest peak at 5755ft/1754m), lies the ancient rose-coloured city of Petra. This was the capital city of the Nabateans, who developed an empire in Jordan during the 1st century BC.

Romans, Arab Muslims, Christian Crusaders, Mamelukes and Ottoman Turks have in turn dominated the area. John the Baptist baptized Christ in the River Jordan, which is holy not only to Christians but also to Muslims and Jews. Jordan became a British protectorate after the First World War. In 1920 it was mandated to Britain as part of Palestine; by 1923, however, the territory east of the Jordan came to be recognized as the separate country of Transjordan, under the Emir Abdullah. In 1946 Transjordan became the independent Hashemite Kingdom of Jordan, a name that came into general use a few years later, and Abdullah became king.

King Abdullah, an architect of the Arab League, invaded the newly proclaimed state of Israel in 1948, in what was the first of the

Arab-Israeli Wars. Israel now occupies most of the area that was Palestine, which caused many thousands of Palestinians to flee to Jordan and elsewhere. However, under a peace agreement with Israel in 1949, Jordan retained the part of Palestine and East Jerusalem that it had captured. Abdullah was assassinated in 1951 and his grandson, Hussein, became king in 1953, after Hussein's father was deposed because of mental illness.

Jordan continued to administer the area until 1967, when the Six-Day War (second Arab-Israeli War) ended in the Israeli occupation of East Jerusalem and what is referred to as the West Bank, an area that had originally been designated for Arab occupation by the UN in 1947. Jordan also went to Syria's aid in the Golan Heights in 1973, which Israel also captured. Jordan continues to oppose the Camp David Agreements of 1979, and in particular the continued settlement of the West Bank by the Israelis; it is also a contentious issue that Israel has pronounced the whole of Jerusalem its capital.

In 1980, Jordan was a supporter of Iraq in the war between Iran and Iraq. It also sided with Iraq during the Gulf War of 1991. In 1988 Jordan surrendered its claim to the Israeli-occupied West Bank to the Palestine Liberation Organization (PLO), then led by Yasser Arafat.

Head of state since 1999, following the death of his father, King Hussein, is King Abdullah II. Head of government since April 2005 is Prime Minister Adnan Badran. Since his accession, King Abdullah has done much to improve living standards, stabilize the economy and introduce political reforms. In 2000 Jordan became a member of the World Trade Organization (WTO), negotiated a free trade accord with the US, and came to an agreement with the EU in 2001: all these have helped to put Jordan firmly on the foreign investment map.

Jordan is predominantly desert, but where there is water, cereals, citrus fruits, olives and grapes are grown and livestock is reared. However, Jordan was deprived of most of its fruit-growing region on the West Bank in 1967. Minerals include potash, phosphates, oil and natural gas. Many of Jordan's inhabitants still live nomadic lives and there is a large Palestinian population.

OPPOSITE: The citadel temple of Hercules, Amman.

ABOVE LEFT: Women in traditional dress, Jerash.

RIGHT: The treasury building at Petra, a city carved out of the virgin rock.

KAZAKHSTAN

Location:	18 G
Capital:	Astana
Area:	1,049,150sq m (2717300km²)
Population:	15,185,844 July 2005
Main Languages:	Kazakh, Russian
Main Religions:	Muslim, Christian
Currency:	1 tenge = 100 tiyn
Climate:	Hot summer, cold winter, dry all year, snow in mountains

A republic of central Asia to the south of Russia, and equivalent in size to Western Europe, Kazakhstan stretches from the Caspian Sea to the Altay Mountains and China. It has land borders to the south with Turkmenistan, Uzbekistan and Kyrgyzstan, and shares the inland Aral Sea with Uzbekistan. (The Aral Sea has shrunk to a quarter of its size following Soviet irrigation schemes that dried up its feeder rivers.) A small portion west of the Ural river also extends into easternmost Europe. The grassy steppe of the north gives way to desert or semi-desert in the south, with a mineral-rich central plateau. A large area south of Koursatov and along the Chinese border was used by the Soviets to test nuclear weapons and has caused radioactive contamination.

Kazakhstan's Turkic tribes, nomads who wandered the great steppes in seach of fresh pastures for their livestock, were overrun by Genghis Khan and his Mongol hordes in the 13th century. Following Genghis Khan's death, the area was divided up into khanates, which eventually became the territories of the Kazakh Khanate, which

OPPOSITE: A rider herding cattle on a collective farm near Astana.

LEFT: A dwelling in Kokchetav.

BELOW: A pedestrian precinct in Almaty.

government is Prime Minister Daniyal Akhmetov since 2003.

Kazakhstan is still a developing country, though it is wealthier than most of its Asian neighbours. For a time, the break-up of the Soviet Union had an adverse effect on exports, but these are now recovering. Agriculture is still important, and includes grain, cotton, wool and livestock production. There are major deposits of petroleum, natural gas and coal, and these provide valuable revenue, while other minerals and metals are in plentiful supply. The opening of an oil pipeline from the Caspian Sea has considerably improved Kazakhstan's export opportunities.

reached its apogee in the 18th century. During the Khanate, medieval cities, such as Aulie-Ata and Turkestan, were founded along the northern route of the Great Silk Road to China.

In the 19th century, the Russian empire began to expand and spread into Central Asia. Eventually, what is known today as Kazakhstan, came under the rule of the Russian tsars. In 1920 it became an autonomous republic within Russia, and in 1936 became the largest constituent republic of the Soviet Union, apart from Russia. There was an influx of Russians and other

displaced persons into Kazakhstan in the 1950s and 60s, following Khrushchev's 'Virgin Lands' plan to develop Kazakhstan's grasslands into a main grain-producing area of the Soviet Union, with the result that the indigenous population were outnumbered. It became an independent republic within the Commonwealth of Independent States on the break-up of the Soviet Union in 1991, when many of the earlier immigrants left the country.

Head of state since 1991 is President Nursaltan Anazarbayev, a former Communist Party leader, while head of

KENYA

Location:	16 K
Capital:	Nairobi
Area:	224,941sq m (582600km²)
Population:	33,829,590 July 2005
Main Languages:	Swahili, English
Main Religions:	Christian 72%,
	Traditional 18%, Muslim 6%
Currency:	1 Kenya shilling =
	100 cents
Climate:	Hot and humid on coast;
	temperate inland; hot and
	dry in north; rains
	Mar–May, Nov–Dec

Mount Kenya gave its name to the country, and at 17,058ft (5199m), is the second-highest mountain in Africa. The Republic of Kenya straddles the equator and has land borders with Uganda, Sudan, Ethiopia, Somalia and Tanzania. From the tropical coastal plain, bordering the Indian Ocean, the land rises to more temperate highlands in the west, that are crossed by the Great Rift Valley.

The British Kenyan-born archeologist, Louis Leakey (1903–72), discovered

gigantic animal fossils at the Olduvai Gorge in 1958, his wife, Mary, having previously found the skull of an ape-man of the Miocene period on Rusinga Island in Lake Victoria in 1948. In 1972, their son, Richard, discovered the earliest human bones ever found near the shores of Lake Turkana (Rudolf) in the north-west; consequently, Kenya can justifiably claim to be the 'cradle of civilization'.

Populated largely by Bantu-speaking peoples, Kenya was settled by Arabs in the

214

8th century. In the 16th century, Portuguese traders dominated the area, but the Arabs regained control in 1729. Britain gained rights to the coastal area in the late 19th century and colonization began at the beginning of the next, on land acquired from the Kikuyu, on which plantations and farms were established. Kenya became a British crown colony in 1920.

The Mau Mau, a Kikuyan terrorist secret society, with nationalist aims, was active during the 1950s, focusing their attacks on European settlers in the south-western Kenyan Highlands. This resulted in a state of emergency being declared, the presence of British troops, and the imprisonment of Jomo Kenyatta for his alleged involvement with the Mau Mau. The conflict ended in 1960, by which time thousands had died, including even more Mau Mau. Kenyatta was released from prison in 1961, when he became president of the Kenya African National Union (KANU), which led Kenya to independence in 1963. A republic was established the following year, and Kenyatta became Kenya's first prime minister, becoming president the following year. Kenyatta's was an authoritarian rule, but he tried to establish unity, though drought and territorial disputes with Uganda and Tanzania caused civil unrest.

The years 1967–68 saw the departure of Asians from Kenya, many to Britain, following a period of intense Africanization. Kenya was a virtual one-party state from 1969–82, under the dominance of KANU. In 1978, Kenyatta died and was succeeded as president by Daniel Arap Moi, who was re-elected in multi-party elections in 1992 and 1997. Moi created the first coalition government in 2001 and was succeeded by President Mwai Kibaki the following year, when he defeated the KANU candidate, Uhuru Kenyatta. Kibaki is head of both state and government.

In 1998 the US embassy in Nairobi was bombed, killing nealy 250 people and injuring thousands more, and a terrorist car-bomb in a Mombasa hotel took more lives in 2002.

Kenya is still a developing country, but it is one of the most agriculturally productive in Africa, and tea, coffee, wheat, sugar, cotton, sisal, tobacco, rice and timber are grown and dairy cattle and beef are raised. There is a luxury trade in flowers, fruit and vegetables that are air-freighted to Europe, providing out-of-season produce when it is unavailable at home. Mineral resources include soda ash, limestone, salt, gemstones, zinc, diotomite and gypsum, while industries include plastic goods, textiles, soap, oil refining, aluminium, lead, steel, batteries and cement. Kenya has an abundance of wildlife and many game reserves. Its beach resorts also attract thousands of tourists every year.

PAGE 214: Modern buildings in Nairobi, Kenya's capital city.

PAGE 215: Flamingoes on Lake Bogoria, a soda lake lying at the foot of the towering Laikipia escarpment. The national park also protects one of Kenya's remaining herds of greater kudu.

RIGHT: Masai dancing in Hell's Gate National Park.

KIRIBATI

Location:	1 K
Capital:	Bairiki
Area:	277sq m (717km²)
Population:	103,092 July 2005
Main Languages:	English
Main Religions:	Roman Catholic 53%, Protestant 39%
Currency:	1 Australian dollar = 100 cents
Climate:	Hot all year

A country of Oceania in the Pacific Ocean, Kiribati, formerly a part of the Gilbert and Ellice Islands, straddles the equator, and consists of 33 small coral atolls, more than half of which are uninhabited. They include the Gilbert, Line, and Phoenix Islands and Banaba (Ocean Island), which was one of three phosphate rock islands in the Pacific, though the phosphate is now exhausted. The capital, Bairiki is located on Tarawa atoll. The islands are subject to occasional tornadoes, and typhoons can occur from November to March. Some of the islands are low-lying and there is the potential for them to be drastically affected by changes in sea level.

Inhabited by Micronesian peoples, who were also the first inhabitants 2,000 years ago, the islands were first seen by the Spanish in the mid 16th century, and were visited by British navigators in the the late 18th century. The Gilbert and nearby Ellice Islands (now Tuvalu) were declared a British protectorate in 1892, becoming a British colony in 1915. The British connection with the Gilbert Islands ended when they became an independent republic within the Commonwealth of Nations in 1979, with the name Kiribati, a local transliteration of 'Gilberts'. At the same time, the US relinquished Phoenix Island and all but three of the Line Islands to Kiribati in a treaty of friendship.

President Anote Tong has been head of both state and government since 2003. There is no tradition of political parties on Kiribati, and its parliament can only be regarded as a loose assembly of 42 representatives who are elected every four years.

The soil of the islands is poor and calcareous, making agriculture difficult. Kiribati has few skilled workers or natural resources and copra and fish are all that are produced and exported. It receives financial aid, largely from the UK and Japan, and relies on money sent home by people who have left the islands to work abroad.

NORTH KOREA

Location:	22 G
Capital:	Pyongyang
Area:	47,402sq m (122771km²)
Population:	22,912,177 July 2005
Main Languages:	Korean
Main Religions:	Traditional 14%, Chondoist 14%, Buddhist 2%, Christian 1%
Currency:	1 won = 100 chon
Climate:	Summer hot, winter cold, snow, rains Jun–Sep

A country in the Far East, North Korea occupies the northern part of the Korean peninsula. It is predominantly mountainous, the capital Pyongyang lying on the western coastal plain. China lies to the north, with South Korea to the south of the demilitarized zone which divides the two countries. To the east is the Sea of Japan, with the Korea Bay and Yellow Sea to the west. There is a short border with Russia along the Tumen river in the far north-east.

The history of Korea goes back 2,000

years BC to its founding by the Tangun dynasty, which was followed by the Chinese Kija dynasty, which ruled from 1122 BC until the 4th century AD. Korea suffered internal wars and invasions until the 7th century AD, when the peninsula became a unified kingdom. Korea again became a vassal of China under the Yi dynasty from 1392.

Following the Russo-Japanese War, Korea was occupied by Japan in 1905, with annexation following in 1910. Thereafter, Japanese colonizers began to arrive, who developed agriculture and industry, but used Koreans as forced labourers. The Japanese surrendered Korea at the end of the Second World War in 1945, when two zones of occupation were formed, divided by the 38th parallel at Panmunjom, the Soviets occupying the area north of the line, the US the south.

North Korea's official name is the

Democratic People's Republic of Korea and it was formed in 1948, after attempts at reunification had failed. The Soviets installed a government, led by the Communist-trained Kim Il Sung, who began a radical programme of land reform and nationalization. In 1950 North Korea invaded South Korea in a further attempt at reunification. UN troops, consisting mainly of US forces, countered the invasion by invading North Korea, with China intervening on the side of the North. Peace was restored in 1953 at a cost of two million lives and the status quo was restored. North Korea became increasingly isolated and millions fled the dictatorial regime.

A new constitution was adopted in 1972, whereby Kim Il Sung became president of

develop a nuclear 'deterrent'. Later that year, however, it began talks on the subject with China, Japan, Russia, South Korea and the United States. US President George W. Bush once described North Korea as part of an 'axis of evil', along with other countries in the Middle East. In February 2005, North Korea withdrew, confirming it had nuclear weapons and declaring it would not resume talks until this description of it had been withdrawn. In May 2005 US spy satellites detected preparations for possible underground nuclear testing; however, possibly because of its failing economy, North Korea agreed to resume talks and negotiate a peace treaty later in the year. Meanwhile, the US is still delivering food aid to North Korea in the hope that it is not being diverted from those who need it most.

OPPOSITE ABOVE: Dancers celebrating 50 years of the Workers' Party in Nampo.

OPPOSITE BELOW: The central military demarcation line at Panmunjom.

LEFT: The Pohyon Temple in the Myohyang mountains.

BELOW: Man with a bull cart, Kaesong.

Head of government since 2003 is Pak Pong Ju.

Although North Korea has rich mineral deposits, natural disasters, corruption and the collapse of the Soviet bloc have all taken their toll on the economy. Moreover, North Korea continues to neglect its agriculture in favour of military spending.

North Korea. In 1991, North Korea became a UN member, when a pact of non-agression was made with South Korea. When Kim Il Sung died in 1994, he was succeeded, unopposed, by his son, Kim Jong Il, when an agreement was made to cease development of nuclear weapons in return for US aid. In 1996, flooding caused severe famine and devastated agriculture. North Korea continued to rely on food aid while maintaining a one-million-strong army.

In 2002 it was discovered that North Korea was violating its 1994 agreement to freeze and eventually halt its plutonium-based nuclear programme; North Korea responded by expelling international weapons inspectors from its territory. In 2003 North Korea declared its withdrawal from the International Non-Proliferation Treaty, announcing that it would continue to

SOUTH KOREA

Location:	22 H
Capital:	Seoul
Area:	38,332sq m (99254km²)
Population:	48,422,644 July 2005
Main Languages:	Korean
Main Religions:	Buddhist 23%,
	Protestant 18%, Roman
	Catholic 7%
Currency:	1 won = 100 chon
Climate:	Summer hot, winter cold,
	snow, rains Jun–Sep

South Korea occupies the southern portion of the Korean peninsula and, though smaller, has twice the population of North Korea. The terrain is mostly hilly, with coastal lowlands in the west and south. Its territory also includes the island of Cheju-do to the south-west, where Mount Halla, at 6,398ft (1950m), is the highest peak.

South Korea shares a common history with North Korea until 1945, when the peninsula was split into two at the 38th

parallel. Thereafter, it was occupied by the US until full autonomy was granted in 1948 and the Republic of Korea was born. America and the UN supported South Korea during the Korean War (1950–53), which ended in stalemate, despite the loss of many lives and devastation of South Korea's infrastructure. The corrupt and repressive Synghman Rhee, the first president, was overthrown in a military coup in 1961, sparked by the massacre of student protesters. General Park Chung Hee seized power and a period of rapid industrial development began; by the end of the 1970s, South Korea had emerged as a major producer of electronic goods and an important shipbuilding nation.

Park was assassinated in 1979, but the years of increasingly stringent military rule

Pyongyang with Kim Jong Il of North Korea, where South Korean investment in the North was discussed. Kim Dae Jung was awarded the Nobel Peace Prize for his efforts at reconciliation, which were derailed two years later by a dispute over coastal waters in the Yellow Sea. With Japan, South Korea also co-hosted World Cup football in 2002. President Roh Moo-hyun has been president since 2003, with Lee Hae-chan the head of government from 2004.

South Korea was deprived of energy and mineral resources by its division from North Korea, and agriculture seemed all that remained. However, this was revolutionized by self-help collective farming. Today, the country is a fully-functioning, stable democracy, with per capita GDP 20 times that of North Korea and an economy that is comparable with the middle-ranking countries of the EU. This has been achieved by a strong labour effort, restriction of consumer goods, and prudent savings and investments, despite a downturn caused by the Asian financial crisis of 1997. Korea continues to export semiconductors, telecommunications equipment, motor vehicles, computers, steel, petrochemicals and ships.

OPPOSITE ABOVE: Kyongbokkung.

OPPOSITE BELOW: A cabin on Mount Halla.

ABOVE LEFT: Mount Taedunsan in autumn.

LEFT: A mask dance, performed in Pongsan.

did not end there, though a more liberal constitution ensured the election of President Roh Tae-woo in 1987. The summer Olympic Games were held in Seoul in 1988. In 1991 anti-government protests were forcibly suppressed, relations with North Korea improved, and South Korea joined the UN, establishing diplomatic relations with China the following year. In 1992 the first civilian government for over 30 years came to power. In 1996 South Korea was admitted to the OECD and Kim Dae Jung, a former dissident, became president the following year. In 2000, Kim Jing Pil, prime minister since 1998, resigned and was eventually replaced by Lee Han Dong. That same year, President Kim Dae Jung had a meeting in

KUWAIT

Location:	16 H
Capital:	Kuwait
Area:	6,880sq m (17819km²)
Population:	2,335,648 July 2005
Main Languages:	Arabic
Main Religions:	Muslim 92%, Christian 6%
Currency:	1 Kuwaiti dinar = 1000 fils
Climate:	Hot and humid in summer, cooler on coast; cool in winter

A country of the Middle East on the north-western coast of the Persian Gulf, between Iraq and Saudi Arabia. Kuwait mostly consists of low-lying desert inhabited by nomadic Bedouin tribes.

Kuwait has been an autonomous sheikhdom since the 18th century. It was founded by the al-Sabah family, while nominally remaining part of the Ottoman Empire. Concerned at growing Ottoman and German influence, the shiekh invited British protection in 1897. The British protectorate lasted until 1961, when independence was restored to Kuwait and it became a member

of both the UN and the Arab League.

This small, barren country, that had previously relied on maritime trading, pearling and simple boat-building for its survival, suddenly leapt to prominence in 1938, when oil was discovered at Burgan, and there were subsequent finds in the Kuwait-Saudi-Arabian Neutral Zone. However, large-scale exploitation did not begin until after the Second World War. Since then, the vast oil revenues the sheikh receives have been redirected into developing the country.

Iraq had long deemed Kuwait to be Iraqi territory. Indeed, a previous abortive attempt had been quelled by British troops in 1961. Kuwait was invaded by Iraq in August 1990, so beginning the second Gulf War. After several weeks of aerial bombardment, a UN-sanctioned coalition of 34 US-led nations began a ground assault in February 1991, liberating the country in a matter of days, but leaving Kuwait with $5 billion-worth of

repairs or replacements to oilfields and equipment that had been damaged or destroyed.

The hereditary monarch since 1977 is the Amir Jabir al-Ahmad al-Jabir al-Sabah. Sheikh Saad al-Abdullah al-Salem al-Sabah was appointed prime minister by the amir in 1978 and the National Assembly was reconstituted in 1981. Kuwait held its first parliamentary elections in 1992. In 1999, however, moves towards giving women a political voice were defeated on the grounds that it was contrary to Islamic principles and the traditions of Kuwait.

Today, Kuwait is one of the world's leading oil-producing countries and oil revenue has enabled it to acquire some of the best medical and educational services in the world, its capital being an enviable example of town planning at its best. Some of the world's most sophisticated desalinization plants provide much of the domestic water, the remainder being imported, along with most of the country's food. More oilfields remain to be developed in the north.

OPPOSITE: Striking architecture in Kuwait City.

ABOVE LEFT: A fish-seller in the souk.

RIGHT: Safat Square, Kuwait City.

KYRGYZSTAN

Location:	18 G
Capital:	Bishkek
Area:	77,180sq m (199900km²)
Population:	5,146,281 July 2005
Main Languages:	Kyrghyz
Main Religions:	Sunni Muslim 70%
Currency:	1 som = 100 tyiyn
Climate:	Hot summer, cold winter, dry all year, snow in mountains

A landlocked, mountainous country in Central Asia, Kyrgyzstan is dominated by the Tian Shan range that borders China to the south. It shares other borders with Kazakhstan to the north, and Uzbekistan and Tajikistan to the east and south.

Formerly the Kyrghyz Republic, or Kirghizia, the region was annexed by Russia in 1864, eventually becoming a constituent republic of the Soviet Union. Following the break-up of the USSR in 1991, Kyrgyzstan became an independent state within the Commonwealth of Independent States. It was a relatively stable country throughout the 1990s under ex-President Askar Akayev,

until recently, when percived manipulation and electoral fraud forced him to flee the country. At first, he maintained that a coup had occurred, but eventually resigned the presidency in April 2005, leaving the country in a state of turmoil. The president since July 2005 is Kurmanbek Bakiev.

Two-thirds of Kyrgyzstan is populated by peoples of Turkic-Mongoloid descent, who migrated south from around Siberia's Yenisey river to the Tian Shan region of China in the 10th century. This migration accelerated following the rise of the Mongol Empire in the 13th century. They arrived in what is now Kyrgyzstan in the 15th–16th centuries. Islam was introduced in the 17th century.

Contact with Russia and Russian settlers had the effect of modifying Kyrgyzstan's nomadic way of life, with only the traditional breeding of livestock persisting to this day. Today, it is a poor country, with a predominantly agricultural economy that produces tobacco and cotton (which are exported), fruit, vegetables, wool and meat. It has good natural resources, including abundant hydro-electric power, gold, uranium, mercury, coal, oil and natural gas, some of which are exported. The production of textiles is also important.

OPPOSITE: Sheep herding by Song-Köl (lake).

ABOVE: Woman tending her animals by Song-Köl.

LEFT: Ysyk-Köl, Kyrgyzstan's largest lake.

LAOS

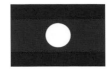

Location:	20 l
Capital:	Vientiane
Area:	91,400sq m (236726km²)
Population:	6,217,141 July 2005
Main Languages:	Lao
Main Religions:	Buddhist 58%, Traditional 34%, Christian 2%, Muslim 1%
Currency:	1 kip = 100 at
Climate:	Hot all year, cool in highlands, rains May–Oct

A landlocked country of South-East Asia, Laos is narrow, mountainous, and densely forested, with a broad plateau in the north that rises to 6,500ft (2000m). Laos shares borders with Myanmar (Burma), China, Vietnam, Cambodia and Thailand. The country's main artery is the River Mekong, which is important in that there is neither a railway system nor adequate infrastructure. Most of the population is concentrated in the plains bordering the River Mekong and Thailand.

Buddhism came to Laos in the 8th century and persists to this day. From the 9th

LEFT: The Mekong river at Luang Prabang.

OPPOSITE LEFT: A Laotian tribeswoman.

OPPOSITE RIGHT: The Patuxai monument, Vientiane.

to the 13th centuries Laos, then a collection of small principalities, was part of the great Khmer Empire, centred around Angkor in Cambodia. In the 14th century the first independent Laotian state was founded by King Fa Ngum, and lasted for the next 400 years. Laos was under the control of Siam (Thailand) from the 18th century until 1893, when it became part of French Indo-China, becoming fully independent from France in 1954.

A sporadic civil war ensued between government forces headed by Prince Souvanna Phouma and the Communist Pathet Lao, headed by his half-brother, Prince Souphanouvong. In the meantime a third (right-wing) force, headed by Prince Boun Oum, entered the fray. Vietnam intervened on the side of the Pathet Lao, which resulted in the Vientiane Agreement of 1973, which gave two-thirds of the country to the Communists. By 1975 the Pathet Lao (now the Lao People's Front) held the balance of power. King Savang Vatthana abdicated in 1980, and Laos became a People's Democratic Republic under the presidency of Prince Souphanouvong.

Laos joined the Association of South-East Asian Nations (ASEAN) in 1997. Head of what is one of the world's few remaining Communist states is President General Khamtai Siphadon, first elected from

1991–98 and re-elected in 2001. Boungnang Volachit has been prime minister (appointed by the president) since 2001.

Private enterprise has been encouraged since 1986, and great strides have been made, checked only by the Asian financial crisis of 1997. However, Laos is still a poor country. Agriculture is at subsistence level and occupies 80 per cent of the population, producing half the country's GDP. Vegetables, corn, tea, sugar, cotton, tobacco, rice, livestock and timber are produced, while natural resources include hydro-electricity and tin (which are exported), gold and gemstones. Industries include mining, food processing, garment-making, tourism (which is growing fast), and the production of wooden objects.

LATVIA

Location:	15 F
Capital:	Riga
Area:	24,595sq m (63701km²)
Population:	2,290,237 July 2005
Main Languages:	Latvian
Main Religions:	Christian
Currency:	1 lats = 100 santimi
Climate:	Warm summer, cold winter

With Estonia and Lithuania, Latvia is one of the so-called Baltic States of northern Europe. It lies on the eastern shores of the Baltic Sea and the Gulf of Riga, with Estonia to the north and Lithuania to the south. It also borders Russia to the east and Belarus to the south-east. Latvia, previously Livonia, is a land of many forests and rivers, that flow through fertile, low-lying terrain with some hills in the east; it also has a multitude of scattered lakes and areas yet to be drained.

Latvia was annexed by Russia in the 18th century after periods of Polish and Swedish rule. It proclaimed itself an independent republic in 1918, when it was apparent how Russia had been weakened by its revolution and the First World War. There followed 20 years of democratic multi-party government until the system ended in a coup in 1934. This was brought about by Latvia's own prime minister, who began a period of authoritarian rule, until Latvia was annexed by the Soviet Union in 1940, becoming a constituent republic of the USSR.

Latvia was occupied by the Germans from 1941–44, but when the Second World War ended, Russia began a process of forcible assimilation: Latvians were deported to Russia and Russians were settled in Latvia, and the Latvian language was suppressed. Latvia became independent once more on the break-up of the Soviet Union in 1991.

Latvia became a member of the World Trade Organization in 1999, and a member of both NATO and the EU in 2004. Head of state since 1999 is President Vaira Vike-Freiberga; Aigars Kalvitis was nominated by the president and appointed prime minister by parliament in 2004.

Traditionally, Latvia is an agricultural

country, but it has become predominantly industrial since the Second World War, producing buses, vans, railway rolling stock, synthetic fibres, agricultural machinery, washing machines and electronics, among other useful commodities. It has benefited from its gradual transition towards trade with Europe, since the Soviet Union came to an end, and since 2000 has enjoyed one of the highest growth rates in Europe.

OPPOSITE: Riga with the River Daugava in winter.

ABOVE: The Ecke Convent in the old town of Riga.

LEFT: A Russian Orthodox church at Liepaja.

LEBANON

Location:	15 H
Capital:	Beirut
Area:	4,036sq m (10452km²)
Population:	3,826,018 July 2005
Main Languages:	Arabic, French
Main Religions:	Muslim 55%, Christian 38%
Currency:	1 Lebanese pound = 100 piastres
Climate:	Hot, humid summer, cooler inland; cold winter

A country in the Middle East, on the eastern shore of the Mediterranean Sea, Lebanon lies between Israel to the south and Syria to the north and east. A narrow coastal plain rises to the Lebanon Mountains that run north to south down the centre of the country, while the Anti-Lebanon Mountains and Mount Hermon lie on the Syrian border to the east. Between the mountain ranges lie the Litani river and the fertile Bekaa Valley, whose cultivable land has been increased by irrigation. Lebanon was once noted for its giant cedar trees, one of which is depicted on the national flag. Sadly, the cedars have all but disappeared.

RIGHT: Anjar, a stronghold built by the Umayyad Caliph Al-Walid bin Abdul Malik in the 8th century, possibly on the site of earlier Roman remains.

OPPOSITE LEFT: The souk at Tarabulus (Tripoli).

OPPOSITE RIGHT: The Crusader castle of St Louis, Sayda (Sidon), thought to have been occupied by the French king, Louis IX.

Lebanon, which takes its name from Mount Lebanon, is regarded as one of the regions of the Middle East where civilization began, being historically the home of Phoenician traders, whose advanced culture flourished in the area over 2,000 years ago. It was also part of the Roman Empire, and was the site of Crusader battles before it was taken by the Ottoman Empire early in the 16th century. On the collapse of the empire, after the First World War, Lebanon was mandated by the League of Nations to the French (evidence of their influence could once be seen in the boulevards of Beirut), eventually achieving independence in 1945.

There followed alternating periods of instability and prosperity, when Lebanon's position as an important financial and trading centre was established. After the first Arab-Israeli War of 1948, large numbers of Palestinian refugees, fleeing from the new Israeli state, entered the country, with even more arriving after the war of 1967. Eventually, there were more than 300,000 Palestinians in Lebanon; they were led by Yasser Arafat and his Palestinian Liberation Organization (PLO).

to the Druse (under Walid Jumblatt) and to Shi'a Muslim forces. Meanwhile, the multinational peacekeeping force had proved ineffectual and was withdrawn in 1984. The Israeli forces withdrew to a buffer zone in southern Lebanon.

There followed a period of chaos until the Arab League-sponsored Ta'if Agreement heralded the beginning of the end of the war in 1989, when the reconstruction of Beirut began, but not before an estimated 200,000 or more had been killed or injured. The year 2000 saw the completion of Israel's withdrawal from the Lebanon, followed by the last of the Syrian forces in 2005. Head of

state since 1998 is President Émile Lahoud, with Fuad Siniora the head of government since June 2005.

Years of civil war have seriously affected Lebanon's economy, and have almost destroyed its tourist industry and its position as an important entrepôt and banking and financial centre in the Middle East. However, with the help of foreign aid, and given the resilience of Lebanon's people, recovery is being made. Agriculture is still important, and fruits, vegetables, sugar beet, olives and tobacco are grown; industries include food processing, textiles, tobacco, electrical goods, petroleum and chemicals.

It had been laid down in the country's constitution that the president of Lebanon should be a Maronite (Christian), who in turn would appoint the prime minister, always a Sunni Muslim, while the elected National Assembly should be headed by a Shi'a Muslim. By now, however, Muslims were in the majority. Moreover, from the late 1960s Palestinian guerillas had been establishing themselves in southern Lebanon, using it as a base from which to attack Israel. These factors sparked the disastrous civil war of 1975–76 between Christians and Muslims. In 1976 Syria, originally a supporter of the guerilla activity against Israel, began military action in conjunction with the Maronite Christians (linked with Bachir Gemayel's Phalangist Party) against an alliance of Palestinians and leftists. Israel invaded

Lebanon in 1978 and again in 1982, with a view to evicting the PLO. It was in the latter period that the first massacre of Palestinians at the refugee camps of Sabra and Shatila by Phalangist forces occurred, followed by the assassination of president-elect Bachir Gemayel, thought to be a secret supporter of Israel.

A multinational force arrived in Beirut in 1982 to oversee the withdrawal of the PLO and Syrian troops from Lebanon. There followed a number of terrorist attacks against US forces, including the destruction of the US embassy. It was also around this time that Hezbollah, an extremist Shi'a Muslim group, previously active in Iran, also established a presence in Lebanon. In 1984 most of the army of President Amin Gemayel, who had replaced his brother Bachir in 1982, defected

LESOTHO

Location:	15 M
Capital:	Maseru
Area:	11,720sq m (30355km²)
Population:	1,867,035 July 2005
Main Languages:	Sesotho, English
Main Religions:	Roman Catholic 63%, Protestant 27%
Currency:	1 loti = 100 lisente
Climate:	Hot summer, cold winter, snow in mountains, rains Oct–Apr

A mountainous, landlocked country, Lesotho forms an enclave within South Africa. There are areas where the valleys have been flooded by the headwaters of the Orange River, causing bogginess and an excess of surface water. The range of the Drakensberg Mountains lies to the south-east.

The Sotho nation was founded by Moshoshoe I, who united the nomadic tribesmen to fight the Zulus in the 1820s. During the years that followed, a losing battle with the encroaching Boer settlers was fought, which led what was now Basutoland to seek the protection of the British in 1868.

Basutoland subsequently became part of the British Cape Colony and was eventually under Britain's direct rule.

During the years that followed, fertile land was lost to South Africa, with the result that most of the population ended up working in the mines or on the farms of South Africa, which continues to this day. Basutoland became an independent kingdom within the Commonwealth in 1966, when its name was changed to Lesotho, the Paramount Chief becoming head of state as King Moshoshoe II. In 1970, the prime minister, Chief Leabua Jonathan, annulled the first post-independence election, refusing to cede power to the Basuto Congress Party (BCP) and imprisoning its leadership. Continuing conflict for many years ended in a military coup in 1986, when executive powers were given to Moshoeshoe II, who until that time had been a king in name only. However, within a few years he was forced

into exile. In 1990, he was deposed and his son Letsie III became king.

In 1992, the BCP won the first multi-party elections, when military rule came to an end. Letsie III tried unsuccessfully to have his father restored as king and in 1994, backed by the military, staged a coup to overthrow the BCP. Eventually, Moshoeshoe II was restored but died in a car accident in 1996, when his son again became king. The BCP, which had also been restored, was now split by leadership disputes. Ntsu Mokhehle and his Lesotho Congress for Democracy party formed a new government, the LCD also winning the next election. However, opposition parties eventually rejected the results, which led to army mutinies and violent demonstrations in 1998. Later that year, South African and Botswanan troops entered the country to put down the mutinies, but retreated the following year. In the meantime, there were many casualties,

LEFT: A Lesotho landscape.

BELOW: A woman from Mokhotlong.

and much looting and destruction. An Interim Political Authority was introduced to review the political system, with the result that peaceful elections were held in 2002. Head of government since 1998 is Prime Minister Pakalitha Mosisili.

Lesotho's economy is based on exporting water (its greatest resource) and electricity to South Africa, also manufacturing, agriculture, livestock and the earnings of its migrant workers. It also produces diamonds, wool and mohair.

LIBERIA

Location:	12 J
Capital:	Monrovia
Area:	43,000sq m (111370km²)
Population:	3,482,211 July 2005
Main Languages:	English
Main Religions:	Christian 68%, Traditional 18%, Muslim 14%
Currency:	1 Liberian dollar = 100 cents ($US legal tender)
Climate:	Hot all year, rains May, Oct

Liberia is Africa's oldest independent state, lying on the coast of the Atlantic Ocean between Sierra Leone and the Côte d'Ivoire. It also has a land border with Guinea to the north-east. Lagoons and mangrove swamps line the flat coastal plain, which rises to a densely forested plateau with low mountains in the north-east. The main settlements are along the coast, where crops are cultivated.

Liberia's beginnings were in 1822, when a settlement was founded, near what is now Monrovia, by the American Colonization Society, as a home for Afro-American freed slaves. In 1847, these Americo-Liberians, as they were now known, declared the country's independence as the Republic of Liberia. This resulted in bitter struggles with the indigenous hostile tribes that lasted for many years and ultimately led to the coup of 1980 and successive civil wars.

However, the settlers regarded Liberia as their Promised Land, literally the Land of the Free, their forefathers having been taken from Africa all those years ago. Moreover, they had no wish to integrate with the natives and still identified with America, preferring a way of life like that of the American South; even their government was modelled on that of the USA. An event of great importance to the economy was the concession, granted in 1926, to the American Firestone Company to develop Liberia's rubber plantations.

In 1980 President Tolbert was assassinated in an army coup by men of tribal origin, led by Sergeant Samuel Doe, who seized control and began a brutal and corrupt regime. In the civil war of 1989–96, Doe was ousted and killed, and Charles Taylor was eventually elected president; but his repressive and autocratic regime led to another civil war in 1999.

In 2003 a peace agreement ended 14 years of civil war, which had killed 200,000 people and displaced thousands more. It had also destroyed the Liberian economy. This prompted the resignation of Charles Taylor, who was exiled to Nigeria, though he vowed he would return. A transitional government, under Gyude Bryant, was given the task of rebuilding Liberia and a programme of disarmament was completed in 2004. However, the situation within the country remains volatile and the process of returning to normality is sluggish.

Liberia is heavily dependent on the export of iron, since it ceased to produce rubber in 1990. It was once also an exporter of timber and diamonds until international sanctions were imposed that have yet to be lifted. Liberia's infrastructure has been destroyed and the majority of the people are now unemployed and heavily dependent on foreign aid.

A mud house in Cape Mount, Liberia.

LIBYA

Location:	14 I
Capital:	Tripoli
Area:	679,358sq m (1759540km²)
Population:	5,765,563 July 2005
Main Languages:	Arabic
Main Religions:	Sunni Muslim 97%
Currency:	1 Libyan dollar = 1000 dirhams
Climate:	Hot summer, mild winter

A North African state on the southern limits of the Mediterranean Sea, Libya is bounded by Algeria and Tunisia to the west, Niger and Chad to the south and Sudan and Egypt to the east. The coastal plains of the north-east and north-west consist of rolling terrain, where fruits and cereals are cultivated, giving way to areas of semi-desert; by far the greater part of Libya is occupied by the Sahara Desert to the south, broken here and there by oases, shaded by date palms, and where the Fezzan Mountains and prehistoric rock paintings are to be found. There are no rivers and rainfall is sparse. However, the largest scheme in the

world has been underway since 1991 to bring water to the coastal cities from aquifers beneath the Sahara Desert. There are magnificent archeological sites at Shahat (Cyrene), Leptis Magna, Sabratha and other locations.

Libya was successively occupied by Romans, Vandals and Arabs until the 16th century, when the Turks arrived. In 1911–12 the Italians ousted the Turks, colonizing the coast and developing the country's agriculture, though Italy lost the colony following its defeat in the First World War. British troops occupied the south-west

during the Second World War and Libya was given a UN mandate in 1951, after which it became a kingdom under Idris I. However, Idris was deposed in 1969, following a military coup, when control passed to the Revolutionary Command Council under Colonel Muammar al-Ghadafi: British bases at Tobruk and El Adem were dismantled soon after.

A strict Muslim regime was imposed under Ghadafi from 1971, when only a single-party Arab Socialist Union was permitted and pro-Palestinian and anti-West policies were pursued. The discovery of oil

in 1959 had brought unprecedented wealth to the country, which Ghadafi used in the 1970s and 80s to promote his ideology beyond Libya, supporting terrorists and subversives abroad to bring about the end of

ABOVE: The ruins of Leptis Magna.

OPPOSITE ABOVE: Unmal Lake, Ubari Sand Sea in the Fezzan area of south-western Libya.

OPPOSITE BELOW: Camels near Benghazi.

All Libyan diplomats were expelled from the US and the Libyan embassy was closed. In 1986 the US bombed Tripoli and Benghazi, following evidence of Libya's continuing implication in international terrorism. The UN imposed sanctions on Libya in 1992, when it was suspected of sheltering the terrorists responsible for bringing down Pan Am Flight 103 over Lockerbie, Scotland, causing great loss of life. Thereafter, Libya's support of terrorism seemed to decrease, as a result of which the UN sanctions were suspended in 1999. The sanctions, together with travel restrictions to Libya, were finally lifted in 2003 after Libya agreed to extradite the terrorists responsible for the Lockerbie atrocity. Ghadafi also announced he was ending his production of weapons of mass destruction

and would allow inspectors to verify the fact. He has worked to improve relations with the West ever since, making his first trip for many years to Western Europe, when he visited Brussels in 2004. He also resolved several claims against his government for terrorist activity, by paying compensation to the families of the victims of the German La Belle disco bombing and the Lockerbie disaster.

Libya's economy under the present prime minister, Shukri Muhammad Ghanem, is undergoing something of a boom, its main revenue coming predominantly from oil. It also produces petrochemicals, iron, steel and aluminium. Its agricultural output is limited by its terrain and climate, which means that three-quarters of its food has to be imported.

Marxism and capitalism, both of which he had rejected. In 1973, Libyan forces occupied the Aozou Strip in northern Chad, with the hope of gaining access to valuable minerals, including uranium, and establishing a base from which Chad's politics could be influenced; however, Libya was forced to retreat in 1987. In 1976, as an experiment in 'direct democracy', Ghadafi established his own political system – a combination of socialism, Islam and tribal practices to be implemented by the people themselves. This General People's Congress comprised popular committees, trade unions and professional organizations, over which Ghadafi himself presided.

In 1979, Libyan mobs sacked the US embassy in Tripoli, though Ghadafi denied

any personal involvement. In 1981 the US shot down two Libyan aircraft that were challenging its warplanes, which caused Libya's relations with the US to seriously deteriorate. The following year, however, there were attempts to improve the situation, when Libya asked Jimmy Carter's brother to mediate with the US on its behalf. However, the US government under Ronald Reagan officially severed all diplomatic ties on the grounds of Libya's involvement with terrorism. This included Libya's support of Palestinian groups and its backing of revolutionary Iran in the Iran-Iraq War of 1980–88 – also its support for guerilla and separatist groups, such as Euskadi Ta Askatasuna (ETA), the IRA and the Palestine Liberation Organization (PLO).

LIECHTENSTEIN

Location:	14 G
Capital:	Vaduz
Area:	61.8sq m (160km²)
Population:	33,717 July 2005
Main Languages:	German
Main Religions:	Roman Catholic 86%,
	Protestant 8%
Currency:	1 Swiss franc =
	100 centimes
Climate:	Warm summer, cold winter

Situated at the end of the eastern Alps, between Austria and Switzerland, Liechtenstein is a tiny, mountainous, landlocked country. Its terrain makes it ideal for winter sports, which attract tourists.

At one time the region that is now Liechtenstein was a tiny part of the ancient Roman province of Raetia. However, its geography had the effect of isolating it from the rest of Europe and its affairs, and for years it remained enfiefed to a minor branch of the Habsburg Empire. This meant it had no power of its own and could have no place in the Imperial government or Reichstag. The matter was rectified in 1699 and 1712

respectively, when the Liechtenstein family purchased Schellenberg and Vaduz, which were added to the territory and ended the feudal state. In 1719, the tiny state of what was now called Liechtenstein, the name of the dynastic family, was declared an independent principality within the Holy Roman Empire, with no one to answer to but the suzerain emperor. In 1806, the Holy Roman Empire was dissolved, which had legal implications for Liechtenstein. In 1815 it became a member of the German Confederation, eventually gaining independent status in 1866. However, it maintained close ties with Austria until the end of the First World War, when it was forced to form a monetary union with Switzerland.

The Liechtenstein family lived in Vienna until 1938. Liechtenstein remained neutral during the Second World War, but when the conflict ended, its hereditary lands in Bohemia, Moravia and Silesia were seized as 'German' possessions by Czechoslovakia and Poland. After the war, the Liechtensteins were in dire financial straits and were forced to sell the family treasures, including a painting by Leonardo da Vinci. Thereafter, Liechtenstein began to prosper and is now a wealthy country.

The current prince is Hans-Adam II, who succeeded his father in 1989. Head of government is Ottmar Hasler since 2001.

Formerly an agricultural country, there was an influx of foreign workers after the Second World War that enabled Liechtenstein to develop various light industries and it is now a highly industrialized country, producing electronics, precision and optical instruments and dental

products. Despite its limited natural resources, low tax rates and generous company law have encouraged many thousands of foreign companies to establish nominal addresses in Liechtenstein, thereby increasing the country's prosperity. Recently, Liechtenstein has been taking steps to reform its banking laws after gaining a doubtful reputation as a centre of international money-laundering. It has been

BELOW: A mountain dwelling, Vaduz.

OPPOSITE: The castle residence of the Prince of Liechtenstein, Vaduz.

a member of the European Economic Area since 1995 and is aiming to harmonize its economic policies with those of the rest of the EU in due course.

LITHUANIA

Location:	15 F
Capital:	Vilnius
Area:	25,170sq m (65200km²)
Population:	3,596,617 July 2005
Main Languages:	Lithuanian
Main Religions:	Roman Catholic 90%
Currency:	litas
Climate:	Warm summer, cold winter

One of the three Baltic States, with Estonia and Latvia, Lithuania is situated on the south-eastern shores of the Baltic Sea. It is the largest and most populous of the Baltic States and has land borders with Latvia to the north, Kaliningrad (Russia) to the south-west and Poland and Belarus to the south. Lithuania is flat and low-lying, with a few hills and numerous small lakes. Most of the land is given over to agriculture, while the rest is covered in forests. The capital city, Vilnius, is thought to lie very near the geographical centre of Europe.

The first unified Lithuanian state emerged in around 1250 and by the next century had grown into the Grand Duchy of Lithuania, which incorporated present-day

Belarus and Ukraine; it stretched all the way to Moscow and eventually as far as the Black Sea. Lithuania was absorbed into the Russian empire in 1795, having been united with Poland since 1386. It was declared an independent republic in 1918, but in 1940 was annexed by Russia, becoming a constituent republic of the Soviet Union. It was occupied by the Germans during the Second World War, when large numbers of Lithuanian Jews were killed in the

holocaust. It fell again to the Soviet Union in 1945, following the Second World War.

Fifty years of Communist rule came to an end when Lithuania, in the spirit of *glasnost*, proclaimed its independence in March 1990, the first Soviet republic to do so. Soviet forces tried to suppress the secession and Lithuanian independence was not conceded by the Soviets until the following year. In 1994, Lithuania became the first Baltic State to apply for membership of NATO and in 2004 joined the European Union. Chief of state since 2004 is President Valdas Adamkus, a US citizen who left Lithuania in 1949, and who was previously president from 1998. The prime minister since 2001 is Algirdas Mykolas Brazauskas.

Although Lithuania's economy is

LEFT: Monument to Adam Mickiewicz in Vilnius, a Polish poet, who regarded Lithuania as his true home.

BELOW: Overview of Vilnius.

OPPOSITE: Trakai Castle.

undoubtedly growing, many people still live in poverty. Today, trade is increasing with the West after years of reliance on Russia, and it is recovering from the 1998 Russian financial crisis. The majority of its businesses have been privatized and manufacturing is now the most lucrative part of the economy, producing chemicals, electronics and machine tools. Dairy products, meat production and fishing are also important sources of revenue.

LUXEMBOURG

Location:	14 G
Capital:	Luxembourg
Area:	999sq m (2587km²)
Population:	468,571 July 2005
Main Languages:	Letzeburgesch, French, German
Main Religions:	Roman Catholic 95%
Currency:	euro
Climate:	Warm summer, cold winter

A country in Western Europe, situated between Belgium, Germany and France, Luxembourg encompasses the Ardennes plateau, an area of low mountains and forests. Most of the country's rivers flow into the Moselle, which defines part of Luxembourg's eastern border with Germany.

The history of the country began in 963, when Luxembourg became autonomous within the Holy Roman Empire under the counts of Ardennes, and gradually evolved into a small state of strategic importance. However, the ruling family had disappeared by the middle of the 15th century. It was occupied successively by dukes of Burgundy, the Habsburgs and became part of

the Spanish Netherlands on the division of the Habsburg Empire in 1555. It was annexed by France in 1795. As a result of the Congress of Vienna in 1815, Luxembourg became a grand duchy under King William III of the Netherlands, who remained head of state until 1890, when Queen Wilhelmina ascended the Dutch throne. This is when Luxembourg's connection with the Dutch crown ended, since Luxembourg's law of succession did not permit a woman to rule. This ruling was amended, however, when Marie-Adelaide became grand duchess in 1912. She later abdicated and was succeeded by Grand Duchess Charlotte.

Luxembourg established close economic links with Belgium in 1922, which in 1948 extended to the Netherlands, when the

Benelux Customs Union was formed. Luxembourg was invaded by Germany in both World Wars. After the Second World War it became a founding member of NATO and the UN, and one of the six founding members of the EEC in 1957; it continues to play an important part in European affairs today.

In 1964 Grand Duchess Charlotte abdicated in favour of her son, Jean. A former prime minister of Luxembourg, Jacques Santer, became president of the European Commission in 1994. In 2005 a referendum to establish a constitution for Europe was held in Luxembourg. Grand Duke Henri has been head of state since 2000, when his father, Grand Duke Jean abdicated in his favour. The head of government is Prime Minister Jean-Claude Juncker since 1995.

Luxembourg has a stable, high-income economy, with steady growth, low inflation and low unemployment. The industrial sector, once dominated by steel, has undergone diversification into chemicals, rubber and other products, while the country depends on foreign workers for a third of its labour force. The financial sector has also grown substantially and the service industry, banking in particular, has become increasingly important. Agriculture is centred around small, family-owned farms.

ABOVE LEFT: The Plâteau du Rham, Luxembourg City.

LEFT: Palace Theatre statues.

MACAU

Location:	21 I
Capital:	Macau
Area:	10sq m (25km²)
Population:	449,198 July 2005
Main Languages:	Cantonese, Hokkien, Mandarin
Main Religions:	Buddhist 50%, Roman Catholic 15%
Currency:	1 pataca = 100 avos
Climate:	Subtropical marine, with cool winters, warm summers

A former Portuguese dependency on the south-east coast of China, Macau lies 40 miles (65km) west of Hong Kong, facing Hong Kong across the Zhu Jiang (Pearl) river. It consists of a peninsula, connected by a narrow isthmus to the Chinese province of Guangzhou, where the capital Macau is sited, and includes the islands of Taipa and Colôane. The peninsula is linked by two bridges to Taipa and by a causeway to Colôane. Two taxiways link Taipa with Macau International Airport that has been built out into the Pearl estuary.

Macau was discovered by Vasco da Gama in 1497. It became the first European settlement in the Far East, when it was colonized by the Portuguese in 1557, and became a trading centre for spices, silk and opium. In 1979, Macau's status was redefined as Chinese territory under Portuguese administration, that would eventually return to China. Portuguese rule accordingly ended on the last day of December 1999, when Macau became a Special Administrative Region of China.

Like Hong Kong, conditions were imposed that there would be no interference in Macau's political system for the next 50 years and that it would continue to have a high level of autonomy in other matters during that time. Head of state since 2003 is the President of China, Hu Jintao, while Edmund Ho Hau-wah has been head of government since 1999, having been re-elected in 2004.

Macau is a free port and enjoys a flourishing economy. It exports textiles, clothing, fireworks, toys and electronic goods. Tourism is also escalating, since China eased travel restrictions, with visitors coming from Hong Kong and abroad to visit Macau's many casinos. Since 2004, a Closer Economic Partnership Agreement with China has allowed tariff-free access of Macau's products to mainland China.

ABOVE LEFT: Lin Fung – Temple of the Lotus, Macau.

LEFT: Women working the Colôane-Macau Ferry service to the outer islands.

MACEDONIA
(THE FORMER YUGOSLAV REPUBLIC OF)

Location:	15 G
Capital:	Skopje
Area:	9,928sq m (25713km²)
Population:	2,045,262 July 2005
Main Languages:	Macedonian
Main Religions:	Eastern Orthodox 66%, Muslim 30%
Currency:	denar
Climate:	Warm summer, mild winter

MACEDONIA

Situated in south-eastern Europe at the northern end of the Greek peninsula, Macedonia is a landlocked country of mountains and steep valleys. It is bisected by the River Vardar and has three large lakes, two of which border Albania and Greece, the other Bulgaria. Besides Greece, Macedonia has borders with Albania to the west, Serbia & Montenegro to the north and Bulgaria to the east.

In antiquity, King Philip II founded Thessaloníki and Alexander the Great, his son, established Macedon as a world power, when he conquered not only the rest of Greece but also seized control of the Persian Empire, Egypt and lands as far east as India.

The process of Hellenization began following Alexander's death in 323 BC, when the Greek culture spread throughout the Mediterranean and into the Near East and Asia. However, whether or not the ancient Macedonians were in fact Greek remains a controversial subject to this day, though succeeding kings of Macedon certainly regarded themselves so.

In the Balkan Wars of 1912–13, Bulgaria, Greece, Serbia and Montenegro forced Turkey to give up Albania and Macedonia, leaving the area around Constantinople (Istanbul) the only part of the Ottoman Empire that remained in Europe. Bulgaria quarrelled with Serbia, Greece and Romania over the possession of Macedonia, which had been partitioned between Greece and Serbia. This resulted in thousands of Macedonians fleeing to Bulgaria, when Macedonia was divided between Greece, Bulgaria and Serbia. At the end of the First World War, Serbian

BELOW: The fishermen's Church of St Jovan Bogolov, Lake Ohrid.

OPPOSITE LEFT: The town of Ohrid.

OPPOSITE RIGHT: Old men at Struga's market.

242

Macedonia, which occupied the larger portion to the north and centre of Macedonia, became part of the Kingdom of the Serbs, Croats and Slovenes (later Yugoslavia), which precipitated armed conflict by Macedonian nationalists.

Between 1941 and 1944 Bulgaria occupied the whole of Macedonia until a peace treaty restored the status quo of 1913. After the Second World War, Marshal Tito established a federal Yugoslavia, with Macedonia a constituent republic. The break-up of the Yugoslav Federation occurred in 1991, when Macedonia declared its independence, renouncing all claims to Greek and Bulgarian Macedonian territory.

Greece objected to Macedonia's use of an Hellenic name, flag and currency and imposed a trade blockade. The EC refused to recognize Macedonia's sovereignty, believing that it harboured territorial ambitions. However, a compromise was reached by which Macedonia was known as the Former Yugoslav Republic of Macedonia (FYROM), recognized as such by the UN and NATO. In 1993 the UN accepted FYROM as a member and all the EU members, apart from Greece, established diplomatic relations with the new state. Greece relented in 1995, on condition that Macedonia remove all claims to Greek Macedonia from its constitution; it also demanded that Macedonia redesign its flag, removing an emblem that had long been connected with Philip of Macedon.

In 1999, war in the neighbouring Serbian province of Kosovo led to the influx of a quarter of a million ethnic Albanian refugees and conflict between government forces and Albanian rebels in 2001, following which a new constitution was formed that recognized the rights of the Albanians in Macedonia. Head of state since May 2004, when President Boris Trajkovski was killed in a train crash, is President Branko Crvenkovski, while head of government is Vlado Buckovski, who has been prime minister since December 2004.

At the time of its independence in 1991, Macedonia was the least developed of the former Yugoslav republics. The collapse of Yugoslavia brought to an end what had been a large free trade area, and UN sanctions and the Greek trade embargo, which was lifted in 1995, had devastated the economy. Add to this high unemployment, inflation and a large national debt, and it is clear that the country has a long way to go.

MADAGASCAR

Location:	16 L
Capital:	Antananarivo
Area:	226,656sq m (587040km²)
Population:	18,040,341 July 2005
Main Languages:	Malagasy
Main Religions:	Roman Catholic 28%,
	traditional beliefs 24%,
	other Christian 41%,
	Muslim 7%
Currency:	1 Malagasy franc = 100
	centimes

The fourth-largest island in the world, Madagascar lies 240 miles (390km) off the south-east coast of Africa, and separated from it by the Mozambique Channel. The narrow coastal plain rises to central highlands, while three great massifs lie in the north, the highest of which is volcanic Tsaratanara, which peaks at 9,468ft (2886m).

What is known of the history of Madagascar tells how Arab trading posts were established in the 7th century, though the first European, a sea captain called Diego Díaz, did not see Madagascar until 1500. The Merina people dominated the island from the

17th century. In 1817 a treaty was made between the Merina leader and the governor of Mauritius, whereby the slave trade was abolished. To compensate for the loss to the economy, the British provided military and financial assistance to the island, with members of the Merina court eventually becoming Christians. In 1885 the British accepted the island as a French protectorate in

return for eventual control of Zanzibar, now part of Tanzania. In 1895–96 the Merina fought the French and lost and the Merina monarchy was abolished. In 1942–43 British troops arrived to overthrow the pro-Vichy administration, restoring a Free-French government to what was by now Malagasy. A national uprising was brutally suppressed by the French in 1947–48, when as many as

80,000 islanders are thought to have died.

Malagasy became a fully independent state within the French Community in 1960, with Philibert Tsiranana of the Social Democrat Party its first president. However, his autocratic rule proved unpopular, especially when he planned to link the economy with South Africa's apartheid regime. In 1972, a Merina-dominated military

1997. In 1998 Tantely Andrianarivo was elected prime minister. In 2000, over half a million people were made homeless when cyclones hit the island, and political and ethnic violence followed the election in 2001. Head of state since 2002 is Marc Ravalomanana, who became president when Ratsiraka fled the island following disputes with his rival, which averted civil war. Jacques Sylla is head of government.

From modest beginnings, Madagascar has achieved slow and steady growth since the middle of the 1990s. Agriculture, forestry and fishing are the mainstays of the economy, though deforestation is a cause for concern. Coffee is a major cash crop. However, the unique diversity of Madagascar's flora and fauna may prove to be the making of the country, by attracting more and more ecotourists to its shores.

OPPOSITE: Typical Malagasy village dwellings.

LEFT: A sensible way of carrying heavy loads.

BELOW: An aerial view of Antananarivo.

overthrew Tsiranana's government, and the economy took a sudden dive. Martial law was imposed in 1975, when Malagasy became Madagascar. A new one-party Marxist state was then adopted, with Lieutenant-Commander Didier Ratsiraka as president. However, he abandoned Marxism, which had involved nationalization and the severing of connections with France in 1980. A multi-party system of government became legal in 1990.

Following anti-government demonstrations, Ratsiraka established a government that included opposition members the following year. Constitutional reform was approved by referendum in 1992, and multi-party elections were held the following year. Ratsiraka was re-elected in

MALAWI

Location:	15 L
Capital:	Liongwe
Area:	45,747sq m (118485km²)
Population:	12,158,924 July 2005
Main Languages:	English, Chichewa
Main Religions:	Christian 64%,
	Muslim 12%, Animist
Currency:	1 kwacha = 100 tambala
Climate:	Hot all year, cooler in
	mountains, rains Nov–Mar

A small country of south-central Africa, lying in the Great Rift Valley, Malawi is essentially a plateau, apart from Lake Malawi (Nyasa), which drains into the Zambezi via the Shire River. Lake Malawi covers half the country, and extends almost its entire length, forming Malawi's borders with Tanzania and Mozambique; Malawi shares the lake with both countries. Mozambique also borders Malawi to the south and south-west, giving way to Zambia in the west.

Malawi grew from what was once a traders' and missionaries' route to the Zambezi river. In the east, the plateau attains 3,000ft (1000m), reaching 8,000ft (2500m) on the Nyika Plateau in the north, and rising to 9,850ft (3000m) in the south-east.

The first Europeans to visit the area were the Portuguese, who began to arrive in the 17th century. By the late 19th century, however, they began to have ideas of linking the territory with the Portuguese colonies of Mozambique and Angola. The British objected and made the area a British protectorate from 1891; it was known as Nyasaland from 1907.

Until then, the difficulty of the terrain and the ferocity of warring tribes had prevented any real exploration of the country, though David Livingstone had reached Lake Malawi in 1859. From 1953 to

1963, against the will of the people, Nyasaland became part of the Federation of Rhodesia and Nyasaland, but became the independent Commonwealth state of Malawi the following year under the leadership of Hastings Kamazu Banda. Banda continued to dominate the country for the next 30 years, establishing a totalitarian one-party system of government and declaring himself president for life in 1971. More than half a million refugees, fleeing the civil war in Mozambique, arrived during the 1980s.

In the mid 1990s, after an improvement in human rights had been made a condition of Malawi's continuing famine relief, Banda

ABOVE: On Lake Malawi.

LEFT: Mother and child.

OPPOSITE: Traditional village huts.

finally gave way to popular and international pressure, and multi-party elections were held in 1994. Banda lost the election, however, and Malawi received its first taste of democracy. Banda's successor was Bakili Muluzi, who proved to be less oppressive, though there were accusations of corruption within the government. He was succeeded by Binguwa Mutharika in May 2004. However, his predecessor still has a hand in running their shared political party, which causes something of a power struggle between the two. So far, Mutharika's efforts to eradicate corruption have led to several high-level arrests but no actual convictions.

Malawi is one of the world's poorest countries. Poverty, and the high rate of HIV/AIDS continue to cause concern and tens of thousands die of AIDS each year. A programme to combat the scourge was launched in 2004, when Muluzi admitted that his brother had also died of the disease.

Malawi has few natural resources, and is a country prone to natural disasters, when food aid is inevitably required. Subsistence agriculture is the main activity, but tea and tobacco are exported and there are reserves of uranium, bauxite and coal that remain to be exploited. Nevertheless, there is much to admire in Malawi's lakes, mountains and forests, and its national parks and game reserves continue to attract visitors.

MALAYSIA

Location: 20 J
Capital: Kuala Lumpur/Putrajaya
Area: 127,317sq m (329751km²)
Population: 23,953,136 July 2005
Main Languages: Bahasa Malay
Main Religions: Muslim 53%,
Buddhist 17%, Chinese
12%, Hindu 7%
Currency: 1 ringgit = 100 sen
Climate: Hot and humid all year,
rains Nov–Feb (east), Aug
(west)

A country in South-East Asia, Malaysia is a federation consisting of East Malaysia (the northern part of Borneo, now Sabah, and Sarawak) and West Malaysia (the southern part of the Malayan Peninsula, formerly Malaya. West Malaysia has Thailand to its north and Singapore to its south, separated from the peninsula by a causeway and bridge. East Malaysia is bordered to the south by Indonesia. On the north-east coast lies the independent Sultanate of Brunei. The two parts of Malaysia are separated by 400 miles

(650km) of the South China Sea. Equatorial rainforest covers three-quarters of the total area, the land rising from coastal plains to mountain regions, the highest point being the 13,435-ft (4095-m) Mount Kinabalu in Sabah.

Various Malay kingdoms, thought to be Hindu or Buddhist, developed from coastal cities in the 10th century, with Islam arriving in the 14th century. The Sultanate of Malacca was established in the 15th century, and controlled what is now the Malayan

Peninsula, southern Thailand and the eastern coast of Sumatra. Portugal captured Malacca in 1511, which led to a struggle for control of the Malacca Strait between the Portuguese and Dutch, which ended in 1641 with the Dutch taking control. After the

which were followed by race riots. Since this time, however, Malaysia has managed to maintain a delicate balance that accommodates not only ethnic Malays but also Islam. In 1998, after publicly calling for Prime Minister Mahathir bin Mohamed's resignation, his deputy, Anwar Ibrahim, was arrested for sodomy and corruption.

Malaysia is a constitutional elective monarchy, 'kings' being selected for a five-year period from the sultans of nine of the 13 states that make up the federation. The present head of state and Paramount Ruler from 2001 is the Raja of Perlis. Following the retirement of Mahathir, Malaysia's longest-serving prime minister, Abdullah bin Ahmad Badawi came to power in 2003.

There was significant economic growth under Prime Minister Mahathir in the 1980s and 90s, when the transition from

OPPOSITE: Temple dragon. Kuching, Sarawak.

LEFT: Iban women from Sarawak.

BELOW: Temple interior, Kuala Lumpur.

agriculture, and the production of rubber, rice, palm oil and timber, was made to an industry-based economy. Growth is now driven by the export of computers and consumer electronics in particular. However, Malaysia did not escape the effects of the Asian financial crisis of the late 1990s. Continued growth rests on the development of exports to the US, China and Japan, which are also Malaysia's chief sources of foreign investment.

Anglo-Dutch Treaty of 1824, the British took control of Malacca and established the British Crown Colony of the Straits Settlements in 1826; these consisted of Singapore, Penang and Malacca, and the territory was gradually increased. They were administered from Calcutta by the British East India Company until 1867, when control was transferred to the Colonial Office in London. Following occupation by Japan during the Second World War, popular support for independence grew, coupled with the insurgency of Communism in the Chinese population. This developed into guerilla warfare, when many Chinese were

forcibly resettled. Independence was achieved in 1957, when the colony's name was changed to the Federation of Malaya, though Singapore's independence was rejected.

A new federation, called Malaysia, was formed in 1963, following the merger of the Federation of Malaya and the British Crown Colonies of Singapore, North Borneo (now Sabah) and Sarawak; Brunei declined to join. The following few years were marred by Indonesia's bid to gain control, and Singapore withdrew from the federation in 1965. There were also claims to Sabah by the Philippines in 1969, which are ongoing,

MALDIVES

Location:	18 K
Capital:	Male
Area:	115sq m (298km²)
Population:	349,106 July 2005
Main Languages:	Maldivian Dhivehi
Main Religions:	Sunni Muslim
Currency:	1 rufiyaa = 100 laari
Climate:	Hot and humid all year, monsoon Nov–Mar (NE), Jun–Aug (SE)

The Maldives archipelago consists of more than 1,000 low-lying islands and coral atolls, of which only 200 or so are inhabited. They are located to the south-west of the Indian peninsula and oriented roughly along a north to south line in the Indian Ocean; the Arabian Sea lies to the west and the Laccadive Sea to the east. Being so low-lying, the islands are prone to flooding if there are changes in the surrounding sea level.

Archeological remnants of ancient cultures have been found on the islands, but particular interest was kindled in 1879, when there were indications that Theravada Buddhism had been practised by the islanders in the 4th century. There were more excavatations in the 1980s by the Norwegian anthropologist, Thor Heyerdahl, whose interest in cultural diffusion led to his most memorable experiment in 1947, when he sailed his balsa raft, *Kon-Tiki*, from Peru to Tahiti, to prove that early migrations were possible. His research in the Maldives led him to believe that as early as 2000 BC, trade routes had been established between the islands and the civilizations of Egypt, Mesopotamia and the Indus Valley.

The islands were a dependency of Ceylon from 1645–1948, coming under British protection from 1887, when they were administered from Ceylon, while retaining their local Islamic sultanates. They

were occupied by the Japanese in 1943, but liberated by the British in 1945. The islands became independent in 1965 and the last sultan was deposed three years later, when they became known as the Republic of Maldives.

Maumoon Abdul Gayyoom was elected president and head of government in 1978 and has held the post ever since, having survived a coup in 1988. Political parties were permitted in 2005, following occasional anti-government demonstrations that began in 2003. In December 2004, the Maldives were devasted by a tsunami caused by an earthquake in the Indian Ocean. Being so flat, the islands were swamped and many were killed. Much of the infrastructure was destroyed, at great cost to the economy, and the islands will also need to be remapped, due to changes in their geography.

Fishing always was and still is the most important occupation of the Maldivians. Steps have been taken to mechanize and develop the industry and a fish-canning plant was installed in 1977, with Japanese help. The next most important earner of foreign exchange is tourism, which has encouraged weaving, lacquer work and other handicrafts. Other industries have also emerged, which include printing, garment-making, repairing marine engines and the manufacture of coir rope.

OPPOSITE: A picture-book Maldivian island.

ABOVE: One of the smaller atolls.

LEFT: The Great Friday Mosque, Male.

MALI

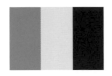

Location:	13 I
Capital:	Bamako
Area:	1,240,190sq m (478838km²)
Population:	12,291,529 July 2005 E
Main Languages:	French
Main Religions:	Sunni Muslim 90%
Currency:	1 CFA franc = 100 centimes
Climate:	Hot all year, rains Jun–Oct, drier in north

A landlocked country of West Africa, Mali has borders with Algeria, Niger, Burkina Faso, Côte d'Ivoire, Guinea, Senegal and Mauritania. It occupies the upper basins of the Senegal and Niger rivers, but for the most part consists of desert, with the Sahara lying to the north. The terrain is mostly flat, rising to undulating plains. There is savannah around the River Niger in the south, where most activity is centred, and where there is sufficient rain for cultivating crops.

Mali was one of the great medieval African empires, together with Ghana and Songhaí, that grew to power in the Sahel (a

vast semi-arid region south of the Sahara), all focused on the legendary city of Timbuktu. In the 14th century, Islam was adopted and Timbuktu became an important centre of learning and trans-Saharan trade. Mali was invaded by the French in 1880, when it became known as French Sudan. In 1959 the Mali Federation was born, following the union of Mali and Senegal. The federation gained independence from

France in June 1960, but Senegal withdrew after only a few months. By September 1960, Mali had withdrawn completely from its autonomous position within the French community, becoming the Republic of Mali under President Modibo Keïta, who was displaced in a military coup in 1968.

In the 1970s, a series of droughts caused the deaths of thousands of people from famine. Mali was ruled by a series of

dictators until a coup prompted the formation of a new constitution in 1992, when Alpha Oumar Konaré became president after Mali's first multi-party elections. After his re-election in 1997, Konaré continued his programme of political and economic reform – also his war on corruption. His permitted term of office came to an end in 2002, when he was succeeded by Amadou Toumani Touré, who

had participated in the uprising of 1991 that had precipitated the adoption of democracy. Head of government since 2004 is Prime Minister Ousmane Issoufi Maiga.

Mali is rich in natural resources, with gold destined to become a major export in the future. Uranium, phosphates, kaolin, salt and limestone are also produced, and there are other resources still to be explored. In spite of this, Mali remains one of the poorest countries in the world, heavily dependent on foreign aid. Some of the people still lead a nomadic life, but by far the majority are engaged in farming, with cotton and livestock by far the most important products.

OPPOSITE: Bani river scene, Mopti.

LEFT: A Mali mother in traditional dress.

BELOW: The streets of Timbuktu.

MALTA

Location:	14 H
Capital:	Valletta
Area:	121.9sq m (316km2)
Population:	398,534 July 2005
Main Languages:	Maltese, English
Main Religions:	Roman Catholic 98%
Currency:	1 Maltese lira =
	100 cents
Climate:	Hot summer, warm winter

Part of an archipelago of Mediterranean islands, Malta, with Gozo and Comino, are the only inhabited islands in the group. They lie 58m (93km) to the south of Sicily and north of the coast of North Africa. In general, the terrain is flat and treeless, but the coasts have numerous bays that provide good harbours.

Malta has evidence of settlements going back to the Stone Age. It was successively colonized by the Phoenicians, Greeks and Carthaginians and became part of the East Roman or Byzantine Empire in 395. St Paul was shipwrecked on Malta during his missonary journeys among the Gentiles after

the death of Christ. Malta fell to the Arabs in 870, when Islam was introduced. In 1530 it became the headquarters of the Knights of St John of Jerusalem, who defended Malta in a Turkish siege. It fell to the French in 1798, but became a British colony in 1814, when it gained strategic importance as a military base. Malta supported Britain during both World Wars.

In 1942 King George VI awarded Malta the George Cross, in recognition of the particular courage shown by its people during the Second World War, after they had been beseiged and attacked from the air by German and Italian aircraft. It became a

NATO base in 1953. Malta remained within the Commonwealth after it became independent in 1964; it became a republic in 1974. Head of state is President Edward Fenech Adami, while Prime Minister Lawrence Gonzi has been head of government since 2004.

Malta has been a member of the EU since 2004. Agriculture and fishing are important activities and lace-making is a traditional craft. Malta also exports machinery and transport equipment, while a major natural resource is limestone. However, Malta has limited fresh water and no energy source of its own. Nevertheless,

LEFT: Grand Harbour dockyard, Vittoriosa.

BELOW: St Agatha, St Agatha's Catacombs, Rabat.

OPPOSITE: Valletta, Malta's capital.

it has developed its dockyards, and has become important for transshipment of freight. It has encouraged new industries, such as textiles, electronics, apparel, plastics and chemicals, as well as financial services and tourism. Malta is in current discussions with Tunisia regarding the presence of oil on the continental shelf that divides the two countries fom one another.

MARSHALL ISLANDS

Location: 25 J
Capital: Delap-Uliga-Djarrit
Area: 70sq m (181km²)
Population: 59,071 July 2005
Main Languages: Marshallese
Main Religions: Independent Protestant
Christian Church 80%
Currency: US dollar
Climate: Hot all year

A Micronesian nation, the Marshalls comprise many islands and coral atolls in the western Pacific Ocean. There are two main chains of islands, Ralik and Ratak. They are located north of Nauru and Kiribati, east of the Federated States of Micronesia and south of Wake Island. Two-thirds of the population lives on Majuro, where the capital is situated, and Ebeye.

Little is known of the early history of the islands, but it seems they were settled by Micronesians in the 2nd millennium BC. Alonso de Salazar, a Spanish explorer, is thought to have sighted the islands in the 16th century, but it was not until 1788 that John Marshall, an English sea captain, visited them, and gave the islands their name. German traders arrived in 1885 and the Marshalls eventually became a German protectorate. They were invaded by Japan during the First World War, which administered them thereafter under a League of Nations mandate.

The US invaded the islands in 1944, during the Second World War, and they were added to the US-administered Trust Territory of the Pacific Islands in 1947, along with several more besides. After the war, the US began nuclear testing on Bikini and Enewetak, which continued into the 1960s. This led to high radiation levels in the population and continuing claims for compensation. The Marshalls became a republic in 1979, when a Compact of Free Association with the US was signed, effective from 1986. They became fully independent in 1991, when the trust given to the US was officially ended and the Marshalls became a member of the UN. The islands host the Reagan Missile Test Site on Kwajalein, which is of great strategic importance to the US defence. Head of both state and government since 2004 is President Kesai Hesa Note.

The US provides revenue to the islands, on which they are heavily reliant. Small farms produce coconuts, breadfruit, melons and tomatoes, while industry is limited to handicrafts, copra and fish processing. It is hoped that tourism will continue to expand after the economic downturn following the Asian financial crisis of the late 1990s.

MARTINIQUE

Location: 9 J
Capital: Fort-de-France
Area: 409sq m (1060km²)
Population: 432,900 July 2005
Main Languages: French, Creole
Main Religions: Roman Catholic 85%,
Protestant 10%
Currency: euro
Climate: Tropical, moderated by
trade winds, risk of
hurricanes

An overseas department of France from 1946, Martinique lies in the Caribbean Sea in the Windward group of the Lesser Antilles. It is volcanic in origin and several of its volcanoes are still active, one of which, Mount Pelée, erupted in 1902, destroying the original capital of St-Pierre and killing more than 30,000 people. Hurricanes and flooding are also prevalent.

Martinique was discovered by Columbus in 1502. It became a French colony in 1635 and has remained attached to France ever since, with only brief periods of occupation by other powers. In 1660, the

French expelled the indigenous Carib Indians, bringing in slaves from Africa to work the sugar plantations. It is from these slaves that the present population is mostly descended.

Chirac of France, represented by Prefect Yves Dassonville. Head of government since 1992 is Claude Lise.

The economy is still based on sugar, most of it nowadays going to rum production, and bananas and light industry are also important. Tourism is a rapidly growing sector.

OPPOSITE: Overview of Case-Pilôte.

BELOW: Morne Piquet, Route de la Trace, one of Martinique's most scenic routes.

The Empress Joséphine, née Marie Josèphe Rose Tascher de la Pagerie, was born on Martinique. She was the widow of a French aristocrat who was guillotined during the French Revolution. She married Napoleon Bonaparte in 1804, but bore him no children, and they were divorced in 1809. The remains of the plantation of La Pagerie can still be seen on the island.

Head of state is President Jacques

MAURITANIA

Location:	12 I
Capital:	Nouakchott
Area:	398,000sq m (1030820km²)
Population:	3,086,859 July 2005 E
Main Languages:	Arabic
Main Religions:	Sunni Muslim 99%
Currency:	1 ouguiya = 5 khoums
Climate:	Hot and dry, rains in south Jul–Sep

Situated in north-west Africa, over two-thirds of the Islamic Republic of Mauritania is covered by desert, much of it by the Sahara Desert, and many of the people still lead nomadic lives, living by their flocks and herds. The rest of the population is concentrated in the south-western Sahel, many of them black Africans; ethnic tensions exist between the minority black African and Arab-Berber populations to this day. The only agricultural land is a relatively small area in the south along the Senegal River. Mauritania has a coastline on the Atlantic Ocean, where Nouakchott the capital is sited, and land borders with Western Sahara, Algeria, Mali and Senegal.

The Romans called their north-west African province Mauretania, after the Mauri or Berber people that inhabited the area. It continued to be the centre of Berber power into the 11th and 12th centuries, when the Almoravid dynasty, which had established empires in Algeria, Morocco and Spain, also brought Islam to the area. In the 14th and 15th centuries it became part of the great Mali Empire. Nomadic Arab tribes became more dominant, while European trading posts sprang up along the coast. Mauritania became a French protectorate in 1903 and a colony within French West Africa in 1920. It became fully independent within the French community in 1960, with Moktar Ould Daddah the first president of the one-party state. Morocco opposed Mauritania's independence and for a time tried to absorb it. However, matters improved when King Hassan II of Morocco revealed his plan to divide Western Sahara. In 1976, Spain withdrew from the territory and Morocco took 66 per cent of Western Sahara and Mauritania the southern third, only to relinquish it three years later after being raided by POLISARIO guerillas seeking the independence of the territory. (See also Western Sahara.)

Moktar Ould Daddah, the only president there had been since independence, was overthrown in a military coup in 1978 and a

military junta took control. In 1984 Maaouiya Ould Sid Ahmed Taya became president, still under a military regime. A new constitution and national assembly were adopted in 1991, with multi-party elections the following year. President Taya continued to preside, now over a civilian government, and later survived several attempts to oust him. However, on 3 August 2005, while he was in Saudi Arabia attending the funeral of the king, there was a bloodless coup, when the Military Council for Justice and

OPPOSITE: Fishing boats on a beach.

ABOVE: Desert landscape, somewhere between Nouadhibou and Nouakchott.

RIGHT: Village scene, between Kiffa and Nema.

Democracy, led by Ely Ould Mohamed Vall, seized power, on the grounds that it was ending a totalitarian regime. Sidy Mohamed Ould Boubacar was appointed prime minister.

Half the population still relies on its livestock and agriculture, growing dates, rice and cereals, though many abandoned the land for the cities after the repeated droughts of the 1970s and 80s. Mauritania has large deposits of iron ore, which makes up nearly half of its exports. Other natural resources are gypsum, copper, phosphate, gold and diamonds, and reserves of oil and natural gas are under investigation. It also has some of the richest fishing waters off its coast, though overfishing is a concern. Recent tensions have arisen with Senegal over both countries' use of the Senegal river that marks the border between the two countries.

MAURITIUS

Location:	17 L
Capital:	Port Louis
Area:	788sq m (2041km²)
Population:	1,230,602 July 2005
Main Languages:	English
Main Religions:	Hindu 52%, Roman Catholic 26%, Muslim 17%
Currency:	1 Mauritius rupee = 100 cents
Climate:	Tropical summer; sub-tropical winter; rain all year, especially Dec–Mar

Lying in the Indian Ocean 500m (800km) or so east of Madagascar, the territory consists of the main island of Mauritius, almost entirely surrounded by coral reefs, the island of Rodrigues, 20 or so nearby islets, and the dependencies of the Agalega Islands; it also includes the tiny Cargados Carajos shoals (Saint Brandon Rocks). The French island of Réunion lies 125m (200km) to the south-west.

Collectively, the archipelago is known as the Mascarene Islands; they were formed by undersea volcanic eruptions when the African plate drifted over the Réunion hotspot. However, they have long since ceased to be volcanically active.

The Portuguese discovered the then-uninhabited islands at the beginning of the 16th century, where they found a previously unknown bird, which they called the *doudo* (dodo) or simpleton, because it had no fear of man and could easily be killed. Sadly, the dodos had all disappeared by 1681, either killed by settlers or by their domestic animals. The Dutch occupied the islands from 1598–1710, and named them Mauritius, after Prince Maurice of Nassau. It was controlled by the French from 1715, until the British took control in 1810, and it was ceded to Britain in 1814. Mauritius was the fifth country in the world to issue postage stamps, the first of which, issued in 1847, are highly prized by philatelists; they are extremely valuable because of their rarity.

BELOW: The Rochester Falls, near Souillac, lie on the River Savanne.

OPPOSITE LEFT: Woman selling vegetables at Triolet market.

OPPOSITE RIGHT: Cap Malheureux.

In 1968 Mauritius achieved independence within the Commonwealth of Nations. More than half the people are Indo-Mauritians, descendants of labourers imported from India after the abolition of slavery in the 19th century; the rest are of African, French, Chinese or mixed descent. Head of state since 2003 is President Sir Anerood Jugnauth; head of government is Prime Minister Paul Berenger, also since 2003.

Mauritius has long enjoyed political and economic stability, with the kind of growth that has attracted investment from abroad. It also has a positive attitude to human rights. Sugar and molasses (the main export), tea and tobacco are produced and textiles are important. However, drought and declining sugar prices have recently taken their toll of the economy. Nevertheless, Mauritius has steadily-growing industrial, financial and tourism sectors and will become a duty-free zone within the next few years.

MEXICO

Location:	6 I
Capital:	Mexico City
Area:	759,529sq m (1967180km²)
Population:	106,202,903 July 2005
Main Languages:	Spanish
Main Religions:	Roman Catholic 90%, Protestant 3%
Currency:	1 peso = 100 centavos
Climate:	Hot and humid on coasts; Inland and mountains cooler and drier

A country in North America, with extensive coastlines on the Gulf of Mexico to the east and the Pacific Ocean to the west. It has land borders with the United States to the north and Belize and Guatemala to the south-east. The Gulf of California divides the mainland of the east from the elongated, mountainous peninsula of Baja California to the west. The two ranges of the Sierra Madre enclose an extensive central plateau (*mesa*) and meet near the isthmus of Tehuantepec, where both coasts converge. The country can be divided into three climatic zones: the *tierra caliente*, a low-lying tropical region adjacent to the coasts and including the Yucatán peninsula; the *tierra templada*, a temperate region that includes most of the plateau; and the *tierra fria*, a colder region rising to 6,000ft (1800m), and where the capital Mexico City is situated. There are also areas of desert in the north, where cactus, yucca and mesquite flourish.

The site of several Mesoamerican civilizations, including those of the Olmecs, Mayans, Toltecs and Aztecs, Mexico is rich in archeological sites; these include the Pyramid of the Sun at Teotihuacán, the Toltec and Mayan ruins at Tula and Chichén Itzá in the Yucatán, and the Zapotec city of Monte Albán near Oaxaca. Montezuma, the last Aztec emperor, was killed by the Spanish under Hérnan Cortéz in 1520, which was followed by the colonization of Mexico as New Spain that lasted for 300 years. During this time, Spanish culture and Catholicism became firmly entrenched and the wealth of the country was established.

After years of war, Spanish rule came to an end in 1821, when the First Mexican Empire was created and Spanish possessions in Central America were incorporated into Mexico. This was short-lived, however, with republicans seizing power in 1824. In 1832 Antonio López de Santa Ana became president. Texas decided to break away from Mexico in 1836, and the rest of Mexican territory north of the Rio Grande was ceded to the US following the Mexican War of 1846–48, becoming the modern states of California, Nevada, Utah, New Mexico, Colorado and most of Arizona. A revolution led to the overthrow of Santa Ana in 1855, which was followed by civil war.

At the beginning of the 1860s, the Habsburg emperor, Maximilian of Austria, supported by the French, was proclaimed Emperor of Mexico. This Second Mexican Empire was challenged by the existing leader, Benito Juárez, supported by the US and the military expertise of General Porfirio Díaz, following which the French army supporting the emperor was defeated in 1862. Although Maximilian was reinstated as emperor for a time, he was eventually executed in 1857 and Juárez continued in office until 1872. He was followed by Porfirio Díaz, who assumed the presidency in 1877, establishing a dictatorship that lasted for many years and achieving peace

RIGHT: The Kukulkan Pyramid, Chichén Itzá, Yucatan.

OPPOSITE LEFT: Guanajuato city skyline.

MICRONESIA

Location:	23 J
Capital:	Palikir
Area:	271sq m (702km²)
Population:	108,105 July 2005
Main Languages:	English
Main Religions:	Christian
Currency:	US dollar
Climate:	Hot all year

and prosperity for Mexico. His fraudulent victory in the 1910 elections led to his downfall and sparked the Mexican Revolution, sparking conflict that lasted for almost two decades. Battles with the peasant armies of Villa and Zapata and intervention by the US ended in the creation of the National Revolutionary Government (later the Institutional Revolutionary Party) in 1929, which remained in power until 2000. The head of state and head of government since 2000 is President Vicente Fox Quesada. It was the first time an opposition party had been voted to power since 1910. In Chiapas in 1994, action by Zapatistas for more rights for indigenous peoples was followed by demonstrations in 2001 that achieved success, and a new bill supporting the minority cause was passed.

Mexico has a free market economy that is a mix of modern and more primitive industry and agriculture. In late 1994, the devaluation of the peso led to economic turmoil, triggering the worst recession in over 50 years, since when an impressive recovery has been made. But problems do exist, such as frequent drought, a large population, underemployment and unequal distribution of wealth, especially among Amerindians living in the poorer southern states. Exports include oil and oil products, manufactured goods, minerals, fuel, coffee and textiles. Beef, dairy cattle and other livestock are also reared. Forestry and tourism are also important, with many visitors coming from the USA to resorts such as Acapulco and the great archeological sites.

A federation of associated, widely dispersed Oceanian island states, comprising the bulk of the Caroline Islands, but excluding Belau, which remains a trust territory of the US. The 607 islands are situated in the western Pacific to the north of the equator and north-east of Papua New Guinea. To the north-west lies the Mariana Trench, the deepest known ocean depth in the world at 36,201ft (11034m) at the Challenger Deep. The islands range from mountainous to low coral atolls, with volcanic outcrops. They are located at the edge of a typhoon belt and severe damage occasionally occurs.

The Portuguese were the first to

discover Micronesia, when they were looking for the Spice Islands (Moluccas) in the 16th century. Spain annexed the islands in 1874, selling them to Germany in 1899. The islands were occupied by Japan in 1914, and was subsequently given a mandate to govern them by the League of Nations in 1920. During the Second World War, a substantial part of the Japanese fleet was based at Truk. In 1944 Operation Hailstone, one of the most important naval battles of the war, was fought, when many Japanese aircraft and support vessels were destroyed. US forces captured the islands and the group was administered by the US as part of the UN Pacific Islands Trust Territory from 1947. It entered into free association with the US as an independent state in 1986, which was amended and renewed in 2004. It became a full member of the UN in 1991.

There are four states, Kosrae, Pohnpei, where the capital Palikir stands, Chuuk (Truk) and Yap. Each has its own culture and traditions that are centuries old. However, a clan system operates throughout the islands and the importance of the extended family is common to all. Head of both state and government since 2003 is President Joseph J. Urusemal.

The economy is almost entirely dependent on US aid. Due to the shortage of land, only a little subsistence farming exists. Fishing is also important to the islanders, though overfishing has become a great concern. There are few mineral deposits, and only a little high-grade phosphate is worth exploiting. There is a potential tourist industry, but the area is possibly too remote for it to be developed.

MOLDOVA

Location:	15 G
Capital:	Chisinau
Area:	13,000sq m (33700km²)
Population:	4,455,421 July 2005
Main Languages:	Moldovan
Main Religions:	Romanian Orthodox,
	Moldovan Orthodox
Currency:	Leu
Climate:	Warm summer, cold winter

A landlocked country in south-eastern Europe, Moldova lies between Romania to the west and Ukraine to the east. Its western border with Romania follows the River Prut, which joins the Danube before flowing into the Black Sea. It consists of a fertile, well-watered plateau, which never reaches more than 1,410ft (430m).

The region that is now modern Moldova was once a major part of ancient Dacia, which was annexed by Trajan in AD 106 as a province of the Roman Empire. Lying as it did on a strategic route between Europe and Asia, it was liable to frequent invasions of Mongol and other tribes. During the Middle Ages most of present-day Moldova, together with Bessarabia and Bukovina, formed the eastern part of the principality of Moldavia (Moldova in Romanian). At the beginning of the 16th century it was conquered by the Turks and was part of the Ottoman Empire until the 19th century. In 1775 Austria gained Bukovina and Bessarabia was annexed by Russia, following the Treaty of Bucharest in 1812. In 1859 the western part of the principality of Moldavia joined with Wallachia to form the old Kingdom of Romania. At the end of the First World War, Bessarabia broke from Russia, and with Bukovina joined with Romania in 1918. Russia refused to recognize this defection and reinvaded Bessarabia in 1940, Romania eventually ceding Bessarabia and Northern Bukovina to the Soviet Union in a peace treaty of 1947. The southern and northern parts, with their sizeable Slavic and Turkic populations, were transferred to the Ukraine SSR, while the Trans-Dneister, where ethnic Romanians then outnumbered Slavs, joined the rest of Moldavia to form the Moldavian SSR. This resulted in the destruction of the Romanian middle classes, when many ethnic Romanians were deported to Siberia and Kazakhstan and were replaced by Soviets, most of whom were Slavs.

The Moldavian SSR became a member of the Commonwealth of Independent States as the Republic of Moldova, following the break-up of the Soviet Union in 1991. The

BELOW LEFT: A small farm growing maize, sunflowers and vines.

OPPOSITE LEFT: A highly-decorated interior in Voldulai-Vode.

OPPOSITE RIGHT: The Cathedral of the Nativity, Chisinau.

Trans-Dneister region, by now heavily populated by ethnic Russians and Ukrainians, also claimed independence in 1991, fearing Moldovan reunification with Romania. Russian and Ukrainian forces intervened on the side of the Trans-Dneister and remained in the area to keep the peace. There were moves towards reunification with Romania, but a referendum in 1994, when a new constitution was also adopted, indicated otherwise. Elections in 2001 voted in a Communist party, the first former Communist state to do so, with a Communist president, Vladimir Voronin. He was re-elected in 2005. Head of government since 2001 is Prime Minister Vasily Tarlev.

Moldova has various sedimentary rocks and minerals, including sand, gravel, gypsum and limestone, but its main attributes are a favourable climate and good soil. It therefore concentrates mainly on agriculture, growing fruit, vegetables, tobacco, and grapes for wine. However, it is still one of the poorest countries in Europe and continues to look to Russia for its energy requirements. Despite recent positive growth and attempts to reduce poverty, foreign investment is not forthcoming.

MONACO

Location:	13 G
Capital:	Monaco-Ville
Area:	0.75sq m (1.95km²)
Population:	32,409 July 2005
Main Languages:	French
Main Religions:	Roman Catholic 90%
Currency:	euro
Climate:	Hot, dry summer; mild winter

The smallest independent state in the world, after Vatican City, Monaco stands on the Mediterranean Côte d'Azur, 11m (18km) east of Nice and in close proximity to the Italian border and Ventimiglia. It is an enclave within the French department of Alpes-Maritimes, which borders it on three sides. It comprises seven *quartiers*: Monaco-Ville (the capital), Monte Carlo (with its famous casino), La Condamine, Fontvielle (an area reclaimed from the sea), Monghetti, Larvotto Terano and Saint-Roman. Monaco is unusual in that the native Monégasques are a minority in their own country, the French being the larger population, and with French the official language. The currency is

Living standards are high and the absence of income tax and low business rates attract not only wealthy tax exiles, whose income derives from outside the principality, but also foreign companies setting up offices in the principality. The state retains monopolies of several sectors, including tobacco and the postal and telephone services. It is not a member of the EU, but its currency is the euro, in harmony with that of France.

OPPOSITE: Oceanographic museum, Monaco.

LEFT: The Royal Palace (Palais de Prince).

BELOW: Port de La Condamine.

that of France, which is also responsible for Monaco's defence. Monaco is the most densely populated country in the world now that Macau has been returned to China.

Previously a colony of Genoa, Monaco has been ruled by the Grimaldi dynasty since 1297, apart from the period from 1793, when it was under French control. It was a protectorate of Sardinia from 1815 until Monaco's sovereign was recognized by the Franco-Monégasque Treaty of 1861. The Prince of Monaco was an absolute ruler until 1911. In 1918 a treaty was signed establishing limited French protection over Monaco, but that its policy should be in line with the political, military and economic interests of France.

Rainier III died in April 2005 after a reign of more than 50 years. He married the Hollywood actress Grace Kelly in 1956 but their fairytale marriage came to a tragic end when she died in a car crash on the Grande Corniche. He was succeeded by his son Albert, Marquis of Baux, as Albert II of Monaco. Head of government since 2005 is Minister of State Jean-Paul Proust.

One of Monaco's chief sources of income is tourism, with visitors attracted to the sophisticated resort by its location, climate and casino. However, care has been taken to expand its economy by developing services and high-value light industries, such as printing and textiles. Major reconstruction now allows cruise ships into the harbour.

MONGOLIA

Location: 20 G
Capital: Ulan Bator
Area: 604,250sq m (1565008km²)
Population: 2,791,272 July 2005
Main Languages: Khalkha Mongolian
Main Religions: Buddhist, Muslim
Currency: 1 tugrik = 100 möngö
Climate: Mild summer,
very cold winter, snow

A large and sparsely-populated country of eastern Asia, present-day Mongolia was previously known as Outer Mongolia to differentiate it from Inner Mongolia, which is a part of China. It is bordered by Siberian Russia to the north and China to the south. There is very little cultivable land, much of the terrain being flat, grassy steppe, with mountains in the north and west and the Gobi Desert occupying much of the south. A third of the population is nomadic or semi-nomadic, and lives by herding livestock, while most of the remainder is concentrated in Ulan Bator, the coldest capital city in the world.

References to Mongols first appeared in Chinese writings in the 6th century, their power reaching its zenith under Ghenghis Khan (1162–1227), who united the Mongolian tribes. His grandson, Kublai Khan (1216–94), was the first Mongol emperor of China. In the 13th century, Mongolia was the centre of a great Mongol Empire that stretched from China to the Black Sea. Separation of the northern Mongols from those of the south occurred in the 14th century, following the overthrow of the Mongol dynasty in China by the Ming in 1368. A long period of internal struggles and feuds led to the Manchu conquest of Inner Mongolia (the south) in 1636 and the submission of Outer Mongolia to China in 1691. After the Chinese Revolution of 1911–12, both declared their independence. In 1919, Chinese troops again took

BELOW: Statue of Sukhbator, Sukhbator Square, Ulan Bator.

OPPOSITE LEFT: On the Mongolian steppe.

OPPOSITE RIGHT: Gandan Monastery, Ulan Bator.

Outer Mongolia, but were driven out in 1921, when the Russian Civil War spread to Outer Mongolian territory. By now allied with the Soviet Union, the Communist Mongolian People's Republic was declared in 1924. In 1928 Horloogiyn Choybalsan came to power, when forced collectivization, purges and the destruction of Lamaist monasteries caused thousands of people to perish or flee to Inner Mongolia. China eventually recognized Outer Mongolia's independence in 1946, retaining the autonomous region of China known as Inner Mongolia.

Multi-party elections in 1990 paved the way for the adoption of a new, more liberal constitution in 1992. In 1996, the Democratic Union Coalition, the first non-Communist government for 70 years, came to power.

Head of state since 2005 is President Nambaryn Enkhbayar, while head of government since 2004 is Prime Minister Tsakhi Elbegdorj.

The Mongolian economy has suffered in its transition from Communism to capitalism, with Soviet aid disappearing almost overnight following the break-up of the USSR in the early 1990s. It has long had traditional industries based on agriculture and herding, but now coal, copper, molybdenum, tin, tungsten and gold production have assumed importance. Mongolia joined the World Trade Organization in 1997, enabling it to export cashmere, minerals and food products to Russia, the US, China, Japan and Italy, among others.

MOROCCO

Location:	12 H
Capital:	Rabat
Area:	177,192sq m (458927km²)
Population:	32,725,847 July 2005
Main Languages:	Arabic
Main Religions:	Sunni Muslim 98%
Currency:	1 dirham = 100 centimes
Climate:	Hot summer, mild winter, more extreme inland

LEFT: Ureka, high up in the Atlas Mountains near Marrakech.

BELOW: The Royal Palace, Rabat.

OPPOSITE: Moroccan musician in traditional dress.

A country in north-west Africa, Morocco or Al Maghrib – the kingdom in the west – has a long coastline on the Atlantic that continues past the Moroccan-controlled Strait of Gibraltar and along the northern coast of the Mediterranean. It has land borders with Western Sahara (of which Morocco claims ownership), Mauritania to the south and Algeria to the east, though the border with Algeria is now closed. The High and Middle Atlas Mountains, that rise to 15,000ft (4570m), traverse the country from south-west to north-east; further south is the Anti-Atlas range, and the Rif Mountains, which are geologically unstable, lie to the north. In the south-east, the Sahara Desert continues into the disputed territory of Western Sahara. The narrow coastal plain in the west is fertile, while coniferous forests clothe the mountain slopes.

Berbers settled the area around 3,000 years ago and Jewish colonies were established under the Romans. There was an Arab invasion in the 7th century, when Islam was introduced. A century after the Arab conquest of North Africa, successive Moorish dynasties began to rule in Morocco, and Berbers and Arabs united in an independent Moroccan state. In the mid-11th century, the Almoravids conquered Morocco and established a vast Muslim empire; they were succeeded by the Almohads. In the 15th century the Moors retreated from Spain, and Spain and

Portugal began to gain footholds in Morocco.

The 16th century, particularly the reign of Ahmad Al-Mansur (1578–1603), was Morocco's golden age, when invaders were repelled from the country, and by the 17th century, the present Alawite dynasty was able to re-claim most of the European-held territory.

In 1860, northern Morocco was occupied by Spain, and its sovereignty was gradually eroded. Morocco was the last of the Barbary States to relinquish its independence, when the sultan, though continuing as ruler, accepted French protection in 1912, under the Treaty of Fès. There followed the division of the country into three zones from 1923: the special international zone of Tangier; a Spanish protectorate in the north; and a French protectorate covering the remainder. This led to armed conflict with indigenous tribesmen, which ended in the surrender of Abd El-Krim in 1926, the leader of the revolt against European rule.

There was widespread unrest following the Second World War. In 1947, Sultan Sidi Mohamed called for independence from France and Spain. In 1956 the struggle for independence ended with Morocco recovering Tangier and most of the Spanish possessions, apart from the northern enclaves of Ceuta, Melilla, Peñón de Vélez de la Gomera and several small off-shore islands, which are still under dispute. The following year, Morocco became an independent monarchy, when the sultan changed his title to King Mohamed V; he was succeeded by his son Hassan in 1961.

There were internal political as well as territorial disputes, especially with Algeria, during the 1960s. In 1976 Spain finally relinquished its claim to Spanish Sahara, which it had held since the 19th century. Morocco virtually annexed the territory, now known as Western Sahara, giving part of it to Mauritania. Mauritania eventually withdrew, leaving the whole of the phosphate-rich region to Morocco; the validity of this has been disputed both internationally and by local independence movements ever since.

Gradual reforms in the 1990s led to the establishment of a bicameral legislation in 1997. In July 1999 King Mohamed VI acceded to the throne on the death of his father, Hassan II. Head of government since 2002 is Prime Minister Driss Jettou. In 2003, Casablanca, Morocco's largest city, was attacked by terrorists linked to Al-Qaeda, leaving 41 civilians dead and more than 100 injured.

Morocco's problems are those of any developing country, in that education and living standards are in urgent need of improvement. On the other hand, Morocco has recently entered into Free Trade Agreements with the EU, with effect from 2010, and with the US, with which it has a long tradition of friendship and which allows almost tariff-free unilateral trade. Fishing and agriculture are important activities, where irrigation makes crop-growing possible, and fruit, olives, grapes, sugar beet and wheat are grown. Tourism is gaining momentum, and the historic cities of Fès, Marrakech, and the capital Rabat, attract many visitors each year.

MOZAMBIQUE

Location:	16 L
Capital:	Maputo
Area:	308,642sq m (799382km²)
Population:	19,406,703 July 2005
Main Languages:	Portuguese
Main Religions:	Traditional 40%, Roman Catholic 18%, Muslim 13%
Currency:	1 metical = 100 centavos
Climate:	Warm all year; cooler and wetter inland, rains Oct–Mar

A country on the eastern coast of southern Africa, Mozambique has a coastline on the Mozambique Channel and the Indian Ocean. It has land borders with Tanzania, Malawi, Zambia, Zimbabwe, South Africa and Swaziland. A wide coastal plain, through which many rivers flow to the sea, including the Zambezi and Limpopo, rises to highlands of up to 8,000ft (2450m; rainforests of ebony and ironwood teem with wildlife. The only real harbour is the capital, Maputo, formerly the city of Lourenço Marques.

The indigenous people of Mozambique are from the Bantu tribes, but by the 10th century Arabs traders in ivory and gold had established themselves along the coast. After the area had been visited by Vasco da Gama in 1498, however, the Portuguese began to arrive and colonization began in 1505, formalized in 1910; in the interim, huge plantations were built. Mozambique was a centre of the slave trade in the 18th and 19th centuries. It achieved independence from Portugal in 1975, after a ten-year struggle by the FRELIMO (*Frente*

BELOW: A railroad cutting through the Mozambique landscape.

OPPOSITE LEFT: Carrying water from the pump.

OPPOSITE RIGHT: Back-breaking work.

de Libertação de Moçambique) liberation movement, which resulted in a mass exodus of Portuguese settlers and the draining of the country's resources. The new FRELIMO government, with the FRELIMO leader Samora Machel its first president, established a one-party Communist state; it also assisted other liberation movements in Rhodesia (Zimbabwe) and South Africa, bringing them into conflict with the Mozambique National Resistance Movement (RENAMO) opposition. Civil war raged for 16 years, when thousands of people lost their lives. Samora Machel died in 1986 and was succeeded by Joachim Chissano. In 1989 FRELIMO abandoned Marxism and a multi-party system was adopted. In 1992, following a period of severe drought and famine, a UN-negotiated peace agreement was signed. In 2000 the Zambezi and Limpopo rivers flooded, leaving vast areas of the country under water, making almost a million people homeless and destroying much of the country's infrastructure. In 2004, Chissano stood down after 18 years in office, and was succeeded by Armando Emilio Guebuza.

Mozambique is one of the world's poorest countries, and civil war and natural disasters have not helped matters. In spite of the hydro-electric power generated by the Cabora Basso Dam on the Zambezi, north-west of Tete, industrial development is still on a small scale, leaving subsistence agriculture as the main source of income. Fishing is also important and shrimp is exported, along with sugar and copra.

MYANMAR

Location:	20 I
Capital:	Rangoon
Area:	261,228sq m (676577km²)
Population:	42,909,464 July 2005
Main Languages:	Burmese
Main Religions:	Buddhist 89%,
	Christian 5%, Muslim 4%
Currency:	1 kyat = 100 pyas
Climate:	Hot all year, cooler
	Oct–Feb, rains May–Oct

Designated Myanmar by the ruling military junta since 1989, and not universally accepted, Burma is a country of South-East Asia on the Bay of Bengal and Andaman Sea. It has land borders with Bangladesh, India, China, Laos and Thailand. The terrain is characterized by central lowlands, where most of the population is centred, bisected by the Ayeyarwady (Irawaddy) river and surrounded by rugged highlands. Earthquakes, cyclones, droughts, flooding and landslides are frequent occurrences.

The history of Burma began with the arrival of primitive tribes from the borders

LEFT: *The palace moat with royal barge, Mandalay.*

OPPOSITE LEFT: *View of temples at Pagan.*

OPPOSITE RIGHT: *Fishing on Inle Lake, Shan state.*

of China and Tibet in the 7th century. Over the next four centuries, however, they developed a distinctive civilization, that extended from the original settlement of Pagan to cover most of present-day Burma; the main characteristics of this civilization were Buddhism and the architectural form of the pagoda. In 1287, Kublai Khan's grandson, Ye-se Timur, occupied the country, when all vestiges of the Pagan dynasty were obliterated. Anarchy reigned after his withdrawal until 1752, when Alaungpaya unified the country, establishing Rangoon as his capital.

Annexed by Britain during the 19th century, Burma was incorporated into the Indian Empire until it was restored to a separate, self-governing colony in 1937. Burma was occupied by the Japanese from 1942–45. Following its liberation, and after negotiations with Britain, it became an independent republic in 1948. In 1962 an army coup, led by General Ne Win, overthrew the government and established an authoritarian regime, leaving the overthrown Prime Minister U Nu to retreat to Thailand to plan revolt; subsequent insurrections in various parts of the

2000–02 and was imprisoned in 2003, following an attack on her convoy in northern Myanmar; in December 2004 the junta declared it would continue to detain her for at least another year. Meanwhile, her supporters and all who strive for democracy and human rights are routinely harassed or imprisoned.

Myanmar is rich in mineral resources and precious stones, rubies in particular, which have remained largely unexploited.

Consequently, most of the people live in abject poverty, relying on the food they grow themselves. Moreover, the treatment of Aung San Suu Kyi has brought to a halt development assistance, investment from abroad and export sanctions. However, timber, gems, illegal drugs and rice find their way to neighbouring countries with which Myanmar has maintained good relations, and finance is forthcoming from China, Thailand and Singapore.

country were thought not to be unconnected with him.

In spite of the victory of the National League for Democracy (NLD) in multi-party elections held in May 1990, the military regime refused to relinquish power. Aung San Suu Kyi, the leader of the NLD and Nobel Peace Prize laureate, had been under house arrest from 1989 and was not released until 1995. She was detained again from

NAMIBIA

Location:	14 M
Capital:	Windhoek
Area:	318,275sq m (824332km²)
Population:	2,030,692 July 2005
Main Languages:	English
Main Religions:	Lutheran 51%, Roman Catholic 20%
Currency:	1 Namibian dollar = 100 cents
Climate:	Hot and dry; rainfall sparse and erratic

Namibia is an arid country, situated in south-west Africa. The Namib Desert lies along its coastline on the Atlantic Ocean in the west, while the Kalahari Desert extends into Botswana in the east. It has other land borders with Angola and Zambia to the north and South Africa to the south. The central plateau is where the capital, Windhoek, is located, while to the north lies an alluvial plain and the marshlands of the Caprivi Strip.

The San were the original inhabitants of the country, but were eventually replaced by Bantu-speakers, such as the Ovambo, Kavango and Herero. The area was annexed

by German South-West Africa in 1884, when it was the scene of the Herero rebellion, which was put down with unnecessary brutality. In 1920 South-West Africa, as Namibia was then called, was mandated to South Africa by the League of Nations; South Africa, however, continued to administer the country after the mandate had expired in 1964, despite international censure. In 1966, the SWAPO (Marxist South-West African People's Organization) guerilla movement launched a war of independence, but it was not until 1988 that South Africa, in accordance with a UN peace plan, agreed to withdraw. Namibia became fully independent in 1990 and has been governed by SWAPO ever since. Head of state since 2004 is President Hifikepunye Pohamba; he replaced Sam Nujoma, who had led the country during its first 14 years of self-rule. Prime minister since March 2005 is Nahas Angula.

Where it exists, Namibia has good grazing, and cattle, goats and sheep are reared, yielding valuable skins. Offshore there is good fishing and crops are grown here and there. Namibia's mineral wealth acounts for the bulk of its exports and consists of diamonds, silver, zinc, vanadium, copper, uranium and tin, and there may be reserves of oil, iron ore and coal.

OPPOSITE: Sand dunes at Sossuvlei in the Namib Desert.

LEFT: Post Street Mall, Windhoek.

ABOVE: A Namibian lion at Mount Etjo Safari Lodge.

NAURU

Location:	24 K
Capital:	Yaren
Area:	8sq m (21km²)
Population:	13,048 July 2005
Main Languages:	Nauruan, English
Main Religions:	Roman Catholic, Nauruan Protestant
Currency:	Australian dollar
Climate:	Hot all year

The world's smallest independent republic, Nauru is an Oceanian phosphate rock island, one of three in the South Pacific, the others being Banaba in Kiribati, and Makatea in French Polynesia. Nauru lies close to the equator and south of the Marshall Islands. It is a raised atoll surrounded by a reef that is visible at low tide. There is a narrow coastal belt, where most of the people live, rising to a central plateau 200ft (60m) or so above sea level. There is no fresh water, apart from rainwater, and a single desalinization plant, or imported water from Australia, supplies the rest.

Nauru's first inhabitants were Polynesian and Melanesian settlers. Discovered by

Europeans in 1798, the island was seized by Germany in 1888 and annexed to German New Guinea, with mining of its phosphate reserves beginning soon after. In 1920 it was mandated to Britain by the League of Nations. It was occupied by the Japanese in 1942–45, then taken into UN trusteeship in 1947, when it was effectively administered by Australia. Nauru eventually achieved independence in 1968, becoming a 'special member' of the Commonwealth and joined the UN as a member state in 1999.

In 2001 a ship with refugees from various countries, including Afghanistan, attempted to dock in Australia, but was diverted to Nauru as part of the Pacific Solution, where the refugees were detained. However, by 2005 all the women and children had been granted asylum, with only about 30 men remaining on the island. Head of state and head of government since 2004 is President Ludwig Scotty

Much of Nauru's prosperity was dependent on the large phosphate deposits present on the island, now seriously depleted. The phosphate is thought to be of marine or guano origin, used as a top-dressing to fertilize the soil; the bulk of it goes to Australia, which is the country to which Nauru looks for support. However, a century or so of mining has turned the centre of the island into a wasteland. Nauru's other great asset, built on the profits from phosphate, was the revenue derived from an office block built in Melbourne, but this had to be sold to pay off some of Nauru's debts. Faced with these problems it may be necessary to look to new sources of income, without which Nauru's future seems uncertain.

NEPAL

Location:	19 I
Capital:	Kathmandu
Area:	56,831sq m (147192km²)
Population:	27,676,547 July 2005
Main Languages:	Nepali
Main Religions:	Hindu 87%, Buddhist 8%, Muslim 4%
Currency:	1 Nepalese rupee = 100 paisas
Climate:	Hot summer, cold winter, snow in mountains, monsoon Jun–Oct

A landlocked country in southern Asia, Nepal is bounded on the north by China, on the south by India. Running parallel with the southern border is a level strip of land, the Terai, that runs along the Gangetic Plain. The Terai rises to the great range of the Himalayas in the north, culminating in Everest (29,035ft/8850m), Kanchenjunga (28,208ft/8598m) and several other lofty mountains, some of the highest in the world.

Around 563 BC, the Buddha, Siddhartha Gautama, was born in Lumbini in the far south. In the 1st century BC, Ashoka ruled a

vast Buddhist empire that covered northern India and the Terai of southern Nepal. However, this empire was displaced by Hindu fiefdoms, including the Licchavis dynasty, which arrived from India in 300, bringing a caste system with it: to this day Nepal remains the only Hindu state in the world. From the 13th to the 18th centuries Nepal was dominated by the Malla dynasty, great patrons of the arts. It emerged as a unified nation under Gurkha rule, when King Prithwi Narayan Shah captured Kathmandu in 1768. However, Gurkha expansion into northern India brought Nepal into conflict with Britain, leading to a permanent British presence in Kathmandu.

The year 1814 was the start of the Anglo-Nepali War, which ended with the Sugauli Treaty of 1816, when Nepal surrendered Sikkim and the southern Terai and the British retreated. Most of the Terai was returned to Nepal after it helped Britain in the Indian Sepoy Mutiny of 1857: Britain eventually recognized Nepal as a sovereign state in 1923. It also recognized the bravery of Gurkha soldiers who fought with Britain in two World Wars.

Meanwhile, following the Kot Massacre of 1846, when several hundred princes and chieftains were massacred, Nepal had fallen into the clutches of the Rana family, which established itself as a dynasty of hereditary chief ministers, succeeding in isolating Nepal from the rest of the world; their domination lasted for over a century until they were overthrown. With the Rana removed from power, the monarchy was restored in 1951,

279

followed by the formulation of a constitution in 1959, followed by free elections. However, in 1960 King Mahendra declared that a system based on village councils or *panchayat* should prevail. Mahendra died in 1972 and was succeeded by his son Birendra Bikram Shah Dev, who continued the *panchayat* system until 1989, when the monarchy was forced to accept constitutional reforms. In 1991 Nepal held its first multi-party elections for many years. Since then, no political party has held power for more than two consecutive years.

In 1996, an attempt by Maoist insurgents to turn Nepal into a Communist state escalated into the 'People's War'. In 2001, Prince Dipendra, the heir to the throne, killed ten members of the royal family, including his father and mother, when they objected to his choice of wife. He then shot himself, but rather than killing himself, ended up in a coma. In spite of what had happened he was still proclaimed king, according to Nepalese custom. He died three days later, however, and his uncle, Gyanendra, became king.

King Gyanendra declared martial law soon afterwards, deploying his troops to contain the People's War. In 2002 he dismissed the government on the grounds of incompetence. An attempt to end the civil war broke down in 2003; the following year the king reinstated the most recently elected prime minister, who formed a four-party coalition government. However, in February 2005 the king, not satisfied with the government's progress in ending the war, again dissolved the government and assumed full power himself.

The People's War between the Nepalese

LEFT: A young girl at a festival in Kathmandu.

OPPOSITE: Durbar Square, Bhaktapur, in the Kathmandu valley.

government and Maoist insurgents, besides killing thousands of people, continues to affect Nepal's economy, as does political instability, lack of technology and the prevalence of natural disasters. However, tourism and hydropower are potential areas of growth. Agriculture and services occupy 80 per cent of the population and account for almost half the national GDP. Most of the industrial activity is centred around Kathmandu and cities in the Terai and mainly involves the processing of what is grown, such as sugar, tobacco, jute, timber and grain. The textile and carpet industries are also providing valuable exports.

NETHERLANDS

Location:	13 F
Capital:	Amsterdam/The Hague
Area:	16,033sq m (41526km^2)
Population:	16,407,491 July 2005
Main Languages:	Dutch
Main Religions:	Roman Catholic 31%,
	Dutch Reformed Church
	14%
Currency:	euro
Climate:	Mild summer, cold winter

A kingdom of western Europe, bounded to the north and west by the North Sea, to the south by Belgium and to the east by Germany. The Netherlands (Holland), with Belgium and Luxembourg, make up what is known as the Low Countries. Strictly speaking, however, the name Holland belongs only to the two coastal provinces of North and South Holland. The plural 'Netherlands', used in English, is a legacy of the past, since the Dutch themselves refer to their country as *Nederland*. The landscape is famously flat: much of it is reclaimed land (polder), lying well below sea level. Dykes have been constructed to prevent flooding and keep the sea at bay.

In 55 BC, the lands south of the Rhine were absorbed into the Roman Empire. From the 4th to the 8th centuries, the Franks subdued the Frisians and Saxons north of the Rhine, and introduced Christianity. After the break-up of the Frankish empire, local feudal lords had a high degree of independence, while nominally belonging to the Holy Roman Empire, a revival of the Roman Empire established at the coronation of Charlemagne in 800. During the Middle Ages many of the towns became prosperous trading centres, ruled by a merchant oligarchy. In the 15th century the Low Countries passed to the dukes of Burgundy and thence by marriage to the Habsburgs,

passing to Spain in 1555 when the Habsburg Empire was divided. Under Charles V, Holy Roman Emperor and King of Spain, the region was part of the 17 Provinces of the Netherlands, which also included Belgium, Luxembourg and parts of France and Germany.

The Dutch united against Spanish rule under William the Silent in 1568, when a long struggle for independence began. The 17th century was a 'Golden Age', when the Dutch led the world in the arts and sciences and founded colonies abroad; the Dutch East India Company was founded in 1602. It was also the age of tulipomania, when tulip bulbs went for enormous sums. In 1648 the northern half of the 17 Provinces became an independent Dutch Republic in the charge of Johann de Witt from 1652. A series of Anglo-Dutch wars also began that year,

caused by commercial and colonial rivalries, with each lasting about two years. In 1672 the French invaded, de Witt was murdered, and William of Orange became stadholder of the Dutch Republic. The years 1672–78 were spent fending off the French; in 1795 Revolutionary France conquered the Netherlands, holding power until 1813.

In 1815 the Dutch Republic united with Belgium and Luxembourg to form the Kingdom of the Netherlands under William I

ABOVE: Dam Square with the Nieuwe Kirk (new church), Amsterdam.

LEFT: Traditional Dutch windmill at Kinderdijk.

OPPOSITE: Amsterdam's Oudeschans canal with the Mint Tower in the background.

of Orange, who also became Grand Duke of Luxembourg. However, Belgium rebelled in 1830 and broke away. In 1890 Queen Wilhelmina succeeded to the throne, causing Luxembourg to secede because, according to its constitution, a female could not inherit the throne. She abdicated in favour of her daughter Juliana after the Second World War; Queen Juliana abdicated in favour of her daughter Beatrix in 1980. Queen Beatrix remains head of state.

The Netherlands remained neutral during the First World War and was occupied by the Germans in the Second, when thousands of Dutch Jews and Roma gypsies were murdered in the holocaust. In 1948 the Netherlands formed the Benelux Custom Union with Belgium and Luxembourg, becoming a founder member of the EEC in 1957. In 1949 Netherlands became a founding member of NATO and most of the Dutch East Indies became independent as Indonesia, following four years of war: the remaining colonies achieved internal self-government in 1954, with Western New Guinea ceding to Indonesia in 1963. Netherlands became a founding member of the EEC in 1958. In 1975 Dutch Guinea became independent as Suriname. In 1994, following an inconclusive general election, a coalition government was formed under Wim Kok. It was dissolved in 1999 after the smallest party withdrew. The Netherlands achieved a double first when it legalized euthanasia in 2000 and homosexual marriage in 2001. In 2002 the government resigned following criticism of Dutch peacekeeping troops in Bosnian Srebenica, where a massacre of

Muslims occurred in 1995. The far-right politician Pim Fortuyn was also assassinated in Hilversum in 2002; following his death, his anti-immigration party joined a coalition government led by Christian Democrat Jan Peter Balkenende, who has been head of government since.

Netherlands is a highly populous and prosperous country and benefits from close ties with the rest of Europe. It is highly industrialized, the main areas of activity being petroleum, aircraft, food processing, chemicals, electronics and machinery. Agriculture is highly intensive and dairy farming is especially important.

NEW CALEDONIA

Location: 25 M
Capital: Nouméa
Area: 7,172sq m (18575km²)
Population: 216,494 July 2005
Main Languages: French
Main Religions: Roman Catholic 60%,
Protestant 30%
Currency: Comptoirs Français du
Pacifique franc
Climate: Tropical, moderated by
south-easterly trade winds

French Oceanian islands in the South Pacific, lying east of Australia, they consist of Nouvelle Calédonie or La Grande Terre (with the capital Nouméa), the Îles Loyauté, Île des Pins, Île Bélep and the Chesterfield and Huon Islands. New Caledonia is an ancient fragment of the vast continent of Gondwana, thought to have included South America, Africa, Arabia, Antarctica, India and Australia, which resulted from the break-up of Pangaea in Mesozoic times. Grande Terre is the only island that is mountainous, the

highest point being Mont Panié at 5,341ft (1628m). The islands have a unique flora and fauna all their own. The New Caledonia Barrier Reef is second only to that of Australia in size and is home to the endangered dugong or sea cow (*Dugong dugon*) and the Green Sea Turtle (*Chelonia mydas*).

The Lapita are thought to be among the first settlers of the islands, skilful navigators who arrived around 1500 BC, followed by Polynesians. In 1774 Grande Terre was sighted by the British explorer, Captain James Cook, who called it New Caledonia, Caledonia being the Roman name for northern Britain. Whalers and traders were attracted to the island, introducing alcohol and new diseases never before experienced by the natives. Some were later taken to

work as slaves in the sugar plantations of Fiji and Queenland, a loathsome trade that did not cease until the beginning of the 20th century. Christian missionaries arrived in the 19th century and eradicated many local customs, making the natives wear clothes.

The islands were annexed by the French in 1853 and served as a penal colony until 1904, becoming French overseas territory in 1946. Today the country is in the unique position of being somewhere between an independent country and a department of France, the inhabitants being French citizens with French passports. From the 1980s a growing separatist movement began to gain momentum, calling for an independent state of 'Kanaky', even though the indigenous Kanak population is now in the minority. However, the agitation subsided after more autonomy was given to the islands in 1988. Head of State since 1995 is the President of France, Jacques Chirac, represented by High

LEFT: Palm-fringed water near Poindimé.

BELOW: A Club Med resort near Nouméa.

Commissioner Michel Mathieu since July 2005. Head of government since 2004 is Marie-Noelle Thémёreau.

Products include nickel (the most important, since new investment in the industry has been received), copra, coffee, cotton, iron, manganese, cobalt and chromium. Only a small amount of land is suitable for cultivation and some food has to be imported. New Caledonia also receives substantial financial support from France.

NEW ZEALAND

Location:	25 N
Capital:	Wellington
Area:	104,454sq m (270536km²)
Population:	4,035,461 July 2005
Main Languages:	English, Maori
Main Religions:	Protestant 42%, Roman Catholic 15%
Currency:	1 New Zealand dollar = 100 cents
Climate:	Hot summer, mild winter (north); mild summer, cold winter, snow (south)

A country in the South Pacific, south-east of Australia, New Zealand consists of a group of islands, the most important being the North, South, Stewart and Chatham Islands. It also includes the smaller Antipodes, Auckland, Bounty, Campbell and Kemadec Islands. Dependencies include the Cook Islands, Niue and Tokelau, and there are claims to areas in Antarctica. New Zealand is rather isolated, being separated from Australia by 1,245 miles (2000km) of

the Tasman Sea. Its closest neighbours are New Caledonia and Tonga to the north. There are compensations, however, in that about 80 per cent of its flora only occurs in New Zealand. It is rich in bird life, including flightless birds such as the kiwi, some now extinct, and there were no non-marine mammals at all before man came to the islands. Reptilian life is present, the most remarkable being the tuatara – a unique creature living in the Cook Islands and

nowhere else. New Zealand's dramatic landscape has made it popular for television programmes and films, including the recent *Lord of the Rings* trilogy.

North Island has excellent harbours at Auckland and Wellington (the capital), unlike South Island, which has a largely unbroken coastline. Apart from the north-western peninsula ending at Cape Maria van Diemen, North Island is mountainous, having active volcanoes and the famous

ABOVE: Art Deco houses, Napier.

PAGE 286: One-Tree Hill, a Maori fortification, Auckland.

PAGE 287: Maori canoists, Waitangi.

district of Rotorua, with its geysers and hot springs. There are many lakes of which the largest is Taupo. South Island has the Southern Alps running its almost entire length and rising to Mount Cook (Aoraki) at 12,313ft (3753m).

Inhabited by Polynesian Maori tribes since about 800, the coasts of New Zealand were explored by Abel Tasman in 1642, who believed it to be land previously discovered off the coast of Chile. Captain Cook began extensive surveys of the islands from 1769,

with whaling and sealing expeditions and European colonization beginning soon afterwards. The Maoris thus came into contact with Europeans as early as the 1780s, when some Maoris were supplied with muskets. This upset the balance of power between the tribes, and led to the Musket Wars of 1815–40, when many thousands of Maoris were killed. The Maoris accepted British sovereignty in 1840 under the Treaty of Waitangi, which promised to recognize Maori land rights, though its real meaning

has since been disputed. In 1975 the Waitangi Tribunal was set up, given the task of hearing claims of violations of the treaty going back to the date of its signing. New Zealand had originally been administered as part of the Australian colony of New South Wales, becoming a colony in its own right in 1841. Thereafter, colonization was more rapid than anticipated and settlers soon outnumbered Maoris.

The first capital of New Zealand was present-day Russell, but shortly afterwards it

was moved to Auckland. However, there were worries that South Island would form a separate colony when gold was found in Central Otago in 1861 and the capital was moved to the more central location of Wellington. In the 1890s it was proposed that New Zealand should confederate with Australia, though this failed to materialize.

In 1893 New Zealand was the first country to enfranchize women. Dominion status was granted in 1907 and 120,000 or so New Zealand troops served in the First World War. During the Second World War, New Zealanders saw active service in North Africa and Italy and many were killed or wounded in action.

Head of state since 1952 is Queen Elizabeth II, represented in New Zealand by Governor-General Dame Silvia Cartwright since 2001. Jenny Shipley was New Zealand's first woman prime minister in 1997, followed in the office by Helen Clark in 1999.

New Zealand's soil is fertile, and forestry and agriculture are important, as is dairy farming and the production of beef, lamb and mutton and wool. The effect of Britain's entry into the EEC was to a large extent cushioned by the excellence of New Zealand's products, which it now exports across the world. It has gradually transformed itself from a largely agrarian society to one that is highly industrialized, with up-and-coming wine and film industries. Also exported is New Zealand's expertise in stock-breeding, animal foodstuffs and seeds. Tourism is a fast-growing sector.

NICARAGUA

Location:	7 J
Capital:	Managua
Area:	50,456sq m (130682km²)
Population:	5,465,100 July 2005
Main Languages:	Spanish
Main Religions:	Roman Catholic 87%
Currency:	1 córdoba =
	100 centavos
Climate:	Hot all year, cooler in
	mountains, rains Jun–Nov

The largest but least densely populated country in Central America, Nicaragua lies between Honduras and Costa Rica, with coastlines on both the Pacific Ocean and the Atlantic/Caribbean Sea. Crossing the country from north-west to south-east is the main cordillera of Central America. The Caribbean Mosquito Coast, with several large rivers running through it, extends up along the Honduran coast, and consists of rainforest and swampland. Near the lowland Pacific coast lie the two large lakes of Managua and Nicaragua, which are situated to the east of a highly unstable volcanic region, interspersed by fertile valleys. It is

an area susceptible to earthquakes, landslides and hurricanes.

Colonized by the Spanish in 1524, Nicaragua broke away from Spanish rule in 1821 and, after brief membership of the Central American Federation and separation from it in 1838, became a sovereign republic in 1854. In the mid-19th century, the country was ravaged by civil war and interference from Britain and the US. When gold was

discovered in California in the 1840s, the US planned to establish a trans-isthmian canal to link the Pacific Ocean with the Gulf of Mexico and Nicaragua has been of strategic interest to the US ever since. Close links with Britain were established during the presidency of José Santos Zemalya, but following his downfall in 1909 the country fell into a state of civil war. In 1912 US Marines were sent to protect the new pro-

American regime and the US gained exclusive rights to the canal in 1916. This sparked a guerilla war led by Augusto César Sandino. In 1933 the US withdrew, but not before setting up a National Guard under Anastasio Somoza to deal with the rebels; the result was that Sandino was assassinated the following year and Somoza became president in 1937, establishing a dynasty of right-wing dictators, supported by the US,

when non-Marxist liberals were rapidly eliminated from the new government, that had been established by the FSLN in 1979. The new left-wing Sandinista regime, led by Daniel Ortega, introduced wide-ranging social reforms, but a counter-revolutionary guerilla campaign waged by US-backed Contra rebels, after government aid had been given to leftist rebels in El Salvador, led to a ten-year civil war that devastated the country.

In the 1990 multi-party elections, the Sandinistas lost power to the National Opposition Union coalition government, led by Violeta Chamorro, though left-wing unions blocked many of her reforms. She was defeated by the Liberal, Arnaldo Aleman, in 1996, who was subsequently found guilty of corruption and imprisoned in 2003. Head of both state and government since 2002 is President Enrique Bolanos.

Impoverished by years of conflict and natural disaster, Nicaragua began to slowly rebuild its economy during the 1990s. However, it was knocked back by Hurricane Mitch in 1998 and is hampered by massive unemployment and a huge external debt, even though it was reduced under the Heavily Indebted Poor Countries (HIPC) initiative in 2004. Agriculture has long been the traditional occupation of the people and coffee, sugar, cotton and bananas are exported. There are reserves of copper, silver, and gold which remain largely unexploited

OPPOSITE: Market boys, Esteli.

ABOVE: Young men on a wooden jetty.

LEFT: A young Nicaraguan girl.

which was to dominate Nicaraguan politics until 1990.

The Sandinista National Liberation Front (FSLN) – named after Augusto César Sandino – led a revolt in 1978–79 against another Anastasio Somoza, the last of the Somoza family to inherit power, after he diverted international relief following the Managua earthquake of 1972. He was assassinated in exile in Paraguay in 1980,

NIGER

Location: 14 I
Capital: Niamey
Area: 489,401sq m (1266999km²)
Population: 11,665,937 July 2005
Main Languages: French
Main Religions: Muslim 97%
Currency: 1 CFA franc = 100 centimes
Climate: Very hot all year, rains Jul–Aug

A landlocked sub-Saharan country in West Africa, Niger is bordered by seven countries: Algeria, Libya, Chad, Nigeria, Benin, Burkina Faso and Mali. It takes its name fom the River Niger. Towards the centre of the country, near Agadez, lie the semi-volcanic Aïr Mountains. Elsewhere, the terrain is predominantly desert with sand dunes, with hillier areas in the north and savannah, suitable for livestock and limited agriculture, in the south. It is hot, dry and dusty.

The area that is now Niger was once occupied by powerful African empires, such

LEFT: Tuareg women in typical dress.

OPPOSITE LEFT: Tahoua was a recipient of the 1986 Aga Khan Award for architecture.

OPPOSITE RIGHT: Market at Boubon.

as those of Mali and Songhai, and several northern Nigerian Hausa states also laid claims. During recent centuries, however, Tuareg nomads from the north have pushed southwards, clashing with the Fulani Empire that had gained control of Hausa territory in the 18th century. In the 19th century, great travellers, such as Mungo Park and Heinrich Barth began to explore the area in their search for the River Niger's source.

In 1922 Niger became a colony within French West Africa, becoming independent of France in 1960, when it was run by a single-party civilian regime under Hamani Diori. However, devastating drought and allegations of corruption led to a military coup in 1974, when Colonel Seyni Kountché took control, ruling the country until his death in 1987. He was succeeded by his chief of staff, Ali Saibou, who was soon removed. A transitional government was installed in 1991 to pave the way for multi-party elections in 1993. Meanwhile, the Tuareg began to agitate for greater autonomy. Rivalries within the coalition government that was elected in the first fair and free elections in 1993 gave Colonel Ibrahim Baré Maïnassara a reason for overthrowing it in 1996, when he won a somewhat tarnished election. Unable to justify his coup and subsequent flawed elections, Baré ignored an international embargo against Libya, and looked to Libya for funds to help Niger's economy. This was followed by widespread violation of the civil liberties of opposition leaders, journalists and others by an unofficial militia composed of both police and military. In the meantime, however, a 1995 peace accord was signed that ended the Tuareg insurgency in the north. In 1999, in a coup led by Major Daouda Malam Wanké, Baré was overthrown. A new constitution restored the

semi-presidential system of government and led to the election of Tandja Mamadou as president and head of government in 1999. Hama Amadou shares some executive power with the president.

One of the poorest countries in the world, Niger's economy is based on subsistence agriculture, livestock and some of the largest uranium reserves in the world, much of it going to France. However, a drop in world demand for uranium, together with the periods of prolonged drought not uncommon in the Sahel, and a growing population, have taken their toll and Niger has to look to its camels, goats, cattle and sheep for survival. It has difficulty feeding its people, due to the shortage of arable land, and relies heavily on food aid and other donations from abroad. However, there are thought to be reserves of oil, gold, phosphates, iron and coal that it has insufficient funds to exploit, but they could very well be the country's future salvation

NIGERIA

Location:	13 J
Capital:	Abuja
Area:	356,669sq m (923773km²)
Population:	128,771,988 July 2005
Main Languages:	English
Main Religions:	Muslim 48%,
	Protestant 17%,
	Roman Catholic 17%
Currency:	1 naira = 100 kobo
Climate:	Hot all year, rains Mar–Nov
	(south), Apr–Sep (north),
	Jul–Oct (inland)

A country in West Africa on the Gulf of Guinea, Nigeria has land borders with Benin, Niger and Cameroon. The south is hot and steamy around the delta of the Niger, with its maze of creeks and mangrove swamps. Further inland is a belt of tropical forest that gives way to savannah, much of which has been cleared for farming. The terrain becomes increasingly treeless and arid towards the north, with the Sokoto plains in the north-west, while to the south-east the rugged Adamawa Highlands extend along Nigeria's border with Cameroon.

Some of the most beautiful examples of African sculpture have been excavated in the region, thought to date from the Nok civilization that began around 500 BC. In the Middle Ages it was the site of highly developed kingdoms, such as that of Kanem-Bornu and the Hausa. The Yoruba kingdom flourished in the 15th century, followed by the Songhai empire in the north, and the Portuguese established trade with Benin. Thereafter, Nigeria became an area of city states under the Igbo, Hausa and Fulani.

The area came under British influence during the 19th century, when the existing slave trade came to an end. By 1906 Britain had conquered all the country, dividing it into two protectorates, those of Northern and Southern Nigeria, the two merging into one in 1914. In 1954 Nigeria federated into three regions. Independence came in 1960 and the state became a federal republic within the Commonwealth. However, the tripartite arrangement was unable to contain rivalries, believed to be rooted in poverty, unemployment and competition for land, between the 250 or so ethnic, linguistic and religious groups that make up Nigeria – now Africa's most populous country. In 1966 a military coup by Igbo officers saw the start of a vicious civil war, when Biafra in the east attempted to split from the rest of the country; this was quelled in 1971. In 1976 the federal states were increased in number and reorganized to obliterate the former social divisions, though the imposition of Islamic law in several states in 2000 was to cause thousands of Christians to flee.

After several more military coups civilian rule returned briefly to Nigeria in

OPPOSITE: Dye pits at Kano, an ancient city state.

BELOW: Local boys at Kurmi market, Kano.

RIGHT: Overview of Kano from Dala Hill.

1979, followed by another military junta in 1983, which declared the presidential election, won by Chief Moshood Abiola in 1993, invalid. General Sanni Abacha continued in power, promising to restore civilian rule by 1998 but continuing an oppressive regime. Following the execution of the writer Ken Saro-Wiwa, with other activists in 1995, Nigeria was suspended from the Commonwealth until 1999, when the ethnic Yoruban and former military ruler, Olusegun Obasanjo, won Nigeria's first civilian-run presidential elections for nearly 20 years. He was re-elected in 2003.

Oil was discovered in the 1960s and 70s, when Nigeria emerged as one of the world's major producers. There have been undesirable side effects, however, and the trade in stolen oil has fuelled violence and revenues have been squandered through general corruption and mismanagement. Moreover, ethnic tensions have not yet been adequately diffused, neither has Nigeria's food production been able to keep pace with the rapid population growth, with the result that food must now be imported. However, Nigeria has economic potential in that manufacturing is diversifying into chemical and clothing production, steel milling and vehicle assembly. It is also a large producer of palm oil, peanuts, cocoa and rubber.

NORWAY

Location:	14 E
Capital:	Oslo
Area:	125,050sq m (323879km²)
Population:	4,593,041 July 2005
Main Languages:	Norwegian
Main Religions:	Lutheran 88%
Currency:	1 Norwegian krone = 100 øre
Climate:	Warm summer, cold winter, snow, more moderate on coast

A kingdom occupying the western part of the Scandinavian peninsula, Norway is bounded on the east by Sweden and by Finland and Russia to the north-east. The terrain is mountainous and glaciated, rising to a high point near the Sogne fjord, the largest and deepest in Norway. To the north-west lies the Norwegian Sea and North Atlantic Ocean, with the Barents Sea and the Arctic to the north and the North Sea further to the west, while Denmark lies across the Skagerrak to the south. Also belonging to Norway are the Arctic islands of Jan Mayen and Svalbard, while Bouvet Island in the

South Atlantic and Peter I Island in the South Pacific are dependencies. There are also claims to Dronning Maud Land in Antarctica. The *aurora borealis* or northern lights can be seen north of the Arctic Circle during the long, dark winter nights.

Norway was originally inhabited by Finns that were gradually ousted by Teutonic invaders. From the 8th to the 11th centuries Norway's great seafaring tradition began, when Vikings began to raid and settle many parts of Europe. Iceland, the Faröe Islands, Greenland and parts of Britain were colonized and attempts were made to settle parts of Newfoundland. Vikings founded several major Irish cities, including Dublin and Cork, and captured the English Anglo-Saxon city of York as well as Normandy in France.

Local chieftains ruled until the 9th century, when Norway was united under Harald Fairhair and a feudal system was introduced. Christianity was introduced by Olav II (St Olav) in the 11th century. Norway and Denmark were united by marriage in 1380, but the royal Norwegian line came to an end on the death of Queen Margarethe's son, aged 17, in 1387. Norway, by now the weaker nation, was united with Denmark and Sweden in 1397 and union with Denmark continued after Sweden became independent in 1523. The Reformed religion (Lutheranism) was introduced three years later.

In 1814 Norway was ceded to Sweden; as a compromise, Norway kept its own parliament but accepted the Swedish monarch as king. Discontent continued until 1905, when a plebiscite declared Norway independent; Prince Carl of Denmark was voted king of Norway as Haakon VII. In 1907, Norway was the first European country to enfranchise women. Despite military resistance, aided by British and French forces, Norway, a neutral country, was invaded by Germany during the Second World War. A puppet regime was established under Vidkun Quisling and king and government fled to Britain. After the war,

Labour governments introduced economic planning and price controls. In 1949 Norway became a founding member of NATO and joined the Nordic Council in 1952. In 1960 it was a co-founder of the European Free Trade Association (EFTA).

In 1981 Gro Harlem Brundtland (Labour) became Norway's first woman prime minister, and held the office for three terms. In 1991 Olav V, who had succeeded Haakon VII in 1957, was succeeded by his own son, Harald V. In 2000, Jens Stoltenberg became prime minister following the resignation of Kjell Magne Bondevik, who had been prime minister since 1997.

Norway has possibly the best quality of life in the world. It has a thriving economy, being richly endowed with petroleum and natural gas (discovered in the North Sea in the 1960s), as well as abundant hydro-electric power, forests, minerals and fish. It comes third in importance, after Saudi Arabia and Russia, as an exporter of oil; however, there are worries about the future when the oil and gas run out and Norway is working to contain its welfare system in the event of this happening. After a referendum in 1972 Norway refused to enter the EEC, but sought trade agreements instead; in a 1994 referendum it again refused to enter, though it does participate in the EU single market.

OPPOSITE: A Naeroyfjord mountain village.

ABOVE LEFT: Stave Church and folk museum, Oslo.

LEFT: View of Bergen and the harbour.

OMAN

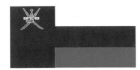

Location: 17 I
Capital: Muscat
Area: 119,499sq m (309502km²)
Population: 3,001,583 July 2005
Main Languages: Arabic
Main Religions: Muslim 88%
Currency: 1 Omani rial = 1000 baiza
Climate: Hot and humid all year, cooler in mountains, rain in winter (north)

A sultanate occupying the south-eastern corner of the Arabian peninsula, the country was known as Muscat and Oman until 1970. Oman borders the United Arab Emirates in the north-west, Saudi Arabia in the west and Yemen in the south-west. A vast desert, part of the 'Empty Quarter' of Rub' al Khali, covers central Oman, and there are mountains running along the north-western and south-eastern coasts. There is a fertile coastal plain bordering the Gulf of Oman to the west of Muscat, the capital, where the famous dates are grown. Also attached to Omani territory

is the enclave of Musandam, which is strategically located on the Gulf of Hormuz, a vital transit point for the world's crude oil; there is another enclave within the United Arab Emirates, known as Wadi-e-Madhah.

It is thought that Oman was the semi-legendary Magan, a thriving seafaring state at the time that the Sumerian civilization, which came to an end around 2000 BC, occupied Mesopotamia (Babylon). For that

reason, Oman, along with adjacent areas of the Middle East, is sometimes referred to as the 'cradle of civilization'. It became a satrap or province of the Persian Empire in around 563 BC, lasting until 632 AD, when Oman's Arab character was established. In 751 an imamate of Ibadhi Muslims was founded in Oman, imams being Muslim leaders that claim direct descent from the prophet Muhammad. The Ibadhis claimed

kinship with the Kharijites, who were among the first supporters of Ali, the fourth caliph of Islam; the Ibadhis practised a stricter form of Islam than the Shi'a or Sunni Muslims and survived in Oman until the 20th century.

The main port of Muscat, a trading centre for centuries, was captured by the Portuguese in 1508, who held it until it was taken by the Ottomans in 1659. The Turks were driven out in 1741, when the present

296

ruling dynasty was founded by Ahmed ibn Said. Oman grew to be a major power in the 19th century, with possessions in Baluchistan and Zanzibar that were eventually lost. In 1891 it became a British protectorate, which lasted until 1951.

The reactionary Sultan Said ibn Taimur was ousted by his son in 1970, who succeeded him as Sultan Qaboos ibn Said (1940–). He continues as head of both state and government to this day. With the help of Britain and Iran, he was able to suppress the activity of left-wing guerillas in the western mountainous province of Dhofur that borders southern Yemen. He also made peace with other Middle Eastern countries and set his country on the road to prosperity. In 2001 US forces, engaged in raids against Afghanistan and Osama bin Laden, utilized military bases in Oman. In 2003 universal suffrage for the over-21s was adopted and the lower house of the bicameral advisory council, established by the sultan in 1996, was freely elected, with two women gaining seats.

Today, oil, discovered in 1964, represents about 90 per cent of Oman's exports and there have been significant finds of natural gas. Other natural resources include copper, asbestos, limestone, marble, chromium and gypsum. Most of the oil

OPPOSITE: Oasis with date palms, Burami.

BELOW LEFT: Bedouin women and child in Burami, a town on Oman's border with the United Arab Emirates.

BELOW: Omani houses in Musandam, an Omani enclave on the Gulf of Hormuz.

revenue has gone into building up the infrastructure, as well as schools, hospitals and electricity- and water-generating plants. However, Oman is the only Middle Eastern oil-producer that is not a member of OPEC, though it has been a member of the World Trade Organization since 2000.

PAKISTAN

Location:	18 I
Capital:	Islamabad
Area:	307,293sq m (795889km²)
Population:	162,419,946 July 2005
Main Languages:	Urdu, Punjabi, Sindhi
Main Religions:	Muslim 97%
Currency:	1 Pakistan rupee = 100 paisas
Climate:	Summer very hot, winter warm, cold in mountains, rains Jun–Sep

An Islamic republic in south Asia, Pakistan lies to the north-west of India, with a coastline on the Arabian Sea. Besides India, Pakistan also has land borders with Iran, Afghanistan and China. It comprises the provinces of Punjab, Sind, Baluchistan and the North-West Frontier. There are mountain ranges to the north and west, while the remainder of the country is a fertile plain, watered by the Indus and its tributaries, with supplementary irrigation that was installed in the late 19th century that is one of the largest systems in the world.

LEFT: A Pakistani craftsman.

OPPOSITE LEFT: The Badshahi mosque, Lahore, Punjab.

OPPOSITE RIGHT: The North-West frontier, with the Khyber Pass.

The Indus Valley was the site of a sophisticated civilization that flourished between 2600 and 1760 BC. Its position, straddling the Greater Middle East and Asia, caused it to be conquered many times, by Aryans, Persians, Greeks, Kushans, White Huns and Scythians, among others. In the 8th century, the first Muslim conquests in Sind and Baluchistan were followed by an increasing influx of Muslims from the 10th century. In 1206 the Delhi Sultanate stretched from north-west Pakistan and across northern India. In the 16th century the Sikh religion developed in Punjab, and from time to time Lahore became the capital of the Mogul Empire, which succeeded the Sultanate and stretched across the northern half of the Indian peninsula. From 1843–49 the Sind and Punjab were annexed by Britain and incorporated into British India. In 1933 'Pakistan' was invented as the name of a future Muslim state, as Muslims in British India began to fear domination by the vast Hindu majority. Pakistan was thus formed in 1947, with Muhammad Ali Jinnah its first president, following the withdrawal of the British from India; this is when the dispute over Kashmir began.

Pakistan originally comprised two regions to the east and west of India, where the population was predominantly Muslim, separated from each other by 1,000 miles of

Indian territory. The drawing of the frontiers resulted in violent religious disruptions, as Muslims, Hindus and Sikhs fled from India to Pakistan and vice versa, with considerable loss of life. But the new country eventually settled down and in 1956 became an independent republic within the Commonwealth. Military rule was imposed from 1958 by General Ayub Khan. By 1970, increasing divergences between the eastern and western parts of the country led to civil war, with the result that East Pakistan (the province lying east of West Bengal, India), with the help of India, became the independent state of Bangladesh in 1971. West Pakistan became the Pakistan that exists today, registering its protest by withdrawing from the Commonwealth.

Power was transferred from the military regime to Zulfiqar Ali Bhutto, who became president of Pakistan following the secession of East Pakistan (now Bangladesh). Under a new constitution, he became prime minister a few years later, but was ousted in a military coup in 1977. The following year he was sentenced to death for alleged conspiracy to murder a political opponent, and despite international pleas for clemency, was hanged. Under the presidency of General Zia ul-Haq elections were postponed and martial law was declared, that was not lifted until 1985. In 1980 three million refugees fled to the North-West Frontier and Baluchistan when the Soviets invaded Afghanistan. The following year there were moves towards the restoration of democracy and the case for Islamization moved forward a pace: Sharia law was adopted in 1988 and the charging of interest on loans was banned in 2001.

The year 1986 saw the emergence of Bhutto's daughter, Benazir, who began to agitate for free elections. In 1988 she became prime minister following the death of General Zia in an air crash. In 1989 Pakistan rejoined the Commonwealth and tensions with India were increased by outbreaks of civil war in Kashmir – the subject of a dispute between the two since 1947. India agreed to peace talks with Kashmir in 1999 only for conflict to erupt once more in 2002.

In 1990 Benazir Bhutto was dismissed following allegations of nepotism and corruption. She was re-elected in 1993 only to be dismissed again three years later, when charges of corruption resurfaced; in 1998 both she and her husband were formally charged, fined and imprisoned. That year Rafiq Tarar became president and nuclear testing began in response to India's nuclear programme, to the consternation of the world. Sanctions were imposed by the US, though tensions have recently begun to lessen. There was a military coup when Prime Minister Nawaz Sharif tried to sack the army's chief of staff, General Pervez Musharraf, with the result that Musharraf assumed full power himself and declared a state of emergency. In 2000 India accused Pakistan of involvement in the hijacking of an Indian airliner by Kashmiri militants and Sharif was subsequently found guilty of hijacking and terrorism. He was subsequently freed and fled the country.

Musharraf supported the US in the war against al-Qaeda and the Taliban in Afghanistan in 2001. His presidency was extended by four years in a referendum the following year. In 2004 Shaukat Aziz became prime minister.

Pakistan has been impoverished by decades of political strife, together with ongoing disputes with India and lack of foreign investment. However, substantial economic reforms have been made since 2000, bolstered by generous assistance from abroad. Recently there have been signs of improvement, and exports of rice, textiles, leather and sports goods, chemicals, carpets and rugs have been expanding.

PALAU

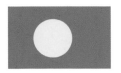

Location:	22 K
Capital:	Koror
Area:	188sq m (487km²)
Population:	20,303 July 2005
Main Languages:	English, Palauan
Main Religions:	Roman Catholic
Currency:	US dollar
Climate:	Hot and humid

Palau (or Belau) consists of a group of 300 or so mostly uninhabited islands and atolls, lying to the west of the Caroline chain of the western Pacific Ocean, south-east of the Philippines. The terrain varies from one island to another, from the mountainous main island of Babelthuap, to low coral atolls fringed by large barrier reefs and the famous uninhabited rock islands. With Babelthuap, the most important islands are Angaur, Peleliu (where a battle was fought in the Second World War), and Koror, where two-thirds of the people live.

In around 1000 BC, Micronesians, and possibly Malayans, settled the islands. In 1543 they were visited by the Spanish navigator Ruy López de Villalobos and later by the British in the 18th century. They were then colonized by Spain, which sold the islands to Germany in 1899.

The islands were seized by Japan, following the outbreak of the First World War, and Japan was given a mandate to administer them by the League of Nations in 1920. In 1944, after the Japanese had been removed, the islands were controlled by the US as part of the Trust Territory of the Pacific Islands. In 1981, having decided not to join the Federated States of Micronesia, the islands obtained autonomy as the Republic of Palau, under a constitution which prohibited the entry, storage or disposal of nuclear or biological weapons.

There followed a long period of transition, during which time two presidents met violent deaths. Full independence was achieved in 1994 and membership of the UN was granted. That year, after 30 years of American trusteeship, a Compact of Free Association with the US at last came into force. This gave the US the right to maintain military facilities on the islands in return for economic aid. The issue had been hotly debated for many years, as many thought it gave the US too much power. The US had already built a submarine base on Guam, the southernmost of the Mariana Islands, and particularly wanted further control of the Mariana Trench for submarine testing, on account of its great depth. Tommy Esang Remengasau became president in 2001, having previosly served as vice-president. He is also head of government.

The economy of Palau is based on tourism, subsistence agriculture and fishing, though overfishing is a concern. It relies heavily on financial help from the US. Natural resources are minerals, especially gold, which are also present in the sea-bed, and forests. An air service to other parts of the Pacific began operations in 2004 but ceased the same year. It has not yet restarted.

BELOW: Palm trees and tropical skies on Palau.

PALESTINE

Location: 15 H
Area (West Bank) 2,264sq m (5860km2)
Area (Gaza Strip) 139sq m (360km²)
Population:
West Bank 2,385,615 July 2005
Gaza Strip 1,376,289 July 2005
Main Languages: Arabic
Main Religions: Muslim 99%
Currency: 1 shekel = 100 agorot
Climate: Hot, dry, summer; mild
winter

Historically, Palestine is the name of a region in south-west Asia, situated between the Mediterranean and the depression of the River Jordan and the Dead Sea, to the north-west of the Arabian peninsula. It is also known as the Holy Land, being of religious significance to Jews, Christians and Arabs.

In Biblical times Palestine comprised the kingdoms of Israel and Judah. Its position on the main route connecting Egypt with the valley of the

Birzeit village on the West Bank.

Euphrates in Asia Minor led to its control at various times by Egypt, Assyria, Babylonia, Persia, Macedonia, the Ptolemys, the Seleucids and Rome. It was part of the Roman Empire at the time of Christ and later belonged to the Byzantine Empire before it was conquered by the Arabs in 636. The Crusaders occupied Jerusalem for almost 100 years from 1099, when it came under the rule of the Mamelukes. From 1516 to the end of the First World War it was part of the Ottoman Empire, after which it came into British hands, when a military administration was

ABOVE: Children of the West Bank.

OPPOSITE: A Palestinian couple, West Bank.

installed, followed by civilian government. In 1922 Britain received a League of Nation mandate to administer Palestine, which included the historical Palestine and what is now Jordan. Thousands of Jewish immigrants were allowed to enter, who began to develop agriculture and industry. The Arabs were dismayed, however, at seeing land that had been theirs since the Arab conquest settled by strangers. In 1948 the state of Israel was established in what had traditionally been Palestine; however, the name Palestine continued to be used by Palestinian Arabs in the context of their struggle for territorial and political rights that exists to this day, the conflict characterized by violence on both sides and terrorism at home and abroad.

There followed a series of Arab-Israeli Wars and the Palestinians developed liberation forces to continue their resistance. In 1974 the Palestinian Liberation Organization (PLO) was formed, led by Yasser Arafat, which was recognized as the Palestinian Authority by the Arab League. The year 1987 saw the first intifada against the Israeli occupation.

In 1993 the Israeli prime minister, Yitzhak Rabin, with Shimon Peres, negotiated a Declaration of Principles (DOP) with Yasser Arafat and the PLO, whereby limited Palestinian autonomy would be granted in the Gaza Strip and West Bank for a transitional period not exceeding five years; Yasser Arafat became head of the autonomous Palestinian Authority the following year.

The signing of the DOP resulted in the award of a Nobel Peace Prize, shared by all three negotiators. New negotiations began in 1999, but were derailed by a second intifada in 2000. This led to the drawing up of a 'road map' by the American president, George Bush, in 2002, whereby Israeli-Palestinian conflict would be resolved once and for all and a two-state system established.

Yasser Arafat died in 2004 and was succeeded as leader by Mahmud Abbas, since when there have been hopeful signs that the matter will finally rbe esolved. In August 2005, Israeli settlements in Palestinian territory in Gaza and the West Bank were officially disbanded. Despite compensation from the Israeli government, to enable the Israeli settlers to establish new homes elsewhere, many resisted and were forced to leave. Some see the withdrawal as a necessary step in the road map to peace, while others view it as a strategy to increase Israel's hold over the West Bank and East Jerusalem.

The West Bank, the larger of the two areas under the Palestine Authority, has seen a general decline in economic growth since the second intifada began in 2000, largely due to border closures, which disrupted movement of the Palestinian labour force working in areas of Israeli settlement. Further Israeli military action in 2001 and 2002 caused destruction of capital plant, business closures and general disruption of the Palestinian administration. However, international aid in 2004 prevented the total collapse of the economy, at least for the time being .

PANAMA

Location:	7 J
Capital:	Panama City
Area:	29,761sq m (77081km²)
Population:	3,039,150 July 2005
Main Languages:	Spanish
Main Religions:	Roman Catholic 85%, Protestant 5%
Currency:	1 balboa = 100 centésimos
Climate:	Hot all year, cooler in hills, rains May/Dec

A country in Central America, between Colombia and Costa Rica, Panama occupies a strategic position at the eastern end of an isthmus that connects North and South America. The country is traversed by a chain of mountains running parallel to the coastal plains. Panama has more rainforest than anywhere else in the West, outside the Amazon basin, and its jungle is home to numerous tropical plants, animals and birds.

Colonized by Spain in the early 16th century, Panama gained freedom from Spanish control in 1821, when it joined the confederacy of Gran Colombia, which

included Colombia, Venezuela, Ecuador, Bolivia and Peru, returning to Colombia when the confederacy came to an end. Ferdinand de Lesseps, who also built the Suez Canal, began to build the Panama Canal in 1869, but it was left to the US Army Corps of Engineers to finish the job, when sickness and financial problems led to the project's collapse. Panama gained full independence in 1903, encouraged by the US, which was interested in obtaining the

Canal Zone. The Panama Canal was constructed at the narrowest part of the Darién isthmus to connect the Pacific and Atlantic Oceans. It was followed by the leasing of the Canal Zone surrounding it to the US in perpetuity, though it was handed back to Panama in 1979. In 1977 an agreement was signed to hand over the canal to Panama, with affect from 1999. This was done, together with the remaining US military bases, the US guaranteeing its

protection together with an annual payment.

A military junta under General Omar Torrijos Herrera, leader of the National Guard, ruled Panama from 1968, when a costly programme of economic reform was initiated. He was followed by General Manuel Noriega from 1983, who ignored calls for his removal, despite the suspension of US military and economic aid. In 1988, charged with drug-smuggling by the US, Noriega declared a state of emergency after

the failure of a coup, announcing a state of war with the US the following year. The US invaded Panama under Operation Just Cause, when Noriega was deposed, though at a cost of 4,000 Panamanian lives. Guillermo Endara was installed as president, abolishing the military in 1990 and creating the Panamanian Public Forces. In 1992 Noriega was found guilty of drug charges and received a 40-year prison sentence. In 1994 the army was abolished and in 1999 Mireya Moscoso, widow of a former president, became Panama's first female head of state. In 2000 a commission was set up to discover what had happened to the 150 people who had disappeared during the military regime. Head of state and government since 2004 is President Martin Torrijos, son of Omar Torrijos, the former military leader.

Panama has an economy based on the

OPPOSITE: A Cunard cruise ship on the Panama Canal.

LEFT: A Cuna Indian woman, surrounded by the colourful needlework typical of the San Blas Islands.

BELOW: The Pedro Miguel locks on the Panama Canal.

dollar that rests squarely on its well-developed service sector, though some agricultural products are exported. Services include operating the Panama Canal and the Colón Free Zone, banking, insurance, container ports and tourism. However, a few families of European descent control most of the country's wealth and much of the population still lives below the poverty line.

PAPUA NEW GUINEA

Location: 23 K
Capital: Port Moresby
Area: 178,703sq m (462840km²)
Population: 5,545,268 July 2005
Main Languages: English
Main Religions: Protestant 58%,
 Roman Catholic 32%
Currency: 1 kina = 100 toea
Climate: Hot all year

A country in Oceania in the south-western Pacific, Papua New Guinea comprises the eastern half of the island of New Guinea, together with the neighbouring islands of the Bismarck Archipelago, the North Solomons (Bougainville), the Trobriand and D'Entrecasteaux Islands and the Louisiade archipelago. The western half of the island is the Indonesian province of Irian Jaya. Papua New Guinea is situated north-east of Australia, of which it is a geological extension, which indicates that the two were once attached. Most of the terrain is mountainous, with a central range that rises in the east to Mount Wilhelm at

14,790ft (4508m). There are frequent earthquakes, landslides and tsunamis. Dense rainforest covers the lowland coastal areas, and there is a large area of swamp on the south-western coast. The country is famous for the diversity and abundance of its flora and fauna.

Archeological evidence indicates that people, possibly from South-East Asia, arrived on New Guinea some 60,000 years

LEFT: Papuan dancers in ceremonial dress.

OPPOSITE LEFT: The plumed bird of paradise, a native of Papua New Guinea.

OPPOSITE RIGHT: Tapping for rubber in the central district.

ago, with later arrivals developing a productive agricultural system. The first Europeans to see the island were Portuguese and Spanish navigators exploring the area in the early 16th century. However, little was known of the inhabitants until the 19th century, when an anthropologist spent several years living among the tribes and described their way of life. South-eastern New Guinea was annexed by Queensland in 1883. The following year the southern coast and the adjacent islands became a British protectorate as British New Guinea, which was annexed by Britain in 1888. It was transferred to the Commonwealth of Australia in 1901 and renamed the Territory of Papua in 1906.

North-eastern New Guinea was annexed by Germany in 1884, when it was administered by a trading company, coming under direct German control in 1899, when the area became known as German New Guinea. It was occupied by Australia in 1914 and was administered by Australia under a mandate from the League of Nations from 1921–42. It was captured by the Japanese from 1942–45, becoming a Trust Territory of Australia in 1946. In 1949 the whole of

eastern New Guinea was combined to form the Trust Territory of Papua New Guinea; the name was changed to Papua New Guinea in 1975.

The first government of Papua New Guinea was headed by Michael Somare, who led the country to self-government, followed by independence within the Commonwealth in 1975. However, from 1980 frequent changes of leadership and government coalitions led to loss of confidence in the political system. In 1989 the operation of the Panguna copper mine, on the island of Bougainville, initially brought land rights and environmental issues to the fore, but escalated into a secessionist civil war claiming 20,000 lives and lasting for nine years. Under the watchful eye of the UN, the government is now looking towards a

referendum, when the question of independence will be resolved. Head of state since 1952 is Queen Elizabeth II, represented locally by Governor-General Sir Paulias Matane. The last general election was held in 2002 when Sir Michael Somare, who was the first to hold the office following independence, was elected prime minister.

Papua New Guinea has a rich supply of natural resources, though their exploitation is hampered by a rugged terrain and lack of infrastructure. Oil, copper and gold account for nearly three-quarters of export revenue and fishing, rubber and timber are also important. In 1997, droughts devastated Papua New Guinea's coffee, cocoa and coconut production. However, recovery has been made, helped by aid from Australia and elsewhere.

PARAGUAY

Location:	9 M
Capital:	Asunción
Area:	157,042sq m (406749km²)
Population:	6,347,884 July 2005
Main Languages:	Spanish
Main Religions:	Roman Catholic 96%
Currency:	1 guaraní =
	100 céntimos
Climate:	Hot summer; wet, mild
	winter

An inland republic of South America, Paraguay is bounded by Bolivia to the north-west, Brazil to the north-east, and Argentina to the south and south-west. The country lies to either side of the River Paraguay, with the River Paraná dividing Paraguay from Argentina in the south-east. The Paraná's impressive Itaipú Dam, which it shares with Brazil, is the largest hydro-electric plant in the world. The Gran Chaco is a flat, grassy plain that extends into Argentina, with scrubland to the north-east. In fact there is not much high ground in Paraguay, the highest point being Cerro Pero at 2,760ft (842m), the remainder being marshy lowland and forest. Most of the population is concentrated in the south.

The indigenous people of Paraguay were the Guaraní. The country was discovered by Sebastian Cabot in 1526 and Asunción, the capital, was founded by Spanish settlers ten years later. From around 1600, most of the country was administered as a virtual theocratic state by the Jesuits (who had come as missionaries to bring Christianity to the Guaraní), until their expulsion in 1767. Paraguay was subject to the viceroyalty of Peru until 1776, when it came under the viceroyalty of Buenos Aires, becoming independent from Spain in 1811.

In 1865 Paraguay was involved in the damaging five-year War of the Triple Alliance, with Brazil, Argentina and Uraguay, when two-thirds of Paraguay's male population and much of its territory were lost. This was followed by a period of stagnation that lasted for half a century, characterized by revolutions and border disputes with Bolivia, which was attempting to gain a port on the Paraguay river. This eventually escalated into the Chaco War of 1932–35. Intervention by the US and five South American republics eventually effected a peace treaty and settlement in 1938, when territory was won back from

Bolivia. The year 1940 saw the beginning of a period of political instability that ended in a military coup in 1954, when General Alfredo Stroessner seized power. He was ousted in another coup in 1989 by General Andrés Rodrigues, who was elected president, since when elections have been relatively regular and free. However, despite a new constitution in 1992, a fully democratic system is slow to emerge and widespread corruption still exists. The present head of both state and goverment is President Nicanor Duarte Frutos since 2003.

Paraguay's most important product is hydro-electricity, other natural resources being iron ore, manganese and limestone. The economy is particularly dependent on Brazil and neighbouring countries, to whom

OPPOSITE: The Palacio de Gobierno, Asunción.

LEFT: An Amerindian in a feathered headdress, Asunción.

BELOW: The Paraná river.

Paraguay re-exports imported consumer goods, such as electronics and television sets; timber, coffee and beef are also exported. The remainder of the population relies on subsistence agriculture and thousands of informal small businesses, such as street vending, for example.

PERU

Location:	8 L
Capital:	Lima
Area:	496,225sq m (1285223km²)
Population:	27,925,628 July 2005
Main Languages:	Spanish, Quechua
Main Religions:	Roman Catholic 92%
Currency:	1 nuevo sol = 100 céntimos
Climate:	Hot on coast, cooler in mountains, hot and rainy in east

A South American republic, bordering the Pacific Ocean and lying wholly within the Tropics of Cancer and Capricorn, Peru has land borders with Ecuador, Colombia, Brazil, Bolivia and Chile. It can be divided from west to east into a narrow strip of desert along the Pacific coast; three ranges of the Andes, the Occidental, Central and Oriental Cordilleras, that peak at Mount Huascarán at 22,205ft (6770m) in the Occidental; and the forested eastern slopes of the Andes, where the headstreams of the Amazon rise at Nevado Mismi and descend to the jungle of the Amazon basin. Between

the western and eastern Andes lies the *altiplano* (high plain), the site of many lakes, including Titicaca, the highest navigable lake in the world, that spans Peru's border with Bolivia.

Peru has a remarkable early history stretching back over 10,000 years. It includes several pre-Inca civilizations, besides that of the Inca itself, which has left behind an impressive legacy at Machu Picchu and Cuzco. Due to civil war among the Inca, Francisco Pizarro was able to seize most of the country before he was assassinated in 1541, by which time Spanish rule had been firmly established and a steady supply of silver and gold was going to Spain. A revolt by Tupac Amaru indians came to nothing in 1780 and while there were successful rebellions against Spanish rule in other parts of South America, Peru was the last to gain independence in 1824, helped by the Argentine army under José de San Martín and by Simón Bolívar. Since then, the main events in Peruvian history are the abortive union with Bolivia in 1836–39, the naval war against Spain (1864–66), the War of the Pacific over the nitrate fields of the Atacama Desert, in which Peru was defeated and lost three provinces to Chile, one of which was returned to Peru in 1929.

all the guerillas in the process. An economic slump in the late 1990s, together with Fujimori's increasingly dictatorial stance, caused general dissatisfaction with the regime and although he was re-elected for a third time in 2000, scandals and international pressure brought an end to his presidency later that year, when a caretaker government was installed. Alejandro Toledo Manrique was elected in 2001 and his presidency has also been tarnished by allegations of corruption. The president of Peru is also head of government.

Peru has one of the better-managed economies of South America, though poverty and unemployment persist, but inflation is down and foreign debt has been reduced since 1990. Sugar, cotton and coffee are major exports and rice, potatoes, beans and maize are also important, as is timber and rubber. Beef is produced and hides are processed and there is a luxury trade in llama and alpaca wools and that of the rarer vicuna. Coca is also produced, used in the production of cocaine. Peru is a leading fishing nation, though most of the catch is converted to fishmeal. Copper is in good supply, as is silver, gold, iron, lead and zinc, and there are onshore as well as offshore supplies of oil and natural gas. There is much to attract tourists to Peru, even if the major Inca sites are discounted.

OPPOSITE LEFT: A fiesta with a procession of the Virgen del Carmen, Cuzco.

OPPOSITE RIGHT: Plaza de Armas, Cuzco.

ABOVE LEFT: The Inca ruins of Machu Picchu.

This was followed by boundary disputes with Bolivia in 1902, with Colombia in 1927 and with Ecuador in 1942, which was to re-emerge in 1981.

A bloodless military coup in 1968 led to the expropriation of American oil and mining interests, and vast estates, ranches and sugar plantations were turned into co-operatives. Military rule that began in 1968 ended with the reinstatement of Fernando Belaunde Terry in 1980, previously ousted in a coup. The election of Alberto Fujimori as president in 1990 heralded a dramatic improvement in the economy, together with more success in curtailing the Shining Path and Tupac Amaru Revolutionary Movement (MRTA), whose activities had claimed more than 30,000 lives. In 1996 MRTA guerillas captured the Japanese embassy in Lima, laying seige to it for four months. It ended when the army stormed the embassy, killing

PHILIPPINES

Location: 22 J
Capital: Manila
Area: 115,300sq m (298627km²)
Population: 87,857,473 July 2005
Main Languages: Filipino, English
Main Religions: Roman Catholic 84%,
Aglipayan 6%, Muslim 4%,
Protestant 4%
Currency: 1 peso = 100 centavos
Climate: Hot summer, dry winter,
rains Jul–Oct

A country in South-East Asia, the Philippines consist of an archipelago of over 7,000 islands, separated from the mainland by the South China Sea. It is bordered to the east by the Philippine Sea/Pacific Ocean and to the south by the Celebes Sea, with the Sulu Sea separating the Sulu Archipelago from Palawan to the west. Directly to the north lies Taiwan, with the island of Borneo to the south-west. Between them, the largest islands of Luzon and Mindaneo occupy over two-thirds of the total area. Most of the islands are mountainous, with coastal lowlands and forested plateaux, and there are many active volcanoes, including those of Mayon and Taal, Mount Apo and Mount Pinatubo, which erupted violently in 1991; typhoons are also common.

The islands were inhabited for thousands of years, first by aboriginal tribes and later by migrants from China, before the first Europeans arrived. Islam was introduced in the 14th century. Ferdinand Magellan, together with Portuguese and Spanish explorers, visited the islands in 1521 and Spanish rule was established from 1565, during the reign of Philip II, in whose honour the islands were named. As well as colonization, the aim of Spain was to bring Catholicism to the islands and to look for gold and spices. However, Spanish rule was harsh and led to several revolts by the native people. The government quelled the uprisings, using the Roman military strategy known as 'Divide and Rule', in which one tribe was played off against the other. In the 19th century, José Rizal, a celebrated intellectual, founded the Propaganda Movement to press for civil rights and later for independence; he was executed in 1896. The Philippine Revolution followed, which almost succeeded in ousting Spain.

The Philippines were ceded to the US following the Spanish-American War in 1898. The Commonwealth of the Philippines

RIGHT: The Basilica of the Black Nazarene, Manila.

OPPOSITE LEFT: Nayong Filipino dancers, Manila.

OPPOSITE RIGHT: The fabulous mountain rice terraces of Banaux.

was established in 1935, with Manuel Luis Quezon its first president, with full independence as a republic coming in 1946. During the Second World War the Japanese overcame Filipino and American troops under General MacArthur and occupied the islands from 1942–45. In 1947 the US was granted a lease on several military bases on the islands. There was a troubled period from 1945, when Communist activity was strong, and a Muslim movement was also active in the 1970s, seeking to establish Mindanao, the Sulu Archipelago and Palawan as an independent Muslim state; Muslim separatists continue to be active.

From 1965 the country was under the increasingly dictatorial rule of President Ferdinand Marcos (1917–89), who was driven from power in 1986, when a popular rebellion forced him into exile. Marcos was replaced by Corazón (Cory) Aquino, the widow of the opposition leader, Benigno Aquino, who was assassinated in 1983. She was president until 1992, though her presidency was blighted by several coups, preventing a full return to political stability. She was followed by Fidel Ramos, when better progress was made. The last American military base on the islands was closed in 1992. In 1996 an agreement with the Moro National Liberation Front ended many years of rebellion on Mindanao and led to the creation of a Muslim state: however, the fragile ceasefire crumbled two years later. Joseph Estrada became president in 1998, but was succeeded by his vice-president, Gloria Macapagal-Arroyo in 2001, after he was ousted in a popular rising. She was re-elected in 2004. Besides being head of state, the president is also the head of government.

In 1998 the economy of the Philippines suffered slightly as a result of the Asian financial crisis and poor weather conditions, particularly agriculture (especially rice and bananas), light industry and service industries, though it had begun to rally by 2000. Efforts are also being made to improve the infrastructure and overhaul the tax system.

PITCAIRN ISLANDS

Location: 4 M
Capital: Adamstown
Area: 1.75sq m (4.6km²)
Population: 46 July 2005
Main Languages: English
Main Religions: Seventh-Day Adventist
Currency: NZ dollar
Climate: Tropical, hot, humid,
moderated by south-east
trade winds.
Rains Nov–Mar

A dependency of Britain, the Pitcairns are a group of islands in the South Pacific, east of French Polynesia. They lie about midway between Peru and New Zealand. The colony's only settlement is at Adamstown, on Pitcairn Island, which is volcanic and the chief island of the group.

The original settlers of the islands were Polynesians, who are thought to have lived there for several centuries before they died out in around the 15th century. The islands were uninhabited when they were rediscovered by the Spanish explorer, Pedro Fernandez de Quiros, in 1606, and remained so until 1767, when a British ship visited them and the largest was named after one of the crew. In 1790, nine mutineers from HMS *Bounty*, accompanied by Tahitians, settled Pitcairn Island and set fire to the *Bounty*, the remains of which can be seen at the bottom of Bounty Bay. The presence of the mutineers did not come to light until 1808. In the meantime, they survived on fishing and farming, fighting among themselves, and occasionally resorting to murder before tensions were eventually resolved. Pitcairn became a British colony

in 1838. By the middle of the century the community was beginning to outgrow the island. Queen Victoria offered it Norfolk Island and all of the islanders set sail in the *Morayshire* in 1856, though some inevitably returned. The nearby coral island of Henderson (where rare species are to be found), the coral atolls of Dulcie and Oeno, and Sandy, a mere sandbar, were annexed and attached to Pitcairn Island in 1902, but are not habitable. Since reaching a peak of 233 in 1937, much of the population has emigrated, mainly to New Zealand, leaving only about 46 on the island. Chief of state since 1952 is Queen Elizabeth II, represented from 2001 by a non-resident governor, Richard Fell, who is UK High Commissioner to New Zealand. He is also head of government.

It is thought that there has long been sexual abuse of girls as young as 10 on Pitcairn. In 2004 seven men on the island, and six now abroad, were charged with sexual offences, including rape. Six men were eventually convicted, including Pitcairn's mayor. He was dismissed after refusing to resign from office.

This tiny economy has only a dozen or so able-bodied men remaining, and the community exists on subsistence farming (fruit and vegetables and sugar cane) and fishing. Barter is practised and handicrafts, postage stamps and honey are sold to passing ships. There are no paved roads, no airstrip and no natural harbour. Supplies, therefore, have to be loaded from ships onto smaller boats before they can be rowed ashore.

OPPOSITE LEFT: A Pitcairn islander with a handmade model of the Bounty.

OPPOSITE RIGHT: Islanders in a longboat.

BELOW: The north-eastern side of Pitcairn Island.

POLAND

Location: 14 F
Capital: Warsaw
Area: 120,728sq m (312685km²)
Population: 38,635,144 July 2005
Main Languages: Polish
Main Religions: Roman Catholic 94%
Currency: 1 zloty = 100 groszy
Climate: Warm summer, cold
                  winter, snow in mountains

A country in central Europe, with a coastline on the Baltic Sea in the north, Poland is bounded to the west by Germany, to the south by the Czech and Slovak Republics, to the east by Ukraine and Belarus, and by Lithuania and the Russian oblast of Kaliningrad to the north. For the most part undulating, Poland is part of the great Northern European Plain, though it rises towards the south through hills that culminate in the Sudeten and Carpathian mountains to form the southern frontier. It also has thousands of lakes, mostly in the north-east of the country,

Poland was first united as a nation over 1,000 years ago under the Piast dynasty. In 1025 Boleslaw I became the first king of Poland. By the 12th century the country had fragmented into several smaller states that were ravaged by Mongols of the Golden Horde. In 1329 Wladyslaw I became king, but his dynasty eventually collapsed under the might of the Teutonic Knights. By the 16th century, Poland had risen to a position of dominance in Europe under the Jagiellonian dynasty, when it united with Lithuania. In 1791 Poland's first written constitution was formulated. Thereafter, it suffered badly from Swedish invasion and the rise of Russian, Prussian and Austrian power; it was partitioned between the three in the late 18th century. Poles resented their diminishing freedoms, which they had long held dear, and there were several Polish uprisings. After the Napoleonic Wars, the Duchy of Warsaw emerged as a reconstituted state. It was ruled by the tsars until it was eventually annexed by Russia.

Poland regained power as a republic after the First World War. In the Polish-Soviet War of 1919 Poland successfully defended its independence. Its invasion by Germany and the Soviet Union in 1939 precipitated the Second World War, when Polish territory was split between the two.

RIGHT: Wawel Castle Cathedral, Krakow.

OPPOSITE LEFT: The Sigismund III Vasa column with the Royal Palace, Warsaw.

OPPOSITE RIGHT: The Long Market and Neptune fountain. Gdánsk.

since 2004 is Prime Minister Marek Belka.

Before the Second World War, Poland was predominantly an agricultural economy, but industry was greatly expanded under Communism. Since its return to democracy, Poland has had many problems coping with its transition to a market economy, and has suffered from a low GDP growth and high unemployment. Since it joined the EU in 2004, however, burgeoning exports to the rest of Europe have seen a surge in growth and farmers are already beginning to reap the benefits of EU agricultural subsidies. Many of Poland's young people now work in other EU countries, such as Ireland, attracted by the higher wages and standard of living. Natural resources are coal, lignite, sulphur, copper, natural gas, silver, lead, salt, amber and arable land. Poland also has nearly 100,000 scientists working in the country today.

Poland suffered more then most in the war; over 6 million perished, half of them Polish Jews. The country also emerged a fifth smaller, due to the shifting of the borders, and led to the migration of many millions more. It eventually became a satellite Communist state under Soviet domination, though with a relatively tolerant and progressive government.

In the 1980s, striking dockers in the Gdánsk shipyards formed the independent trade union movement, Solidarity, which eventually became a political force under Lech Walesa. It was instrumental in eroding Communism in Poland and contributed to its collapse all over the Eastern bloc. In 1989 Solidarity was elected and Walesa became president the following year. In 1996 Poland joined the Organization for Economic Co-operation and Development (OECD), and a new democratic constitution was drafted the following year. In 1999 Poland became a part of NATO, along with Hungary and the Czech Republic. In 2001 Solidarity suffered a major defeat, when it failed to return a single deputy to the lower house which, as a trade union, caused it to reconsider its political role. Head of state since 1995 is President Aleksander Kwásniewski, while head of government

PORTUGAL

Location: 12 H
Capital: Lisbon
Area: 35,516sq m (91986km²)
Population: 10,566,212 July 2005
Main Languages: Portuguese
Main Religions: Roman Catholic 95%
Currency: euro
Climate: Hot summer, mild winter

A country that occupies the western part of the Iberian peninsula in south-west Europe, Portugal borders the Atlantic Ocean to the west and south, and Spain to the east and north. It also includes two Atlantic archipelagos, the Azores and Madeira, that occupy strategic points along the approaches to the Strait of Gibraltar. The overseas territory of Macao (Macau) was returned to China in 1999. Portugal is an elongated oblong, crossed from north-east to south-west by several parallel ranges of mountains, through which the valleys of the Minho, Douro, Tagus and Guadiana rivers pass. There are coastal plains and much of the country is covered in forests of pine and cork oak.

Many different cultures have left their stamp on the area during the past 3,000 years, including that of the Iberians, Celts, Phoenicians, Carthaginians, Greeks and Romans. The Romans called their Iberian province, Lusitania, which roughly corresponded to present-day Portugal. After the fall of the Roman Empire in the 5th century, Iberia was overrun by Vandals and Visigoths, the Moors dispelling the Visigoths from the south in 711. In the 10th and 11th centuries, Christians resettled the north under the rule of Castile and León. Portugal emerged as a nation when Alfonso, son of Henry of Burgundy, captured Lisbon and assumed the title of king in 1143; with the help of the Knights Templar, he began the expulsion of the Moors, though the Portuguese *Reconquista* was not completed until 1250. A commercial treaty with

BELOW: Praca do Comercio Square, Lisbon.

OPPOSITE LEFT: The Castelo São Jorge in Lisbon dates from the 14th century.

OPPOSITE RIGHT: The River Minho at Valenca do Minho.

1908 King Carlos and his eldest son were assassinated, and his younger son, Manuel II, was driven from the country by insurrection in 1910, when Portugal was declared a republic. However, the republic proved unstable, violent and corrupt.

During the First World War Portugal declared war on Germany in 1916 and its troops fought in France and Africa. (It remained neutral in the Second World War but provided British air bases in the Azores.) A long period of semi-fascist dictatorship under António de Oliveira Salazar, prime minister from 1932–68, and his successor Marcello Caetano, came to an end in a military coup in 1974, when the army seized power to end a stalemate situation in the African colonial wars. This led to Portugal's rapid withdrawal from its African colonies

and eventually to democratic reform in 1976, when the appointment of Mario Soares as prime minister restored civilian rule. He resigned two years later, but was elected president in 1986 and again in 1991. Head of state since 1996 is President Jorge Sampaio; José Socrates has been prime minister since March 2005.

Portugal has developed a diverse and increasingly service-oriented economy since joining the EEC (EU) in 1986. It qualified for the European Monetary Union (EMU) in 1998 and began to use the euro on 1 January 2002, along with 11 other member countries. Portugal exports textiles, clothing, footwear, paper, wood products, cork, tinned fish, wine, electrical equipment and refined petroleum. Tourism is another area that has seen rapid growth.

England was signed in 1294 and an alliance established. The Aviz dynasty was founded in 1385 by John I; his son, Henry the Navigator, captured the Azores and Madeira.

The 15th century was Portugal's great age of exploration. Portuguese navigators surveyed the African coast, Vasco da Gama opened up a sea route to India, and Pedro Cabral reached Brazil. The 16th century consolidated Portugal's position as a great colonial power and its power and wealth continued to increase. By then, the kings of Portugal were absolute monarchs; however, in 1580 the Aviz male line was extinguished and Philip II of Spain seized the crown. The Portuguese rebelled against Spanish rule in 1640 and the Duke of Braganza became king as John IV. However, it was not until a long period of war had elapsed that Spain recognized Portugal's independence in 1668.

Portugal fought on the side of Britain in the War of the Spanish Succession from 1701–14. In 1755 Lisbon was destroyed in an earthquake, heralding the loss of much of Portugal's wealth and status. Napoleonic France invaded Portugal in 1807, when John VI fled to Brazil. Thus began the Peninsula War that ended in 1814, when Wellington expelled the French from Portugal. In 1820 John VI was forced to accept a constitutional government and return from Brazil. In 1822, his son, Pedro I, declared Brazil independent from Portugal. In 1828, Dom Miguel prevented the succession of his niece, Queen Maria, and assumed the throne himself. After civil war, she regained the throne in 1834, when a constitutional government was established.

The late 19th century saw the rise of socialist, anarchist and republican parties. In

PUERTO RICO

Location:	8 I
Capital:	San Juan
Area:	3,425sq m (8871km²)
Population:	3,916,632 July 2005
Main Languages:	Spanish, English
Main Religions:	Roman Catholic 85%
Currency:	US dollar
Climate:	Tropical marine, mild

Together with a number of smaller islands, Puerto Rico is the most easterly of the Greater Antilles in the Caribbean. It is separated from the island of Hispaniola and the Dominican Republic by the Mona Passage in the east, giving it direct access to the Panama Canal and the Pacific Ocean. In the north, the capital, San Juan, is one of the best harbours in the Caribbean. The country can be described as a rough rectangle in shape, with a range of mountains, interspersed by valleys, running east to west across its surface. It has fertile coastal plains in the north and sandy beaches elsewhere.

One of the earliest Spanish settlements in the New World, Puerto Rico was discovered by Christopher Columbus in 1493, when it was known to the Arawak inhabitants as Boriquen. It was annexed by Spain in 1509; over the next 400 years of colonial rule, its indigenous population was almost totally wiped out and African slave labour was introduced to work the plantations. It was ceded to the US in 1898, following the Spanish-American War, and became a commonwealth in voluntary association with the US, with full powers of local government, in 1952. It has voluntarily opted to retain the status quo ever since. Head of state since 2001 is President George W. Bush; head of government since January 2005 is Governor Anibal Acevedo-Vila.

Puerto Rico has one of the most thriving economies in the Caribbean. Industry, such as pharmaceuticals, electronics, clothing and food products, now far outstrip the more

traditional agriculture as the prime source of revenue, though dairy farming and livestock rearing are still important. Unrestricted by wage laws and attracted by tax incentives and Puerto Rico's duty-free status, US companies have been encouraged to invest heavily in the country and tourism is fast gaining momentum

LEFT: San Juan's colonial architecture.

TOP: El Morro Fort in old San Juan.

ABOVE: The cruise ship, Allegra, San Juan.

QATAR

Location: 17 I
Capital: Doha
Area: 4,416sq m (11437km²)
Population: 863,051 July 2005
Main Languages: Arabic
Main Religions: Muslim
Currency: 1 Qatari riyal =
100 dirhams
Climate: Very hot summer, humid on
coast, warm winter

A Middle Eastern emirate, the Qatari peninsula extends for 100 miles (160km) or so into the Persian Gulf; where it meets the rest of the Arabian peninsular in the south, it borders Saudi Arabia, otherwise it is surrounded by water and a few scattered coral islands. The terrain is predominantly low-lying stony desert, with barren salt flats. Along the coast to the south-east is the dramatic Khor al Adaid, an area of spectacular sand dunes. Water is in short supply and is supplemented by desalination plants.

The area developed into an important trading centre during the Baghdadi Abbasid empire in the eighth century. In the late 18th century, the al-Khalifa clan migrated to the area from the Arabian peninsula and settled on the neighbouring Bahrain Island, from where it ruled the peninsular. When the al-Khalifa suppressed a Qatari revolt, destroying the town of Doha, it violated an Anglo-Bahraini Treaty of 1820 that led to British censure and intervention. The British nominated Muhammad ibn Thani al-Thani, a member of a distinguished local family, as sheikh or emir of the area, now distinct from Bahrain, that would eventually be known as Qatar. In the meantime, a British Resident was installed to keep the peace and resolve neighbouring disputes.

From 1871–1914 Qatar was nominally part of the Ottoman Empire, but it became a British protectorate from 1916. In 1939 oil and offshore natural gas were discovered and Qatar's fortunes dramatically changed.

In 1968 the British announced they would politically withdraw from the Gulf by 1971, which prompted Qatar to negotiate a federation of Gulf states; this was ultimately unsuccessful. In 1970 a constitution was adopted, when the emirate was declared an absolute monarchy, and the following year Qatar became a sovereign independent state. In 1991, Qatar joined the UN coalition in the Gulf War against Iraq. In 1995 the ruling sheikh, who had been siphoning off oil revenues that should by rights have gone to the country, was ousted by his son, Hamad bin Khalifa al-Thani. Since then, a new constitution has been introduced, social liberalization achieved, including votes for women, and *Al Jazeera*, the controversial television news channel, has been created. In 2001 the International Court of Justice's ruling on long-standing territorial disputes with Bahrain and Saudi Arabia was implemented. In 2005 a suicide bombing of a theatre in Doha killed a British teacher; this was shocking in a country that had never experienced terrorism before. Head of government is the monarch's brother, Muhammad bin Khalifa al-Thani.

Before oil was discovered, Qatar was wholly reliant on fishing and pearling. Nowadays, Qatar's revenue comes almost entirely from oil and natural gas, giving it a standard of living comparable with nations of Western Europe. There has been some diversification into cement, fertilizers and steel, and the economy relies heavily on its immigrant workforce. Most of the country's food has to be imported.

ABOVE: Doha National Museum.

LEFT: Qatari dhows.

RÉUNION

Location: 17 M
Capital: St-Denis
Area: 968sq m (2507km²)
Population: 776,948 July 2005
Main Languages: French
Main Religions: Roman Catholic 86%
Currency: euro
Climate: Tropical, cooler in hills.
Rains Nov–Apr

The largest of the Mascarene Islands, Réunion is a volcanically-active, subtropical island in the Indian Ocean, east of Madagascar. It is rugged, mountainous and forested in the interior, surrounded by a fertile coastal plain that is intensively cultivated. The highest point is the Piton des Neiges at 10,076ft (3070m). Piton de la Fournaise, on the south-eastern coast, is still volcanically active, and devastating cyclones occur from time to time. Their progress in Réunion and the rest of the Indian Ocean is monitored from a station at Saint-Denis, the capital.

Discovered by the Portuguese in 1513, Réunion was annexed by Louis XIII of

France in 1642, becoming part of France overseas in 1972. Until 1869, when the Suez Canal was opened, the island was important as a stopover on the trade route to the East Indies. Head of state since 1995 is the President of France, Jacques Chirac, represented by Prefect Laurent Cayrel. Head of government since 1998 is Jean-Luc Poudroux.

The white and Indian populations are far more prosperous than other segments of the population, and this causes social tensions, an example being the riots of 1991.

Moreover, the high unemployment that exists on the island is predominantly among the poor. It is not surprising, then, that Réunion is still heavily reliant on subsidies from France. Natural resources are fish, arable land and hydropower, and products include rum, maize, tobacco and vanilla. Sugar cane was once the most important crop by far, but services are now predominant and tourism is being encouraged.

Réunion's lush vegetation.

ROMANIA

Location: 15 G
Capital: Bucharest
Area: 91,699sq m (237500km²)
Population: 22,329,977 July 2005
Main Languages: Romanian
Main Religions: Romanian Orthodox 70%,
Greek Orthodox 10%
Currency: 1 leu = 100 bani
Climate: Hot summer, cold winter,
snow, more moderate
along coast

A republic of south-east Europe, Romania is bounded by Bulgaria, the Black Sea, Moldova, Ukraine, Hungary and Serbia & Montenegro. Romania is traversed from north to south by the Carpathian Mountains, which span the border with Ukraine, from east to west by the Transylvanian Alps, and by two ranges that form a great arc separating Transylvania in the north-west from the plains of Moldavia and Wallachia. There are numerous lakes along the length of the River Danube that flows through Romania on its way to the Black Sea.

The Romans under the Emperor Trajan conquered Dacia in 101–07, and many of them intermarried with the existing population, which explains the country's name. When the Romans left, Romania was occupied by Goths, Huns, Bulgars, Slavs and other invaders. By the 11th century, Transylvania had fallen to Hungary. (See also Hungary.) By the 14th century, the principalities of Moldavia in the east and Wallachia in the south had emerged, with Wallachia falling to the Ottoman Empire in the 15th century and Moldavia a century later; they both went to Russia after the Russo-Turkish War of 1828–29. In 1859 Moldavia and Wallachia united to become the independent state of Romania; it became a kingdom in 1881, when the Hohenzollern Carol I became King of Romania.

Romania fought on the side of the Triple Entente (Britain, France and Russia) during the First World War and was occupied by the Germans from 1917–18. When victory went to the Allies, it received Transylvania and Bukovina from the dismembered Austro-Hungarian Empire, and Bessarabia from Russia in 1918. Michael became king in

LEFT: *The 13th-century Petru Voda monastery in Neamt – the oldest in Romania.*

BELOW LEFT: *A Romanian gypsy wedding.*

BELOW: *A village of wooden houses.*

1927, but surrendered the throne in 1930 to his father, Carol II, who dispensed with democracy and established a dictatorship. During the 1930s, political instability and economic inequalities led to the growth of fascism and anti-Semitism. In 1940 northern Bukovina and Bessarabia were occupied by the Soviet Union, northern Transylvania by Hungary, and southern Dobruja by Bulgaria; Carol II abdicated, returning the throne to Michael, his son. Ion Antonescu became dictator in 1941 and Romania joined the German invasion of Russia in the Second World War; meanwhile, more than half the Jews in Romania were exterminated. The Antonescu regime was toppled in 1944 and Romania joined the war against Germany.

In 1945 Romania was occupied by

Soviet troops and a Communist government was installed. By the Treaty of Paris in 1947, Transylvania was returned to Romania, but lost southern Dobruja to Bulgaria and Bessarabia and northern Bukovina to the Soviet Union. King Michael was forced to abdicate later that year and a People's Republic of Romania was declared, under the direct control of the Soviets. Industry was nationalized and farming collectivized. In 1955 Romania joined the Warsaw Pact. In 1965 Nicolae Ceausescu became leader of the Romanian Communist Party, his Securitate police state became increasingly repressive throughout the 1980s. His regime collapsed in a bloody revolution in 1989, when 10,000 lost their lives. Ceausescu and his wife were tried and executed and a new

democratic constitution was introduced. Former Communists continued to dominate the government until 1996, when they were replaced by a coalition of centrist parties. Head of state from 2004 is President Traian Basescu, with Calin Popescu-Tariceanu the head of government, also since 2004.

Membership of the EU has been tentatively set for 2007, but this cannot hope to be achieved until the prevailing corruption, poverty, and tardy economic and political reforms have been addressed. Romania's economy was greatly harmed by a concentration on heavy industry during the period when the Communists were in power. This left it with an industrial capacity wholly unsuited to its needs. Today, oil, natural gas and antimony are the chief resources, with agriculture producing nearly a quarter of GDP. Romania is a large producer of wine, timber, textiles and fruit.

RUSSIA

Location:	19 E
Capital:	Moscow
Area:	6,592,849sq m
	(17075479km²)
Population:	143,420,309 July 2005
Main Languages:	Russian
Main Religions:	Russian Orthodox,
	Muslim
Currency:	1 rouble = 100 kopeks
Climate:	Mild summer, hot in south-
	east, very cold winter,
	mild on Black Sea

RUSSIAN FEDERATION

A country in northern Asia and eastern Europe, the Russian Federation, even after its emergence from the USSR, is still the largest country in the world. It has borders with Norway, Finland, Estonia, Latvia, Lithuania, Poland, via the Kalinigrad oblast, Belarus, Ukraine, Georgia, Azerbaijan, Kazakhstan, China, Mongolia and North Korea. It also has maritime borders with the United States, Canada and Japan, while to the north lies the Arctic Sea.

From the 9th to the 10th centuries, Vikings established themselves in Novgorod

LEFT: St Basil's Cathedral, Moscow

OPPOSITE: Horses pulling a sleigh on the Angara river in eastern Siberia.

and Kiev and other cities and temporarily united the other tribes into the empire of Kievan Rus. Christianity came from the Byzantine Empire in Constantinople in 988. The modern state evolved from the expansion of medieval Muscovy, a principality centred on Moscow. As Muscovy expanded, its princes became rulers of Russia. In 1472 Ivan III (Ivan the Great), grand duke of Muscovy, completed the unification of the country and adopted the title 'Ruler of all Russia'. He was ultimately responsible for driving out the Golden Horde of Mongols and Turkics (Tatars), invaders from the east, which had been plundering the area since 1237. In 1547 Ivan IV, known as Ivan the Terrible, who killed his eldest son in a fit of rage, became the first tsar of Russia. He also began the colonization of Siberia which, by 1700, stretched to the Pacific Ocean. Boris Godunov, a former advisor to Ivan the Terrible, succeeded Ivan's son as tsar from 1598 to 1605.

The Romanov dynasty, the last to rule Russia, began with Tsar Michael in 1613, when Russia was still largely undeveloped. However, it was playing an increasing role in Europe by the time of Peter the Great, who ruled from 1682 to 1725. Peter's plan to make Russia the equal of the countries of Western Europe was continued by Catherine

LEFT: *Red Square and the Kremlin, Moscow.*

OPPOSITE: *Palace Square, St Petersburg.*

PAGE 328: *Listuyanka village, by Lake Baikal, Siberia.*

PAGE 329: *The beautiful Kamchatka peninsula in the Russian far east.*

Stalin died in 1953, and there seemed no one to succeed him. Eventually, Nikita Khrushchev emerged as the new leader of the USSR, but the reforms he made were generally unproductive, and Soviet relations with the US and China became very much worse. In 1961 Yuri Gagarin made the first space flight, orbiting the earth in 108 minutes. In 1964 Khrushchev was ousted under the collective leadership of Alexei Kosygin and Leonid Brezhnev, with Brezhnev gaining prominence in the 1970s. In 1985 President Mikhail Gorbachev introduced openness (*glasnost*) and restructuring (*perestroika*) in his efforts to modernize the Soviet economy, inadvertently beginning the process that would lead to the break-up of the Soviet Union six years later.

In June 1991, Boris Yeltsin became president of Russia in the first direct presidential election in the country's history. In August 1991, Communist hardliners arrested Gorbachev and attempted to capture the Russian parliament in Moscow, but democratic forces rallied around Yeltsin and

the Great (r.1762–96). This was achieved, however, at the expense of the serfs, who were beginning to rebel, so that by the beginning of the First World War the position of Nicholas II (r.1894–1917) seemed precarious indeed. Following the overthrow of the Romanov dynasty in the October Revolution of 1917, Vladimir Lenin and the Bolsheviks seized power and Russia became the largest constituent republic of the Soviet Union, renamed the Union of Socialist Republics (USSR) in 1922. In 1918, Tsar Nicholas and his family were killed while imprisoned. Lenin died in 1924, and by 1928 Joseph Stalin had emerged as absolute ruler, after ousting Leon Trotsky. Stalin's plan for a socialist economy entailed rapid industrialization, which he forced on a largely rural country; farms were collectivized and millions died of famine. The purges began in 1938, when Stalin began to dispose of his critics and sent millions to the *gulags* on trumped-up charges.

Despite a non-agression pact, made in 1939 between the Soviets and Nazi Germany, Germany invaded the Soviet Union in 1941, but was halted at the Battle of Stalingrad in 1943, surrendering in 1945. This resulted in the domination of Eastern Europe by the Soviet Union, now acknowledged as a great power. It was also the start of the Cold War with the West.

the coup was defeated. On 25 December 1991 Gorbachev resigned as president of the USSR, yielding power to Boris Yeltsin, and on 31 December the Soviet Union was dissolved, to be replaced by the Commonwealth of Independent States (CIS). In 1998 Yeltsin sacked the government, when the financial cris in Asia devastated the Russian economy; he also sacked Viktor Chernomyrdin, and appointed Serge Kiriyenko prime minister. When the stock market collapsed and the rouble was heavily devalued, Kiriyenko was replaced by

Yevgeny Primakov. The US promised to send grain and meat after GDP contracted by five per cent in 1998. Yeltsin dismissed Primakov's government in 1999, followed by that of Stepashin, appointing Vladimir Putin prime minister. President Yeltsin resigned and Putin replaced him as president the following year, with Mikhail Kasyanov as prime minister.

Since secessionist Chechnya announced its independence in the early 1990s, intermittant guerilla warfare has been in progress between various Chechen groups

and the Russian military, with some of the groups becoming increasingly Islamist over the course of the struggle. It is estimated that over 200,000 people have died in the conflict, and there have been minor skirmishes in Ingushetia and North Ossetia. In 1999 Putin relaunched the war with Chechnya. In August 2000 a nuclear-powered submarine, the *Kursk*, sank after an explosion, caused when a torpedo misfired, and the crew of 118 died. In 2002 Chechen rebels entered a Moscow theatre and took 750 people hostage. In a rescue operation by

the Russian army, 129 lost their lives. That year President George W. Bush went to Moscow to sign a Strategic Offensive Reduction Treaty to reduce US and Russian nuclear arsenals by two-thirds by the end of 2012. In 2003, Russia opposed the invasion of Iraq by the US and its allies.

Since 1991, the struggle to achieve democracy and a market economy, after the rigours of the Soviet era, have not been easy. From 1999, however, there have been signs of recovery, though economic development throughout the country is uneven.

RWANDA

Location:	15 K
Capital:	Kigali
Area:	10,169sq m (26338km²)
Population:	8,440,820 July 2005
Main Languages:	Kinyarwanda, French, English
Main Religions:	Roman Catholic 65%, Protestant 9%
Currency:	1 Rwanda franc = 100 centimes
Climate:	Hot all year, cooler in mountains, rains Jan–Apr, Oct–Dec

A landlocked country in central Africa, Rwanda has borders with the Democratic Republic of Congo, Burundi, Tanzania and Uganda. It includes part of the beautiful Lake Kivu in the west, which has volcanic mountains to its north-east. Eastern Rwanda forms part of the Great Rift Valley and is bounded by the Kagera National Park and the Kagera river. The remainder of the country is rolling savannah grassland.

In the 10th century, Hutu people settled the area that was previously inhabited by Pygmy and Twa hunter-gatherers. In the 14th and 15th centuries the Hutu came under the domination of the immigrant cattle-owning Tutsi people, even though they were in the majority. The Tutsi established control throughout the land, almost as an aristocracy, and eventually founded a kingdom near Kigali. By the late 18th century, Ruanda and Burundi had united into a single Tutsi-dominated kingdom with a centralized military structure. The area was claimed by Germany in 1890, and was administered as part of German East Africa until 1918. It was occupied by Belgium forces during the First World War, eventually becoming part of the Belgian League of Nations mandate territory of Ruanda-Burundi.

Rwanda became independent as a republic in 1962, a few years after the Tutsi king had been violently overthrown by the majority Hutu people, and the Hutu Grégoire Kayibanda was made president. Over the next few years, thousands of Tutsi were killed and 200,000 were driven into exile in neighbouring countries. Kayibanda was ousted in a military coup under General Juvénal Habyarimana in 1973, who became

ABOVE: Hillside houses at Keah.

OPPOSITE LEFT: The countryside around Kigali.

OPPOSITE RIGHT: Rwandan women peeling yams.

800,000 people, largely Tutsi and Hutu moderates, were slaughtered by predominantly Hutu supporters of the government. Fearing Tutsi retribution, over two million fled, including some responsible for the massacre, to Zaïre (the Democratic Republic of Congo) and neighbouring countries. In 1997 Rwandan troops supported Laurent Kabila's successful overthrow of President Mobutu in Zaïre, but Kabila failed to expel Hutu militia from Congo. In 1996–97 Rwanda and Zaire came to the brink of war after there were Tutsi killings of Hutu in Zaire. A Hutu refugee crisis was averted as thousands were allowed to return to Rwanda. In the first elections since the genocide, Paul Kagame of the RPF became president, with Bernard Makuza prime minister in 2000; both were re-elected in 2003. A peace deal was made in 2002 with the Democratic Republic of Congo, in which Rwanda promised to withdraw its troops from the east if Congo expelled the Hutu militias that had been hiding there since the early 1990s.

The most densely populated country in Africa, Rwanda has few natural resources and very little industry. Around 90 per cent of the population is engaged in subsistence agriculture, which has trouble keeping pace with the growing population. The main exports are coffee, tea, pyrethrum, tin and hides, though exports are hampered by inadequate infrastructure. The 1994 genocide decimated Rwanda's already fragile economy, making the people far poorer than they already were; consequently, Ruanda receives substantial foreign aid and qualified for Heavily Indebted Poor Country (HIPC) debt relief in 2000.

president five years later. Drought devastated Rwanda during the 1980s, followed by a period of inter-ethnic conflict after Tutsi exiles launched a raid, in which many thousands were killed. In 1990 the government was attacked by the Rwanda Patriotic Front (RPF), a Tutsi military-political organization, formed by the children of exiles and based in Uganda, when Habyarimana was forced to adopt a multi-party constitution. The period following was characterized by ethnic tensions and political and economic upheavals, which culminated in 1994 in the deaths of President Habyarimana and the president of Burundi, who were assassinated when their aircraft was shot down, though it is uncertain who was responsible for the deed. This triggered the Rwanda Genocide – a seemingly organized attempt to eliminate the Tutsi population. It ended in defeat for the Hutu regime, but not before more than

ST KITTS & NEVIS

Location:	9 I
Capital:	Basseterre
Area:	101sq m (262km2)
Population:	38,958 July 2005
Main Languages:	English
Main Religions:	Christian
Currency:	1 East Caribbean dollar = 100 cents
Climate:	Hot all year, hurricane risk Aug–Oct

ST KITTS
AND NEVIS

Adjoining members of the Leeward Islands, St Kitts and Nevis lie about a third of the way between Puerto Rico and Trinidad & Tobago, within the arc of the Lesser Antilles. Basseterre on St Kitts is the capital and the territory also includes the nearby island of Sombrero. The islands have mountainous, volcanic interiors, with fertile plains along the coast.

The islands were inhabited by Carib Indians when Christopher Columbus visited them on his second voyage in 1493. He

with both holding it jointly from 1628 to 1713. This led to intermittent conflict that damaged the islands' economy, though Nevis, which was only ever settled by the English, did eventually grow prosperous.

St Kitts was ceded to Britain in 1713, but both islands were seized by the French in 1782; however, both definitively went to Britain following the Treaty of Paris in 1783. A self-governing union between St Kitts and Nevis (and briefly Anguilla) was created in 1967, which became a fully independent member of the Commonwealth in 1983. Nevis is currently trying to separate from St Kitts, a previous referendum in 1998 having failed to obtain the required votes. Head of state since 1952 is Queen Elizabeth II, represented by Governor-General Cuthbert Montraville Sebastian since 1996. Head of government is Dr Denzil Douglas, who has been prime minister since 1995.

Until the 1970s, sugar was the mainstay of the economy, but continued losses led to its abandonment following the bad harvest of 2005. Instead, the islands have decided to concentrate on tourism (now the most important earner), ways of attracting businesses to the islands, offshore banking, and manufacturing.

OPPOSITE: Nisbet beach, Nevis.

ABOVE: The south-eastern peninsular of St Kitts.

RIGHT: Basseterre, St Kitts.

named the larger island after his patron saint, St Christopher, and the other, Nevis, because the shape of the island reminded him of a mountain capped with snow (*nieve*). The island of St Christopher was colonized first by English settlers in 1623, who shortened the name to St Kitts, and then by the French,

ST LUCIA

Location:	9 J
Capital:	Castries
Area:	238sq m (616km²)
Population:	166,312 July 2005
Main Languages:	English
Main Religions:	Roman Catholic 80%
Currency:	1 East Caribbean
	dollar = 100 cents
Climate:	Hot all year,
	rains May–Dec

St Lucia is one of the Windward Islands that lies in the chain of the Lesser Antilles, north of St Vincent and the Grenadines and south of Martinique. To the west lies the Caribbean Sea, with the Atlantic Ocean to the east. St Lucia is a volcanic island, the peak of Mount Gimie rising to 3,150ft (960m), and it has lush, fertile valleys and tropical forests. The volcanic Gros and Petits Pitons, near Soufrière in the west, are the island's most famous landmarks. Around a third of the population is concentrated in and around the splendid port of Castries, the island's capital.

LEFT: The Pitons above Soufrière.

OPPOSITE ABOVE LEFT: Rodney Bay.

OPPOSITE BELOW LEFT: Dennery, a quiet fishing village.

OPPOSITE RIGHT: A waterfall in the Diamond Botanical Gardens, Soufrière.

Europeans first got to hear of the island in the 1500s, but it was not settled by the French and British until the 17th century, due to the ferocity of the indigenous Carib Indians. Its possession was long disputed, and the island changed hands 14 times before France ceded St Lucia to Britain in 1814. In 1838, around 13,000 slaves, that the French had originally brought in to work the sugar plantations, were freed.

St Lucia was part of the short-lived West Indies Federation until 1962. It achieved self-government in 1967 and full independence within the Commonwealth in 1979. Head of state is Queen Elizabeth II, represented on the island by Governor-General Dame Pearlette Louisy; head of government since 1997 is Dr Kenny Anthony. St Lucia is a full member of the Caribbean Community (CARICOM) and the Organization of Caribbean States (OECS).

The island's main source of revenue is tourism and offshore banking and it has been able to attract foreign business and investment. This diversification has become all the more important due to increased competition from Latin American bananas, though steps are being taken to revitalize St Lucia's own banana industry, for a long time its principal export crop.

ST VINCENT & THE GRENADINES

Location:	9 J
Capital:	Kingstown
Area:	150sq m (389km²)
Population:	117,534 July 2005
Main Languages:	English
Main Religions:	Christian
Currency:	1 East Caribbean dollar = 100 cents
Climate:	Hot all year

ST VINCENT AND THE GRENADINES

An independent state in the Windward Islands of the Lesser Antilles, which comprises the island of St Vincent and some of the Grenadines, the remaining islands in the south being administered by Grenada. The best known of the Grenadines is the island of Mustique, an exclusive holiday resort, where the late Princess Margaret had a villa; Mick Jagger and David Bowie also visited Mustique.

The islands lie north of Trinidad and Tobago, with the Caribbean Sea to the west

and the Atlantic Ocean to the east. They are volcanic, mountainous islands, and the volcano of Soufrière in the north of St Vincent poses a constant threat.

In the 18th century, attempts were made by the French, Dutch and British to establish settlements on the islands, though they finally went to the British in 1783, who deported most of the indigenous Carib population and replaced them with African slave labour. The state achieved autonomy in 1969 and full independence with a limited form of membership of the Commonwealth in 1979. Head of state is Queen Elizabeth II, represented by Governor-General Sir Frederick Nathaniel Ballantyne since 2002; head of government since 2001 is Prime Minister Ralph E Gonsalves.

Agriculture is the predominant occupation and major exports are bananas, coconuts and arrowroot. However, tropical storms have devastated crops several times within recent years. Tourism is also important, though there have been fewer visitors following the American disaster of 11 September 2001.

OPPOSITE: A Tobago cay, Grenadines.

ABOVE: A shopping area on the privately-owned island of Mustique.

LEFT: An arrowroot factory on St Vincent.

SAMOA

Location:	1 L
Capital:	(Samoa) Apia
Area:	1,093sq m (2831km²)
Population:	177,287 July 2005
Main Languages:	Samoan, English
Main Religions:	Protestant 62%, Roman Catholic 22%
Currency:	1 tala = 100 sene
Climate:	Hot, humid summer, cooler winter

Location:	1 L
Capital:	(American Samoa) Pago Pago
Area:	77sq m (199km²)
Population:	57,881 July 2005
Main Languages:	Samoan, English
Main Religions:	Congregationalist 50%, Roman Catholic 20%
Currency:	US dollar
Climate:	Tropical marine

The Oceanian volcanic island group of Samoa, in the South Pacific, lies to the north-east of Fiji, and consists of the independent state of Samoa to the west, and US-administered American Samoa to

OPPOSITE: Coastal view of Tapu Tapu, Tutuila, American Samoa.

RIGHT: Trying on a sarong in Pago Pago, American Samoa.

BELOW: View of Samoa from Vailima, Robert Louis Stevenson's house.

BELOW RIGHT: Knife dance, Samoa.

the east. The islands are predominantly mountainous, with narrow coastal plains. They are fringed by coral reefs and are subject to devasting storms and active volcanism. The majority of the population is indigenous Polynesian. The islands were discovered by European explorers in 1722, though there is a history of occupation that stretches back into prehistory.

Western Samoa (the 'Western part of the name was dropped in 1997) comprises the islands of Savaii and Upolu and several

other smaller, uninhabited islands. Samoa belonged to Germany before the First World War, but when the war ended, it was administered by New Zealand under a League of Nations mandate, before coming under the trusteeship of the UN. In 1962 Samoa became the first Polynesian nation in the 20th century to re-establish its independence. Head of state is Chief Tanumafili II Malietoa since 1963, with Prime Minister Sailele Malielegaoi Tuila'epa the head of government since 1996.

The economy of Samoa is dependent on development aid, money sent home by relatives working overseas, agriculture and fishing, with agriculture providing most of the export revenue. The most important exports are coconut cream, coconut oil and copra. Fish stocks are on the decline, which is a worry, but tourism is fortunately a growing industry.

In a treaty of 1899, the islands of Tutuila (with its excellent harbour of Pago Pago), Ta'u, and the coral atolls of Rose Island, with Swains Island to the north, now known as **American Samoa**, were acquired by the US, when Britain and Germany divided the Samoan archipelago into two. Head of state since 2001 is President George W. Bush; Governor Togiola Tulafono has been head of government since 2003.

The economy of American Samoa is still traditionally Polynesian and most of the land is in communal ownership. However, it is strongly linked to the US in terms of remittances and trade, with tuna fishing and tuna processing providing the most important exports. Agriculture is limited, though tourism promises much for the future.

SAN MARINO

Location: 14 G
Capital: San Marino
Area: 24sq m (61km²)
Population: 28,880 July 2005
Main Languages: Italian
Main Religions: Roman Catholic
Currency: euro
Climate: Hot summer, mild winter

were elected in 2003. Head of government and Secretary of State for Foreign and Political Affairs, also since 2003, is Fabio Berardi. San Marino's foreign policy is aligned with that of Italy, which is also responsible for its smaller neighbour's defence.

The economy is largely agricultural, and while manufacturing is important, tourism is a vital source of income. The key industries are banking, clothing, cement, building stone, electronics and ceramics; wine and cheeses are also produced. The standard of living is comparable with the most prosperous areas of Italy, which supplies much of San Marino's food.

San Marino is the smallest republic in the world, after Vatican City and Monaco, and forms an enclave within Italy, lying 12 miles (19km) south-west of Rimini, that lies on the Adriatic Sea. San Marino also claims to be the oldest state in Europe, having been founded in the 4th century. The capital, also San Marino, stands on Mount Titano, a spur of the Apennines; its inaccessible mountain location has played an important part in maintaining the country's long history of independence. San Marino possesses its own legislative assembly, the Great and General Council, which elects Captains Regent as heads of state. The present incumbents are Cesare Gasperoni and Fausta Morganti, who

TOP: The Basilica of San Marino.

ABOVE: Piazza della Libertà.

LEFT: The old fortress of San Marino, perched high on Mount Titano.

SÃO TOMÉ & PRÍNCIPE

Location:	13 K
Capital:	São Tomé
Area:	387sq m (1001km²)
Population:	187,410 July 2005
Main Languages:	Portuguese
Main Religions:	Roman Catholic 90%
Currency:	1 dobra = 100 centimos
Climate:	Hot, humid all year, rains Jun–Sep

SAO TOME AND PRINCIPE

A republic consisting of the two main islands of São Tomé and Príncipe, about 90 miles (145km) apart and lying close to the equator in the Gulf of Guinea, off the north-western coast of Gabon in north-west Africa; it also includes several smaller islands. The extinct volcanic islands are mountainous, fertile, heavily forested, and crossed by swiftly-flowing streams.

The islands, then uninhabited, were discovered and settled by the Portuguese in the late 15th century, who imported convicts and slaves to work the sugar plantations, making the islands Africa's most important

LEFT: Beach with dugout canoe.

BELOW: Young girls from São Tomé.

producer of sugar. However, the slaves successfully revolted in 1530, when the islands became a centre of the Congo-Americas slave trade. In the 19th century, cocoa and coffee were introduced and forced labour from Africa was used to work the plantations. By the beginning of the 20th century, São Tomé was the world's largest producer of cocoa, still the case today.

In 1953 1,000 striking plantation workers were gunned down in the Batepá Massacre by Portuguese troops. By the late 1950s the forerunner of the Movement for the Liberation of São Tomé e Príncipe (MLSTP) had been formed. In 1974 a military coup in Portugal, when Salazar and Caetano were overthrown, caused strikes, demonstrations and an army mutiny in São Tomé, when it was realized that Portuguese colonies abroad were to be dissolved;

thousands of settlers fled the country. São Tomé e Príncipe became independent in 1975, when Manuel Pinto da Costa of the MLSTP became president; close links were forged with the Communist bloc and the plantations were nationalized. Mindful of the collapse of Communism in Eastern Europe, Marxism was abandoned in 1990 and the first, free multi-party elections were held the following year, when Miguel Trovoada, a former prime minister, in exile since 1986, was elected president.

In 2001 Fradique de Menezes became president, and a coalition government was formed the following year. In 2003, the government was taken over in a military coup by Major Fernando Pereira, whose forces detained Prime Minister Maria das Neves. After international mediation, Menezes and Neves were reinstated, though Neves was removed from power in 2004, when a new government was formed by Damião Vaz d'Almeida. Almeida resigned in June 2005 and was succeeded by Prime Minister Maria do Carmo Silveira.

São Tomé e Príncipe has become increasingly reliant on cocoa since 1975, though production is now in decline, due to drought and bad management. However, oil has recently been discovered in the Gulf of Guinea, which will undoubtedly have a significant effect on the economy, especially as the islands rely on aid and rescheduling of their external debt. There are also hopes of expanding the tourist industry.

SAUDI ARABIA

Location:	16 I
Capital:	Riyadh
Area:	849,400sq m (2200000km²)
Population:	26,417,599 July 2005
Main Languages:	Arabic
Main Religions:	Sunni Muslim 98%
Currency:	1 rial = 100 halalah
Climate:	Hot, dry inland, cooler, humid on coast

Occupying 80 per cent of the Arabian peninsula, Saudi Arabia is the largest state in the Middle East. It is predominantly desert, the Rub' al Khali (the Empty Quarter) in the south being the largest and most desolate expanse of sand in the world. It has land borders with Jordan to the north, Iraq to the north and north-east, Kuwait, Qatar, Bahrain and the United Arab Emirates to the east, and Yemen and Oman to the south and south-east. In the west is the coastal plain of the Hejaz, while in the south-west is the Asir, a highland region that rises to Mount Sawda at 10,279ft (3133m). In the centre lies the Najd plateau, with Riyadh the capital. Saudi Arabia has

coastlines on the Gulf of Aqaba and Red Sea to the west and on the Persian Gulf to the north-east, where the Hasa lies.

Saudi Arabia has two of Islam's holiest places within its boundaries – Mecca, the birthplace of the Prophet Muhammad in 570, and Medina, where he was buried. The country's origins lie in the 18th century,

when the Al Saud family united the tribes of the Najd in support of the Wahhabi Islamic movement, establishing Riyadh as the capital in around 1830. By 1870 Hejaz and Hasa were under the control of the Ottoman Empire. In the late 19th century, the rival dynasty of Ibn Rashid became rulers of the Najd. Abdul Aziz ibn Saud responded with a

Bedouin revolt, regaining Riyadh in 1902. By 1913, Hasa had been recovered from the Turks and two years later Britain recognized Abdul Aziz as Sultan of Najd and Hasa. During the First World War, the British-backed Arab revolt effected the final expulsion of the Turks and the emergence of the present kingdom. This was achieved

succeeded by King Fahd. In 1987 diplomatic relations with Iran suffered when Iranian pilgims on a *hajj* to Mecca began to stampede, causing 1,400 deaths.

In 1991, Saudi Arabia sided with the Allies against Iraq in the Gulf War; however, it did not support the US-led invasion of Iraq in 2003. In 1992, under international pressure to make democratic progress, King Fahd formed a consultative council; he died of a stroke in 1996. In 2003 terrorist attacks, possibly involving al-Qaeda, killed 35 people in the capital, prompting the Saudi government to consider the growth of extremism at home, which coincided with more media freedom. There are also plans for more political representation in a country that adheres to Shari'a (Islamic Law) and is governed strictly according to

OPPOSITE: An oasis with mud-built house, Najaran.

LEFT: Oil storage tanks, Yanbu.

BELOW: The Prophet's Mosque, Medina.

its tenets. The present head of both state and government is King Abdullah ibn Abd al-Aziz Al Saud.

Saudi Arabia has a fast-growing population, which is a cause for concern in an economy almost entirely dependent on petroleum. However, the government is encouraging growth in other areas to lessen this dependency and provide more employment. The large number of pilgrims that make the *hajj* to Mecca each year also contribute to the economy.

when the Najd and Hejaz were united under Abdul Aziz ibn Saud, who was proclaimed ruler of both in 1926. In 1932, the sultanate was renamed the United Kingdom of Saudi Arabia, though there are those who question the legitimacy of the Saud dynasty, that continues to this day, and decline to refer to it as a true monarchy.

In 1933 the US-owned Standard Oil Company was permitted to prospect for oil, which was found in Hasa in 1938. This transformed the economy, and Saudi Arabia became the largest producer of oil in the Middle East. In 1953 Abdul Aziz died, and

was succeeded by King Saud, who sent his troops into Yemen when it looked as though its monarchy was about to be overthrown. He was overthrown himself in 1964, when Crown Prince Faisal became king. Faisal was assassinated in 1975 and Crown Prince Khalid became king; his reign saw the growth of Islamic fundamentalism in Iran. In 1979, Shi'a fundamentalists tried to capture the Great Mosque at Mecca, an act that was brutally suppressed. Saudi Arabia supported Iraq during the Iran-Iraq War of 1980–88; this led to retaliation, with Iran attacking Saudi shipping. In 1982 Khalid died and was

SCOTLAND

Location:	13 F
Capital:	Edinburgh
Area:	30,079sq m (77905km²)
Population:	5,062,011 2001
Main Languages:	English
Main Religions:	Church of Scotland, Roman Catholic
Currency:	1 pound = 100 pence
Climate:	Mild summer, cool winter

Scotland is the part of Great Britain lying to the north of the border with England. In addition to the mainland, it comprises numerous islands, including Arran and Bute in the Firth of Clyde; the Inner and Outer Hebrides off the west coast; and the Orkneys and Shetlands in the north. The western coastline is highly fragmented, while that of the east is comparatively regular. Most of Scotland is highland, apart from the centre and extreme north-east.

In AD 140 the Romans built the Antonine Wall, that stretched for 37 miles (59km) between the Rivers Forth and Clyde. It was intended to mark the northern limit of the Roman province of Britain, but was abandoned in 200 in favour of Hadrian's Wall, nearly twice as long and begun in 122, which marks the present border between Scotland and England. The Romans called the area north of the wall, Caledonia, which was inhabited by a war-like tribe of Picts, thought to be of Celtic origin. In the 6th century the 'Scots'came from Ireland and settled the west of Scotland, having been Christianized by St Columba (c.521–97), who established the monastery of Iona in the Inner Hebrides in around 563, and converted the Picts to Christianity.

In 844, after centuries of internecine strife, Kenneth MacAlpin became king of the Scots and Picts. Malcolm Canmore ruled Scotland from 1057 to 1093, having previously lived in England and absorbed the English culture. He and his queen (St Margaret) brought this English influence

with them to the Scottish court, together with the English language, which attracted English settlers. A French element was also introduced around this time, the Normans having conquered England in 1066 and were beginning to gravitate towards Scotland.

In the 14th century Edward I of England, known as the 'Hammer of the Scots', tried to annex Scotland; this led to a series of revolts, led by William Wallace and Robert the Bruce from 1296. The defeat of Edward II at Bannockburn in 1314 was a great Scottish

ABOVE: The 13th-century Urquhart Castle, located on the banks of Loch Ness.

LEFT: Edinburgh Castle.

OPPOSITE: The capital city of Edinburgh.

victory, though England did not recognize Scotland's independence until 1328. The next 300 years were characterized by bloody warfare, and included the Battle of Flodden in 1513, when James IV was killed. The Reformation in Scotland was dominated by John Knox, who was instrumental in establishing the Church of Scotland within a Scottish Protestant state. He also opposed the Catholic Mary, Queen of Scots, when she returned from France to rule Scotland in her own right in 1561. England and Scotland were linked, when James VI of Scotland acceded to the English throne as James I of England, following the death of Elizabeth I. Elizabeth signed the death warrant for James'

ABOVE: Shags on Foula, the Shetlands.

LEFT: The University of Glasgow.

OPPOSITE ABOVE LEFT: The Inverary Woollen Mill.

OPPOSITE ABOVE RIGHT: The Forth rail bridge.

OPPOSITE BELOW: A stone bridge at Carrbridge, a Highland village.

mother and her own cousin, Queen Mary, but herself died childless. In 1689, the Jacobites, the supporters of the deposed Stuart king of England, James II, with the help of Scottish Catholic Highland clans, tried to recover the throne for the Stuarts, whose dynasty had been founded by Robert II in 1371.

Opposition to the Act of Union of 1707, when the Scottish and English parliaments were united, led to further Jacobite risings, in which James, the 'Old Pretender', led a rebellion in Scotland and the north of England in 1715. His son, Charles Edward Stuart, led a Scottish invasion of England in 1745 that stopped short of Derby. Bonnie Prince Charlie was finally defeated at the

Battle of Culloden in 1746. The Highland Clearances began soon after, when the clan system was destroyed and thousands were evicted from their rented crofts to make way for sheep and deer; this was repeated in the 19th century. It also began the mass migration of Scots to other parts of the world, including the Americas. During the 20th century a strong nationalist movement developed. In 1999 the first Scottish parliament for 300 years was elected, following devolution from London. It sits in Edinburgh and is responsible for the majority of Scottish affairs, while responsibility for defence, foreign affairs and taxation still lie with Westminster.

SENEGAL

Location: 12 J
Capital: Dakar
Area: 75,954sq m (196720km²)
Population: 11,126,832 July 2005
Main Languages: French
Main Religions: Sunni Muslim 90%
Currency: 1 CFA franc =
100 centimes
Climate: Hot, dry all year in north;
Hot, wet May–Nov,
cooler Dec–Apr in south

Senegal is the most westerly country in Africa. With a coastline on the Atlantic Ocean, it has land boundaries with Mauritania, Mali, Guinea and Guinea-Bissau. Gambia forms a virtual enclave within Senegal, in a narrow strip that follows the Gambia river inland for 190m (300km). In the north of Senegal there is scrub and semi-desert, while the south is wetter and more fertile, rising to foothills in the south-east. It has several protected wildlife parks.

From the 10th to the 14th centuries, the Tukolor (*Toucouleur*) state of Tekrur dominated the area, though Senegal took its name from the Zenega Berbers, who brought Islam to the region in the 11th century from North Africa; it is still the dominant religion, though all religions and cultures are respected. Part of the great Mali empire in the 14th century, the Jolof (Wolof) empire was established in the 15th century. In the 1400s, the Portuguese reached Cape Verde and trading posts were opened. By the 17th century, the export trade in slaves, ivory and gold had been established by European traders, though the slave trade was dominated by the French from 1658, whose first colony was St-Louis in the north-west. The French were temporarily expelled by the British in 1763, the British forming the colony of Senegambia, their first in Africa. The French regained control in 1783 and by 1902 Senegal was part of French West Africa. In 1946 it became French overseas territory, with representation in the French parliament.

Briefly a partner in the Federation of Mali (1959), Senegal withdrew and became a fully independent republic in 1960. Its first post-colonial president from 1960 to 1980 was Léopold Sédar Senghor, a well-known poet and promoter of African culture, as well as a former campaigner for democracy. He was also a Senegalese deputy to the French National Assembly from 1946–58 and the founder of the Senegalese Progressive Union (UPS). He handed power over voluntarily to Abdou Diouf in 1980. In 1982, Senegal joined with Gambia to form the confederation of Senegambia, but the union was abandoned in 1989.

Since 1982 a long-running, low-level separatist war in the southern Casamance region has claimed hundreds of lives, though there have been hopes of peace since 2004.

The conflict concerns the Dioula people, who consider themselves marginalized by the Wolof, Senegal's main ethnic group. The 40-year rule of Senegal's Socialist Government came to a peaceful end in 2000, when Abdoulaye Wade of the Senegalese Democratic Party was elected president; the head of government since 2004 is Macky Sall.

Senegal has a long history of international peace-keeping, having had a presence in the Democratic Republic of Congo, Liberia and Kosovo. It also has a good political record of peaceful changes of leadership and economic corruption is low. Therefore, although poverty is widespread and unemployment high, it is one of Africa's more stable economies. Agriculture is the main industry and peanuts, petroleum products, phosphates and cotton are exported, while fishing is also important. In 1996 Senegal was connected with the Internet, leading to expanding information technology-based services.

ABOVE: A woman ironing, Dakar.

LEFT: Overview of Dakar.

SERBIA & MONTENEGRO

Location:	14 G
Capital:	Belgrade
Area:	39,449sq m (102173km²)
Population:	10,829,175 July 2005
Main Languages:	Serbian
Main Religions:	Serbian Orthodox 65%,
	Muslim 19%
Currency:	dinar (Serbia)
	euro (Montenegro)
Climate:	Warm summer, cold winter

A Balkan republic in south-eastern Europe, formerly part of the now-defunct Yugoslavia. Serbia is landlocked, and only Montenegro has a coastline on the Adriatic Sea. To the north are rich, fertile plains watered by the Danube, but Kosovo and Montenegro in the south are rugged and mountainous.

Serbia, then known as Moesia Superior, was conquered by the Romans in the 3rd century BC, though the area did not extend to Belgrade until the time of the Emperor Augustus. In the 6th century, Slavic tribes,

including Serbs, Croats and Slovenes, crossed the Danube and settled in the Balkan peninsula. In 879 the Serbs were converted to Orthodox Christianity by St Cyril and St Methodius. From the mid-10th to the 11th centuries, Serbia extricated itself from the Byzantine Empire to form an independent state that reached its apogee in the 14th century under Stefan Dushan, when it controlled much of Albania and northern Greece. In the Battle of Kosovo in 1389 the Serbs were defeated by the Turks, and Serbia came under the Ottoman Empire; Montenegro remained independent, though Croatia and Slovenia were absorbed into the Habsburg Empire. Serbia regained its independence in 1878, after Russia defeated the Turks in the war over Bulgaria.

During the Balkan Wars of 1912–13, Serbia expanded its territory at the expense of Turkey and Bulgaria, which contributed to the outbreak of the First World War. In 1918 Serbia was absorbed into the Kingdom of Serbs, Croats and Slovenes under Peter

ABOVE: View of Budva, Montenegro.

Karageorgevic (Peter I). In 1929, during the reign of Alexander I, the name Yugoslavia was adopted; Alexander was assassinated in 1934 and his son, Peter II, became king. In 1941, Yugoslavia was invaded by the Germans, though pro-royalist *chetniks* and Communist partisans under Marshal Tito offered armed resistance. In 1945 a Communist constitution was formed under Tito's leadership; Yugoslavia split from the Soviet Union in 1948. In 1953 Tito became president. He died in 1980, when a collective leadership assumed power.

Armed forces suppressed demonstrations by Albanians demanding full republican status in Kosovo in 1981–82. In 1986 Slobodan Milosevic became leader of the Serbian Communist Party. Strikes, inflation, economic difficulties and ethnic unrest in Montenegro and Vojvodina, and separatist demands in Croatia and Slovenia, erupted in 1988. In 1989 the reformist Croatian Ante Markovic became prime minister. There were ethnic riots over Serbian attempts to end the autonomy of Kosovo and Vojvodina, when a state of emergency was imposed, though Kosovo and Vojvodina were stripped of their autonomy the following year.

In Slovenia, Croatia, Macedonia and Bosnia, non-Communist governments came to power, aiming for a looser federation, while multi-party systems were established elsewhere. In 1991, four out of the six Yugoslav republics seceded, with Slovenia, Croatia and Macedonia declaring their independence. Bosnia-Herzegovina announced its independence the following year, but ethnic conflict between Muslims, Serbs and Croats reduced Bosnia to civil war.

War came to an end with the signing of the Dayton Peace Accord in 1995.

Meanwhile, the remaining republics of Serbia and Montenegro had declared a new Federal Republic of Yugoslavia (FRY), though it failed to be recognized as such until 2000 by the UN and others. This was due to Milosevic's continuing military efforts to unite ethnic Serbs in neighbouring republics into a 'Greater Serbia'. In 1998–99, massive expulsions by FRY forces and Serb paramilitaries of ethnic Albanians in Kosovo, provoked an international response, including the bombing of Serbia by NATO and the stationing of a NATO-led force in Kosovo; since 1999 Kosovo has been governed under the authority of the UN, pending determination of its future status.

In 2000, after claims of ballot-rigging, followed by mass demonstrations, Milosevic conceded electoral defeat and Vojislav Kostunica became president. In 2001 Milosevic was arrested for crimes against humanity, and his trial began in The Hague, Netherlands, the following year. In 2003, what was left of the Federal Republic of Yugoslavia became the loose commonwealth of Serbia & Montenegro, though each may seek independence in a referendum to be held every three years. President Svetozar Marovic has been head of both state and government since 2003.

The economy has suffered greatly due to war, mismanagement and economic sanctions during the Milosevic era, and corruption and unemployment, as well as Serbia's complicated political relationship with Montenegro, continue to hamper progress.

SEYCHELLES

Location:	17 K
Capital:	Victoria
Area:	175sq m (453km²)
Population:	81,188 July 2005
Main Languages:	Creole, English, French
Main Religions:	Roman Catholic 90%,
	Anglican 8%
Currency:	1 Seychelles rupee =
	100 cents
Climate:	Tropical, hot, wet
	Dec–May, cooler Jun–Nov

THE SEYCHELLES

An archipelago of 115 or so islands, located in the Indian Ocean to the north-east of Madagascar. Only 33 islands are inhabited; those around Mahé, where the capital Victoria is situated, and where most of the population is concentrated, are mostly granite, with a narrow coastal strip, and there are coral atolls elsewhere.

The islands are home to many endemic plant species, one of which – the coco-de-mer palm – has the largest seed of any plant. The Seychelles largely escaped the tsunami of 2004, though there was flooding and a

Economic growth is led by the tourist industry, which provides 70 per cent of revenue, though there have been recent moves to lessen dependency on tourism by developing light industries, farming and tuna-fishing.

OPPOSITE: Anse-à-la-Mouche, Mahé.

LEFT: Fisherman's Cove harbour, and the Beau Vallon Hotel Meridien, Mahé.

BELOW: The coastline of Anse Patates, La Digue.

loss of marine life and three people lost their lives.

The islands were explored by the Portuguese in the early 16th century. Colonized by the French from the mid-18th century, the Seychelles were seized by the British in 1794 and were made a dependency of Mauritius in 1810, becoming a separate crown colony in 1903. Independence as a republic within the Commonwealth was achieved in 1976, and the islands of Aldabra, Farquhar and Des Roches, that had detached themselves in 1965, to form the British Indian Ocean Territory, were returned to Seychelles. It was declared a one-party state in 1979, which lasted until 1992, with the first free elections coming the following year. In 2001 France-Albert René was re-elected, having been president since the coup d'état in 1977. In 2004 he stepped down, and his vice-president, James Michel, became president and head of government.

SIERRA LEONE

Location:	12 J
Capital:	Freetown
Area:	27,925sq m (73326km²)
Population:	6,017,643 July 2005
Main Languages:	English
Main Religions:	Traditional 51%, Muslim 39%, Protestant 6%, Roman Catholic 2%
Currency:	1 leone = 100 cents
Climate:	Hot, humid all year, cooler on coast

Located in West Africa, between Guinea and Liberia, Sierra Leone has a coastline on the Atlantic Ocean to the south-west. The interior consists of forested plateaux and mountains to the east, while mangrove swamps line the coastal plain. To the north lies tropical savannah.

Portuguese explorers arrived in 1460 and gave the area its name, possibly struck by the mountainous peninsula of what is now Freetown, the capital. In 1787, in an area that had previously been a source of slaves, a settlement for freed slaves was

established at Freetown. Sierra Leone became a British crown colony in 1808, eventually gaining independence in 1961, with Sir Milton Margai its first prime minister. It was briefly a one-party state in the early 1980s.

The year 1991 saw the start of the Sierra Leone Civil War, when the Revolutionary United Front (RUF) of Foday Sankoh, seeking to end foreign interference and nationalize the diamond mines, rebelled against the government. The result was tens of thousands of deaths, with the perpetrators of unspeakable atrocities eventually facing charges of war crimes. Over two million people, well over a third of the population, were displaced, many of them now refugees in neighbouring countries.

Major Johnny Paul Koromah ousted the then-president, Ahmad Tejan Kabbah, in a military coup in 1997. In 1998 Kabbah was reinstated after the junta was overthrown by Nigerian-led intervention forces, and

OPPOSITE LEFT: The slave trail from Bunce Fort.

OPPOSITE RIGHT: Girl with manioc root.

LEFT: Women and children, Freetown.

continues to lead the country today. In July 1999, a peace agreement, bolstered by peace-keeping forces, raised hopes that the country would rebuild its devastated economy and infrastructure. By the following year, however, the situation had deteriorated to such an extent that British troops were deployed to evacuate foreign nationals. In 2002, Sierra Leone emerged from a decade of civil war, helped by Britain, UN peace-keepers, and financial contributions from abroad. However, the gradual withdrawal of peace-keeping forces in 2004 and 2005, and deteriorating conditions in Guinea and Liberia, throw doubts on Sierra Leone's future stability.

Sierra Leone is a poor country, and what wealth that exists is not distributed equally. It is now faced with the task of reconstruction, and the tribal rivalry and official corruption that led to the conflict have still not ended. The illicit trade in diamonds is known to have funded and perpetuated the war, and their mining has long been exploited at the expense of agriculture and industrial development, to the nation's cost. However, there are plans to re-open bauxite and titanium mines, closed down during the conflict, and to explore other mineral reserves, To date, however, foreign investment has not been forthcoming.

SINGAPORE

Location:	20 K
Capital:	Singapore City
Area:	247sq m (641km²)
Population:	4,425,720 July 2005
Main Languages:	Chinese, Malay, Tamil, English
Main Religions:	Buddhist 51%, Christian 15%, Muslim 15%
Currency:	1 Singapore dollar = 100 cents
Climate:	Hot, humid all year, heavy rains Nov–Jan

An island republic lying off the southern tip of the Malay Peninsula and joined to the mainland by a causeway crossing the Strait of Johore. The terrain is mostly lowland, with a gently undulating central plateau. It was once covered by rainforest, though little of it remains today and agriculture is relatively unimportant.

A settlement was founded in 1299, its original name being Temasak, but it was destroyed in the 14th century, probably by the Javanese. It arose again as Singapura (city of the lion), and was later absorbed into the sultanate of Malacca (Melaka). In 1819, the island was leased from the Sultan of Johore by Sir Stamford Raffles of the British East India Company, which founded the capital, Singapore City. In 1826 it became part of the Straits Settlements, together with the British possessions of Penang and Malacca, and was administered by the governor of Bengal; by 1832 Singapore had become the capital of the Straits Settlements, attracting Chinese and Indian immigrants to its busy port. In 1858 the British government undertook the administration of the Straits Settlements, which in 1867 became a crown colony of the British Empire. During the Second World War Singapore was seized by the Japanese, when tens of thousands of British and Australian prisoners were taken. British

BELOW: View of Singapore from Kusu Island.

OPPOSITE LEFT: The Sultan Mosque, Muscat Street.

OPPOSITE RIGHT: Singapore skyline with ships.

354

rule was restored after the defeat of Japan and by 1946 Singapore was a separate crown colony, gaining independence in 1959. It joined the Malaysian Federation, with Malaya, Sabah and Sarawak, in 1963, seceding to become a republic within the Commonwealth in 1965.

Lee Kuan Yew and his People's Action Party came to power in 1959, and he retired after 31 years as prime minister in 1990. Singapore owes much of its success to Lee Kuan Yew, who initiated an ambitious, if rigid, policy of industrialization; his successor, Goh Chok Tong, seems to have continued in his footsteps. Head of state since 1999 is President Sellapan Rama Nathan; head of government since 2004 is Prime Minister Lee Hsien Loong.

Singapore has a highly developed and successful economy, with a per capita GDP equal to that of the Big Four countries of Western Europe. Historically, its wealth was based on transshipment and this is still the case, but it also relies on exports, particularly of electronics, machinery and chemicals, and banking, insurance and oil refining are also important. Singapore was adversely affected by the global recession of 2001–03, however, and by the outbreak of Severe Acute Respiratory Syndrome in 2003, which damaged its tourist industry, though this was largely counteracted by vigorous growth in 2004.

SLOVAKIA

Location:	14 G
Capital:	Bratislava
Area:	18,932sq m (49034km²)
Population:	5,431,363 July 2005
Main Languages:	Slovak
Main Religions:	Roman Catholic 60%,
	Protestant 20%
Currency:	1 koruna = 100 haliers
Climate:	Hot summer, mild winter,
	cold inland

A landlocked country in central Europe, Slovakia has land borders with the Czech Republic, Poland, Ukraine, Hungary and Austria. The country is rugged and mountainous in the north and central areas, and much of it is forested. The Carpathian Mountains dominate the north, giving way to the range of the High Tatras, popular with skiers, that are interspersed with scenic lakes and valleys. There are fertile lowlands in the south. However, the extent of the danger to the environment caused by the Gabickovo dam, that diverts water from the River Danube, is still under debate.

What is now Slovakia was settled in the 5th and 6th centuries by Slavs. It was part of the empire of Greater Moravia in the 9th century, and was conquered by Magyars in the 10th century, when Roman Catholicism was adopted. By the 11th century it was part of the Kingdom of Hungary, and then of Austria-Hungary until 1918, during which time a process of Magyarization was enforced and the national identity was stifled. Following the break-up of the Austro-Hungarian Empire, and the chaos that ensued, Slovakia declared its independence and united with the Czech-speaking areas of Bohemia and Moravia to form the state of Czechoslovakia.

Germany annexed Czechoslovakia in 1939 and it became a puppet state of the Axis under the leadership of Josef Tiso. The 'Slovak Uprising' of 1944 saw a popular revolt against German rule, and the following year Czechoslovakia was liberated by Soviet troops. The Communists emerged as the strongest party in 1946, and by 1948 had tightened their grip; however, there followed a brief period of liberalization (the Prague Spring) in 1968, that survived the Soviet invasion, when the Slovak-born Communist leader, Alexander Dubcek, introduced reforms. In 1969, under a new federal constitution, a Slovak Socialist

LEFT: Gypsy musicians at Bardejov's three-day market.

OPPOSITE LEFT: A Ruthenian landscape, East Slovakia.

OPPOSITE RIGHT: St Martin's Cathedral, Bratislava.

Republic was created, with autonomy in local affairs. The peaceful 'Velvet Revolution' of 1989 marked a relatively easy transition towards a non-Communist government and in 1989 a new government was elected, with former dissident playwright, Václav Havel, as president. In multi-party elections in 1990, there was strong Slovak representation and Vladimir Meciar, a champion of Slovak democracy, became prime minister. By 1991 there was increasing Slovak separation as the economy deteriorated, and the Slovak parliament's declaration of sovereignty led to Havel's resignation. In 1993 the Slovaks and Czechs agreed to part company and Slovakia joined the UN and Council of Europe as the Slovak Republic. In 1994 it joined NATO's 'Partnership for Peace' programme, signing a treaty of friendship and co-operation with Hungary the following year. Slovakia joined both NATO and the EU in 2004. Head of state since 2004 is President Ivan Gasparovic; head of government since 1998 is Prime Minister Mikulas Dzurinda.

Slovakia has successfully completed the difficult transition towards a market economy and its economic growth has exceeded expectations since 2001, though unemployment remains a concern. Exports include vehicles, machinery and electrical equipment, chemicals, minerals and plastics.

357

SLOVENIA

Location:	14 G
Capital:	Ljubljana
Area:	7,819sq m (20251km²)
Population:	2,011,070 July 2005
Main Languages:	Slovene
Main Religions:	Roman Catholic 75%
Currency:	1 tolar = 100 stotinas
Climate:	Hot summer, mild winter, colder inland

A country of south-central Europe, Slovenia has a short coastline on the Gulf of Trieste and Adriatic Sea, and land borders with Italy, Austria, Hungary and Croatia. A mountainous region lies to the north and includes the Julian and Karavanke Alps, with the great limestone Karst (*Kras*) to the west; little of the Karst's pine forests remain – said to have gone to making the piles on which Venice was built. In the centre and east are areas of hills and plains, drained by the Sava and Drava rivers, while the Dinaric Alps lie to the south. Half the land is forested – a major resource – and there are extensive farms and vineyards.

Part of the Roman Empire until the 4th

century, the first stable Slavic Slovenian state was formed in the 7th century, though it was largely under Frankish, then Bavarian rule, during the 8th and 9th centuries. In the 13th century much of Slovenia's territory passed to the Habsburgs, later becoming part of the Austro-Hungarian Empire, which collapsed in 1918. The following year, Slovenia was ceded to the Kingdom of the Serbs, Croats and Slovenes, called Yugoslavia from 1929. It was occupied by Nazi Germany and partitioned between Germany, Italy and Hungary during the Second World War, during which time an anti-Nazi Liberation Front was formed, allying itself with Marshal Tito's Communist-led partisans. After the war its status changed to that of a republic of the renewed Yugoslavia, declared in 1945. By the mid 1980s, the Communist government became more liberal and agreed to free elections. In 1990 a coalition government secured victory in the first multi-party elections and Milan Kucan, a reform Communist, became president. Sovereignty was declared and independence was overwhelmingly approved in a referendum. Following the collapse of Communism in Eastern Europe, Slovenia seceded from Yugoslavia, along with Croatia, in 1991, despite intervention by Yugoslav forces, when 100 people were killed; it joined the UN the following year. President Janez Drnovsek has been head of state since 2002, having had previous periods as prime

ABOVE LEFT: Lake Bled.

LEFT: View of Ljubljana.

OPPOSITE: Lake Bohinj, in the Julian Alps.

minister, while Janez Jansa has been prime minister since 2004.

Slovenia can be regarded as one of Europe's most successful economies, given its recent entry into the EU in 2002. Exports include manufactured goods, machinery, transport equipment, chemicals and textiles, while fruit, maize, potatoes and wheat are major crops.

SOLOMAN ISLANDS

Location:	24 K
Capital:	Honiara
Area:	10,954sq m (28371km²)
Population:	538,032 July 2005
Main Languages:	English
Main Religions:	Protestant 75%,
	Roman Catholic 19%
Currency:	1 Solomon Island
	dollar = 100 cents
Climate:	Hot all year

An Oceanian Melanesian archipelago consisting of many hundreds of islands in the South-Western Pacific, the Solomon Islands lie to the east of Papua New Guinea. The largest island is Guadalcanal, and other inhabited islands include Choiseul, the Shortland Islands, the New Georgia Islands, Santa Isabel, the Russell Islands, the Florida Islands, San Cristobal, Malaita, Sikaiana, Maramasike, Ulawa, Uki, Santa Ana, Rennell and Bellona, and the Santa Cruz Islands. The northern members of the group, formerly a

German protectorate, form part of Papua New Guinea. Most of the islands are mountainous and covered in rainforest, while the coastal plains are used for subsistence farming on which most of the population relies.

The islands were discovered by the Spanish in the 16th century, though they were not colonized until the 19th century, when the southern islands were placed under British protection from 1893. In 1899 Germany ceded its possessions in the islands, which had been held since 1895, to Britain, in return for British recognition of its claims to Western Samoa. In 1900 the islands were named the British Solomon Islands Protectorate. They were occupied by Japan in 1942–43, triggering one of the fiercest battles of the Second World War off Guadalcanal. The islands were liberated by US forces in 1944, after the loss of tens of thousands of lives on both sides. They were renamed the Solomon Islands in 1975 and became fully independent from Britain in 1978.

Rivalry, sometimes bitter and intense, together with crime and political corruption, had always existed on the islands, but fighting began in earnest in 1998 when the Isatabu Freedom Movement accused the Malaitans of monopolizing land and jobs in Guadalcanal, and began to force them out. In 2000 a rival militant group, the Malaitan Eagle Force, effected a coup and the prime minister was overthrown. In the first election after the coup, Allan Kemakeza became prime minister in December 2001, having previously been sacked as deputy prime minister for allegedly helping himself

to funds meant for civil war victims. But his government failed to control the growing violence and in 2003 the Governor-General appealed for international help. But the trouble continued, and an Australian-led multi-national peace-keeping force was deployed later that year, when rebel leaders were arrested and illegal weapons confiscated. Since then, law and order have effectively been restored and government institutions and the economy are being slowly rebuilt.

Civil war caused the virtual collapse of the economy and timber, the main export commodity, remains vulnerable to fluctuating prices. Despite financial assistance from Australia, the hope for the future is that gold mining and palm oil production, which are among the islands' most important products, will be speedily resumed.

SOMALIA

Location:	16 K
Capital:	Mogadishu
Area:	246,200sq m (637657km²)
Population:	8,591,629 July 2005 E
Main Languages:	Arabic, Somali
Main Religions:	Sunni Muslim 99%
Currency:	1 Somali shilling = 100 cents
Climate:	Hot all year, rains Mar–Jun, Sept–Dec

A country of East Africa that extends along the Gulf of Aden and the Indian Ocean, Somalia, previously known as the Somali Democratic Republic, occupies a strategic position on the Horn of Africa. It is bounded by Ethiopia and Djibouti to the west and north and by Kenya to the south-west. Predominantly dry grassland and semi-desert, the terrain is undulating in the north but flat in central and southern areas; irregular rainfall gives rise to recurrent drought.

Arab traders began to migrate to the coastal areas from the 7th century and mingled with the indigenous Cushitic peoples. The Arabs brought Sunni Islam with them and established Mogadishu as a centre of trade and eventually a sultanate in the 10th century.

The protectorate of British Somaliland was established in the north from 1884–87 and Italian Somaliland in the centre and south from 1889. Italian Somaliland was established as a colony in 1927, and was incorporated into Italian East Africa in 1936. It was occupied by the British during the Second World War, who administered it until 1950, when it was again administered by Italy under UN trusteeship. Both became independent in 1960, when the two joined to form the United Republic of Somalia.

In 1969 the president was assassinated in a military coup, led by General Mohamed Siad Barre; the constitution was suspended, political parties were banned and Siad Barre became president of a socialist Islamic state, beginning a programme of large-scale public works. In 1972, 20,000 people perished during a period of severe drought. In 1977, with the help of Soviet arms, Somalia began an eight-month war with Ethiopia, when it made an unsuccessful attempt to seize the Ogaden Desert, that was inhabited by Somali nomads. Somalia would not withdraw, however, and hundreds of thousands of

BELOW: The Somalian desert.

OPPOSITE LEFT: Saltworks at Gizera.

OPPOSITE RIGHT: A health centre in Mogadishu decorated with graffiti.

Puntland, and Prime Minister Ali Muhammad Ghedi. The government includes several leading warlords but remains exiled in Kenya. The internationally recognized government is the Transitional National Government, originally led by Abdulkassim Salat Hassan, which controls only a part of the capital city of Mogadishu.

Somalia has relatively few resources and much of the economy has been devastated by civil war, deep political divisions and natural disaster. In 2004 Somalia was one of the many countries devastated by the tsunami, which struck areas around the Indian Ocean, destroying entire villages and killing around 300 people. Around 60 per cent of the population is nomadic or semi-nomadic and lives by its livestock.

refugees fled to Somalia. By the late 1980s, guerilla activity had increased in the north and civil war intensified. In 1991 Siad Barre was overthrown by opposing clans and the country was plunged into a state of lawlessness. That same year north-western Somalia declared its independence as the Somaliland Republic, though it remains largely unrecognized as such. In 1993, after widespread famine, convoys bringing food aid were hijacked by warlords. UN peace-keeping forces, led by US Marines, tried to help matters, but by the time they withdrew two years later, order had still not been restored. In 1998 the self-proclaimed state of Puntland in the north-east declared its

autonomy, as did Jubaland. The territory of Jubaland is encompassed within the state of South-Western Somalia and its present status is unclear. The fourth self-proclaimed succession, led by the Rahanweyn Resistance Army, came in 1999 and led to the autonomy of South-Western Somalia.

In 2000 clan elders appointed Abdulkassim Salat Hassan president at a conference in Djibouti. A transitional government was set up with the aim of reconciling warring militias, though little real progress was made. In October 2004, a Transitional Federal Government was elected in Nairobi, Kenya, led by President Abdullahi Yusuf Ahmed, the leader of

SOUTH AFRICA

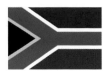

Location: 15 M
Capital: Pretoria/Cape Town
Area: 471,647sq m (1221566km²)
Population: 44,344,136 July 2005
Main Languages: Afrikaans, English
Main Religions: Protestant 54%, Roman
Catholic 15%, Hindu 3%
Currency: 1 rand = 100 cents
Climate: Hot summer; warm winter
in east, cool in north, mild
in south

A country
occupying the
southern extremity
of the African
continent, most of
South Africa is
covered by
highveld, a natural grassland that gives way
in the south to the lesser plateaux of the
Little and Great Karroo. These are bordered
to the south and east by the ranges of the
Swarteberge, Sneeuberge, Stormberge and
Drakensberg mountains, then by a lowland
coastal margin. In Transvaal, the veld is
crossed by the long ridge of Witwatersrand
and its goldfields, on which Johannesburg
stands, while Table Mountain, at 3,550ft

(1082m) overlooks the city of Cape Town in
the extreme south-west. South Africa has
coastlines on the South Atlantic and Indian
Oceans and land borders with Namibia,
Botswana, Zimbabwe, Mozambique and
Swaziland; Lesotho is an enclave to the
south-east, and lies totally encompassed
within South African territory.

In 1652 the Dutch East India Company
established the Cape of Good Hope as a
port of call for shipping on the way to the
Indies. The area had expanded by the 18th

century into a Dutch possession, by which
time half the population were Cape
Coloureds or Cape Malays, descendants of
indigenous peoples and slaves imported by
the Dutch, who had intermarried. In 1797
Britain seized the Cape during an Anglo-
Dutch War and annexed Cape Colony in
1805. In 1836 some 10,000 Boers (Dutch
farmers), in an attempt to escape British
rule, set out on the 'Great Trek', meeting
fierce resistance from the Zulu kingdom on
the way, and founding the Boer republics of
Transvaal and the Orange Free State from
1852–54. The discovery of diamonds in
Kimberley and gold in Transvaal attracted
prospectors and led to the subjugation of the
natives and conflict with the Dutch farming
community. In 1877 Britain annexed
Transvaal and overcame the Zulus in the
Zulu War of 1879. In the first Boer or South

African War, Transvaal Boers defeated the British at Majuba in 1881 and regained their independence. Denial of the rights of citizenship to British immigrants in Transvaal, and the imperialist ambitions of Cecil Rhodes, led to the Jameson Raid and the second Boer War (1899–1902). The Boers, led by Jan Smuts and Louis Botha, continued to resist until the British, by reason of superior numbers, seized the Boer republics at last.

In 1910 the Union of South Africa was formed, comprising the Cape of Good Hope, Natal, Orange Free State and Transvaal, with Botha as prime minister. In 1912 the African National Congress (ANC) was formed to improve the rights of the majority black population. The outbreak of the First World War was marked by a Boer rebellion that was speedily crushed by Smuts. German South-West Africa (Namibia) was occupied and later mandated to the Union and Union forces served in East Africa and France. Between the wars there were alternating periods when the (Boer) Nationalist Party, under General Hertzog (who wished to further racial segregation and sever ties with the British Empire), and the South African Party under Smuts (who wished to maintain the Commonwealth connection), were in power. They merged to form the United Party in 1934, in an attempt to reconcile Afrikaner- and English-speaking whites, but split over the Union's entry into the Second World War on the side of the Allies, the right-wing National Party having sympathies with Nazi Germany.

In 1948, when the National Party under Daniel Malan came to power, a stringent policy of apartheid (separate development of the races) was adopted. (This was continued under Johannes Strijdom (1954–58), Hendrik Verwoerd (1958–66), B.J. Vorster (1966–78) and P.J. Botha (1978–89.) In 1950 the entire population was classified by race and blacks and whites were segregated. The ANC responded with a campaign of civil disobedience, culminating in the massacre at Sharpville in 1960, when 70 black demonstrators were killed and the ANC was banned. The following year, in the face of Commonwealth opposition to apartheid, South Africa left the Commonwealth and became a republic. In 1964 the ANC leader, Nelson Mandela, was sentenced to life imprisonment; detention without trial was introduced three years later. In the 1970s over three million people were forcibly resettled in black 'homelands' and many were killed in clashes between black protesters and security forces in Soweto. A new constitution in 1984 gave segregated representation to coloureds and Asians, but continued to exclude blacks. Growing violence in black townships led to a state of emergency from 1985 to 1990, and sanctions were imposed by the Commonwealth and the USA.

In 1989 F W de Klerk succeeded Botha as president; public facilities were desegregated, and many ANC activists were released. The following year, the ban on the ANC was lifted and Mandela was released. In 1991 the remaining apartheid laws were repealed and sanctions were lifted, though clashes continued between the ANC and

Chief Buthelezi's Zulu Inkatha movement. In the first multi-racial elections in 1994, Mandela became president and membership of the Commonwealth was restored. In 1995 a Truth and Reconciliation Commission, headed by Archbishop Desmond Tutu, began to investigate crimes committed under apartheid. In 1999 Mandela retired from the presidency and was succeeded by Thabo Mbeki, who is also head of government.

Daunting economic problems still exist, hangovers from the apartheid era, and include poverty, high employment and lack of empowerment in disadvantaged groups; AIDS and crime are also major problems. On the other hand, South Africa has abundant natural resources, with mining forming the basis of its economy. It also has well-developed financial, communications, energy and transport sections, as well as a stock exchange that is among the largest in the world. It is the world's largest producer of platinum, gold and chromium, and produces diamonds and machinery. Agricultural products include wine, fruits, maize, meat and sugar.

OPPOSITE LEFT: Victoria and Albert Waterfront, Cape Town.

OPPOSITE RIGHT: Ndebele tribeswoman.

ABOVE: Union government buildings, Pretoria.

SPAIN

Location:	13 H
Capital:	Madrid
Area:	194,884sq m (504750km²)
Population:	40,341,462 July 2005
Main Languages:	Spanish
Main Religions:	Roman Catholic 97%
Currency:	euro
Climate:	Temperate in north; hot, dry summer, mild winter in south

A kingdom of south-west Europe, Spain occupies most of the Iberian peninsula, which it shares with Portugal, Gibraltar, and Andorra. Spain consists of a vast plateau that slopes to the south-west and is crossed by several mountain ranges. The plateau is bounded to the south by the Sierra Nevada range and to the north by the Cantabrian mountains and the Pyrenees, that separate Spain from France in the north-east. The Mediterranean Balearic Islands, the Atlantic Canary Islands, and Ceuta and Melilla, two enclaves in Morocco, together with a few islands, are also included in the territory.

The first inhabitants of the area were known collectively as Iberians, and may have included the Basques. Celtic tribes from beyond the Pyrenees eventually mingled with the Iberians, and were known as Celtiberians. Before the Romans arrived in the 2nd century BC, when the area became the Roman province of Hispaniola, the Mediterranean coast had been successively colonized by Phoenicians (Cádiz), Greeks (Emporion) and Carthaginians (Cartagena). After the fall of the Roman Empire in 414, Visigoths established a kingdom that lasted until the invasion of the Moors in 711. Over the next few centuries, Islamic art and culture were firmly established in Spain, evident in the splendour of the Great Mosque at Córdoba and the Alhambra of Granada. By 1250, however, most of southern Spain, apart from Granada, had been reconquered by the Christians, and a

number of small Christian kingdoms that had survived in the north were absorbed into Castile and Aragón. The marriage of Ferdinand of Aragón to Isabella of Castile in 1469, united their kingdoms: the conquest of Granada in 1492 completed the *Reconquista* and made them rulers of all Spain.

Under the patronage of Ferdinand and Isabella, Columbus made three voyages of discovery to the New World, and most of Central and South America went to Spain. By 1519 Ferdinand and Isabella's grandson, Charles I, was not only king of Spain, but also Holy Roman Emperor, Archduke of Austria, and ruler of Naples, Sicily and the Netherlands. But rebellion in the Netherlands, the defeat of the Armada by the

OPPOSITE LEFT: Retiro Park, Madrid.

OPPOSITE RIGHT: The Obradorio, Santiago de Compostela, Galicia.

LEFT: Port de Soller, Majorca.

BELOW LEFT: View across the River Guadalquivir to the Torre del Oro, Seville.

English in 1588, together with war, inflation and corruption, saw Spain's power begin to ebb, and by the 17th century it was a shadow of its former self. Following the War of the Spanish Succession (1701–14), when the Bourbon dynasty was established, and the Treaty of Utrecht in 1713, Spain lost its possessions in Europe, including Gibraltar. France overthrew Spain's Bourbon king, and Napoleon's brother was installed as King of Spain in 1808. With Britain's help, Spain was eventually liberated and the Bourbons were restored at the end of the Peninsular War in 1814.

Spain had already lost its South American colonies during the period 1810–30 and had also ceded Cuba and the Philippines to the USA after the Spanish-American War of 1898. Republicanism, socialism and anarchism came to the fore after 1900; General Primo de Rivera's dictatorship of 1923–30 failed to save the monarchy and a republic was declared in 1931. In 1936 the election of the left-wing Popular Front sparked the Spanish Civil War between the Nationalists, that included monarchists and members of the Falange Party, and the Republicans, which included socialists, Communists and Catalan and Basque separatists. The Nationalists, headed by General Franco and assisted by Italian and German forces, gained control of the countryside but failed to capture Madrid, while the Republicans received minimal assistance from Russia, and volunteers from many countries formed the International Brigade in support of the government. Bilbao and the Basque country were bombed into submission by the Nationalists in 1937 and in 1938 Catalonia was cut off from the main Republican territory. Barcelona fell in January 1939 and the war ended with the surrender of Madrid a few months later, with Franco now the dictator of a fascist regime. Franco died in 1975 and King Juan Carlos became head of state; the Nationalist movement was abolished. In 1977 Adolfo Suarez won Spain's first democratic election in 41 years, but in 1982 the Union of the Democratic Centre (UCD) lost heavily, and Felipe González Márquez headed the first left-wing administration since 1936. In 1982 ETA, the Basque separatist organization, stepped up its terrorist activities and despite a ceasefire, which ended in a bombing in Madrid in 2000, the violence continues. In 2002 Batasuna, a Basque nationalist party, was outlawed on the grounds that it was ETA's political wing.

Spain's economic revival began in the 1950s, based on tourism and manufacturing. It has since transformed itself from a poor agricultural economy into a prosperous industrial nation, producing cars, ships, electronics, chemicals and textiles. However, it still exports fruit and vegetables and is the third-largest wine-producer in the world. Spain entered the EC (EU) in 1986.

SRI LANKA

Location:	19 J
Capital:	Colombo
Area:	25,343sq m (65638km²)
Population:	20,064,776 July 2005 E
Main Languages:	Sinhala, Tamil
Main Religions:	Buddhist 73%, Hindu 15%, Muslim 7%, Christian 5%
Currency:	1 Sri Lankan rupee = 100 cents
Climate:	Hot all year, cooler in hills, monsoons May–Jul, Dec–Jan

Formerly Ceylon, Sri Lanka is an island state in the Indian Ocean, lying off the south-eastern tip of the Indian peninsula and separated from India by the Gulf of Mannar and the Palk Strait. The coastal plain is low-lying, lined with swamps and many lagoons. The land rises in the centre and south towards Adam's Peak (7,359ft/2243m) and Mount Pidurutalagala, which at 8,280ft (2524m) is the highest point on the island, while the wetter south-west supports rainforest and tea plantations. It is one of the most biologically diverse places on earth.

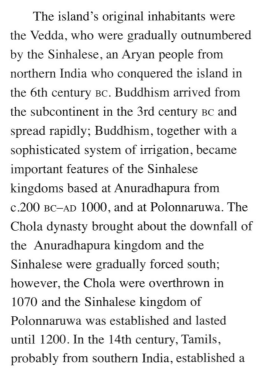

The island's original inhabitants were the Vedda, who were gradually outnumbered by the Sinhalese, an Aryan people from northern India who conquered the island in the 6th century BC. Buddhism arrived from the subcontinent in the 3rd century BC and spread rapidly; Buddhism, together with a sophisticated system of irrigation, became important features of the Sinhalese kingdoms based at Anuradhapura from c.200 BC–AD 1000, and at Polonnaruwa. The Chola dynasty brought about the downfall of the Anuradhapura kingdom and the Sinhalese were gradually forced south; however, the Chola were overthrown in 1070 and the Sinhalese kingdom of Polonnaruwa was established and lasted until 1200. In the 14th century, Tamils, probably from southern India, established a

LEFT: Beach at Mount Lavinia.

BELOW: Festival of the Golden Tooth, Kandy.

OPPOSITE: Tea-pickers, Eliya.

kingdom in the north. Starting in the 16th century, the island was dominated successively by the Portuguese, Dutch and British, who developed the plantations. Ceylon was finally annexed by Britain in 1796. It was formally ceded to Britain in 1815 and became a member of the Commonwealth from 1948, becoming independent in 1972, when it reverted to its traditional name of Sri Lanka; at this time,

and government forces. In the meantime, the conflict between Tamil separatists and the Sinhalese majority, which even Indian intervention has been unable to resolve, continues. In 2002, after two decades of fighting, a ceasefire mediated by the Norwegian government, was at last agreed, but not before tens of thousands had perished on both sides and many Tamils had fled the country. The Tamils, however, were forced to accept autonomy, rather than a separate state. Late in 2005 Sri Lankar's Foreign Minister, Lakshman Kadirgamar, was assassinated, and the LTTE was blamed. This has had the effect of hampering the peace process and the future of the country is currently as uncertain as ever.

In 1960 Sirimavo Bandaranaike became the world's first woman prime minister, succeeding her husband, Solomon Bandaranaike, who was assassinated in 1958. Chandrika Bandaranaike Kumaratunga was elected president of Sri Lanka in 1994, and remains head of state to this day. Also in 1994, her mother, Sirimavo Bandaranaike, was elected prime minister for the third time, holding the office until her death in 2002. The present prime minister is Mahinda Rajapakse, who assumed the office in 2004.

The Tamils' struggle for independence continues to affect the economy, while the tsunami of 2004 took a heavy toll in terms of tens of thousands of human lives and widespread damage to property. However, Sri Lanka is a large producer of tea, spices and rubber. It is developing its industrial base, and is also producing ceramics, textiles and garments, and tourism, insurance and banking are growing industries.

administrative and legislative power was transferred from Colombo, the commercial capital, to Sri Jayewardenepura Kotte.

In the 1950s, following the declaration of Sinhalese as the official language, violence erupted between the Sinhalese Buddhist majority and the Hindu Tamils. Since independence in 1972 there have been increasing demands for a separate Tamil state and in 1983 these erupted into civil war between Tamils, led predominantly by the Liberation Tigers of Tamil Eelam (LTTE),

SUDAN

Location:	15 J
Capital:	Khartoum
Area:	967,500sq m (2505815km²)
Population:	40,187,486 July 2005
Main Languages:	Arabic
Main Religions:	Muslim 73%, Roman Catholic 6%, Protestant 2%
Currency:	1 Sudanese pound = 100 piastres
Climate:	Hot, dry summer, cooler winter in north and west; hot all year, cooler on coast, rains Apr–Oct in south

The largest and most diverse country in Africa, Sudan lies in northeast Africa, south of Egypt and north of Uganda, with a coastline on the Red Sea to the north-east. The fertile valley of the Nile separates the Libyan Desert in the north-west from the high, rocky Nubian Desert in the north-east, otherwise the terrain is flat and featureless.

In ancient times, Meroë, near Khartoum, was the capital of the Nubian empire that

LEFT: The volcano at Jebel Marra, the fourth-largest in the world.

OPPOSITE LEFT: A nomadic herdsman, Omdurman.

OPPOSITE RIGHT: Kitchener's Gate, a coral building in the old port of Suakin.

covered southern Egypt and northern Sudan. From the 11th century BC to around AD 350, it was part of several Kushite kingdoms. Christianity had already been introduced in around the 4th century, but Islam arrived in 640, when Arab merchants became the economically dominant class. In 1820 Sudan was invaded by Muhammad Ali and came under the control of Egypt. In 1881 a nationalist revolt was led by the self-proclaimed Mahdi (Messiah) Muhammad Ahmad, which led to the capture of Khartoum and the death of the British General Gordon in 1885. In 1898 Lord Kitchener led an Anglo-Egyptian offensive, subduing the Mahdi revolt at the Battle of Omdurman, in which 20,000 Sudanese died. Thereafter, the north and south were treated as two separate and segregated colonies: they were ruled by an Anglo-Egyptian condominium until independence was granted in 1956.

Around this time, civil war erupted between the dominant Arab Muslim north and the secession-seeking black Christian and Animist south, which saw itself as increasingly marginalized. After continuous conflict lasting for nearly 17 years, plans to form a Federation of Arab Republics, to include Egypt, Syria and Sudan, were abandoned, and it was agreed in 1972 that

2005 granted the southern rebels autonomy for six years and an equal share in oil revenue, after which time a referendum to determine independence will be held. An unrelated intertribal war in Dafur, that broke out in 2003 and which is still current, has also resulted in tens of thousand of deaths and the displacement of many more.

Overall head of both state and government since 1993 is Lt Gen Omar Hassan Ahmad al-Bashir, though Salva Kiir heads an interim administration in the south.

In 1991 Osama bin Laden arrived in Sudan, attracted by what was claimed to be a purely Islamic state. He is thought to have lost a sizeable amount on business ventures in the country, including road-building, and received a defunct tanning factory as compensation from the government. This was confiscated, when, at the request of the US, he was forcibly expelled in 1996 and ended up in Afghanistan.

Sudan faces formidable economic problems, and years of civil war will keep its population poor for many years. However, it began to turn the situation around by applying sound economic policies, and achieved its first surplus in 1999, when the export of crude oil began. For the time being, however, agriculture is the most important sector, with cotton one of Sudan's main exports. Drought is a perennial problem.

the three southernmost regions would become autonomous, with a capital at Juba. However, successive military regimes, the first of which seized power in 1958, favouring Islamic-oriented governments, led to the creation of a Federated Sudan in 1983, which included these three states; but the imposition of Shari'a (Islamic) law sparked another outbreak of civil wars. The second of these wars, and the famine it caused, has resulted in more than two million deaths and the displacement of over four million southerners over a period of two decades. However, a final peace treaty in January

SURINAME

Location:	9 J
Capital:	Paramaribo
Area:	63,278sq m (163890km²)
Population:	438,144 July 2005
Main Languages:	Dutch
Main Religions:	Hindu 27%, Roman Catholic 23%, Muslim 20%, Protestant 19%
Currency:	1 Suriname guilder = 100 cents
Climate:	Hot all year, rains May–Oct

A country near to the equator in the north of South America, Suriname (Surinam) has a coastline on the North Atlantic Ocean. It has land borders with Guyana to the west, Brazil to the south and French Guiana to the east; the most southerly parts of the borders with Guyana and French Guiana are currently in dispute. The narrow, flat, coastal plain is cultivated and most of the relatively small population is concentrated in and around the capital, Paramaribo. The interior is mainly rainforest and savanna and is largely uninhabited, with ranges of mountains lying towards the south and south-west. There is a great diversity of flora and fauna; the Central Suriname Nature Reserve is a UNESCO World Heritage site, and there are several other national parks elsewhere.

A Spanish explorer discovered the area at the end of the 15th century, but it was the Dutch who first established settlements. A colony was founded by the British in 1651, to which settlers from Barbados were sent. In exchange for the Dutch colony of New Amsterdam (New York), the country was ceded to the Netherlands by the Treaty of Breda, which brought the second Anglo-Dutch War to an end in 1667. By the 1680s coffee and sugar plantations had been established, worked by imported African slaves; when slavery was abolished, labour was brought in from China, Java and India instead. The country reverted to Britain for short periods in the late 18th and early 19th centuries. In 1915 bauxite was discovered, which became Suriname's most important product; the large reservoir lake south of Brokopondo was constructed in 1964 to provide hydropower for the bauxite industry as well as for domestic use.

In 1954 Suriname became an autonomous part of the Kingdom of the Netherlands as Dutch Guiana. From 1958 to 1969 the country was dominated by Johan Pengel, the leader of the predominantly Creole Suriname National Party (NPS), becoming president of the country in 1975. Independence was also granted that year, when nearly half the population emigrated to the Netherlands. In 1980 there was a military coup and although a civilian government was tolerated, the military was essentially in control. In 1982 the army, led by Lt Col Dési Bouterse, seized power, setting up a socialist state. That year, economic aid from the US and the Netherlands was withdrawn after opposition leaders, charged with plotting a coup, were executed. In 1987 international pressure finally forced democratic elections, but the military overthrew the civilian government in 1989 and a democratic government was not returned until 1991. That year, Ronald Venetiaan, leader of the New Front for Democracy and Development, became president, when the power of the military was curtailed. He remained president until 1996, when a coalition government, led by Jules Wijdenbosch, came to power. Venetiaan was re-elected president in 2000.

Bauxite (aluminium) accounts for 70 per cent of Suriname's export earnings. However, its future prosperity depends on responsible monetary and fiscal policies, liberalization of markets, and increased competition.

LEFT: Courtyard of Fort Zeelandia, Paramaribo.

SWAZILAND

Location: 15 M
Capital: Mbabane
Area: 6,705sq m (17366km²)
Population: 1,173,900 July 2005
Main Languages: Swazi, English
Main Religions: Christian 60%,
 Traditional 40%
Currency: 1 lilangeni = 100 cents
Climate: Warm all year, cooler in
 Highveld, with winter
 frosts; light rain Oct–Mar

A landlocked country of south-east Africa, Swaziland takes its name from the Swazi, a Bantu tribe. It is bordered on the north, west and south by South Africa, and to the east by the Lebombo Mountains and Mozambique. The terrain consists of a central valley (Middleveld), with the eastern Drakensberg mountains (Highveld) to the west and the Lowveld to the east.

Swaziland has one of the oldest monarchies on the African continent. Towards the end of the 16th century, according to tradition, Ngwane II, a Bantu chief, founded a dynasty that dominated the indigenous Nguni and Sothi tribes. By the beginning of the 19th century, his descendant, Sobhuza I, had established a powerful Swazi kingdom, and by the mid 1880s the warrior king, Mswati I, ruled an area three times the size of the present country. In 1882 gold was discovered in the north-east, attracting fortune-hunters from Europe; these succeeded in gaining land concessions, usually by coercion. In 1894 Swaziland came under the joint rulership of Britain and the Boer republic of Transvaal. Following the South African War of 1899–1902, Swaziland, against the wishes of South Africa, became a British protectorate in 1903. In 1922 King Sobhuza II ascended the throne, and when Swaziland became an independent kingdom within the Commonwealth in 1968, he became hereditary head of state. In 1973, however, the struggle began between a totalitarian monarchy and those seeking democracy. The king reacted by suspending the constitution, banning political activity and assuming absolute power, substituting a traditional tribal system for parliamentary rule. He died in 1982, when one of his numerous wives became regent until the crown prince came of age. The regent, Queen Dzeliwe, was ousted by a younger wife the following year as real power passed to the prime minister, Prince Bhekimpi Dlamini. In 1986 the crown prince came to the throne as King Mswati III; he grudgingly reinstated a parliamentary system in 1990, following agitation from students and workers, and promised political reform. In 1993 elections of candidates were held for the first time, and again five years later. Prime minister since 2003 is Absolom Themba Dlamini.

Being practically an enclave of South Africa, Swaziland is heavily dependent on its powerful neighbour, both for imports and exports, and the money Swazi workers in South Africa send home is vital to their families. Over 80 per cent of the population relies on subsistence agriculture, since the exhaustion of iron ore reserves in 1978, with sugar and wood pulp the chief products. Overgrazing, soil depletion and drought, however, meant that a quarter of the population needed food aid in 2004, added to which Swaziland has recently surpassed Botswana in having the highest incidence of HIV/AIDS.

ABOVE LEFT: Thatched huts being repaired at Belegang.

ABOVE: Swazi woman in traditional dress, near Piggs Peak.

SWEDEN

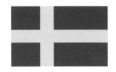

Location: 14 E
Capital: Stockholm
Area: 173,806sq m (450157km²)
Population: 9,001,774 July 2005
Main Languages: Swedish
Main Religions: Lutheran 89%,
Roman Catholic 2%
Currency: 1 Swedish krona =
100 öre
Climate: Mild summer, cold winter,
snow

A kingdom of northern Europe, Sweden occupies the eastern portion of the Scandinavian peninsula, bordering Finland in the north-east. It has a coastline on the Gulf of Bothnia and the Baltic Sea to the east and the Skagerrak and Kattegat Straits lie to the south-east. A mountain range runs along most of Sweden's border with Norway to the west, and there are more mountains in the north. In the centre is a lowland area, with the fertile Skane in the extreme south. There are numerous lakes, the largest being Vänern, Vättern, Mälaren and Hjälmaren, that lie to the centre in the south. Of Sweden's numerous islands, Öland and Götland in the Baltic Sea are the largest. Two-thirds of the country is covered in forests and there is very little arable land. The climate is moderated by the Gulf Stream in the south, but it is subarctic in the north.

Although a Swedish tribe of *Suiones* was mentioned by Tacitus, the Roman historian, in the 1st century, little is known of the earliest inhabitants until the 8th century, when Svears are known to have lived in the east (Svealand), from which the name Sweden derives, with Goths (*Götars*) in the south. During the 9th and 10th centuries, Swedish Vikings ventured east and south into the Baltic countries, Russia, Europe and as far as the Black Sea and Constantinople. In around 1000 Christianity was adopted and much of Sweden was united, apart from the extreme south, which was ruled by Denmark until 1660. Beginning in the 11th century, a series of forays into the wilds of Lappland, Finland, and the rest of the peninsula,

Germany) in the Thirty Years' War, which, in spite of Sweden's victory and swift elevation to power in Europe, left it depleted and impoverished. Ruled by a corrupt oligarchy, Sweden sank into insignificance thereafter, until Gustav III (1771–91) established an enlightened despotism and introduced wide-ranging reforms.

Sweden lost Finland to Russia in 1809, but was granted Norway in 1814 – a union that was not dissolved until 1905; since then, Sweden has preserved it neutrality and refrained from making alliances, policies it adhered to in both World Wars and the Cold War that followed. Because the Vasa line was by now extinct, the crown passed to the

French marshal, Jean Bernadotte, who reigned as Charles XIV (1818–44) and established the present dynasty. King Carl XVI Gustav has been head of state since 1973. In 1980 Salic law, that prevented succession through the female line, was abrogated and his daughter, Crown Princess Victoria (1977–) became his heir-apparent. Göran Persson has served consecutive terms as prime minister since 1996. In 2003, Anna Lindh, Sweden's popular foreign minister, was killed in a motiveless attack.

Sweden, assisted by a long period of peace and neutrality, together with an almost continuous Social Democrat government since 1932, has an enviable standard of living, having adopted high-tech capitalism married with an extensive social welfare system. By the 1920s Sweden had been transformed itself from an agricultural to an industrial economy, with the result that timber, iron and steel (developed in the late 19th century), machinery, motor vehicles and hydropower are now the mainstays of an economy oriented towards foreign trade. However, indecision as to its precise role in Europe delayed Sweden's entry into the EU until 1995. In 2003 it declined to join the euro system for the second time, having concerns over the diminishment of its sovereignty.

brought Finland under Swedish rule in 1362. The Riksdag, a parliament of nobles, clergy and burgesses, was founded in 1359, and peasants were included 80 years later; it survives to this day though with various reforms.

By the Union of Kalmar in 1397, Denmark, Norway and Sweden were united beneath the rule of the Danish queen, but Swedish nationalism led to revolts, the last

of which brought an end to the union in 1520–23. This brought Gustavus Vasa, the leader of the rebellion, to the throne of an independent Sweden as Gustav I, and Lutherism, which was encouraged by him, became the national religion a few years later. In the 17th century, Sweden's ambition to dominate the Baltic brought it into conflict with Denmark, Poland, Russia and Brandenburg (then a state of eastern

OPPOSITE: Riddarholmen, Stockholm.

FAR LEFT: A fjord-side house in the Nynashamn archipelago.

LEFT: Lake Mälaren, Stockholm.

SWITZERLAND

Location:	14 G
Capital :	Bern
Area:	15,943sq m (41293km²)
Population:	7,489,370 July 2005 E
Main Languages:	German, French, Italian
Main Religions:	Roman Catholic 46%,
	Protestant 40%
Currency:	1 Swiss franc =
	100 centimes
Climate:	Warm summer, cold
	winter, snow

A landlocked federal republic of Western Europe, bounded by Germany to the north, Austria and Liechtenstein to the east, Italy to the south and France to the north-west. Switzerland is extremely mountainous, its central plateau contained by the ranges of the Jura in the north-west and by the Alps in the south. The upper Rhine and Rhône rivers lie between the Bernese Oberland and the main chain of the Alps, whose highest point is Monte Rosa at 15,217ft (4638m). There are many lakes, the largest being Lake Geneva, which lies partly in France and into which the Rhône flows.

Lake Constance (Bodensee), in the north-east, is shared with Germany and Austria, and Lakes Maggiore and Lugano with Italy.

The Celtic Helvetii were conquered and the area was occupied by the Romans in 58 BC. It was ruled by the Franks in the 6th century and was later divided between Swabia and Burgundy. According to legend, the origins of the Swiss Federation date to

1291, when three forest cantons formed the Swiss or Everlasting League, traditionally led by William Tell, to defend themselves from their foreign Habsburg rulers. After a struggle, the league achieved independence from the Habsburgs in 1388 and the Swiss victory over the Swabian League in 1499 effectively freed Switzerland from the suzerainty of the Holy Roman Emperor

BELOW LEFT: View of Lake Geneva.

OPPOSITE LEFT: The Castle of Chillon and the Dents du Midi, Lake Geneva.

OPPOSITE RIGHT BELOW: The Breithorn, Zermatt.

Maximilian. In 1506, due to the past successes of Swiss mercenaries, Julius II began the tradition of the Vatican's Swiss Guard, that has protected the papacy ever since.

By 1513, the acquisition of new territory, including Lucerne, Bern and Zürich, brought the number of cantons to eight; these have increased over the years and today number 26 relatively autonomous cantons. The Reformation of Ulrich Zwingli, which differed from that of Luther, in that he regarded the communion as a commemoration, rather than a repetition of Christ's sacrifice, was accepted by Zürich, Bern and Basel, but rural cantons remained Roman Catholic. This led to conflict between Protestants and Catholics in 1529 and 1531, and further violence erupted in the Battles of Villmergen of 1656 and 1712.

The Treaty of Westphalia recognized Switzerland's full independence in 1648. After the suppression of the Peasants' War in 1653, the cantons fell increasingly into the hands of small oligarchies. A French invasion in 1798 established a centralized government and rendered Switzerland a mere satellite of France, though Napoleon's Act of Mediation in 1803 largely restored Swiss autonomy. The Congress of Vienna in 1815 re-established Swiss independence and Switzerland received Geneva and other

territories: a new constitution was adopted, whereby Switzerland became a federation and its neutrality was guaranteed. In 1847, following a further outbreak of civil war between Protestants and Catholics, which was to be the last conflict on Swiss soil, a revised constitution, giving the central government wider powers, was announced, and the principle of the referendum was introduced in 1874. The constitution received further revision in 1891, since when there have been continuous social, political and economic improvements.

In 1999 Ruth Dreifuss became Switzerland's first woman president. In 2002 Switzerland became a full member of the UN. Despite being a member of the European Free Trade Association, it is not a member state of the EU, though it is broadly in agreement with its principles, and many aspects of Swiss life, including the law, have been brought into line with those of Europe. Head of both state and government since January 2005 is President Samuel Schmid.

Switzerland maintained its neutrality throughout two World Wars and has a strong tradition of international co-operation, that has enabled it to remain peaceful and prosperous, with a stable economy, a skilled workforce and low unemployment. It is a country lacking natural resources, but has a well-developed industrial sector, producing chemicals, electrical equipment, machinery, precision instruments, watches and textiles. Dairy farming and tourism are also important, as is international banking.

SYRIA

Location:	16 H
Capital:	Damascus
Area:	71,498sq m (185180km²)
Population:	18,448,752 July 2005 E
Main Languages:	Arabic
Main Religions:	Muslim 90%
Currency:	1 Syrian pound = 100 piastres
Climate:	Temperate on coast; summer hot and dry inland; cold winter, snow in hills

A Levantine country in the Near East, Syria is for the most part a plateau, drained in the north-east by the Euphrates and its tributaries, and rising in the south-west to the Anti-Lebanon Mountains and Mount Hermon, and the Golan Heights. It has land borders with Israel, Lebanon, Turkey, Iraq and Jordan. The Syrian Desert covers the south-west, the north-east is semi-arid grassland, and there is a narrow plain bordering the Mediterranean in the west.

Situated on a trade route between the

LEFT: Overview of Aleppo city.

OPPOSITE LEFT: The Citadel, Aleppo.

OPPOSITE RIGHT: Ruins at Apamea.

Mediterranean and Mesopotamia, the area that is now Syria at one time included Lebanon, part of Jordan, Israel, Saudi Arabia and Iraq. It was settled by various peoples in antiquity, including Semitic Amorites, Canaanites, Hebrews and Phoenicians, who established trading posts along the coast. Aramaeans built their capital at Damascus in the 11th century BC, making it the oldest continuously inhabited city in the world. Syria was also occupied by Egyptians, Hittites, Assyrians, Babylonians (Chaldeans) and Persians, before control fell to Alexander the Great in 333 BC. After his death, Alexander's general, Seleucus Nicator, took control, bringing a Hellenistic culture to the country and founding Antioch, where St Paul eventually established Syria's first Christian church. In 63 BC Syria was conquered by the Romans under Pompey, and became part of the Roman Empire. It passed to the Byzantine Empire in AD 395, following the fall of the Roman Empire, when it was fully converted to Christianity.

In 633 Syria was conquered by Arabs and was gradually converted to Islam. By the middle of the 7th century, Damascus had grown prosperous under the Ummayad caliphate, but declined when the Abbasids moved the caliphate to Baghdad in 750. In 1055 Syria was overrun by Seljuk Turks. Syria was a target of the Crusades that began in 1096, though Saladin eventually won the

crisis and the second Arab-Israeli War, Syria merged with Egypt to form the United Arab Republic in 1958; conscious of being the lesser power, it seceded in 1961, re-establishing itself as a Syrian Arab Republic. In 1963 the Ba'ath Socialist Party established a military dictatorship, and there was a further military coup in 1966. In the Arab-Israeli Six-Day War of 1967, Syria lost the Golan Heights to Israel. In 1970 the Ba'athist Minister of Defence, Hafez al-Asad, assumed power in a bloodless military coup, becoming president by referendum the following year. Asad formed the National Progressive Front, a coalition of parties led by the Ba'athists. However, his authoritarian but stable regime was not without its critics, both at home aand abroad, and there was domestic dissension and insurgency in the 1970s that was promptly quashed. A new constitution in 1973 declared Syria a democratic socialist state.

After the Yom Kippur War of 1973, when Syria invaded the Golan Heights, and succeeded in recapturing only a small part, UN troops occupied a demilitarized zone between Syria and Israel. In 1986 Britain broke off diplomatic relations, having accused Syria of international involvement in terrorism, though contact was restored four years later. In 1991 Syrian troops joined the US-led coalition in the Gulf War against Iraq. In 1994 talks were held between Syria and Israel regarding the Golan Heights, and there were further discussions which came to nought. In 1998 relations with Israel deteriorated after land cultivated by Arabs in the Golan Heights was seized by the Israelis. President Asad died in 2000, after 30 years

in power, and was succeeded in the office by his son Bashar al-Asad. Head of government since 2003 is Prime Minister Muhammad Naji al-Utri. Syria completed a full withdrawal of its troops from Lebanon in May 2005; they had been stationed there since 1976, ostensibly in a peace-keeping role.

Syria's main resources are oil, hydropower and fertile agricultural land, which produces wheat and cotton, among other crops. The worry is, however, that the oil will soon run out, and industrial diversification is now under way.

day. In the 13th century the Mameluke sultans of Egypt took control, setting up their headquarters in Damascus. In 1516 the Ottoman Turks established their rule, which lasted for 400 years, broken only by the Egyptian, Ibrahim Pasha, who ruled as governor from 1832–39, after which the Turks returned.

The turn of the 19th century saw the rise of Arab nationalism in Lebanon and Syria. Separatist movements, rebelling against Ottoman rule, were supported by Britain and France during the First World War, and the end of Ottoman control came in 1918, when

an Arab kingdom was briefly restored. Syria, with Lebanon, however, became a French protectorate in 1920, when the king was exiled. Following the fall of France in 1940, Syria came under a Vichy regime that was expelled by Britain and the Free French in 1941. In the face of French opposition, Syria gained full independence in 1946. In the first Arab-Israeli War of 1948–49 Syria joined the unsuccessful invasion of the newly-created Israeli state.

After a series of coups d'état, and admiring the leadership shown by the Egyptian President Nasser during the Suez

TAHITI & FRENCH POLYNESIA

Location:	3 L
Capital:	Papeete
Area:	1,608sq m (4167km²)
Population:	270,485 July 2005
Main Languages:	French, Polynesian
Main Religions:	Protestant 54%,
	Roman Catholic 30%
Currency:	Comptoirs Français du
	Pacifique franc
Climate:	Tropical, but moderate

Stats apply to French Polynesia as a whole

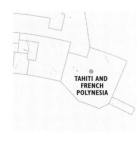

TAHITI AND FRENCH POLYNESIA

Tahiti is the largest and most populated of the French Polynesian islands, that lie to the east of Australia, Vanuatu and Fiji. The native population are Polynesians, and the islands are situated within the archipelago of the Society Islands in the South Pacific. Tahiti itself is mountainous and volcanic, but has fertile soil supporting tropical fruits, copra, sugar cane and vanilla, as well as luxuriant rainforest. Some of the

other islands have a terrain similar to Tahiti's, while others are low-lying and surrounded by coral reefs. Papeete, on Tahiti, is the capital of French Polynesia.

Seen by a Spanish ship in 1606, Tahiti was charted by Samuel Wallis, an English sea captain, in 1767. He was followed in 1768 by Louis-Antoine de Bougainville, who was making the first circumnavigation

of the world for France. Bougainville described Tahiti as an earthly paradise, where the people live happy, uncorrupted lives, far removed from the evils of civilization. Thus the concept of the noble savage was born, and was developed by philosophers such as Jean-Jacques Rousseau in their Utopian writings. Captain James Cook visited the island in the 1770s and

there were other visiting ships from Europe, including HMS *Bounty*, whose crew later mutinied; with Tahitian companions, they colonized the nearby Pitcairn Islands that lie to the south-east.

Needless to say, the beautiful idyll was destroyed with the coming of the Europeans, who introduced Christianity, prostitution, venereal diseases and alcohol, with smallpox

BELOW: Musicians in Moorea.

OPPOSITE and RIGHT: Bora Bora on the Society Islands.

and typhus decimating the indigenous population. In 1842 the kingdom of Tahiti was declared a French protectorate and had ceded sovereignty to France by 1880; various other islands in the group were annexed later. The French post-Impressionist painter, Paul Gauguin, lived and painted here in the 1890s. In 1995 there was widespread protest when France resumed nuclear testing on the Mururoa atoll, after a moratorium lasting three years; the tests were suspended in January 1996. In 2004 Tahiti and the rest of French Polynesia became overseas territories of France and French citizenship was accorded to the islanders, as well as full civil and political rights. Head of state since 1995 is President Jacques Chirac of France, locally represented by High Commissioner of the Republic Michel Mathieu. Head of government since March 2005 is Oscar Temaru.

Since 1962, when France began to station its military personnel in the region, French Polynesia has diversified from subsistence agriculture, and much of the workforce is employed by the military (at least until the end of nuclear testing), or by the tourist industry, which is now the country's greatest earner. Other sources of income are pearling, deep-sea fishing, handicrafts and phosphates; Makatea in French Polynesia is one of the three great phosphate islands in the Pacific, the others being Banaba in Kiribati and Nauru.

TAJIKISTAN

Location: 18 H
Capital: Dushanbe
Area: 55,250sq m (143100km²)
Population: 7,163,506 July 2005
Main Languages: Tajik
Main Religions: Muslim 85%
Currency: somoni
Climate: Hot summer, cold winter, dry all year, snow in mountains

Landlocked Tajikistan is centrally located in south-eastern Asia, bordered by Uzbekistan, Kyrgyzstan, China, Pakistan and Afghanistan. In the north is the westernmost part of the great range of Tian Shah, while the snow-capped Pamirs lie in the south-east. To the north-west lies part of the Fergana valley and the ancient route to Samarkand.

The Tajiks are descended from Persians, who settled the area about 2,500 years ago. The region was conquered by Alexander the Great in the 4th century BC, when it became part of his Eastern empire, and in the 7th century by Arabs, who introduced Islam to the area. In the 9th century, the country fell to the Persian Empire, and was conquered by Genghis Khan and added to the Mongol Empire in the 13th century. The north came under the rule of tsarist Russia from 1860 to 1900, while the south was annexed by Bukhara that lay to the west. However, the Russian Revolution of 1917 weakened Russia's hold on Central Asia and its power was not fully re-established until 1925.

In 1924 Tajikistan became an autonomous part of the Soviet Socialist Republic of Uzbekistan, but was made a separate contituent republic in 1929, though Uzbekistan retained Bukhara and Samarqand. Tajikistan suffered greatly during the period of Stalinist collectivization and remained backward compared with other SSRs, though vast irrigation schemes greatly improved agriculture in the 1930s. In the 1970s Islamic underground movements began to form, setting the Tajiks against the Soviet Union, though serious disturbances did not begin until the 1990s.

There was a resurgence of Tajik nationalism in the late 1980s; the Rastokhez (Revival) Popular Front was established in 1989, Tajik was declared the state language, and new mosques were built. The Soviet Union collapsed in 1991, when Tajik independence was declared and Tajikistan joined the new Commonwealth of Independent States (CIS).

A civil war began almost immediately, when tensions between the new government (that consisted mainly of former Communists) and Islamic and democratic groups came to a boil. The government looked to Russia for assistance and by 1993 the Islamic rebels were forced to retreat to Afghanistan. However, fighting continued along the Afghan border and frequent incursions were made by the rebels into Tajikistan. In 1995 the civil war resumed in earnest, and air attacks on rebel bases in Afghanistan were launched by Russia. In 1996 pro-Islamic rebels captured towns in the south-west, though there was a UN-sponsored ceasefire later that year. In 1997 a four-stage peace plan was signed and a peace accord was reached with the Islamic rebel United Tajik Opposition (UTO); as part of the peace plan, members of UTO were appointed to the government.

In 2001 Tajikistan joined the post-11 September U.S.-led anti-terror coalition, following which borders were tightened to prevent al-Qaeda members from leaving Afghanistan. A referendum in 2003 allowed President Rakhmonov two further seven-year terms in office from 2006. Head of government since 1999 is Prime Minister Oqil Oqilov.

Tajikistan is the poorest of the ex-Soviet republics, though it has a high rate of literacy. With foreign revenue dependent on cotton and aluminium, the economy is highly vulnerable to external shocks, and protracted civil war, a heavy external debt, and a second year of drought have done little to help the overall situation. However, there are reserves of oil, gold, silver and uranium, though they appear somewhat limited. Tajikistan is in the process of seeking World Trade Organization membership and has joined NATO's Partnership for Peace.

Hissarsky Mountains and the Hissar Valley.

TANZANIA

Location: 15 K
Capital: Dar es Salaam/Dodoma
Area: 364,881sq m (945041km²)
Population: 36,766,356 July 2005
Main Languages: Swahili, English
Main Religions: Christian 34%,
Muslim 33%
Currency: 1 Tanzanian shilling =
100 cents
Climate: Hot all year, cooler in
mountains, rains Nov–Apr
(inland), Mar–May (coast)

A republic of East Africa, formed by the union of Tanganyika and Zanzibar in 1964, Tanzania has a coastal plain that rises to a fertile plateau of savannah grassland, with the mass of Kilimanjaro to the north-east and the Livingstone Mountains to the south-west. It is bordered by Kenya, Uganda, Rwanda, Burundi, DR Congo, Zambia, Malawi and Mozambique. It is bordered on the east by the Indian Ocean and parts of Lakes Victoria, Tanganyika and Nyasa (Lake Malawi) lie within its borders. Half the country is forested and it is home to ecologically-important wildlife parks, including the famous Serengeti National Park in the north.

Trading posts appeared along the coast, following the area's settlement by Omani Arabs in the 8th century. In 1499, Vasco da Gama visited the island of Zanzibar, and it was occupied by the Portuguese in the 16th century, together with the coastal states. In 1840, Sultan Seyyid bin Sultan moved his capital to Zanzibar and the trade in slaves and ivory flourished, though the sultanates of Zanzibar and Oman separated when the sultan died in 1861. In the 19th century European explorers began to venture inland, followed by Christian missionaries. In 1884, in defiance of Zanzibar, German colonization of the mainland began. In 1890 Zanzibar became a protectorate of Britain and German claims to the mainland were recognized. During the First World War, Tanganyika (part of German East Africa since 1897) was again taken by Britain and held until 1946.

In 1954 Julius Nyerere organized the Tanganyikan African National Union (TANU) to campaign for independence, becoming prime minister in 1960. Independence from Britain was achieved in 1961, though the country remained part of the Commonwealth, and Nyerere became the first post-colonial president of Tanganyika, with Zanzibar achieving independence the following year. In 1964 there was a violent revolution, in which the Arab-dominated sultanate of Zanzibar was overthrown by the Afro-Shirazi Party, merging with Tanganyika the following year, to eventually become the United Republic of Tanzania. Nyerere introduced African socialism, and initiated a programme of self-help and equality by means of nationalization and collective farming. However, a decade later, and despite technical and financial help from abroad, the programme was a singular failure, due to lack of co-operation, inefficiency, corruption and a rise in the price of imported petroleum. This was compounded in 1979 by a costly military intervention to overthrow Idi Amin in Uganda.

The first multi-party elections were held in 1995, producing a comfortable win for Benjamin Mkapa. In 1999 Nyerere died and Tanzania withdrew from Africa's largest trading block. In 2000, President Mkapa, who had improved the economy over the preceding five years, was re-elected. The following year violence broke out between opposition supporters and troops on Zanzibar, after elections had been partially rerun, following allegations of irregularities.

One of the poorest countries in the world, most of the population of Tanzania is rural and heavily dependent on agriculture: however, the system is primitive and topography and climate limit production. Nevertheless, Tanzania does receive technical and financial aid from abroad, and has been successful in attracting investment.

Masai tribespeople, Tanzania.

THAILAND

Location:	20 J
Capital:	Bangkok
Area:	198,114sq m (513115km²)
Population:	65,444,371 July 2005
Main Languages:	Thai
Main Religions:	Buddhist 95%, Muslim 4%, Christian 1%
Currency:	1 baht = 100 satang
Climate:	Hot, humid all year, monsoon May–Oct

An independent kingdom of South-East Asia, long familiar to the West as Siam. The name Thailand was adopted in 1939, and definitively in 1949, after a brief period of reversion to Siam in the 1940s. Thailand is bordered in the east and south by Laos and Cambodia and by Myanmar (Burma) in the north and west. The Andaman Sea lies to the west and the Gulf of Thailand and South China Sea to the south. It is mountainous in the north-west, with the Khorat plateau in the north-east stretching to the Mekong river. The central, fertile plain is highly populated, with the capital, Bangkok, located in the south. A narrow, hilly strip in the south makes up part of the Malayan peninsula, with Malaysia and Singapore at its southern end.

In the 13th century Siamese (Thai) people fleeing the Mongols left south-west China and settled in the valley of the Chao Phraya river, in what was then Khmer imperial territory. In 1238 the Khmer were ousted by the Siamese, who formed a new kingdom based at Sukhothai. The capital was moved to Ayutthaya and a new kingdom was established in 1350. The Thai monarchy, which was absolute until 1932, is thought to have stemmed from this time, the present dynasty dating from 1782. Portuguese traders reached Siam in 1511, followed by the Dutch in the 17th century: the British East India Company also had a presence in Ayutthaya around this time, though at no time did Siam lose its sovereignty to a European power. In 1767 Burmese invaders destroyed Ayutthaya and massacred the ruling family, having occupied the city during the previous century, when it left the country in a state of anarchy.

In 1782 General Phraya Chakri founded the new capital of Bangkok, pronouncing himself King Rama I. The 19th century was a period of modernization and Siam, after its period of isolation, began to open up to the West. A treaty of trade and friendship was made with Britain in 1826, and treaties with other European powers followed. Increasing national awareness during the First World War, together with a bloodless revolution, brought changes to the constitution in 1932, when a constitutional monarchy with little direct power was established; it is a moral

OPPOSITE: Buddhist nuns praying, Bangkok.

LEFT: Klong *(canal) dwellings on the Chao Phraya river, Bangkok.*

force, however, and remains the protector of Thai Buddhism and the national identity.

In 1938 Field Marshal Phibun Songkhram became premier and changed the country's name to Thailand. During the Second World War, Thailand was a puppet state of Japan under Phibun; once the Japanese had withdrawn in 1945, Thailand was obliged to return territory taken from Kampuchea (now Cambodia), Laos and Malaya. In 1946 King Ananda Mahidol was assassinated and was succeeded by his brother, Phumiphon Adunyadet. A series of mostly bloodless coups d'état, the first of which was led by Phibun, brought a military junta, which was overthrown in 1973, and a

democratic constitution was adopted the following year.

Communist guerillas had been active since 1965, not only in the north and east on the Laotian border, but also on the Malaysian border in the south. From 1967 to 1972 Thai troops fought on the side of the USA in the Vietnam War. Following the further military coup of October 1976, Thailand remained a monarchy, the new constitution providing for a Senate appointed by the king, on the prime minister's recommendation, and a House of Representatives elected on universal suffrage. All US forces were withdrawn, though some co-operation continued, but

relations with Kampuchea, Laos and Vietnam remained uneasy. By 1979 the Communists had claimed control of many 'liberated zones'. General Prem Tinsulanonda ruled for much of the 1980s. In 1991 a coup imposed a new military-oriented constitution, in the face of mass protest, but an election the following year saw the establishment of five-party coalition. Riots forced Prime Minister Suchinda Krapayoon to flee and Chuan Leekpai formed a new coalition, that collapsed in 1995–96, only to be replaced by a six-party coalition led by Chavalit Yongchaiyudh. In 1997 a major financial crisis led to a floating currency. An austerity rescue plan was

agreed with the International Monetary Fund (IMF) and Chuan Leekpai was re-elected prime minister. In 1998 foreign workers were repatriated as the economy contracted sharply due to the rescue plan. The opposition Chart Patthana party was brought into the coalition to increase the majority and facilitate economic reforms. In 2001 the Thai Rak Thai party won general elections, but failed to obtain an absolute majority. Thailand is currently facing separatist violence in its three predominantly Muslim southernmost provinces. King Phumiphon is still head of state, having occupied the throne since the Second World War. Head of government since 2001 is Prime Minister Thaksin Chinnawat.

Thailand had the world's highest growth rate from 1985–95. However, the Asian financial crisis of 1997–98 led to a contraction of the economy from which the country has fully recovered. Exports include textiles and footwear, rice, rubber, jewellery, motor vehicles, computers and electrical appliances; tourism is increasing year on year. On 26 December 2004 Thailand was devastated by a tsunami, triggered by an earthquake beneath the Indian Ocean. It claimed 50,000 lives, half of them tourists, and caused massive destruction to property in the southern provinces.

LEFT: Wat Sri Rong Muang Buddhist Temple, Lampang.

OPPOSITE: Phi Phi Don Island, Krabi Province.

Location:	22 K
Capital:	Dili
Area:	5,794sq m (15007km²)
Population:	1,040,880 July 2005
Main Languages:	Portuguese, Tetum
Main Religions:	Roman Catholic 90%
Currency:	US dollar
Climate:	Tropical; Hot and humid, with distinct dry and rainy seasons

Stats refer to East Timor only

Timor-Leste, otherwise East Timor, is a republic of South-East Asia, consisting of the eastern half of the island of Timor, the largest and easternmost of the Lesser Sunda Islands. It lies within the Malay archipelago and includes the islands of Atauro and Jaco, together with the enclave of Oecussi-Ambeno within West Timor. It is a mountainous island; to the north lie the Ombai and Wetar Straits, with the Timor Sea separating Timor from Australia to the south.

Portuguese spice traders were the first Europeans to arrive in the area in the 16th century. By mid-century they had established a colony on Timor, while the surrounding islands were controlled by the Dutch, with Portugal ceding the western part of the island to the Netherlands in 1859. During the Second World War, East Timor was occupied by the Japanese and was the scene of the Battle of Timor, that resulted in tens of thousands of deaths. After their defeat, the Japanese withdrew, and Portugal regained control. The process of decolonization began in 1974, following a change of government in Portugal; but due to more pressing matters in Angola and Mozambique, East Timor was virtually abandoned and declared its own independence from Portugal in 1975. However, before this could be recognized by the rest of the world, East Timor was invaded by Indonesia on the grounds that the East Timorese FETILIN Party, that had received some support from China, was Communist. With the American cause in South Vietnam lost, and fearing the spread

BELOW: Monsoonal land, cleared for grazing cattle, East Timor.

OPPOSITE ABOVE: A concrete house, wrecked by a cyclone.

OPPOSITE BELOW: A mountain stream carrying silt from overgrazed highlands.

of Communism in South-East Asia, the US failed to raise objections, even though

new nation. However, Australian peace-keeping forces eventually brought the violence to an end. Independence was recognized by Portugal in May 2002 and East Timor joined the UN later that year. Since 2002 the head of state has been President Kay Rala Xañana Gusmão, while head of government is Prime Minister Mari Bin Amude Alkatiri.

Before and during colonization Timor was known primarily for its sandalwood, but by late 1999 the economic infrastructure had been destroyed by Indonesian troops and anti-independence militias, and much of the population had fled. However, a massive international effort has achieved substantial reconstruction, and there is the prospect of oil and gas production being developed in territorial waters. Coffee, sandalwood and marble are exported, and there is the potential of exporting vanilla in the future.

West Timor is politically part of the Indonesian province of Nusa Tenggara Timur. It comprises the western half of the island of Timor, with the exception of Oecussi-Ambeno. During colonial times, when it was occupied by the Dutch East India Company, West Timor was known as Dutch Timor and was home to Dutch loyalists during the Indonesian War of Independence (1945–49). It has approximately one-and-a-half million inhabitants, some of which are the refugees that fled from Timor-Leste in 1999.

West Timor has a mainly agricultural economy, using slash-and-burn methods to produce corn, copra, rice, coffee and fruit. Timber, including sandalwood, is also cultivated.

Portugal was a founding member of NATO. The territory was declared a province of Indonesia in July 1976 and Indonesian rule was brutal in the extreme: during the invasion and subsequent occupation, an estimated 100,000 to 250,000 out of a population of 600,000 lost their lives. In 1999 a UN-supervised referendum was held, when East Timor voted overwhelmingly for full independence. There were violent clashes almost immediately, as anti-independence militias, backed by Indonesian forces, began to operate a scorched-earth campaign, with a view to destabilizing the

TOGO

Location:	13 J
Capital:	Lomé
Area:	21,934sq m (56809km²)
Population:	5,681,519 July 2005
Main Languages:	French
Main Religions:	Traditional 60%, Christian 29%
Currency:	1 CFA franc = 100 centimes
Climate:	Hot all year, long rains Apr–Jul, short rains Oct–Nov

A country in West Africa, between Ghana and Benin, Togo also has a border with Burkina Faso to the north, and a short coastline on the Bight of Benin and the Gulf of Guinea to the south. It consists mainly of savannah grassland, divided by highland that crosses the country from north-east to south-west. There is a fertile plateau in the south, giving way to a marshy coastline with many lagoons.

The area was originally the province of Kwa and Voltaic peoples, with later influxes of Ewe and Mina clans from Nigeria, Ghana

Ramatou Beach, Lomé.

and the Côte d'Ivoire. The slave trade flourished in the 16th century and several of the tribes, the Mina in particular, procured slaves for European traders. From 1884 to 1914, Togoland was a German protectorate, after a deal was made with the local king, Mlapa III, and cocoa, coffee and cotton plantations were developed. During the First World War, Togoland was captured by Anglo-French forces and was divided between France and Britain when the war ended. It came under UN trusteeship from 1946 until 1956, when British Togoland chose to integrate with Ghana. In 1960 French Togoland chose independence as the Republic of Togo, with Sylvanus Oympio its first president..

Togo was the first African country to undergo a military coup following

independence: in 1963 Togolese veterans of the French army, many of whom had served in Indo-China and Algeria, overthrew the president when he refused to let them join the Togolese army. Olympio was shot the next day by Sgt Etienne Eyadéma, and Olympio's brother-in-law, Nicolas Grunitzky, assumed power. However, Grunizky was deposed in 1967 by Eyadéma, who became president in his place, allowing only one party, the Rassemblement du Peuple Togolais (RPT). After surviving what he believed to be an attempt on his life, he nationalized the phosphate mines and made all Togolese take African names, changing his own name to Gnassingbé Eyadéma.

From the late 1960s to 1980 Togo's economy boomed, thanks to phosphates, and Eyadéma's plans for Togo grew ever more

grandiose, so that when recession came and the price of phosphates plummeted, the economy was left in tatters. There were many coup attempts thereafter. In the early 1990s there was international pressure for Eyadéma to democratize, which he resisted, and pro-democracy activists were brutally put down. This caused outrage at home and abroad and Eyadéma was forced to recapitulate; he was stripped of power and became president in name only. However, hardline tactics by the army, that was loyal to Eyadéma, continued and the transition to democracy came to a halt. Using blatant intimidation, Eyadéma somehow managed to claim most of the votes and was elected president again in 1993. By now the opposition seemed to have run out of steam, and Eyadéma held the reins as firmly as ever until 2005; at the time of his death later that year he was the longest-serving ruler Africa had ever had. The speaker of the Togolese parliament should have succeeded him, but being temporarily absent, the army appointed Eyadéma's son, Faure Gnassingbé, as interim president, and elections were deferred to 2008. This caused uproar and he resigned, only to be elected president of Togo on 24 April 2005. The prime minister is Edem Kodjo.

Togo relies heavily on agriculture and foreign aid. Cotton is the most important cash crop, but cocoa and coffee are also exported. Togo is one of the world's largest producers of phosphates, though production has fallen over the last few years, owing to the cost of developing new deposits.

TONGA

Location:	1 L
Capital :	Nuku'alofa
Area:	289sq m (748km²)
Population:	112,422 July 2005
Main Languages:	Tongan, English
Main Religions:	Christian
Currency:	1 pa'anga = 100 senti
Climate:	Hot all year

United as a Polynesian kingdom from 1845, and the only monarchy in the Pacific, Tonga is an archipelago in the South Pacific. It comprises 170 or so islands, 36 of which are uninhabited, and lies 1,320 miles (2120km) north-east of New Zealand. Most of the islands have a limestone base, formed from uplifted coral, while others are limestone over a volcanic base.

The first settlers appear to have come from the Santa Cruz Islands to the north-west, being part of a migration that originated in South-East Asia thousands of years ago. By the 12th century, Tongan navigators and adventurers had explored many of the other Pacific islands and could be said to have achieved an empire of sorts. There were

LEFT: The Royal Palace on Tongatapu, the largest Tongan island.

BELOW: A coral-rock trilithon, built c.1200 AD, Tongatapu.

of government since 2000 is Prime Minister Prince Lavaka ata Ulukalala.

Tonga is a small island economy based on agriculture and fishing. The main crops are coconuts, bananas, squash and vanilla, much of which is exported, while tourism is the second most important source of revenue. There is imbalance in the distribution of wealthon Tonga, with a wealthy elite and poverty elsewhere; the effects are mitigated, however, by free education and medicine, while half the people grow their own food and keep their own animals.

outbreaks of civil war in the 15th and 17th centuries, after which, Europeans began to arrive. The explorers Willem Schouten and Jacob Le Maire arrived in 1616 and Abel Tasman in 1643. The islands were visited by Captain Cook three times from 1773, who called them the Friendly Islands, and the first Wesleyan missionaries also came that year. Tonga came under British protection in 1900 and became a sovereign member of the Commonwealth of Nations in 1970, joining the UN in 1999.

Head of state since 1965 is King Taufa'ahau Tupou IV, the son of Queen Salote Tupou III, who came to the throne in 1918. Like the Tu'i Tonga, the sacred paramount chiefs from whom they are descended, the monarch is held in great reverence and criticism is not an option. Head

TRINIDAD & TOBAGO

Location:	9 J
Capital:	Port-of-Spain
Area:	1,978sq m (5123km²)
Population:	1,088,644 July 2005
Main Languages:	English
Main Religions:	Christian 47%, Hindu 24%, Muslim 6%
Currency:	1 Trinidad & Tobago dollar = 100 cents
Climate:	Hot all year, rains Jun–Oct

Lying 7 miles (11km) off the coast Venezuela in the Caribbean Sea, Trinidad & Tobago form an independent state within the British Commonwealth. It comprises Trinidad, the largest and most southerly of the islands, Tobago, that lies north-east of Trinidad, and 21 smaller islands. Trinidad is the most highly populated and is where the main towns are located, including the capital, Port-of-Spain. The terrain is a mixture of plains, hills and low mountains. Trinidad's Pitch Lake, on the south-western coast, is the largest natural source of ashphalt

in the world; it is said that the Elizabethan adventurer and explorer, Sir Walter Raleigh, used the ashphalt from this lake to mend his ships.

Trinidad was peopled by various Amerindian tribes before the arrival of the Europeans, while Tobago was inhabited by Carib Indians. Columbus discovered Trinidad in 1498 and named it after the Holy Trinity, while the name Tobago probably derives from tobacco. Trinidad was colonized by the Spanish in 1532, while Tobago changed hands among various European sea powers, though settlement of both islands remained sparse. In 1797 Trinidad was taken by the British and it was ceded to them in 1802.

Tobago was ceded to Britain by France in 1814, and the islands amalgamated in 1889. Trinidad & Tobago, with Jamaica, belonged to the West Indies Federation from 1958, as a preparation for independence in 1962, when the federation was dissolved; it became a republic in 1976. Its chequered history is reflected in the place names, and the fact that Indian, Portuguese, Chinese and African indentured labourers were imported to work the sugar and cacao plantations in the 19th century, after slavery had been abolished, while immigrants from Syria and Lebanon have also added to the ethnic mix. Head of state since 2003 is President George Maxwell Richards; head of government since 2001 is Prime Minister Patrick Manning.

LEFT: A Tobago beach.

BELOW: A steel band, Grafton, Tobago.

RIGHT: Pigeon Point, Tobago, one of the most beautiful beaches in the Caribbean.

The economy of Trinidad & Tobago is not quite as prosperous as it was during the oil boom that lasted from 1973 to 1983, but petroleum, natural gas and petrochemicals are still the main revenue earners. Tourism is also important, though there were less visitors after the terrorist attacks of 11 September 2001 in New York. Trinidad & Tobago is rapidly becoming known as an international centre of finance and investment.

TUNISIA

Location:	14 H
Capital:	Tunis
Area:	63,378sq m (164150km²)
Population:	10,074,951 July 2005
Main Languages:	Arabic
Main Religions:	Sunni Muslim 99%
Currency:	1 Tunisian dinar =
	1000 millimes
Climate:	Hot summer, mild winter,
	hotter inland, rain Nov–Apr

An independent republic in North Africa, Tunisia is located between Algeria and Libya, with the Mediterranean Sea to its north and east. There is fertile arable and forested land bordering the Mediterranean, which is backed by the easternmost part of the Atlas Mountains, while to the south of the salt lake of Chott Djerid lies the Sahara Desert. The fertile island of Djerba, to the east, is thought to be the Island of the Lotus-Eaters of Homer's *Odyssey*, and is linked to the mainland by a causeway.

In 814 BC, Phoenicians from the ancient port of Tyre in modern Lebanon founded

LEFT: *Ghorfas built between the 15th and 19th centuries at Ksar Soltane.*

BELOW: *Place de la Kasbah monument, Tunis.*

OPPOSITE: *Kebili Oasis, Nefzaoua.*

from Sicily. Berber Hafsids ruled from 1230, while Spain was occupying most of the coast; to combat this, Tunisia became a part of the Ottoman Empire in 1574. In the late 16th century Tunisia was the stronghold of pirates, who were the scourge of the Barbary coast until the 19th century. Under its Turkish governors (beys), Tunisia achieved virtual independence within the Ottoman Empire: the local dynasty founded by Hussein Bey in 1705, lasted until 1957.

Carthage, near to the modern-day capital, Tunis, with Dido as its legendary queen. By the 6th century BC, Carthage was a force to be reckoned with throughout the Mediterranean. During the third Punic War with Rome in 146 BC (the first began in 264 BC), Carthage was destroyed and became part of Rome's African province, producing wheat for the rest of the empire. The area was held by Vandals in the 5th century AD and in 533 became part of the Byzantine Empire. It was invaded by Arabs in the 7th century, when Islam was introduced, and was ruled by Islamic dynasties, interrupted by Berber rebellions, from the 9th to the 12th centuries, the last dynasty being that of the Almohads. Coastal areas were held for a brief period in the 12th century by Normans

A programme of economic modernization, begun by Ahmad Bey in the 19th century, almost ruined the country. In 1881, Tunis became a protectorate of France. In 1920 a campaign began for equal Tunisian participation in the French-dominated government, and Habib Bourguiba founded a radical splinter group, the Socialist Destourian Party (PSD), as a nationalist movement in 1934. Tunisia was a major battleground in the North African campaign, during the Second World War, and there was a brief period of German occupation from 1941 to 1942. In 1956 independence under the rule of the bey was achieved with Bourguiba as prime minister; he was to dominate Tunisian politics for the next 31 years, clamping down on Islamic fundamentalism and establishing women's rights to a degree unusual in an Arab state. However, the bey was deposed the following year and Tunisia became a one-party state under the now-President Bourguiba; he was made president for life in 1975. In 1979 the headquarters of the Arab League was moved to Tunis after Egypt signed the Camp David Accords. The first multi-party elections were held in 1981, but were won by Bourguiba's PSD. In 1982 the Palestinian Liberation Organization (PLO) was permitted to move its headquarters to Tunis. In 1985 diplomatic relations with Libya were severed and Israel bombed the headquarters of the PLO. In 1987 Zine el-Abidine Ben Ali declared Bourguiba, now 84, incompetent, and seized power himself. He was re-elected in 1989, when the PSD became the Constitutional Democratic Rally (RCD); the continuation of the one-party system in an emerging democracy is something of a problem

In 1990 the headquarters of the Arab League was returned to Cairo. In 1994 Zine el-Abidine Ben Ali was re-elected and the PLO transferred its operations to Gaza in Palestinian territory. In 1999 Ben Ali was re-elected president and Muhammad Ghannouchi prime minister. In 2002 al-Qaeda was blamed for bombing a synagogue on the holiday island of Djerba, killing 19 people, 11 of them German tourists.

Tunisia has a mixed economy, and agriculture, fishing, livestock, mining, energy, tourism and manufacturing have ensured steady growth. Tunisia's agreement of association with the EU came into force on 1 March 1998, and was the first of the accords with non-European Mediterranean countries to take effect. By 2008 Tunisia will be a fully associated member of the EU, on a par with countries like Norway or Iceland.

TURKEY

Location:	15 H
Capital:	Ankara
Area:	300,947sq m (779453km2)
Population:	69,660,559 July 2005
Main Languages:	Turkish
Main Religions:	Muslim 99%
Currency:	1 Turkish lira = 100 kurus
Climate:	Very hot summer, cooler on coast; cold winter in north, mild in south

A strategically-located republic in both Europe and Asia, Turkey in Europe (Thrace) is separated from the Anatolian peninsula of Asia Minor by the Bosphorus, the Sea of Marmara (Aegean Sea), and the Dardanelles. To the south lies the Mediterranean, with the Black Sea to the north. Turkey has eight neighbours: Bulgaria, Greece, Georgia, Armenia, Azerbaijan, Iran, Iraq and Syria. The Anatolian plateau is mostly mountainous, rising to Mount Ararat at 16,945 (5165m) near the Armenian border. The Taurus and Anti-Taurus Mountains lie to the south, with the Pontine range bordering the Black Sea to the north. Ankara (Angora),

LEFT: Roman remains at Ephesus.

BELOW: The Grand Bazaar covered market, Istanbul.

OPPOSITE: The Istanbul waterfront with the Galata tower.

situated towards the centre of the plateau, is the capital, and Istanbul, that lies in Europe, is the largest city.

Asia Minor was part of the Roman Empire in the 1st century BC, passing to the Byzantine Empire in 398. At the Battle of Manzikert in 1071, Seljuk Turks conquered the Byzantines, establishing their empire in Asia Minor and bringing Islam to the area. Ottoman Turks, driven west by the Mongols, became vassals of the Seljuks, but Osman I founded a small kingdom of his own in 1299, which quickly displaced that of the Seljuks to include the whole of Asia Minor. The Ottomans began their European conquests by capturing Gallipoli in 1354. In the Battle of Kosovo in 1389 the Turks defeated the Serbs, taking control of the

Balkan peninsula. In 1453, Constantinople, the capital of Byzantium, fell to the Turks, becoming the capital of the Ottoman Empire as Istanbul. The Ottoman Empire reached its zenith under Suleiman the Magnificent in the 16th century. By the middle of the century it had conquered Egypt, Syria, Arabia, Mesopotamia, Tripoli, Cyprus and most of Hungary, taking Crete in 1669.

The Christian counter-offensive began to take effect in 1683 after the Siege of Vienna failed. In 1699 the Turks lost

Hungary and in 1774 Russia ousted Turkey from Moldavia, Wallachia and the Crimea. There was an unsuccessful revolt in Serbia in 1804, but from 1821–29 Greece was able to free itself of Turkish rule. Russia's attempts to exploit the situation were resisted by Britain and France, which fought on Turkey's side in the Crimean War (1854–56). The Bulgarian rising of 1876 led to a new war between Turkey and Russia and by the Treaty of Berlin (1878) Turkey lost Bulgaria, Bosnia and Herzegovina.

A militant group, the Young Turks, secured a constitution for the country in 1908. Italy took advantage of the ensuing crisis to seize Tripoli in 1911–1912, while the Balkan states expelled the Turks from Albania and Macedonia over the next few years. Turkey entered the First World War on the side of Germany in 1914, only to lose Syria, Arabia, Mesopotamia and its tenuous hold on Egypt.

The Greek occupation of Smyrna (Izmir) in 1919 caused a surge of patriotism: Mustapha Kemal Pasha (later to adopt the surname Atatürk – the father of the Turks) established a provisional government at Ankara in 1920, expelled the Greeks, and proclaimed Turkey a republic in 1923, becoming its first president. He began a sweeping programme of Westernization, Islam ceased to be the state religion, polygamy was banned, and a new legal code was introduced. Atatürk died in 1938 and was succeeded by Ismet Inönü. The first free elections were held in 1950, but instability set in thereafter.

The position of the Turkish population in Cyprus had been a burning issue since the

early 1960s. In 1974 Turkey invaded Northern Cyprus to prevent a Greek takeover of the island. However, the 'Turkish Republic of Northern Cyprus' is still not recognized. The 1980s and 1990s saw years of civil war between Turkish forces and the secessionist Kurdistan Workers' Party (PKK ⊾ now KGK), in which 30,000 people lost their lives; in 2004, however, the violence re-erupted after a five-year ceasefire.

In May 2000, Ahmet Necdet Sezer

succeeded Suleiman Demirel, becoming the first non-military president in modern Turkish history. The prime minister since 2003 is Recep Tayyip Erdogan

An associate member since 1964, in 1999 Turkey became an official EU candidate and in an effort to succeed, introduced substantial social, political and educational reforms, as well as improving women's rights. The death penalty was abolished and tougher measures were adopted to prevent torture. Talks resumed in

October 2005, but Turkey's eventual accession to the EU is likely to remain a major issue over the next ten years.

After being close to economic collapse, Turkey has made impressive strides since 2002, when a tough recovery programme was agreed with the IMF. Textiles and clothing are its most important industrial sectors, though it is beginning to diversify into other areas, such as electronics. It is also a producer of chromium and phosphate fertilizers.

TURKMENISTAN

Location:	17 H
Capital:	Ashgabat
Area:	188,450sq m (488085km²)
Population:	4,952,081 July 2005
Main Languages:	Turkmen
Main Religions:	Sunni Muslim 90%
Currency:	1 manat = 100 tenesi
Climate:	Hot summer, cold winter, dry all year

A republic in central Asia, situated to the east of the Caspian Sea, Turkmenistan is dominated by the Kara Kum Desert, which occupies 90 per cent of the country, though irrigation allows crops to be grown. The terrain is predominantly flat to undulating, except for low mountains in the south-west and east along the borders with Iran and Afghanistan. Turkmenistan also borders Kazakhstan and Uzbekistan.

Alexander the Great conquered the area in the 4th century BC, on his way to India. It was then part of Parthia, a kingdom that ruled in Persia from 250 BC to AD 230. In the 7th century it was conquered by Arabs, who brought Islam with them. It was occupied by

Seljuk Turks in the 11th century, seeking to expand their empire into Afghanistan, but Genghis Khan gained control in the 12th century. It subsequently became part of Tamerlane's Mongol Empire until the end of the Timurid dynasty, when it came under Uzbek control. It was annexed by Russia in the 19th century and became the Turkmen SSR from 1925, when the borders of modern-day Turkmenistan were formed. It

remained a constituent republic of the USSR until the break-up of the Soviet Union in 1991, when it became part of the Commonwealth of Independent States (CIS). Saparmurad Niyazov, who was president under the Communist regime from 1985 and was re-elected in 1990, remains head of state and government for life. He retains absolute power and opposition is not tolerated.

Turkmenistan is a large producer of

cotton and has substantial reserves of oil and natural gas that remain to be fully exploited.

ABOVE: An apartment block in Merv.

OPPOSITE LEFT: Turkmen girls, typically dressed.

OPPOSITE RIGHT: Boy with a donkey cart.

TURKS & CAICOS ISLANDS

Location:	8 I
Capital:	Cockburn Town
Area:	192sq m (497km²)
Population:	20,556 July 2005
Main Languages:	English
Main Religions:	Baptist 40%, Anglican 18%, Methodist 16%
Currency:	US dollar
Climate:	Tropical marine, moderated by trade winds

A British dependency in the Caribbean, comprising two groups of about 40 islands between Haiti and the Bahamas, eight of which are uninhabited. The islands are mostly low-lying and composed of limestone, with extensive marshes and mangrove swamps. There is limited fresh water and private cisterns are used to collect rainwater.

The islands were part of the Jamaican colony until 1962, assuming the status of a British crown colony when Jamaica became independent. They were administered locally by the Bahamian governor until 1973, when the Bahamas became independent and the Turks & Caicos received a governor of their own. Independence was originally scheduled for 1982, but this did not happen, and they remain a part of British overseas territory. A union of the Turks & Caicos with Canada has been suggested from time to time, owing to historical links between the two and the amount of Canadian visitors that come each year. In 2004 Nova Scotia voted for the Turks & Caicos to join the province, though nothing has been decided yet. Head of state since 1953 is Queen Elizabeth II, represented locally by Governor Richard Tauwhare since July 2005. Head of

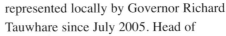

LEFT: A beach on Grand Turk.

BELOW LEFT: Local lizard.

BELOW: A local musician, Turks & Caicos Islands.

government since 2003 is Chief Minister Michael Eugene Misick.

The economy is based on tourism (with most of the visitors coming from the USA and Canada), fishing (lobster and conch), and offshore financial services, while food and capital goods are imported. There is some agriculture and cassava, corn, beans and fruits are grown.

TUVALU

Location:	1 L
Capital:	Funafuti
Area:	10sq m (26km²)
Population:	11,636 July 2005
Main Languages:	Tuvaluan, English
Main Religions:	Congregationalist 97%
Currency:	Australian dollar
Climate:	Tropical marine

Located in Oceania in the south-western Pacific Ocean, Tuvalu consists of a group of nine densely-populated coral atolls, formerly known as the Ellice Islands. The soil is poor, restricting crops to coconut palms, breadfruit and bush, and the terrain is low-lying in the extreme, making the islands sensitive to changes in sea levels. Fortunately, tropical storms are rare, though three cyclones did occur in 1997, and global warming is of some concern to the population. There is a lack of fresh water and the inhabitants have to rely on catchment and storage systems; however, a desalinization plant was built by the Japanese government and another is planned.

The islands were once a part of the

British colony of the Gilbert & Ellice Islands, but separated from the Gilberts (now Kiribati) following a referendum in 1975, which arose due to ethnic differences between the Polynesians of the Ellice Islands

and the Micronesians of the Gilbert Islands. As Tuvalu, the Ellice Islands achieved independence within the Commonwealth in 1978. Head of state is Queen Elizabeth II, represented by Governor-General Filoimea Telito since April 2005. Head of government since 2004 is Prime Minister Maatia Toafa.

Tuvalu has no mineral resources and few exports, leaving agriculture, keeping pigs and chickens, fishing, money sent home by relatives working abroad, and foreign aid as the main sources of income. In 1998, however, Tuvalu began to gain some revenue from the use of its area code for '900' lines and in 2000 by leasing its '.tv' Internet domain name.

ABOVE LEFT: A church on Niutao.

ABOVE: Thatched house, Nanumea Island.

LEFT: A wedding party on Funafuti.

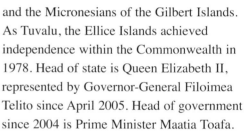
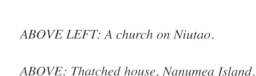

UGANDA

Location:	15 K
Capital:	Kampala
Area:	93,072sq m (241056km²)
Population:	27,269,482 July 2005
Main Languages:	English, Swahili
Main Religions:	Christian 62%, Muslim 6%
Currency:	1 Ugandan shilling = 100 cents
Climate:	Warm all year, cooler in mountains, rains Mar–May, Oct–Nov

A landlocked republic of East Africa, Uganda has borders with Kenya to the east, Tanzania and Rwanda to the south and south-west, the Democratic Republic of Congo to the west, and Sudan to the north. The terrain consists of a savannah platform, rimmed by mountains and drained by the White Nile and Lakes Albert, Victoria, Kyoga and Edward, all of which, apart from Kyoga, are shared with neighbouring countries. Uganda is still predominantly agricultural and most of the population lives in rural areas.

In the 16th century the Bunyoro

LEFT: A Ugandan landscape.

OPPOSITE LEFT: Shopping in Kampala.

OPPOSITE RIGHT: A Ugandan girl.

kingdom was founded by immigrants from south-eastern Sudan. The 17th century saw the rise of the powerful Buganda kingdom in the south, from which Uganda gets its name. By the middle of the 19th century, Arab traders in ivory and slaves had reached Uganda, and European explorers, such as Speke and Stanley, and the first Christian missionaries, had begun to arrive, leading to conflict with the pre-existing Muslim population. Uganda was placed under the charter of the British East Africa Company in 1888 and was ruled as a British protectorate from 1894, becoming independent within the Commonwealth in 1962. The following year it was pronounced a federal republic with the Kubaka (King) Mutesa II of Buganda its head of state and Milton Obote of the Uganda People's Congress its prime minister. The king, who was opposed to a one-party state, was ousted in a coup by Obote in 1967, who ended the federal status of the country and became president himself, banning all opposition parties after an assassination attempt was made on his own life in 1969.

In 1971 Obote was deposed in a military coup led by Maj-Gen Idi Amin Dada, who suspended the constitution and established a ruthless dictatorship. Under Amin's rule, nearly 50,000 entrepreuneurial Ugandan Asians were expelled, many of them fleeing to Britain, and the 300,000 who opposed the

regime were murdered. Amin also terrorized his own people, the economy was brought to near ruin, and relations with other African states, Kenya in particular, to which Amin was making territorial claims, deteriorated. In 1978 the Kagera region of north-western Tanzania was annexed, but the following year Amin was defeated by combined Ugandan exile and Tanzanian invading forces, who expelled him from the country.

After a period of great political instability, Obote was returned to power in the elections of 1980, when guerilla warfare and abuses of human rights claimed at least 100,000 lives, with twice as many fleeing to Rwanda and Zaïre (Democratic Republic of Congo). After opposition by the National Resistance Army (NRA), he was overthrown in a military coup in 1985 and replaced by

Brigadier Tito Okello, the head of the armed forces, who entered into a power-sharing agreement with Lt-Gen Yoweri Kaguta Museveni, the leader of the NRA. Museveni seized power the following year, headed a broad-based coalition government, and was re-elected in the first direct presidential elections in 1996: since becoming president, Museveni has improved human rights by cutting abuses perpetrated by the army and the police. Since 1987, the cult-like Lord's Resistance Army (LRA), a paramilitary group operating mainly in northen Uganda, but which has overflowed into southern Sudan, has been conducting an armed rebellion against the government. The LRA is accused of violating human rights, which includes abductions, the use of child soldiers and a number of massacres and mutilations.

The aim of the LRA is to run the state according to its leader's eccentric interpretation of the Bible's Ten Commandments, but to further this cause, nearly two million have been killed or kidnapped in the course of two decades.

In 1993 the Kubaka, in the person of Ronald Muwenda Mutebi II, was reinstated. In 1997, Uganda, along with other countries, became embroiled in the Democratic Republic of Congo's civil war, in an effort to depose President Mobuto, but DR Congo accuses Uganda of maintaining its influence in DR Congo's mineral-rich east, while Uganda accuses DR Congo of failing to disarm Ugandan rebels present in its territory.

President Museveni, in power since 1986, was re-elected in 2001, and Apolo Nsibambi is the current prime minister, though his role is to assist the president in his supervision of the cabinet.

Uganda has substantial natural resources, including fertile soil, adequate rainfall and deposits of copper and cobalt. Agriculture is the most important sector of the economy, with coffee the principal export. Economically, great strides have been made, but war, corruption, debt, failure to industrialize, and the slowness of the government to press home reforms, raise doubts as to its long-term prosperity. Uganda has had some success in its fight against HIV/AIDS.

UKRAINE

Location:	15 G
Capital:	Kiev
Area:	233,089sq m (603700km²)
Population:	47,425,336 July 2005 E
Main Languages:	Ukrainian
Main Religions:	Ukrainian Orthodox 80%
Currency:	1 hryvna = 100 kopiykas
Climate:	Warm summer, cold winter, snow

A country in Eastern Europe, Ukraine borders Russia to the north-east, Belarus to the north, Poland, Slovakia and Hungary to the west, Romania and Moldova to the south-west and the Black Sea to the south. The Ukrainian landscape is mostly one of fertile steppe and plateaux crossed by several rivers, including the Dnieper, Seversky Donets, Dneister and Bug, that flow into the Black Sea and the Sea of Azov. The only true highlands are a section of the range of the Carpathians in the west. Ukraine is subdivided into 24 oblasts or provinces and one republic, Crimea, that was granted autonomy in 1995.

The ancient Scythian empire was

LEFT: St Andrew's Church, Kiev.

OPPOSITE LEFT: Ivan Franko Opera and Ballet Theatre, Lvov.

OPPOSITE RIGHT: Ukrainian girl in traditional dress.

centred on the northern shores of the Black Sea, and stretched as far as Persia, lasting until about 200 BC. Goths settled in the 3rd century before eventually moving on and defeating the Roman Empire. By the 9th century, Ukraine was a state, founded by the Rus and centred on Kiev. This was a model of East Slavic culture that lasted into the 13th century, when the Mongol-Tatar Golden Horde sacked Kiev and destroyed the Kievan state. During the Middle Ages the area was subsequently divided between a variety of powers, including Poland, Lithuania, Austria, Romania and the Ottoman Empire. After the union of Poland and Lithuania in 1569, much of Ukraine passed to the new Polish Commonwealth.

In the 17th century, Ukrainians and runaway Polish serfs, known as Cossacks (outlaws), formed an autonomous military state in central Ukraine, but further Polish suppression caused the Cossacks to switch their allegiances to Russia. In 1648, the largest of the Cossack uprisings led to Ukraine being divided between Poland and Russia. Eastern Ukraine was eventually integrated into Russia as the Cossack Hetmanate in 1667, though Cossack identity was later suppressed by tsarist Russia.

By 1922 most of central and eastern

Communist Party leader, Leonid Kravchuk, was declared its prospective president. Independence was achieved in 1991, following the collapse of the Soviet Union, and Ukraine joined the newly-formed Commonwealth of Independent States. In 1993 President Kravchuk eliminated the office of prime minister. He was defeated by Leonid Kuchma in 1994, who fostered ties with the West, encouraged privatization and was re-elected in 1999. In 2001 Pope John II made his first visit to Ukraine. A peaceful mass protest in December 2004 ended in the overturn of a rigged election, when the reformist Viktor Yushchenko, having been relieved of power in 2001, was legitimately voted in as president. There is hope that freedom and prosperity will be shortly within Ukraine's grasp.

As part of the Soviet Union, Ukraine was by far the most economically important of the republics, its fertile soil providing a quarter of the Soviet agricultural output. The transition to a free market has not been easy, and resistance to the implementation of reforms within the government has led to backtracking. However, Ukraine is rich in natural resources and is one of the largest producers of sugar beet, wheat and barley, while the Donets basin is one of the most important industrial regions in the world. In 1992 Ukraine joined the Conference on Security and Co-operation in Europe (CSCE) and steps were taken to end its dependency on Russian natural gas and oil. Rapid economic growth in 2002–04 is largely due to a surge of steel exports to China.

Ukraine had become the Ukrainian SSR. However, the Soviets' programme of collectivization had a disastrous effect when applied to the Ukraine, and many slaughtered their livestock rather than hand them over to the authorities. The two engineered famines of 1921–22 and 1932–33 resulted in the deaths of over 8 million Ukrainians and many who rebelled were sent to Siberia. The Ukrainians initially regarded their German invaders as liberators during the Second World War. However, the collective farms were not abandoned and systematic genocide began instead. More than five million ethnic Ukrainians and Ukrainian Jews were deported or exterminated. Of the estimated 11 million Soviet troops that fell against the Germans,

nearly three million were ethnic Ukrainians. After the war, by way of compensation, Ukraine was given a seat in the UN. By now, Soviet rule had been restored and the boundaries of Soviet Ukraine were extended to the west, uniting most Ukrainians within a single state.

The Ukrainian Uniate Church had been founded in 1569 to avoid Catholic persecution, after Ukraine had been absorbed into the Polish Catholic Commonwealth. In 1946 the Uniate Church was outlawed, and was forced to merge with the Russian Orthodox Church. However, the Ukrainian People's Movement was established in 1989 and the ban on the Uniate Church was lifted. In 1990 Ukraine announced its sovereignty, and the former

UNITED ARAB EMIRATES

Location: 171
Capital: Abu Dhabi
Area: 32,300sq m (83657km²)
Population: 2,563,212 July 2005
Main Languages: Arabic
Main Religions: Muslim
Currency: 1 dirham = 100 fils
Climate: Hot summer; humid, mild winter

An independent Middle Eastern state, between Saudi Arabia and Oman, the UAE has coastlines on the Persian Gulf and the Gulf of Oman. The terrain consists of a flat coastal plain, giving way to sand dunes and desert, with mountains in the east.

Islam was introduced into the area in the 7th century. In the 16th century the Portuguese established trading links with the Gulf states. In the 18th century, the ancestors of the current rulers, the Qawasim and Bani Yas, developed their trading and seafaring activities in Ras al Khaimah and Sharjah in the north and Abu Dhabi and

Dubai in the south. In the early 19th century, treaties (or truces – hence trucial) were made between the British and local rulers to ensure that British shipping would be able to pass through the Gulf, unmolested by pirates, in return for British protection. In 1892 the trucial sheikhs agreed with Britain that they would not cede, sell or mortgage their territory to any other power.

In 1952 the Trucial Council was established by the seven sheikhdoms of Abu Dhabi, Ajman, Dubai, Fujairah, Ras al Khaimah, Sharjah, and Umm al Qaiwain, with a view to eventual federation. In 1958 large-scale exploitation of local oil reserves led to rapid economic progress. In 1968 the announcement that Britain would be removing its forces from the Gulf by 1971 led to an abortive attempt to arrange federation between the seven Trucial States, together with Bahrain and Qatar. The United Arab Emirates was formed in 1971 by the federation of six of the states, Abu Dhabi, Ajman, Dubai, Fujairah, Sharjah, and Umm al Qaiwain, with Ras al Khaimah joining the following year. The ruler of Abu Dhabi, Sheikh Zayed, became the first president, a provisional constitution was adopted, and the UAE joined the UN and the Arab League. In 1985 diplomatic and economic links were established with the Soviet Union and China, and diplomatic relations with

LEFT: Burj al Arab, Dubai.

OPPOSITE LEFT: Children racing camels on the Camel Race Track, Dubai.

OPPOSITE RIGHT: Man with a hawk.

Egypt were restored in 1987. In 1990 Sheikh Maktum bin Rashid al-Maktum of Dubhai was appointed prime minister. The UAE opposed Iraq's invasion of Kuwait and sent their troops to join the UN coalition in the war of 1990–91. In 1991 the Bank of Commerce and Credit International (BCCI), partly owned and controlled by Abu Dhabi's ruler, Zayed bin Sultan al-Nahayan, collapsed at a cost to the UAE of $10 billion; Abu Dhabi agreed to pay BCCI creditors $1.8 billion in 1994. In 2001 financial institutions were ordered to freeze the assets of suspected terrorist-funding organizations. In 2004 Sheikh Zayed died and was succeeded as head of state by his son, Sheikh Khalifa bin Zayed al-Nahayan. Sheikh Maktum bin Rashid al-Maktum, the ruler of Dubhai, who was the UAE's first prime minister in 1990, remains head of government.

The traditional occupations of pearling and fishing are still practised today. However, large-scale exploitation of local oil reserves began in the early 1960s, which transformed what was once a collection of poor desert sheikhdoms into a modern state, with a broad social welfare system and one of the highest per capita incomes in the world. As a safeguard for the future, when the oil eventually runs out, the UAE has diversified into international banking and financial services, and tourism is becoming increasingly important. Imports include food, manufactured goods, machinery and chemicals.

UNITED STATES OF AMERICA

Location:	6 H
Capital:	Washington, DC
Area:	3,794,088sq m (9826688km²)
Population:	295,734,134 July 2005
Main Languages:	English
Main Religions:	Protestant 55%, Roman Catholic 30%, Jewish 3%
Currency:	1 US dollar = 100 cents
Climate:	Hot summer, cold winter in north; hot summer, mild winter in south

Forty-eight states of the Union lie within the central mass of North America, between Canada and Mexico. Alaska, which was bought from Russia in the 19th century, is not contigious with the USA, but is connected to northern Canada, separated from Russia by the Bering Sea; Alaska's terrain is predominantly tundra. The 50th state, Hawaii, was the last to be admitted to the Union in 1959; it comprises an archipelago of volcanic islands in the North Pacific. In addition, there are a number of territories, districts and possessions that belong to the United States of America overseas.

The USA consists of vast central plains bounded by the great mountain ranges of the Rockies in the west and the Appalachians in the east. To the east of the Appalachians lie the lowlands of the Atlantic coast, while to their west lies the Central Valley, extending from the five Great Lakes (four of which are shared with Canada) to the Gulf of Mexico, and which occupies about half the entire area of the country: it is here that the Prairies and the Great Plains, America's granary, are located – one of the most important areas of agriculture in the world. The only break in this level uniformity is the range of the Ozarks in Arkansas and Oklahoma.

West of the plains rise great parallel ranges of mountains, with a plateau that is mostly desert in between. The eastern part consists of the Rockies, while to the west lie the Sierra Nevada and the Cascade Mountains. Beyond the Coastal ranges, a narrow strip of land borders the Pacific. The highest point in both the USA and North America is Mount McKinley, in Alaska; it stands at 20,320ft (6194m), while the lowest

RIGHT: Capitol Hill, Washington, DC.

OPPOSITE: The White House, Washington, DC.

OPPOSITE: *The Mendenhall Glacier,
Juneau, Alaska.*

RIGHT: *Seattle Space Needle, Washington.*

BELOW: *The coast of Oregon.*

point is Death Valley in California, at 282ft
(86m) below sea level. The most important
river system is that of the Mississippi-
Missouri, that forms an enormous delta
where it flows into the Gulf of Mexico.

The USA can be divided into ten regions
comprising 50 states: New England, the
historic heart of the Union, includes Maine,
Vermont, New Hampshire, Massachusetts,
Rhode Island and Connecticut, and covers
most of the area originally colonized by the
British; New York, the 'Empire State'; the
Middle Atlantic States include Pennsylvania,
New Jersey and Delaware; the Middle West
includes Ohio, Indiana, Illinois, Michigan
and Wisconsin; the Prairie States include
Minnesota, Iowa, North Dakota, South
Dakota, Nebraska and Kansas; the Mountain
States include Montana, Wyoming,
Colorado, New Mexico, Utah, Arizona,
Nevada and Idaho; the Pacific States include
California, Oregon, Washington, Alaska and
Hawaii (the only state outside the American
continent); the Southern States include
Virginia, North Carolina, South Carolina,
Georgia, Alabama, Mississippi, Louisiana
and Florida; the South-Western States
include Texas and Oklahoma; and the
Border States include Maryland, West
Virginia, Arkansas, Kentucky, Tennessee and
Missouri.

Each state is self-governing in local
matters, such as the police, public health and

FAR LEFT: The Seattle Waterfront, Washington.

LEFT: The Empire State Building, New York City.

BELOW: The United Nations Building, New York City.

OPPOSITE: Aerial view of New York's East River with the Brooklyn and Manhattan Bridges.

Quaker, William Penn, founded Pennsylvania in 1682. The Dutch settlement of New Amsterdam on Manhattan Island was renamed New York after it was taken by the British in 1664.

Throughout most of the 18th century the British colonies were threatened by French

education, but foreign affairs and the armed forces come under the jurisdiction of the central government in Washington. Executive power is vested in the President of the United States, elected by popular vote every four years and eligible to stand for only two terms. Legislative power is vested in Congress, which comprises two houses: the Senate and the House of Representatives. The Senate has two elected members from each state, who are elected for six years, while the House of Representatives has 435 members, distributed in accordance with the size of state that is being represented and serving for two years. Judicial power is the province of the Supreme Court.

Around 12,000 years ago, the ancestors of the Native Americans migrated from Asia by crossing the Bering land bridge and occupying what is now the USA. Here, they developed advanced societies, such as those of the Anasazi and Woodland Indians, who built Chaco Canyon and Cahokia. There were an estimated ten million Native Americans by the time the Europeans arrived, but introduced diseases greatly reduced their numbers. European exploration began with the discovery of the New World by Christopher Columbus in 1492. Spaniards arrived in 1565 and established the first European settlement at St Augustine in Florida. The first British colony was at Jamestown, Virginia, in 1607. In 1620 the Puritan Pilgrim Fathers, who arrived from England in the *Mayflower*, landed at Cape Cod, Massachusetts and founded the Plymouth Colony. Maryland was founded in 1634 and the English

LEFT: Atlanta, Georgia.

OPPOSITE: Bryce Canyon National Park, Utah.

expansion from the north, but the French and Indian War (1756–63), in which Wolfe's capture of Québec was an incisive victory, ended with the French ceding Canada and the Great Lakes to Britain. The heavy tax burden imposed by the British government led to the War of Revolution (War of American Independence) of 1775, when the 13 colonies of New Hampshire, Massachusetts, Rhode Island, Connecticut, New York, New Jersey, Pennsylvania, Delaware, Virginia, North Carolina, South Carolina, Maryland and Georgia, led by George Washington, defeated the army of George III. By their Declaration of Independence on 4 July 1776, the 13 states pronounced themselves the first constitutional and democratic federal republic and George Washington was its first president. The Treaty of Paris of 1783, brought British rule in the colonies finally to a close. The Constitution of the United States replaced the Articles of Confederation in 1789, when a more centralized government was substituted, and though amended down the years, the Constitution remains valid to this day.

In 1803 President Thomas Jefferson effected the Louisiana Purchase, when he bought a vast tract of land from the French. This eventually added the states of Louisiana, Arkansas, Missouri, Iowa, Nebraska, part of Oklahoma, Kansas, Colorado, Wyoming, Montana, North and South Dakota and Minnesota to the Union.

The war with England of 1812 led to the Monroe Doctrine of 1823, and ensured America's future protection from European interference. Expansion westwards later carried US territory as far as the Pacific. In 1845 Oregon was acquired and the war with Mexico (1846–48) added the states of California, Utah, New Mexico and Texas to the Union – often at the expense of Native Americans, who were forced into reservations as a result. Alaska was

ABOVE: Showboat on the Mississippi River, Mississippi.

RIGHT: Cinderella's Castle, Disney World, Orlando, Florida.

OPPOSITE: The Epcot Center with geosphere and fountains, Orlando, Florida.

purchased from Russia in 1867.

There had been a shortage of labour since early colonial times, which had done much to encourage slavery. The Missouri Compromise of 1820 was an attempt to calm the growing conflict between North and South over the South's right to secede and expand slavery. In 1861–65 the Civil War, or War between the States, was fought between 11 Confederate States in the South that had seceded, and wished to retain black slaves to work their plantations, and the Federal States in the North, which were anti-slavery and wanted to preserve the Union. The South chose Jefferson Davis as president, and the North Abraham Lincoln. The Confederates were at first successful in the Battles of Bull Run in 1861 and 1862, but lost at Gettysburg in 1863. On 9 April 1865, the Confederate General Lee

LEFT: *Dallas skyscrapers, Texas.*

OPPOSITE LEFT: *The Golden Gate Bridge, San Francisco, California.*

OPPOSITE ABOVE RIGHT: *Hollywood Boulevard, Los Angeles, California.*

OPPOSITE BELOW RIGHT: *The famous Hollywood sign.*

surrendered to General Grant at Appomattox Courthouse and the war ended a month later, with 600,000 casualties on both sides and utter devastation to the country. The war effectively ended the right of states to secede but also slavery, but the bitterness that remained lasted for 100 years.

However, the war also stimulated industrial development of the North and led to the construction of roads and railroads in the late 19th century that encouraged economic expansion and exploitation of the country's vast natural resources. The displacement of Native Americans also remained an issue, and many tribes continued to assert their rights to traditional land. The Spanish-American War of 1898 confirmed America's role as a great power; it also came to be regarded as the 'Land of Opportunity', and millions of Europeans were to pour into the country, many of them fleeing persecution. Despite occasional depressions, it seemed as though the country's wealth would go on increasing, until the Great Depression of the 1930s arrived and everything changed. When Franklin D Roosevelt became president in 1933 he embarked upon the 'New Deal', in

an attempt to restore America's prosperity.

America entered the First World War in 1917 and the war ended with the Treaty of Versailles in 1919, when President Woodrow Wilson's League of Nations was established. However, the Senate refused to ratify the treaty because of a constitutional clause, and a period of isolationism ensued. America's entry into the Second World (1939–45) was precipitated by the Japanese attack on Pearl Harbor in 1941, to which America responded by dropping atomic bombs on Hiroshima and Nagasaki; this led to the Japanese surrender and the end of the war. But post-war tensions saw the development of the Cold War between the West and the USSR, that lasted until the Soviet collapse in 1991, when the US emerged as the world's leading military and economic power; the war also encouraged the space race.

The USA was a founder member of NATO in 1949. By now it was conscious of the spread of Communism, and American forces were sent to both Korea (1950–53) and

ABOVE: San José de Gracia, an adobe church from 1760, Las Trampas, New Mexico.

RIGHT: Totem Pole, Monument Valley, Arizona.

OPPOSITE: New York Hotel, Las Vegas, Nevada.

Vietnam (1954–75). In 1955 Martin Luther King launched the Civil Rights movement. The Cuban Missile Crisis of 1962 was the closest America ever came to a nuclear war with the Soviet Union and it was narrowly avoided, though it marred the beginning of John F Kennedy's presidency, and his assassination in 1963 shocked the world. In 1969 Neil Armstrong became the first man to land on the Moon. The trauma of Watergate, a political espionage scandal, caused President Richard M Nixon to resign in 1974 and the presidency of Gerald Ford saw a shift in power from president to Congress. Jimmy Carter was elected in 1977, but despite successfully negotiating the Camp David Accords in 1979, and making a significant contribution to Arab-Israeli reconciliation (See Egypt), there was a landslide victory for the Republicans and Ronald Reagan in 1981, with re-election for him four years later. The beginning of Reagan's presidency was marked by the worst economic depression since that of the 1930s, though recovery saw more spending on defence. His mission was a stronger America in terms of military power, with more personal choice and less taxation. Since this time, the government has continued to provide less social welfare services than most industrialized nations, relying on the free market and private charities instead.

The scandal of Irangate in 1987, when arms were covertly sold to Iran, the proceeds going to fund anti-Communist Contras in Nicaragua, illustrated Reagan's loosening grip on power. In spite of victory in the Gulf War of 1991, Saddam Hussein was not removed, and domestic recession led to George H W Bush losing the presidency to Bill Clinton in 1992. Clinton was re-elected in 1996, in spite of the personal scandal that surrounded him, and escaped impeachment in 1999. In 2000 George W Bush was elected president in an election beset by controversy. On 11 September 2001, more than 3,000 American citizens were killed in attacks on the Pentagon and World Trade Center, thought to be the work of terrorists connected with Osama bin Laden. America sent troops into Afghanistan to topple the Taliban regime, but failed to dislodge bin Laden, who was believed to be in hiding there. In 2003 US and British troops invaded Iraq and deposed Saddam Hussein and his regime. Saddam was

eventually captured and is currently undergoing trial for war crimes. The US and Britain continue to occupy Iraq until peace is restored and the Iraqis are able to govern themselves, an aim that continues to be frustrated. Many on both sides of the Atlantic claimed the war to be illegal, and that American, British and other troops should be sent home. In 2005 a devastating hurricane hit New Orleans, causing widespread destruction and loss of life. Most of the population had to be evacuated and it will take many years to repair the levées and restore the city. A second hurricane followed within a few weeks, but missed New Orleans and hit the coast of Texas instead.

The leading industrial power in the world, the USA has service, petroleum, steel, automobile, aircraft, aerospace, telecommunications, chemicals, electronics, food processing, consumer goods, lumber and mining industries and many of its products are exported, together with the products of its advanced agriculture, such as cotton, soya beans, fruit, wheat and corn. The American economy is marked by steady growth, low unemployment and low inflation, together with rapid increases in technology. The economy weathered the terrorist attack of 11 September 2001 with great resilience. However, the war in 2003 between a US-led coalition and Iraq, and the subsequent occupation of Iraq, have necessitated major transference of national resources to the military. There are also long-term problems associated with pensions and medical care in an ageing population, poverty in lower income groups, and trade and budget deficits.

URUGUAY

Location:	9 N
Capital:	Montevideo
Area:	68,037sq m (176216km²)
Population:	3,415,920 July 2005
Main Languages:	Spanish
Main Religions:	Roman Catholic 60%, Protestant 3%, Jewish 2%
Currency:	1 Uruguay peso = 100 centésimos
Climate:	Warm summer, mild winter

The smallest of the South American republics, after Suriname, Uruguay lies between Brazil and the Río de la Plata estuary, and is separated from Argentina to the east by the River Uruguay; the main river, the Negro, traverses the interior. Uruguay has a coastline on the South Atlantic Ocean that is broken by several lagoons. The north of the country is hilly, but the remainder is essentially an extension of the Argentinian pampas, with fertile coastal lowland. The original inhabitants of the area, the Charrúa Indians, had largely disappeared by the 19th century, having been decimated by Europeans or introduced diseases. Today, about half the population, most of which is of European descent, lives in the largest city, which is the capital Montevideo.

The area that is modern Uruguay was settled by the Spanish and Portuguese in the 17th century, though Spain secured the whole of the country in the 18th century, founding Montevideo in 1726 as a military stronghold from which to repel the Portuguese. By the end of the century, Uruguay, with Argentina, Paraguay and parts of Bolivia, Brazil and Chile, had become part of the Spanish Viceroyalty of La Plata, with its capital at Buenos Aires. In 1815, under the leadership of the dictator José Gervasio Artigas, the Spanish were driven out at last, but Artigas himself was overthrown by Brazil in 1820. Uruguay was annexed as a province of Brazil in 1821, though its ownership was disputed between

BELOW: Traditionally-constructed church, with mud walls and straw roof, Uruguay.

OPPOSITE LEFT: Children dancing to the music of a bandoneon, a type of concertina popular in South America.

OPPOSITE RIGHT:
The Río de la Plata estuary, seen from Colonia.

Argentina and Brazil, even after Uruguay had declared its independence in 1825, a fact unrecognized by the two until 1828. Since independence, the Liberal Colorado and Conservative Blanco Parties have dominated Uruguayan politics. From 1865–70 Uruguay fought successfully alongside Argentina and Brazil in the War of the Triple Alliance against Paraguay.

Early in the 20th century, after conflicts with neighbouring states and political and economic fluctuations, when there were large incursions of immigrants, mainly from Europe, the administrations of President Jorge Battle y Ordóñez of the Colorado Party, established widespread political, social and economic reforms. A tradition of democracy was maintained until this stable society began to disintegrate as the economy took a downward turn after the Second World War.

The government began to lose popularity, and the Tupamaros, a Marxist urban guerilla movement in the 1960s, aggravated the crisis with violent activity. The Tupamaros were eventually crushed by the army in 1972, which led to the suspension of human rights under Juan María Bordaberry Araceno and his successor Jorge Pacheco Areco, and ushered in a military junta that lasted for 11 years. Democracy was restored in 1985, after violent anti-government protests, when the Liberal Julio María Saguinetti was elected president. In 2000 Sanguinetti was succeeded by Jorge Battle Ibáñez. Head of both state and government since March 2005 is President Tabaré Vázquez.

Uruguay's prosperous economy is based on the export of beef, meat products, leather and wool, the Merino sheep having been introduced by British traders in 1840, who established meat-processing factories and started off the export trade. It also has an educated workforce, high levels of social spending, and a well-developed industrial sector; its political and labour conditions are among the most liberal in South America. However, there was a major downturn in 1999–2002, caused largely by the economic problems of its closest neighbours, especially the massive withdrawals by Argentinians of dollars deposited in Uruguayan banks, which led to devaluation of the Uruguayan peso and massive unemployment. However, the repayment dates on nearly half Uruguay's external debt were extended in 2003 and public confidence was restored as the economy began to rally in 2004.

UZBEKISTAN

Location:	17 G
Capital:	Tashkent
Area:	172,741sq m (447400km²)
Population:	26,851,195 July 2005 E
Main Languages:	Uzbek
Main Religions:	Muslim 75%
Currency:	som
Climate:	Hot summer, cold winter, dry all year, snow in mountains

An independent republic, Uzbekistan is the most highly-populated country in Central Asia. It is bordered by Kazakhstan to the west and north, by Kyrgysztan and Tajikistan to the east, and by Afghanistan and Turkmenistan to the south. The terrain is mostly desert, apart from the broad, flat, intensely irrigated river valleys of the Amu Darya and Syr Darya rivers. These drain into the Aral Sea in the north-west, which Uzbekistan shares with Kazakhstan. The eastern spur of Uzbekistan culminates in the Fergana Valley, which is almost engulfed by the surrounding mountains of Tajikistan and Kyrgysztan.

What is now modern Uzbekistan was part of the Persian Empire for thousands of years. In the 1st century BC, Samarkand (Samarqand) developed as an important caravanserai and trading post on the Great Silk Road, the strategic route that linked the Mediterranean with China in the east. Tashkent (Toshkent), the modern capital, was founded in the 7th century, and the next century saw the spread of Islam to the area. Genghis Khan and his Mongol hordes arrived in 1220 and the region became a part of the Mongol Empire. In 1369, Timur (Tamerlane) destroyed the power of the Golden Horde and made himself ruler of Samarkand; this became the capital of his great empire, that included Persia, Syria and northern India.

Turkic Uzbek people conquered the area in the 16th century, when khanates, such as those of Bukhara and Samarkand were established. In 1865 Tashkent was seized by Russia and became the capital of the Governor-Generalship of Turkestan. In 1868 Russia annexed Bukhara, and other khanates were acquired by 1876. After Russia's Bolshevik Revolution of 1917, a Communist government was established in Tashkent, when, despite nationalist resistance, life in Uzbekistan became more regulated, religious freedom was denied, but social improvements were made. In 1921 Uzbekistan became part of the Turkestan SSR, and a constituent republic of the USSR from 1924.

As industry developed in the 1930s, ethnic Russians moved into the towns. In 1944 Stalin, the Soviet dictator, forcibly removed 160,000 Meskhetian Turks from their native Georgia, transporting them into Uzbekistan. From the 1950s, major irrigation

projects facilitated the growing of cotton and grain, but drained the Amu Darya and Syr Darya rivers, causing the Aral Sea to recede; the overuse of agricultural chemicals also poisoned the land. In the late 1980s there was a rebirth of Islamic consciousness, stimulated by Gorbachev's *glasnost* in Russia.Uzbekistan became an independent state within the Commonwealth of Independent States (CIS) on the break-up of the Soviet Union in 1991, and Islam Karimov of the People's Democratic Party (formerly the Communist Party) became president. In 1992 Karimov banned the Unity and Freedom parties and large numbers of opposition leaders were arrested, accused of activities against the state. In 1999 bomb blasts in Tashkent killed more than a dozen people, for which Karimov blamed the Islamic Movement of Uzbekistan (IMU). IMU responded by declaring a *jihad* in a radio broadcast from Iran and demanded Karimov's resignation, while IMU insurgents attacked government forces from their mountain hideouts.

President Karimov was re-elected in 2000; human rights observers declared the elections unfair and accused Uzbekistan of widespread violations. In 2001 73 people were jailed for helping Islamic extremists that had infiltrated the south the previous year. Following the 11 September attacks on New York, Uzbekistan permitted the US to use its air bases in the war on terror in Afghanistan. In May 2005, Andijan was the scene of protests against the imprisonment of 23 Muslims accused of extremism. The protestors took 30 hostages and soldiers began to fire on the protestors, leaving several hundred civilians dead. That same day, in Tashkent, a man mistakenly believed to be a suicide bomber, was shot dead outside the Israeli embassy. Head of government since 2003 is Prime Minister Shavkat Mirziyayev.

The rigidity of political control is reflected in Uzbekistan's economy, which is tightly controlled by the government. Uzbekistan is the world's second-largest exporter of cotton, and it is a large producer of gold and oil. However, it is reported to have the lowest standard of living and the lowest growth rate of the former Soviet republics.

OPPOSITE: Minaret and tile detail of the Tashkent mosque.

ABOVE LEFT: Public gardens in Tashkent.

ABOVE: Children in traditional dress.

VANUATU

Location:	24 L
Capital:	Port-Vila
Area:	4,706sq m (12188km²)
Population:	205,754 July 2005
Main Languages:	Bislama, English, French
Main Religions:	Christian 80%
Currency:	vatu
Climate:	Hot, rain all year

Formerly the New Hebrides, Vanuatu is an archipelago of more that 80 South Pacific islands, most of them uninhabited, situated east of Australia. Most of the islands are mountainous and some are volcanically active. Many are densely covered in tropical rainforest, with narrow coastal plains and coral reefs. The main islands are Espíritu Santo, Malekula, and Éfaté, where the capital Port-Vila is located.

The islands were visited in the early 17th century by the Portuguese explorer Pédro Fernández de Quiros, who called them Espíritu Santo, after the Holy Spirit. Captain James Cook visited them on his second voyage in 1774, changing their name to the New Hebrides after the Scottish islands.

Other Europeans arrived in the 1880s, to exploit the trade in sandalwood, but many were attacked by the indigenous Ni-Vanuatu, who in turn were ravaged by the foreign diseases that were inevitably introduced. In the 19th century government of the islands was disputed between British and French settlers; at that time, many of the indigenous islanders were shipped to Australia, Fiji, Samoa and New Caledonia to work the plantations. In 1906 it was agreed that the islands should be administered as an Anglo-French Condominium.

In the 1960s there was a move towards independence. In 1978 a national government was formed, led by Gérard Leymang. There was a brief insurrection in 1980, when separate independence for the island of Espíritu Santo was sought, which delayed the general move towards independence: this was achieved later that year, when the New

Hebrides became Vanuatu. There was a period of political instability in the 1990s, when several coalitions were formed. These proved problematical, owing to language differences between French- and English-speaking members. The controversial prime minister, Serge Vohor, who had previously held the office in the 1990s, and tried to switch diplomatic recognition from China to Taiwan, was ousted after a no-confidence vote in 2004. Ham Lini took his place, revoking Vohor's agreement with Taiwan. Head of state since 2004 is President Kalkot Matas Kelekele.

The economy is based on small-scale agriculture, while fishing, offshore financial services and tourism, which is under development, are also important, in the absence of oil or mineral deposits. Australia and New Zealand are the main suppliers of aid and tourists. Tax revenue is derived from import duties and there is no tax on personal or company income.

LEFT: Local boy, Pentecôte Island.

ABOVE: The Yasur volcano erupting, Tanna Island.

VATICAN CITY

Location:	14 G
Capital:	Vatican City
Area:	0.17sq m (0.44km²)
Population:	900 2000
Main Languages:	Latin, Italian
Main Religions:	Roman Catholic
Currency:	euro
Climate:	Hot summer, warm winter

An independent sovereign state, of which the pope is head. Vatican City is administered by the Holy See, the governing body of the Roman Catholic Church and its Eastern Rites, and includes the Vatican Palace, the pope's official residence, and the basilica and square of St Peter. Situated on the Vatican Hill in the north-west of Rome, on the west bank of the River Tiber, it is an enclave within Italy's capital city. The territory of the Vatican also includes several other basilicas in and around Rome, and the pope's summer residence at Castel Gandolfo.

The area on which the Vatican now stands was long considered sacred, even before the arrival of Christianity. In 326 the Emperor Constantine built his basilica over the supposed tomb of St Peter, the first pope. The first papal residence was established in the 5th century, and apart from a brief spell in the 14th century, when it was transferred to Avignon, it has remained in Rome ever since. The Papal States can be traced to the 8th century, when the popes as secular princes ruled parts of the Italian peninsula for more than 1,000 years. This lasted until the mid 19th century, when many of the states were seized by the recently united Kingdom of Italy. Rome itself was annexed in 1870 and the matter of the pope's holdings was not resolved until the Lateran Treaties were signed in 1929, during the dictatorship of Benito Mussolini, which established the Vatican as an independent state. It also confirmed Italy's unique status within Roman Catholicism, a religion professed by one billion people worldwide.

The present head of state, since April 2005, and elected for life, is Pope Benedict XVI (Joseph Ratzinger). The Pope rules the Holy See through the Roman Curia and the Papal Civil Service. The Holy See plays an active part within most international organizations, with areas of interest extending to diplomacy, the UN, world health and education, ecology, the plight of refugees, space and nuclear technology and much more; it also sends a delegate to the Arab League in Cairo.

This is a non-commercial economy, unique in the world, funded by contributions from Catholics throughout the world, by the sale of postage stamps, coins and medals, by admission fees to museums, and by the sale of publications. Investments, income from

LEFT: St Peter's Basilica.

BELOW: St Peter's Square.

property, international banking (the Vatican Bank) and financial services also contribute to the exchequer and provide salaries for lay workers within the Vatican. It has its own radio service, post office, police and rail station. Italy is responsible for the defence of the Vatican, the 100-strong Pontifical Swiss Guard being limited to ceremonial occasions and security. It has a population of only 900 or so, which is tiny compared with the millions of visitors that flock to see the Sistine Chapel and the treasures of the Vatican each year.

VENEZUELA

Location:	8 J
Capital:	Caracas
Area:	353,857sq m (916490km²)
Population:	25,375,281 July 2005
Main Languages:	Spanish
Main Religions:	Roman Catholic 94%
Currency:	1 bolívar = 100 céntimos
Climate:	Hot all year, cooler in hills, rains May–Dec

A South American federal republic on the Caribbean coast, between Brazil and Colombia, Venezuela occupies the whole of the lower basin of the Orinoco, the country's largest river. In the west, the coastal plain borders Lake Maracaibo, where the Indians of the Guajira peninsula once lived in houses raised on stilts above the water, reminding Amerigo Vespucci, the first to map the area, of the city of Venice. Spurs of the High Andes lie in the north of the country, that continue southward into Colombia and the rest of South America. In the centre lies a vast plain (*llanos*) that rises to over 3,000ft (1000m) in the Guiana Highlands in the south-east, and includes the

Angel Falls – at 3,212ft (979m) the world's highest waterfall. The jungles of Amazonia lie to the south. Venezuela is currently in dispute with Guyana over the area west of the Essequibo river.

The indigenous inhabitants of Venezuela were Carib, Arawak and Chibcha Indians. Christopher Columbus explored the area in 1498 and was enchanted by its diversity and beauty. In 1522 Spanish settlements were established along the north-eastern coast and were absorbed into the Spanish administrative area of New Granada.

After several unsuccessful uprisings, the country declared independence from Spain in 1811, under the leadership of Simón Bolívar, but full sovereignty was not achieved until after the naval Battle of Maracaibo in 1823. Bolívar led other countries to freedom and founded what are now Colombia, Panama, Ecuador, Peru and Bolivia. Venezuela, with Colombia and Ecuador, became part of the Republic of Gran Colombia, until the rebellion led by General José Antonio Paéz led to its collapse in 1830; Venezuelan independence was

declared and Paéz became Venezuela's first president.

Under the dictatorship of Juan Vicente Gómez from 1910, Venezuela's oil reserves were exploited, possibly more for Gómez's own benefit and that of the oil companies, though the country also benefited. Following his death in 1935, the struggle for democracy eventually succeeded and military rule came to an end in 1958. The Democratic Action Party held power almost continuously from 1959, but was defeated in 1978, when Luis Herrera Campins (Social Christian) became

1998 the populist left-wing Chávez became president, and inspired by Venezuela's national hero proclaimed a 'Bolivian revolution'. But radical reforms and political unrest led to deep divisions, attempts to remove him (both by coup and referendum, which he survived), and strikes; he appears to be loved by the poor and loathed by the rich. His close ties with President Castro of Cuba are seen as attempts to antagonize the US, and he makes no secret of his aim to promote socialism in Venezuela. He was forced out of office by the army in 2002, only to be reinstated 48 hours later, following massive loyalist protests. Opposition pressure intensified over the next few years until a referendum in 2004 confirmed his position: he is likely to run for a further term in 2006.

Venezuela's emergence as a major South American power is due to the abundant oil reserves in and around Lake Maracaibo and the heavy oil belt on the northern bank of the Orinoco. Not only has Venezuela some of the largest deposits of oil in the world, it also has huge reserves of iron ore, coal, gold and bauxite, as well as a strong agricultural sector. However, fluctuations in the price of oil continue to be of concern, and unemployment and inflation are perennial problems. Despite the oil boom of the 1970s, which mostly benefited the better-off, most Venezuelans live in poverty, many of them in shanty towns such as the one that spreads its tentacles around the capital city of Caracas.

OPPOSITE: Pui Puy beach, Paria peninsula.

ABOVE: Caracas' skyline.

ABOVE LEFT: El Sapito waterfall, Canaima National Park.

president. In 1992 there were attempts by the military to remove President Carlos Andrés Pérez, who had already been democratically elected twice. This proved ultimately unsuccessful and the perpetrators were jailed for treason; however, Pérez himself was later impeached and convicted of corruption.

The current president of Venezuela, Hugo Chávez Frías, was one of the military leaders involved in the failed coup, and he and the others were released from prison by Pérez's successor, Rafael Caldera, in 1994. In

VIETNAM

Location:	21 J
Capital:	Hanoi
Area:	127,301sq m (329566km²)
Population:	83,535,576 July 2005
Main Languages:	Vietnamese
Main Religions:	Buddhist 55%,
	Roman Catholic 7%
Currency:	1 dong = 10 hao
Climate:	Hot all year, monsoon
	May–Oct

A country of South-East Asia, Vietnam borders China, Laos, Cambodia, and the South China Sea. Only about a fifth of the land is level, and includes the low, flat deltas of the Red river in the extreme north, and the Mekong in the south; the rest is predominantly mountainous or hilly, and densely forested.

Legends abound regarding the origins of Vietnam: what is true is that it was ruled by China from 208 BC until the 10th century AD. It became independent in 939, when the Chinese were defeated in battle, despite which it continued to look to China for protection. Buddhism was introduced in the 11th century. By now, a Vietnamese dynasty had been established, which extended its rule to the south, repelling Mongol invasions and defeating Kublai Khan in the 13th century.

France invaded Vietnam in 1858, completing its conquest in 1884. Vietnam was divided into the protectorates of Tonkin (North Vietnam) and Annam (South Vietnam), becoming part of French Indo-China (with Cambodia/Kampuchea and Laos), in 1887. During the late 19th and early 20th centuries, a colonial economy, based on rubber and rice, was established in the south, which drew its labour force from the north. In 1930 Ho Chi Minh founded the Indo-Chinese Communist Party (ICP). Vietnam was occupied by the Japanese during the Second World War, which led to

BELOW: Vinh Trang pagoda and gardens, My Tho.

OPPOSITE LEFT: Paddyfields along the Mekong delta.

OPPOSITE RIGHT: Boats on the Mekong river.

Vietnamese 'boat people' escaped as refugees. In 1976 the country was reunited under the government of North Vietnam as the Socialist Republic of Vietnam and thousands of southerners were imprisoned. In 1978, Cambodia, with the help of Vietnamese forces, toppled the regime of the Khmer Rouge in Cambodia, to which China, partly in retaliation, responded with a 17-day Sino-Vietnamese border war a few months later. Diplomatic relations with China were not restored until 1991. During the period 1994 to 1997, the 30-year-old trade embargo imposed by the US was lifted, diplomatic relations with the US were restored and Tran Duc Luong and Phan Van Khai became president and prime minister respectively, both of them to be re-elected in 2002; the size of the standing army was also reduced.

During the last 30 years, Vietnam has been recovering from years of war, the loss of Soviet support, and a rigid, centrally-planned economy. Progress has been made, especially in the period 1986–1997, when free-market reforms were introduced; this was checked by the Asian financial crisis of 1997–98, but progress has been made following Vietnam's membership of the ASEAN Free Trade Area, and a bilateral trade agreement made with the US in 2001 has led to more rapid changes still. Vietnam's most important agricultural product is rice. It also produces oil, natural gas, coal and phosphates. In 2005, along with other South-East Asian states, Vietnam had the task of preventing the spread of avian flu throughout the world.

the formation of the Vietminh guerilla force, which overthrew both the Japanese and the puppet regime of Bao Dai, the former Emperor of Annam. By now, Ho Chi Minh was in control of most of the country and declared its independence.

France's attempts to re-establish control of the south led to the Vietnam War of 1946–54 and the final defeat of the French at Dien Bien Phu. Following the Geneva Conference, Vietnam was divided along the 17th parallel of latitude into North Vietnam, under the Communist government of Ho Chi Minh (who died in 1969, and was succeeded by Le Duan), and the French- and US-backed South Vietnam, separated by a demilitarized zone. However, the Viet Cong,

the Communist guerilla National Liberation Front, began to gain control of the south, helped by China and the Soviets: this led to direct US intervention after American destroyers were allegedly attacked in the Gulf of Tonkin in 1964. Peace was restored by the Paris Peace Accords of 1973, following negotiations by Henry Kissinger and Le Duc Tho. US forces began to withdraw, following domestic opposition to American involvement in the war, and concern about the growing number of casualties.

Peace was short-lived, however, and fighting between North and South resumed in 1975, when Saigon was captured by North Vietnam and tens of thousands of

VIRGIN ISLANDS
(BRITISH & US)

Name: British Virgin Islands
Location: 9 I
Capital: Road Town
Area: 59sq m (153km²)
Population: 22,643 July 2005
Main Languages: English
Main Religions: Protestant 86%,
Roman Catholic 10%
Currency: US dollar
Climate: Subtropical, humid,
moderated by trade winds

Name: US Virgin Islands
Location: 9 I
Capital City: Charlotte Amalie
Area: 131sq m (339km²)
Population: 108,708 July 2005
Main Languages: English
Main Religions: Baptist 42%, Roman
Catholic 34%, Episcopalian
17%
Currency: US dollar
Climate: Subtropical, moderated by
easterly trade winds.
Rains Sep–Nov

A group of small islands in the Caribbean, the Virgin Islands were originally inhabited by Caribs and Arawaks. The islands were named by Christopher Columbus for St Ursula, who was said to have been martyred by the Huns, along with 11,000 virgins, while on a pilgrimage to Cologne. The islands to the east, that had been acquired by Britain in 1672, continued to be called the Virgin Islands until the end of the First World War, when islands to the west, that had since become the Danish East Indies, were bought by the US in 1917, and renamed the United States Virgin Islands. The remaining Virgin Islands, belonging to Britain, were then renamed the British Virgin Islands. The islands are mostly volcanic in origin and are famous for their white, sandy beaches.

The British Virgin Islands is an overseas territory of the UK. It consists of over 50 islands, around 16 of which are uninhabited, the largest being Tortola, Virgin Gorda, Anegada and Jost Van Dyke. The islands were first settled by the Dutch in 1648 and were annexed by Britain in 1672. The BVI has one of the most prosperous economies in the Caribbean, with substantial revenues coming from the registration of offshore companies and from tourism. Its economy is closely linked to that of the US Virgin Islands and the US dollar has been its currency since 1959.

The United States Virgin Islands is a dependency of the US and consists of the

main islands of St Thomas, St John, St Croix, and Water Island, with other small islands within the territory. Following the advent of Christopher Columbus, they were successively held by Spain, England, Netherlands, France, the Knights of Malta, and Denmark. The Danish West India Company settled on St Thomas in 1672, on St John in 1694 and bought St Croix from the French in 1733; they became Danish colonies in 1754. Sugar plantations were worked by slave labour during the 18th and 19th centuries, until slavery was abolished in 1848. During the First World War, the US, fearing Germany would seize the islands as a submarine base, bought the islands from Denmark for $25 million in 1917. US citizenship was granted to the islanders in 1927. Tourism is the most important activity and financial services are increasing. There is also an industrial sector that includes rum distilling, textiles, pharmaceuticals and electronics. One of the largest oil refineries in the world is located on St Croix.

OPPOSITE: The port of Charlotte Amalie on St Thomas, US Virgin Islands. The tower dates from 1679.

LEFT: Gorda Island, British Virgin Islands.

WALES

Location:	13 F
Capital:	Cardiff
Area:	8,016sq m (20761km²)
Population:	2,925,000 2005
Main Languages:	Welsh, English
Main Religions:	Protestant, Catholic
Currency:	1 pound = 100 pence
Climate:	Mild summer, cool winter

The principality of Wales is one of the four constituent parts of the United Kingdom, the other three being England, Scotland and Northern Ireland. Wales is located in the south-west of Britain, bordered by England to the east, the Bristol Channel to the south, and the St George's Channel and the Irish Sea to the west and north, which separate Wales from the island of Ireland. The terrain is predominantly mountainous, except for flatter areas near the coast, the valleys of the larger rivers, and Anglesey, an island located off the north-west coast. The main massif of the Cambrian Mountains traverses the country from north to south, and includes Snowdon (3,560ft/1085m), the highest point

in England and Wales, Cader Idris, Plinlimmon, the Black Mountains, and the Brecon Beacons in the south.

During the Roman conquest of Britain, the Romans established a presence in Wales, building forts throughout the south. This included the fortress of Caerleon (Isca), with its splendid amphitheatre. The fortress was first occupied in AD 75 by Sextus Julius Frontinus, who was sent by the Emperor

Vespasian to pacify the Welsh. St David introduced Christianity in the 5th century.

The history of Wales, as distinct from that of England, began with the Anglo-Saxon conquests, when Wales became more isolated from England. Due to its mountainous terrain and the fierce resistance of its people, Wales was never conquered, but retained its Christianity and remained a Celtic race; it has also preserved its own

ABOVE: Cardiff Castle, South Wales.

OPPOSITE: The Gower Peninsula, South Wales.

Welsh language to this day. Offa, the Anglo-Saxon King of Mercia (757–96), constructed a series of earthworks, known as Offa's Dyke, which marked the boundary between England and Wales that he had established during his wars with the Welsh. It ran from the mouth of the River Wye, almost to the mouth of the River Dee, and remnants of it are still visible.

During the 9th–11th centuries, Vikings raided the coast. At this time, Wales was divided into small states or chiefdoms, though princes such as Rhodri (844–78), Howel the Good (904–49), and Griffith ap Llewelyn (1039–63) united the country from time to time. After the Norman Conquest, Norman barons began to occupy the borderlands (Marches), but in the north, Llewelyn I (1194–1240) and his grandson, Llewelyn the Last (1246–82), the last independent Prince of Wales, maintained a spirited resistance, though Edward I of England conquered Wales in 1282. Owen Glendower, a Welsh chieftain, led a final uprising against Henry IV, defeating the English in 1401 and proclaiming himself Prince of Wales. The English responded by denying the Welsh the right of assembly, and other repressive measures were taken.

The way having been paved by the accession of the Welsh Tudor dynasty to the English throne, Wales was politically incorporated into England. This was ratified in the Act of Union of 1536, during the reign of Henry VIII, when the Marcher Lordships were abolished, leaving Wales with 13 counties. English became the official language and English law was imposed. The Welsh largely ignored the Reformation, and supported the Royalist cause during the English Civil Wars. Since the Evangelical Revival of the 18th century, however, nonconformity has become a powerful factor in Welsh life: in 1914, the Church of England was disestablished in Wales.

some. Prince Charles was invested as the 21st Prince of Wales by Queen Elizabeth II at Caernarvon Castle in 1969.

Wales was once heavily industrialized, producing coal, iron, lead, copper and gold, but these industries have since declined, the last coal mine having closed in 1996. Light engineering is still an important sector in parts of the country, but the main focus is now on services and electronics and many Japanese-owned plants are located in Wales. Most of Wales is given over to the rearing of sheep, other livestock, and dairy farming, its

LEFT: A Snowdonia landscape, North Wales.

BELOW: Abergavenny's pony market.

OPPOSITE: An old cottage in a South Wales valley.

terrain and poor soil being unsuitable for crops. Wales has three National Parks that preserve the natural beauty of the landscape, and the unique Welsh culture atracts tourists from all over the world.

By the 19th century a strong coal and iron industry had developed in the south. Miners and ironworkers were militant supporters of Chartism, a movement for parliamentary reform, and Wales has long been a stronghold of trade unionism and socialism. Between the World Wars, Wales suffered greatly from industrial depression and high unemployment, and many left the country to seek work elsewhere. Wales recovered during and after the Second World War, which also saw the growth of nationalism. The Welsh Nationalist Party (Plaid Cymru), founded in 1925, returned its first member to Westminster in 1966. Since

the passing of the Welsh Language Act in 1993 all official documents must be in both English and Welsh. In 1999, the National Assembly for Wales was at last formed, with some powers devolved to it from London.

Wales has a strong tradition of literature and music and the Welsh National Opera is one of the best in Europe. The title, Prince of Wales, has been held by the British heir-apparent since Prince Edward (Edward II) received it from his father, Edward I, in 1301. However, the title is purely ceremonial, there being no direct involvement in the government of the country, and the custom is unpopular with

WESTERN SAHARA

Location:	12 I
Capital:	Laâyoune
Area:	103,000sq m (266769km²)
Population:	273,008 July 2005
Main Languages:	Arabic
Main Religions:	Sunni Muslim
Currency:	1 dirham = 100 centimes (as Morocco)
Climate:	Hot all year

A region of north-west Africa, Western Sahara is located on the Atlantic coast between Morocco and Mauritania. Western Sahara is mostly low, flat desert, with rocks rising to low mountains in the north-east and south.

Western Sahara, previously Spanish Sahara, was formerly an overseas colony of Spain. After the Spanish withdrew in 1975, the northern two-thirds was annexed by Morocco and the rest by Mauritania. Mauritania withdrew in 1979, when Morocco extended its control over the whole area. Morocco continues to claim and administer the area, though its claim is not internationally recognized. The UN regards it as non-decolonized territory, which makes it the last colony in Africa.

The Popular Front for the Liberation of the Saguia el Hamra and Río de Oro (POLISARIO), a liberation movement that had launched a previous guerilla attack against Spain in 1973, continued its struggle against Morocco, in an attempt to establish an independent Sahrawi Arab Democratic Republic in Western Sahara, the Sahrawi Arabs being the indigenous people of the area. A UN-brokered ceasefire came into effect in 1991, since when, a referendum to decide the sovereignty and legal status of the territory has been repeatedly postponed.

Due to lack of arable land and the scarcity of water, Western Sahara can only rely on phosphate mining and fishing, while the rest of the population consists of nomadic herdsmen, who wander the desert, tending their camels, sheep and goats. Some fruit and vegetables can be grown in oases, but food is mainly imported. Standards of living are substantially below those of Morocco. In 2001 Morocco began to explore for oil off-shore, though the results remain inconclusive.

YEMEN

Location:	16 J
Capital:	Sana'a
Area:	205,035sq m (531041km²)
Population:	20,727,063 July 2005 E
Main Languages:	Arabic
Main Religions:	Sunni Muslim 65%, Shi'a 35%
Currency:	1 rial = 100 fils
Climate:	Coast hot and dry; warm summer, cold winter in highlands, rain Mar–Sep

A Middle Eastern country situated to the south of the Arabian peninsula, Yemen borders the Arabian Sea and Gulf of Aden to the south, and the Red Sea to the west. It occupies a strategic position on the Bab el Mandeb strait, that links the Red Sea with the Gulf of Aden, one of the world's busiest shipping areas. Yemen has land borders with Saudi Arabia to the north and Oman to the east. There is a narrow coastal plain, and the fertile Hadramaut valley is backed in the south and west by hills and mountains, while behind them, desert uplands slope towards the barren Empty Quarter (Rub' al

Khali) and Arabia. Fresh water is scarce.

The legendary home of the Queen of Sheba (Saba), fortunate, fertile Yemen was known to the Romans as *Arabia Felix*, in contrast with barren *Arabia Deserta* to the north. An Islamic country from the 7th century, Yemen was part of the Ottoman Empire from the 16th century. Following the defeat of the Ottomans in the First World War, Iman Yahya, a member of the Hamid al-Din dynasty, came to power. In 1839 the

British captured Aden; it became a British protectorate in 1937, when the port of Aden was developed as a British military base. After the Second World War, Yahya was assassinated and Prince Ahmed became ruler. From 1958 to 1961 Yemen formed part of the United Arab Republic with Egypt and Syria. In 1962 the monarchy was ousted in a military coup, followed by civil war between republicans and royalists. In 1967 Britain was forced to withdraw from

Aden and Yemen was partitioned into north and south. By now, the south was Marxist, and declared itself the People's Democratic Republic of Yemen, the more traditionalist north becoming the Yemen Arab Republic. There followed a massive exodus of hundreds of thousands of Yemenis from the south to the north, which led to two decades of hostility between the two; to this day, tensions still exist between the more affluent north and the poorer south.

In 1990 the two states reunited to form the Republic of Yemen. In 1994 the south seceded, but was defeated in a brief civil war (their leaders have since been pardoned by the president and some are beginning to return from exile). In 2000 terrorists attacked the USS *Cole* in the Gulf of Aden: following this, Yemen offered to support the US in its war against terror.

OPPOSITE: View of the old city of Sana'a.

ABOVE: Acacia trees near the Empty Quarter, Yemen.

RIGHT: Part of the ancient Marib dam, dating from the 6th century BC. Saba. Saba.

President Ali Abdallah Salih has been head of state since 1990, having led northern Yemen since 1978, following a military coup; he is Yemen's longest-serving leader in recent times. Head of government since 2001 is Prime Minister Abd al-Qadir Ba Jamal.

Even though a degree of modernization has occurred, Yemen retains something of its old tribal character. It is one of the less affluent of the Arab countries, and its economy is dependent on oil. Most of the population lives by agriculture, growing grains, fruits, coffee, cotton, vegetables, and *qat* – a mildly narcotic shrub; livestock are also herded. However, the economy has been growing since 2000 and there are moves towards diversification into other areas, including tourism.

ZAMBIA

Location:	15 L
Capital:	Lusakaπ
Area:	290,586sq m (752614km²)
Population:	11,261,795 July 2005
Main Languages:	English
Main Religions:	Christian 54%, traditional beliefs 29%
Currency:	1 kwacha = 100 ngwee
Climate:	Hot all year, cooler in highlands, rains Nov–Apr

A landlocked republic of south-central Africa, Zambia, formerly Northern Rhodesia, is divided from Zimbabwe and Botswana in the south by the Zambezi river, from which Zambia takes its name. It is also bordered by Mozambique and Malawi to the east, Tanzania to the north-east, DR Congo to the north, Angola to the west and Namibia to the south. The terrain mostly consists of a vast expanse of high plateaux. In the south the Zambezi occupies a low-lying rift valley of rugged escarpments, and the Muchinga Mountains lie to the north.

There were major influxes of Bantu-speaking immigrants from the 12th century and others followed into the 19th century, including the Luba and Lunda tribes of DR Congo and Angola, who were joined by Ngoni peoples from the south. The area was visited by Portuguese in the 18th century and by missionaries, traders, and explorers in the mid 19th century. In 1855, the Scottish missionary and explorer, David Livingstone, was the first European to see the magnificent waterfalls on the Zambezi, naming them after Queen Victoria. In 1888 Cecil Rhodes and his British South Africa Company obtained mineral rights from local chiefs, drew northern and southern Rhodesia into the British sphere of influence, and gave the country his name. Southern Rhodesia was formally annexed and granted self-government in 1923, and Northern Rhodesia became a British protectorate in 1924. Local rebellions were quashed and mining began in the north-eastern Copperbelt in 1934.

In 1953, both Rhodesias joined Nyasaland (now Malawi) to form the Federation of Rhodesia and Nyasaland, Northern Rhodesia becoming independent within the Commonwealth as Zambia after the federation was dissolved in 1963. (Southern Rhodesia became independent as Rhodesia in 1965, becoming Zimbabwe in 1979.) Kenneth Kaunda had led the campaign for independence and was Zambia's first president from 1964 to 1991. He tried to bring a measure of humanism and co-operation to his government, and there was increased control of the economy. The constitution of 1973 provided for a National Assembly and a consultative House of Chiefs. It also made his United National Independence Party (UNIP) the only political party, where before there had been three, the UNIP, the African National Congress (ANC), and the United Progressive Party (UPP).

Growing opposition to the UNIP's monopoly of power gave rise to the Movement for Multi-party Democracy

(MMD), which included UNIP defectors and labour leaders. This resulted in the end of one-party rule in 1991 and victory for the MMD, when Frederick Chiluba was elected president. The subsequent re-election of Chiluba in 1996 was achieved after Kaunda was effectively barred from further elections by a change in constitution. In 1997 there was an abortive anti-government coup; Kaunda was suspected and arrested, but charges were subsequently dropped. The election of President Levy Mwanawasa in 2001 was also widely challenged; Mwanawasa began an anti-corruption campaign in 2002, which resulted in the

OPPOSITE: Hippos in the Luangwa river, Luangwa Valley.

ABOVE: Men playing drums.

RIGHT: Mother and child by their traditional straw-built house.

prosecution of former President Chiluba and many of his supporters. Opposition parties currently hold a majority of seats in the National Assembly.

In spite of its considerable copper wealth, Zambia has been facing major problems following independence in 1964. There were few Zambians capable or educated enough to run the country and the economy had been founded on foreign expertise. Zambia was also affected by its involvement in Zimbabwe's struggle for independence (1965–1979). In 1975 world copper prices collapsed, further devastating the economy, with the result that Zambia is currently one of the world's poorest nations and much of its population is decimated by disease (HIV/AIDS and malaria). However, copper prices have lately recovered and the government has accepted that diversification is required if it is to exploit Zambia's other resources, such as agriculture, tourism, gemstones and hydropower.

ZIMBABWE

Location:	15 L
Capital:	Harare
Area:	150,873sq m (390761km²)
Population:	12,746,990 July 2005 E
Main Languages:	English
Main Religions:	Christian 44%, Animist 40%
Currency:	1 Zimbabwe dollar = 100 cents
Climate:	Warm all year, rains Nov–Mar

A landlocked country of south-central Africa, Zimbabwe is bordered by Zambia to the north, Mozambique to the east, South Africa to the south, and Botswana to the west, and lies between the Zimbabwe and Limpopo rivers. The broad central plateau (High Veld) rises in the north-east to 5,000ft (1500m), and highlands along the eastern border rise to 8,504ft (2592m) at Mount Inyangani.

The area was occupied by Bantu peoples, notably Shona, who began to settle around 2,000 years ago. By the 11th century Great Zimbabwe, the centre of the Shona

culture, was famous for its gold and metalwork, but had noticeably declined by the 1400s. In 1837 the warlike Ndebele (Matabele), after unsuccessful skirmishes with the Boers in the Transvaal, seized Shona land in the west, where Matabeleland was established. In 1888, Cecil Rhodes obtained mineral rights from King Lobengula, and the territory became a British protectorate, administered by the British South Africa Company. From 1895 Matabeleland, Mashonaland and Zambia, across the Zambezi river, were collectively known as Rhodesia. Thereafter, white colonization was encouraged and the country's precious metal and mineral resources were plundered.

In 1923 the area south of the Zambezi became a self-governing colony. From 1933 to 1953, a policy of black exclusion from

government was followed, and white immigration had nearly doubled the population by the 1950s. Southern and Northern Rhodesia became members of the Federation of Rhodesia and Nyasaland (now Malawi) from 1953 to 1963. In 1961, meanwhile, the Zimbabwe African People's Union (ZAPU) had been formed by Joshua Nkomo. In 1963, following the dissolution of the federation, the white minority demanded independence, contrary to British policy that African majority rule should come first. That year, the Zimbabwe African National Union (ZANU) was formed by Robert Mugabe. Southern Rhodesia was known simply as Rhodesia from 1964, following the creation of Zambia (Northern Rhodesia): the white nationalist leader, Ian Smith, became prime minister that year, rejecting the British terms on which

LEFT: Harare's skyline.

OPPOSITE LEFT: An elephant in Mana Pools National Park.

OPPOSITE RIGHT: The Victoria Falls.

independence should be based. In 1965, unilateral independence was proclaimed, which Britain declared illegal. Negotiations between the two came to nothing, despite the imposition of UN sanctions, and Rhodesia declared itself a republic in 1969, which was not recognized internationally.

Resistance to white rule intensified from the late 1960s, characterized by attacks on white famers. In 1974 Mugabe and Nkomo were released from prison, having been incarcerated since 1964, and formed the Patriotic Front (PF) ito fight the Smith regime. With his regime near to collapse, in 1978, Smith signed an accord with Mugabe, Nkomo and Bishop Abel Muzorewa, though the Muzorewa government soon faltered, and guerilla warfare intensified. At the height of the civil war, 1,000 white Rhodesians were leaving the country every month, taking vital capital with them.

Following the Lancaster House Agreement of 1979, Rhodesia was granted transitional independence as the Republic of Zimbabwe (Zimbabwe-Rhodesia), when a new 'majority' constitution was formed, still favouring whites. In 1980 Zimbabwe received full independence from Britain, having agreed to a transition to African majority rule. The Reverend Canaan Banana became president and Robert Mugabe prime minister. In 1982 Nkomo was ousted from the cabinet, which sparked fighting between ZAPU and the ruling ZANU; this was marked by the genocide of the Ndebele by ZANU's infamous Fifth Brigade, which resulted in Nkomo's capitulation and the merger of ZAPU with the ZANU Patriotic Front. In 1984 the principle of a one-party state was agreed, with Mugabe abrogating all power to himself three years later. Mugabe was re-elected president in 1996 and bans on strikes and political gatherings were issued; projected land reforms sparked violent demonstrations. In 2000 veterans of the war of independence, with government approval, began to invade and claim white-

owned farms without compensating their owners. In 2002 the EU imposed sanctions following the expulsion of observers sent to monitor the general elections; despite the elections being declared illegal, Mugabe is still in power. In 2003 Zimbabwe formally withdrew from the Commonwealth.

In 1992 Mugabe announced the drought and famine in southern Africa a national disaster. This compounded the country's debt and led to IMF adjustment of the economy and a programme of austerity causing further hardship. The government's chaotic land reforms have badly damaged the farming sector, which was once a major source of export revenue. In 2001 2,900

white farmers, whose farms had been targeted for seizure and redistribution, were ordered to stop work under threat of imprisonment. This resulted in no crops being produced, which led to Zimbabwe's worst food shortages in 60 years, in a situation already exacerbated by drought.

Zimbabwe has the fourth-highest

incidence of HIV/AIDS in the world, which continues to drain resources, as did its involvement in DR Congo's war (1998–2002). It was reported in 2005 that Zimbabwe has made a deal with China to provide mineral and other concessions in return for economic aid, and it is said to be looking to South Africa for further help.

INDEX

AA Photo Library: page 112 left
© Eye Ubiquitous/Hutchinson: page 129

Art Directors & TRIP Photo Library: pages 8, 12, 13, 38, 39 both, 72 right, 149 above right, 163 below left, 195 right, 220 both, 221 both, 253 left, 273 right, 290, 291 both, 297 right, 298, 299, 300, 321 both, 323 above and below right, 343, 418 left, 426, 427 both. Art Directors & TRIP Photo Library/the following photographers:
Adina Tovy: pages 40, 41 both, top right, 169, 200, 201 all, 250, 336, 337 right, 434, 435
Alexander Kuznetsov: page 325
Andrew Turner: page 349
Bb Holdings BV: page 372
Bob Turner: pages 3, 23 right, 25, 26 left, 68, 69, 74, 75, 113, 116, 117, 118, 119, 121, 139 below and right, 140 and 141, 142, 144, 152, 154, 155 both, 157, 189 above and below left, 202, 204 below, 228, 229 both, 240 both, 266, 267 left, 270 above, 319 left, 324, 326, 329, 332, 333 both, 344, 335 all, 366, 367 below, 394 above, 396 above, 410, 411, 414 above right, 419, 429 both, 436
Chris Rennie: page 47 right
Constantia Treppe: page 91 below
Dan Cole: pages 338, 339 both below
Dave Saunders: pages 92 above, 175
David Davis: page 337 left
David Hoey: page 46
David Morgan: page 381 right
David Tunnicliffe: pages 360, 361 left
Dimitri Mossienko: page 407 below
Edward Parker: pages 115 both, 173 above
Flora Torrance: page 47 left
George Spenceley: pages 242, 243 right
Grant Fleming: page 114
Howard Sayer: pages 330, 331 both
Ivor Burgandinov: pages 212, 213 both
Jane Sweeney: pages 48, 57 above right and below, 58, 59, 66 both, 67, 86, 81, 132, 133, 176, 177, 194, 195 left, 214, 216-7, 218 both, 219 both, 234, 235 both, 252, 253 right, 258, 259 both, 292, 293 both, 308, 309 left, 348 both, 388, 389, 392, 400, 401 both, 404, 405 both, 412, 430, 431 left, 444, 445 left
J.A. Scott: page 352
J Doe: pages 77 below, 110, 149 top and below, 384
Jim Love: page 384
Joan Batten: page 63 left
Joan Wakelin: pages 24 above, 26 right, 31, 163 above both and below right, 179, 180, 181 both,

190 both, 191, 198 above both, 246 both, 247, 248, 249, 285, 286, 287, 302, 354, 355 both, 368 both, 369, 386, 387, 432, 433 both, 443, 443 both
Jody Denham: pages 232 below, 244, 245, 260, 261 both, 272, 273 left, 322, 373
Helene Rogers: pages 18, 19 all, 24 below, 27, 28, 29, 30, 36, 37, 44, 45 both, 60, 61, 62, 79 all, 90 both, 100, 101, 109 both, 112 right,120, 122, 123, 124, 125, 126, 127, 138, 139 above left, 143 both, 145, 146, 148, 164, 165 both, 173 below, 178, 184 both, 185 left, 186, 187 both, 188, 196, 197, 198 below, 199, 210, 211, 222, 223, 230, 231 both, 241 both, 267 right, 270 below, 271, 282 above, 296, 297 left, 318, 319 above, 323 below left, 342, 344 above, 346, 347 all, 367 above, 370, 371 both, 382, 383 both, 394 below, 395, 396 below, 397, 398 both, 399, 408, 409 both, 418 right, 420, 437, 438 both, 439, 440, 441 both
Hilary Bower: pages 15 below, 233
Ivor Burgandinov: pages 212, 213 both
Jan and Fiona Teede: pages 106, 107
Julian Thomas: page 403 all
Juliet Highet: pages 35 above, 49, 206, 207 both
Laura Gayer: pages 421 all, 423
Maureen Lines: page 9
Mark Gleeson: pages 15 above, 88, 89 both, 341 both
Martin Barlow: pages 52, 53, 54 both, 150, 151, 162 both, 224, 225 both, 232 above, 264, 265 right, 268, 269 both, 309 right, 328, 340 all, 356, 357 left, 358, 413 both, 414 left, 422 left, 424, 45 both
Mary Jelitte: pages 51 above left, 63 right, 78 both, 91 above, 94 both, 95, 135 both
Matthew Turner: pages 406, 407 left
Maxwell Mackenzie: pages 402 all
Mike Feeney: pages 14 all, 375 left
Norman Price: page 73, 136 both, 166 all
Peter Treanor: pages 10, 11, 35 below, 312, 313
Ramzi Musallam: pages 301, 303
Robert Belbin: pages 17, 76 all, 77 top left, 81, 108 all, 134, 147 all, 167 both, 168 both, 304, 305, 314, 315, 320, 339 above, 380, 393 both, 431 right
Robin Smith: pages 92 below, 284 both, 306, 307 both, 428 both
RS Daniell: page 93 both
Terry Knight: pages 390, 391 both
Tibor Bognar: pages 2, 4, 5, 20 both, 21, 23 left, 32, 33, 50, 51 below and above right, 55, 56, 57 left, 65, 70, 71, 72 left, 80 both, 82, 83 all, 84 both, 85, 96 both, 97, 98 both, 99, 102, 103, 104,

105 both, 111, 131, 137, 153, 156, 158, 159, 160, 161, 170 both, 171, 174, 182, 183 both, 192, 193, 203, 204 above both, 205, 208, 209 both, 215, 226, 227 both, 236, 237, 238 both, 239, 251 both, 254 both, 255, 256-7 both, 262, 263, 274, 275 both, 276, 277 both, 279, 280, 281, 282 below, 283, 294, 295 both, 310, 311, 316, 317, 327, 344 below, 345, 350, 351 both, 357 right, 359, 364 both, 365, 374, 375 right, 376, 377 both, 378, 379 both, 381 left, 385, 415, 416, 417, 422 right, 445 right
Tonu Noorits: pages 130, 243 below
Victor Kolpakov: pages 22, 42, 43 both, 265 left
Viesti Collection Inc.: page 16
V. Slapinia: pages 34 both
Zoe Rogers: page 185 right

COVER PICTURES

FRONT COVER: Left, below centre left and right: Art Directors & TRIP Photo Library/ Bob Turner.
Above centre: Directors & TRIP Photo Library/Juliet Highlet.
Far right: Directors & TRIP Photo Library/Tibor Bognar.

BACK COVER & SPINE: Directors & TRIP Photo Library/Tibor Bognar.